Evangelicals and Israel

— end-times theology = <u>13</u>   — "a view of history developed 2000 yrs ago" tasteless.

pre-millennial dispensationalism → 13-14, 20, 112

(does he acknowledge the usual red herring — but that end-times scenario is OT?)   seems contradicted regularly — 23   113

~~But he drops it almost as soon as he has raised it.~~

— political considerations: Israel as front line ~~in~~ of defense ag. ~~Islamic terrorism~~ — 34-35

— thumbnail history of evangelicals   36 f

— Esther — <u>65</u>

Ahmadinejad — 95 f

— Christian anti-Zionists — 111 f
D. Wagner — 108 f   North Pale 125 → 178

who is responsible for 9/11? — p <u>279</u>

— Burge & Wagner 124 f
— Jimmy Carter — 127, 149, 208, 246.

C Rice - 211

Benny Elon 217 - 218

Christ Tourism - 218

Bush / Sharon — 240 - 242

G.W. Bush — 234f

Gaza withdrawal - 242f

Bill Clinton - 243

Herbwith vote - 245

Meiersheimer + Walt - 246

G/H.W. Bush - 248

Evangelicals and Israel

The Story of Christian Zionism

STEPHEN SPECTOR

OXFORD

UNIVERSITY PRESS

2008

Handwritten annotations:

- ICEJ - 143 — Jerry Falwell - 142f, 16
- Pat Robertson - 150f, 163
- M. Hedding - 166
- Hedding joked about Messiah) — 158-159
- Malcolm Hedding - 166
- Abe Foxman 159-160
- Sharon's withdrawal from Gaza - 165-167
- J. Hagee - 167f
- CUFI
- Jerusalem - 174
- Yechiel Eckstein — 191
- the 3rd Temple - 204f — red heifer 204-205
- Shlomo Cohen - 202
- Karen Armstrong - 208
- George Bush — 208f, esp 209

OXFORD
UNIVERSITY PRESS

Oxford University Press, Inc., publishes works that further
Oxford University's objective of excellence
in research, scholarship, and education.

Oxford New York
Auckland Cape Town Dar es Salaam Hong Kong Karachi
Kuala Lumpur Madrid Melbourne Mexico City Nairobi
New Delhi Shanghai Taipei Toronto

With offices in
Argentina Austria Brazil Chile Czech Republic France Greece
Guatemala Hungary Italy Japan Poland Portugal Singapore
South Korea Switzerland Thailand Turkey Ukraine Vietnam

Copyright © 2008 by Oxford University Press, Inc.

Published by Oxford University Press, Inc.
198 Madison Avenue, New York, New York 10016

www.oup.com

Oxford is a registered trademark of Oxford University Press

Library of Congress Cataloging-in-Publication Data
Spector, Stephen, 1946–
Evangelicals and Israel : the story of Christian Zionism / by Stephen Spector.
p. cm.
Includes bibliographical references and index.
ISBN 978-0-19-536802-4
1. Christian Zionism—History.   2. Christian Zionism—United States—History.
3. Religion and politics—United States.   4. Islamophobia—United States.   I. Title.
DS150.5.S64 2008
320.54095694088'28040973—dc22   2008026681

1 3 5 7 9 8 6 4 2

Printed in the United States of America
on acid-free paper

Contents

Preface

This book is a study of the confluence of religion and politics in evangelical Christian attitudes toward Israel and the Jewish people. My goal is to explore Christian Zionists' convictions with understanding and respect, though not necessarily with agreement. I am Jewish and I do not share the fundamental beliefs that lie at the heart of evangelicalism. I have spent my career studying and teaching Christianity and the Bible, however, and I try here to represent evangelicals' views in a way that they will consider accurate and fair. At the same time, I offer perspectives that contradict and balance theirs. The issues I address are passionate. The Israeli-Palestinian dispute is one of the most hotly contested questions in the world, freighted with existential fears and elemental indignation and rage. Adding the conservative Christian marriage of faith and politics to that dangerous mix heightens the intensity of the debate.

That is all the more true because many Christian Zionists consider themselves to be naturally allied with Jews against a radical Islamist movement bent on worldwide domination. They cite the Palestinian graffito "First the Saturday people, then the Sunday people" to illustrate the global danger that extremist Muslims pose: jihadists, they assert, plan to conquer Israel and the Jews first, then the Christians. Especially after 9/11, some prominent evangelical leaders have made assertions about this putative conflict of civilizations that have seemed outrageous to many people. I attempt in Chapters 4 and 5 to discover the theology that underlies this point of view.

The alliance that many born-again Christians offer to Israel and the Jewish people is astonishing to many Jews. Bible-believing Christians are among the

last people whom Jews expect to love, defend, and even idealize them. Polls
have shown just how much the Jewish community distrusts them. In 2004,
when asked to give a "thermometer rating" of their feelings toward groups of
people (from 0 degrees for very cold to 100 for extremely warm), American
Jews gave evangelicals a frigid average rating of twenty-four degrees. More than
one-third of them (37%) rated evangelicals at zero![1] That stands in startling
contrast to the warmth that the overwhelming majority of American evangelicals feel toward Jews. Their thermometer rating of Jews in 2004 was a balmy
68 degrees. In 2005, 75 percent of them expressed favorable or very favorable
attitudes about Jewish people.[2] John Green, a distinguished senior fellow at the
Pew Forum on Religion and Public Life, notes that white evangelicals' positive
feelings about Jews have only grown stronger over the last forty years.[3] But
most American Jews haven't gotten that message. Instead, they see evangelicals
as second only to Muslims in the extent of their anti-Semitism.[4] Much of that
feeling owes to Jews' general tendency to oppose conservative Christians on
many domestic issues, and to fear the loss of acceptance and opportunity that a
more Christianized society might bring. But very many Jews also are aware of
the unhappy fate that awaits them in classical Christian Zionist eschatology.

Many media reports and books have argued that there is good reason for
Jews to distrust evangelicals. Millions of conservative Protestants, they say,
have a hidden agenda. They may love Jews and support Israel now, but their
true goal is the Jewish people's conversion to Christianity, and ultimately the
destruction of all the others in the end times. Moreover, according to many accounts, because these Christian Zionists see current issues through a biblical
lens, they insist that Israel must refuse to give up one inch of the "covenant
land" that God promised to Abraham and his descendants in the book of
Genesis. The Jews must inhabit that land, in this view, in order for Christ to
return. Former president Jimmy Carter succinctly expressed this dark portrait
of those evangelicals: "There's a fairly substantial and very influential group of
Christians" who seek "the complete eradication of any non-Jews from the West
Bank and Gaza, the ultimate coming of Christ, the death or conversion of all
Jews," said Carter. "That's what they espouse."[5]

In examining evangelical beliefs, I expected to find a theological rigidity,
especially about the end times, that issued in political obduracy of the kind
that Carter described. Many commentators have argued, moreover, that these
religious convictions helped define U.S. foreign policy under George W. Bush.
I was prepared to discover that influence too. I found instead an unexpected
pragmatism, flexibility, and nuance in evangelicals. That was true even of many
of the most ardent Christian Zionists. I also found a lot of disagreement and
uncertainty about the end of days. Even born-again leaders who are sure in their

convictions and invoke God's wrath for anyone who divides His Land, never-
theless showed a wholly unanticipated humility about knowing God's plan.
Bush's top aides and Israeli prime minister Ariel Sharon found that out when
they asked evangelical leaders how conservative Christians would react if Israel
gave up the Gaza Strip and portions of the West Bank in the hope of achieving peace. Evangelical leaders assured them that Israel has a right to make its
own mistakes. If the democratically elected government in Jerusalem chose to
commit national suicide, as some of them put it, they would not abandon Bush
or Israel. That does not mean that Christian Zionists have no eschatological
purpose in supporting the Jewish state, as some advocates claim, however. The
issue is too complex and evangelicals are too varied in their beliefs for such
broad generalizations.

One conclusion I reached again and again in this research was that for evangelicals, politics almost always comports with faith. But born-again Christians
are radically individual. Any examination of their beliefs requires a nuanced
understanding of the way that their faith prescribes and accords with policy.
That applies to Bush as well, and to the influence that Christian Zionists, and
his own convictions, had on his Middle East policy.

In researching this study, I interviewed evangelical leaders, pastors, and
laity in Jerusalem and the United States. I spoke with officers of Jewish organizations and with Israeli and American government officials and diplomats.
I attended evangelical worship services and Christian Zionist prayer events
and conferences. I went to meetings between prominent Jews and evangelicals.
I talked with specialists on Christianity, Judaism, and Islam, as well as survey experts. Several present and former White House advisers gave me their views as
well, mostly off the record. I spoke, too, with people who have known George
W. Bush since childhood, and with some who studied Bible with him. My research is based on what I learned from all of them and from Christian Zionist
books, Web sites, mailings, and other publications. I draw as well on a range of
scholarly studies and newspaper reports. I am grateful to all of those who gave
me their time in interviews, and often in subsequent e-mail correspondence
and phone calls. I especially thank John Green, David Frum, Richard Land,
and the leaders of Eagles Wings for generously sharing their perspectives with
me. I am indebted as well to those who read sections of my manuscript and
made welcome suggestions: Yaakov Ariel, Ethan Felson, Amir Shaviv, Paul
Nussbaum, and Howie Schneider.

I've been lucky enough to have as my editor Cynthia Read, whose judgment is invaluable. I am indebted to her, Keith Faivre, Meechal Hoffman, and
the others at Oxford University Press who helped see this book through to
publication.

Abbreviations

AIPAC	American-Israel Public Affairs Committee
BFP	Bridges for Peace
CBN	The Christian Broadcasting Network
CFI	Christian Friends of Israel
CIA	Central Intelligence Agency
CUFI	Christians United for Israel
DPPJ	Day of Prayer for the Peace of Jerusalem
FSU	Former Soviet Union
ICEJ	International Christian Embassy Jerusalem
IDF	Israel Defense Forces
IFCJ	International Fellowship of Christians and Jews
ISNA	Islamic Society of North America
NAE	National Association of Evangelicals
NCLCI	National Christian Leadership Conference for Israel
NIE	National Intelligence Estimate
NSC	National Security Council
PA	Palestinian Authority
PFLP	Popular Front for the Liberation of Palestine
PLO	Palestine Liberation Organization
SBC	Southern Baptist Convention
UCI	Unity Coalition for Israel

Evangelicals and Israel

1

⚜

"We Are with the Jewish People"

Christian Zionism

"A growing group of us is prepared to lay our lives down for Israel and the Jewish people," Robert Stearns told me. That took me by surprise. Robert is an evangelical Christian pastor from upstate New York and an ardent Zionist. He had just explained the genesis of his deep personal commitment to Israel. While living in Jerusalem in the early 1990s, he had told me, he stopped at a favorite bookstore and fell into conversation with a young Orthodox Jewish man who was studying Torah and Talmud at a local yeshiva. The student had a zeal for God. As they spoke, Robert realized that this young man loved the same patriarchs and prophets that he did. Robert had been reborn in Jesus Christ and his faith was strong, but praying with this student at the Kotel (the Western or Wailing Wall), worshipping the same God, triggered a profound shift in Robert's spiritual understanding. It confirmed him on his lifelong journey. From that moment, Robert dedicated himself to discovering the Jewish roots of the Christian faith and to learning how he as a Christian was called to support and defend Israel and the Jewish people.

That was impressive, I thought, but it didn't explain Robert's willingness to die for Israel. Offering his life for the Jewish state was so strong a statement that it seemed to come from some other place, I told him (probably insensitively). Robert paused for a moment, then replied honestly: "Frankly, I'm very concerned about the world my son will grow up in." The danger is Islamic extremism. The world is changing, Robert told me. Europe is all but lost. Western values are at stake and Israel represents the front line.[1] In this brief conversation, Robert conveyed much of the essence of evangelical support for Israel: empathy and pragmatism, deep devotion and a sense of imminent danger, all grounded in reverence for Scripture. These qualities, and the heartfelt impulse to cherish the other in oneself, crystallized the wedding of faith and politics that informs Christian Zionism.

The term "Christian Zionist" is relatively new. It did not come into widespread use until the 1990s, and there is no generally accepted definition for it. It is not in the *Oxford English Dictionary.* The phrase dates to at least 1903, when it began to appear in the *New York Times,* first in letters to the editor and obituaries, then, twenty years later, in news stories. In 1919, Nahum Sokolow used it in his *History of Zionism 1600–1918.* Writers sometimes cited the term in the decades that followed, occasionally dismissing it as a less-than-useful metaphor.[2] In 1967, Claude Duvernoy employed it respectfully in his *Le Prince et le Prophete,* offering a bibliography of "Christian Zionist" publications. In 1975, G. Douglas Young, a pro-Israel evangelical, observed in the *Jerusalem Post* that some of his co-religionists had accused him of being a "Christian Zionist." He thanked them for the compliment.[3] In 1980, the *Times* reported on a large Christian Zionist rally in Jerusalem, and by 2003 it used the term to refer to "a formidable voting bloc of conservative Republicans whose support for Israel is based on biblical interpretations."[4]

Definitions of the term tend to be too narrow or too broad. Church of Scotland minister Walter Riggans, in his 1988 book, *Israel and Zionism,* defined a Christian Zionist very inclusively, as any Christian who supports the Zionist aim of building the state of Israel, its army, government, and other institutions. He added that the term could apply even more generally, to any Christian who supports Israel for any reason.[5] Defined in that way, the phrase is so generic that it can denote, for example, liberal Protestants who sympathize with the Palestinians over the Israelis but who support the Jewish state's existence because of guilt over the Holocaust.[6] That definition is too broad for the purposes of the present study, which will analyze a more specifically faith-based Christian Zionism. Donald Wagner, a Presbyterian minister, professor of religion, and, incidentally, outspoken critic of Christian Zionism, defines it more narrowly, as "a movement within Protestant fundamentalism that understands the modern state of Israel as the fulfillment of Biblical prophecy and thus deserving of political, financial, and religious support."[7] That definition is incomplete. Many evangelicals and other Christians who back Israel are not fundamentalists. And although evangelical Zionists' beliefs usually are rooted in biblical prophecy, their convictions and motives, theological and otherwise, are typically far more complex than that, as we shall see.

I asked Richard Booker, a Christian Zionist and the author of over twenty books on Jewish-Christian relations, to define the term. He offered the broadest understanding, recalling Riggans': "It applies to every Christian who supports Israel, though they may not be familiar with the terminology," he said.[8] Booker, who is the founding director of the Institute of Hebraic-Christian Studies in Woodlands, Texas, exemplifies an especially dedicated variety of Christian Zionist. In the 1970s, he and his wife fell in love with the God of Israel, who put the love of the Jewish state in their life. He left a very successful business career and, with no savings or insurance, set out to educate Christians and Jews about the need to learn about each other and reach out to one another in love. After years of struggling, Booker now leads tour groups to Israel, raises money for Jewish causes, and helps Jews make aliyah (emigration, literally "ascension," to Israel). A very different kind of Christian Zionist is Ted Haggard, who was the head of the National Association of Evangelicals until his very public fall from grace in 2006. Haggard supports Israel, but not because of biblical prophecy, which he doesn't believe applies to modern Israel, and not because God put love for the Jewish state in his heart. Rather, he backs Israel because it is the home to over five million Jews, and God promised to bless those who bless the Jews (Genesis 12:3).[9] The term "Christian Zionist" needs to comprehend Booker and Haggard, and many others as well. I'll use it here to denote Christians whose faith, often in concert with other convictions, emotions, and experiences, leads them to support the modern state of Israel as the Jewish homeland.[10] Robert Stearns is an excellent example.

Electric Guitars and Shofars

I first met Robert in February 2005, at a conference called "Rend the Heavens," at the Calvary Tabernacle in Cranford, New Jersey. The event was sponsored by Eagles' Wings, a nondenominational ministry that he founded after his life-changing experience in Jerusalem. Eagles' Wings had invited a delegation from the Israeli consulate in New York to attend the conference, and a young consul had asked me if I wanted to tag along. It was the first evangelical service that I, a Jewish man from Long Island, had ever attended and I was a little nervous. As I entered the tabernacle, I heard Christian rock music emanating from the sanctuary (which didn't reduce my anxiety at all). In the large lobby were tables with Christian books for sale, along with tapes and CDs—but also, astonishingly, shofars (rams' horns used in Jewish ceremonies)! Then, amazingly, pretty girls carrying large Israeli flags on six-foot-long poles marched from the lobby into the sanctuary. The sound of electric guitars and drums escaped as the doors opened. I followed them in. Inside the massive room sat and stood 700 evangelical Christians who'd traveled from all around the Northeast to be there. It was a Sunday evening service and they were mostly in jeans, many with hands raised in the air, swaying to the music. In the front row were four men, conspicuous in their dark suits: the delegation from the Israeli consulate. I joined them with some relief. Now there were five men in dark suits, sitting stiffly before a crowd in casual dress who moved with the music and the spirit that filled the room.

Robert stood on the large stage at the front. In his mid-thirties, microphone in hand, smiling confidently, he looked a little like a rock star. "We're so honored tonight to have the new Israeli ambassador," he said, introducing the Israeli consul general, Arye Mekel, who sat two seats to my right. Mekel (who has the title of ambassador) had recently left the Israeli consulate in Atlanta to head the important one in Manhattan. "Let Ambassador Arye Mekel know we love him," Robert called to the congregation and the 700 people in the hall cheered. "We are with the Jewish people, against the spirit of anti-Semitism!" Robert declared and the crowd roared, "AMEN!" "Do you want to learn some Hebrew?" he asked them. The words *"Hinei ma tov uma naim, Shevet achim gam yachad"* were projected on a large screen onstage in English transliteration, and the Christians behind us sang them out joyously as the musicians played. The song, meaning "How good and how pleasant it is for brothers to dwell together," is a traditional one in Jewish services and has a sweet, lilting quality. Some people danced in place while others waved their arms to the rhythm. Girls walked down the aisles with white banners emblazoned with the biblical inscription, "ISRAEL, I WILL MAKE YOU A GREAT NATION." Then the music changed and the projector put onscreen the words to *"Sholem Aleichem,"* a high-spirited Hebrew song. Next it switched back to *"Hinei ma tov,"* as hundreds of people danced and clapped with warmth and happiness.

When the singing was over, Robert had everyone cheer us. Then we all sat and he addressed the congregation, and the five of us in front in particular. "We fully recognize that there has been a tragic and unspeakable past in the treatment of the Jewish people in Lutheran Germany," he said in a straightforward yet confessional tone. The crowd uttered their assent and Robert looked at us with compassion, maybe even love. "But we recognize that a new generation has arisen," he said. "And we have made a solemn pledge: 'NEVER AGAIN!'" Those are meaningful words to Jews, declaring that we've learned a cruel lesson of history, that we'll never again be silent as any of our people are slaughtered. But these were evangelical Christians rising to their feet. They were applauding enthusiastically as we looked back at them, trying to conceal our amazement. "That's right," they said in agreement. "NEVER AGAIN! Yes, yes."

"We stand with the Jewish people because you are the root of our faith," Robert declared, and I heard scattered amens behind us. "We know our God because David stood strong and Esther stood strong!" said Robert. I found out later that an Israeli deputy foreign minister had suggested to Robert and other evangelical leaders that, just as God had sent Esther in the Bible to deliver the Jews from annihilation, conservative Christians had been brought to a position of power in America for such a time as this. Now, at the mention of Esther's name, the people across the hall replied, "Yes! Yes!" "Israel stands as a democracy in a sea of Islamic dictatorships!" Robert told them. "Yes! That's right!" came the response. "He has kept his covenant with your people for a thousand generations!" Robert then said to the five of us. There is a rising anti-Semitism in Europe right now, he warned, but he assured us that American Christians will stand with us. Then came a surprise: "We applaud Ariel Sharon's courage, his convictions to make hard decisions in order to achieve peace," he said. That was unexpected. From everything I'd read, evangelical Christians were dead-set against Prime Minister Sharon's plan to disengage from the Gaza Strip and part of the West Bank. I made a mental note to explore this further.

Next, Robert called Ambassador Mekel up to the stage to speak. Mekel was accustomed to addressing evangelicals. He often had done so in Atlanta and the Southeast, so he was comfortable in this setting. "I bring you greetings from Jerusalem!" he roared. The congregation cheered in response. Mekel then told them of his birth to a twenty-one-year-old father and a seventeen-year-old mother, Holocaust survivors who were on a train leaving Russia. I was born on the floor of the train, he said. Luckily a woman passenger had a pair of scissors and she cut the umbilical cord. I know there are mothers here who wouldn't mind at all if nobody had ever cut the umbilical cord with their babies, Mekel said, smiling. Some people laughed appreciatively.

Robert then called another member of our delegation, Rabbi Gerald Meister, up to the stage. "Our rabbi of rabbis," Robert called him affectionately. "He danced a little jig coming in, so I suppose he's Rabbi McMeister," Robert joked. Gerald Meister is British, in his sixties. He has his own pulpit in Brooklyn but also is the Israeli Foreign Ministry's adviser on Israel-Christian affairs. The evangelical congregation here in New Jersey already knew him from his earlier appearances before them. In a sense, he really is their rabbi. "This guy is a trip," a man sitting behind me said good-humoredly, perhaps to no one in particular. It was instantly apparent that Meister is a mesmerizing speaker. Brilliantly, he seized on Mekel's story of his birth, using it extemporaneously as a metaphor to represent the close spiritual kinship between Christians and Jews. "God conceived us in the same divine womb," he declared to the born-again audience. "We have an umbilical connection. We are the root,

you are the branch. The root needs that branch and the branch needs the root."
The image was from Paul's Epistle to the Romans, but there are some theological problems in this interpretation. Paul says that the Jews have been cut off
from the tree, until a remnant will recognize Christ and be grafted back on. I
resolved to return to the rabbi's imagery later.

The congregation seemed awestruck. "They love you," I told Meister when
he descended to his seat and rejoined us. "Theater of the absurd," he joked in
the ironic, self-effacing manner of a British academic. But his dedication to this
group, and theirs to him, was obvious. Our delegation exited through a side
door as the music marked the resumption of the service. Arye Mekel had been
a hit and Rabbi Meister's eloquence had been dazzling, but as we left I heard
a couple of the organizers say that they'd run a little long. Although these big
events are filled with love and joy, they have to be stage-managed carefully.
Mekel and the others from the consulate got into a car and hurried back to New
York and I left as well. But Rabbi Meister stayed behind. These were his people
and he was going to visit with them.

A Plan to Redeem All Mankind through the Jews

The Rend the Heavens conference and my conversation with Robert illustrate
some of the foundational elements of Christian Zionism. Many evangelical
Christians not only support Israel but love it. Some are willing to die for it.
They are adopting Jewish religious customs as their own, recognizing and priz-
ing the Judaic roots of their faith. The high authority with which they endue
Scripture impels them to honor God's love of the Jews as the apple of his eye.
They affirm His promises to ingather the Jewish people to their ancient home
in Zion and they rejoice in the fact that this is happening now. They believe
that God, in his love for mankind, has a plan to redeem all peoples through the
Jews. He revealed it millennia ago, in biblical promises and prophesies that are
coming to pass only in our lifetime.

These evangelicals also openly confess their grief, and their guilt, over the
persecution that Christians have inflicted on Jews over the span of centuries.
They are horrified that it was Christians who perpetrated the destruction of
the European Jews in the 1940s. As we shall see, many of them attribute the
Holocaust to Satan, seeing it as a demonic attempt to frustrate God's providential design. And Christian Zionists are determined to defend and protect
the Jewish people against their current enemies, the Arabs and Iranians, whom
many of them also see as Satan's agents. This is not only a matter of religious
conviction. Many evangelical leaders, like Robert, regard Israel as America's

crucial ally in a war against Islamic extremists. Israeli officials not only accept this support but solicit and encourage it, as was clear that night in the Calvary Tabernacle.

The Day of Prayer for the Peace of Jerusalem

Christian Zionism is only one aspect of Eagles' Wings' ministry. The organization also does outreach to born-again communities, some of them in underground or house churches in places like Honduras, Cuba, and China. But over the past few years especially, connection to Israel has become a major part of their mission.[11] Their huge annual project is to organize an annual international Day of Prayer for the Peace of Jerusalem (DPPJ), following the commandment in Psalm 122:6–7: "Pray for the peace of Jerusalem! May they prosper who love you! Peace be within your walls and security within your towers."[12]

I traveled to Wayne, New Jersey, on a Sunday in October 2005 to attend that event. On that day, Stearns's group had arranged for services to pray for Israel in over 100,000 churches around the word, with coordinators in eighty-nine nations, including several Muslim countries. Millions of born-again Christians prayed at once for the peace of Jerusalem. That enormous organizational achievement makes Robert Stearns a central figure in the international Christian Zionist movement.

The event I attended was in the sanctuary of Calvary Temple, an elegant space with about a thousand seats. Inside were perhaps 150 people of all ages, racially and ethnically diverse. For the first thirty minutes, a five-piece band and piano player, led by a pastor with a booming singing voice and a six-person choir, rocked and inspired the congregation. Their songs included "The Mighty One of Israel" and "I Belong to Jesus, Free from Sin." As I entered the hall, the audience was jumping up and down to the music, some with arms high in the air and backs arched. A lone woman danced down the aisle and nobody seemed to notice. The lyrics were projected high on opposite walls. An Israeli flag with the word *Yerushalaim* ("Jerusalem") written in Hebrew script was draped over the front of the sanctuary.

As the music softened, the mood in this elegant hall became somber, decorous. A woman placed her face in her hands and lowered herself to her seat, crying. Another glided slowly up behind her, caressing her back gently to comfort her. A young black woman stood silently in the row in front of me, her head lowered. Then the pastor, Thomas Keinath, invited people to welcome each other and the young woman beamed as she turned to welcome and bless me. Some people hugged each other. I noticed Rabbi Meister in a large prominent seat up front and off to the right, facing the congregation. I'd chosen to come to Calvary Tabernacle because he was representing the Israeli consulate here and I wanted to hear him again. He hadn't been announced yet and he sat Buddha-like, looking serene and contemplative. Behind him hung a large, shimmering blue banner with a drawing of Jerusalem and the legend "Till He makes Jerusalem a praise in all the earth."[13] As the ushers discreetly took a collection, a mystical-sounding taped rendition of "Hatikvah," the Israeli national anthem, played in the background. Then a hauntingly lovely song played, beginning with "Dear Yeshua" (the Hebrew name from which "Jesus" was derived), and continuing with words taken from Isaiah:

> O Jerusalem, Jerusalem, a child wept for you.
> For Zion's sake I will not be silent,
> For Zion's sake, for Yerushalaim
> I will not rest, I will not rest.
> I'll set watchmen on the walls, O Jerusalem.

Pastor Thomas addressed us. "We are uniting with churches around the globe in accordance with the words of David, Psalm 122," he said and reminded us of the reward that awaits those who pray for the peace of Jerusalem. "We are gathered to pray to the God of Abraham, Isaac, and Jacob, our God, the one true God," he said.

Rodlyn Park, an Eagles' Wings official whom I'd met at the Rend the Heavens conference, rose to speak. I had interviewed her after that earlier event and she had told me how the plans were coming along for the DPPJ. The coordinator from India had said that probably 25,000 churches in his country would participate. Christians in the nation of Jamaica had heard about it and said that they would have churches praying as well. Nine to twelve predominantly Muslim states, including Mongolia and the United Arab Emirates, would join in too, she said, and Singapore had come on board. Even Palestinians were represented. A year earlier, at the Feast of Tabernacles, an annual event that evangelicals celebrate in Jerusalem to mark the Jewish holiday of Succoth, a Palestinian Baptist pastor from Bethlehem named Naim Khoury had spoken very strongly in support of Israel, Rodlyn told me. Muslims had bombed his church dozens of times, he had been shot once, and his brother had been killed, she said. But Pastor Khoury is a Bible-believing evangelical and he responds to the scriptural injunctions to bless Israel and to pray for the peace of Jerusalem.

Rodlyn herself grew up in a nonbelieving Gentile home in Philadelphia. She went to a high school that was 99 percent Jewish, and when her parents moved away, she lived with a Jewish family for her junior and senior years. At thirty-two she became a Christian, which is to say she was spiritually reborn through a personal experience with Jesus. When she came to her faith, she already had a deep appreciation of its Jewish roots, but she couldn't find a church that shared that view. Then she discovered the Eagles' Wings ministry and started to work for Robert, creating a manual that would teach Christians how to pray for Israel. People who have a heart for the Jewish people often need to be given a language to express it, she told me. She wanted to help provide that. Is Eagles' Wings interested in converting Jews? No, she said. That has given too much offense and pain to the Jews throughout history. Nor is her organization motivated by end-of-days theology. Her mission is to defend the Jews, "loving, speaking the truth even when it's dangerous," she said. "I do my job description and I'll let God do his."[14]

Now, at the day of prayer event, Rodlyn rose to update the congregation on the DPPJ worldwide. Over 100,000 fellowships around the globe had prayed for the peace of Jerusalem that morning, then many people had gathered again for additional special evening services like this one, she told them.[15] Robert Stearns and representatives from the Israeli Knesset had come together in Germany to pledge solidarity with Israel as they prayed. Churches in every state in America, plus Guam and Puerto Rico, had participated. Eagles' Wings also had set up a worldwide telephone network and Christians had called in their prayers from Nigeria, Israel, Egypt, South Africa, Germany, the United Kingdom, Kenya, and Canada. People had prayed for Jerusalem in Hebrew, German, and Swahili, as well as English. One woman from Ohio had blown a shofar over the phone. They were fulfilling their biblical responsibility, Rodlyn said, to stand in the gap for Israel and the Jewish people. "Now maybe God can bless America," she declared. Rodlyn was referring to a biblical verse that was so familiar to her audience that she didn't even need to cite it: Genesis 12:3. In it, God promises Abraham, "I will bless those who bless you and curse him who curses you." This prayer vigil, then, like so much of Christian Zionism itself, was inspired by two biblical injunctions, both of which offer rewards to those who obey them: Psalm 122, which wishes for the prosperity of those who pray for the peace of Jerusalem, and Genesis 12:3, which offers blessing to those who bless Israel and the Jewish people. Some people in the congregation were driven by other motives as well, as we shall see.

Pastor Thomas delivered a brief sermon, which he closed against the sound of "Hatikva" playing softly in the background. "Breathe, O God," he said again and again in soothing tones. "Breathe, O God." Then he called Rabbi Meister up to speak.

"For 2,000 years we have never ceased to pray for Zion and for the peace of Jerusalem," the rabbi said magisterially. "In 1948, salvation history began to turn in the direction of the fulfillment of Scripture, the gathering in of the exiles from the Western world, the Near East, the Far East, and Africa. And you, as faithful Christians who believed in God's word as truth, share with us not only the promise but also the reward: you are to be planted among the righteous."

The rabbi continued, extemporizing with the beauty and eloquence that I'd come to expect of him. "Words eternally true and free of error are written for you in the Scriptures that you carry in your hands and in your hearts," he told his Christian listeners. He was invoking the inerrancy of the Bible, one of the defining beliefs of American Protestant fundamentalism. "Those are the only words that ever ring true," said Meister. He now went on to allude to another core conviction of Christian Zionists: that the establishment of the state of Israel and the ingathering of the Jews represent the living fulfillment of biblical prophecy. "The gift of the covenant that God granted to Abraham, Isaac, and Jacob is now being redeemed in contemporary history," he said. "All of us are instruments of his words and of his will. To use Christian signs, we are all called to a special discipleship. An act of fidelity. An act of recognition that God reigns in Jerusalem. A covenant to which you, by your will and your faith, attach yourselves indeed."

The rabbi concluded by speaking of the Jewish people's gratitude for Christian support. "We are grateful for it," he told the congregation, "and we acknowledge it as a blessing for us all." This was an important reassurance in view of American Jews' widespread distrust of Christian Zionists' motives. Only weeks after this event, in fact, several prominent Jewish leaders renewed their attacks on the Christian right. "And so, as we approach this holy season," said the rabbi, "we impart a blessing that Rabbi Abraham Yitzhak HaCohen Kook imparted to his flock in the eternal and most holy city when he said, 'May the old be renewed and may the new be made holy.'" Meister had used his audience's spiritual vocabulary brilliantly, just as they used Hebrew words and Jewish concepts. He had woven Christian theology into his language allusively, elegantly.

When Pastor Thomas spoke again, he was explicit and direct about his religious conviction. "We believe that we are living in the last days," he said. The harvest of souls will take place in these days, he noted. Then, as the piano played softly in the background, he invited people to come forward and "pray out." Rodlyn Park came up first. "Lord, your prophet Isaiah said that there would be a day when you would set watchmen on the walls of Jerusalem [Isaiah 62:6]. Father, this is that day. And we are those people who have said, 'Yes, Lord, here am I.' We will stand for Jerusalem. We will stand in the gap for the Jewish people. We will stand in the gap for Israel. We will be those watchmen on the walls, Lord, whether it's popular or not. It's not about what the world thinks. It's about what you do, what you've asked for, what you're looking for."

A young woman, virtually in tears, took the microphone to pray out next: "Lord, I thank you that you love your Jewish people and Israel. And Lord, I thank you that you have all of these promises for the apple of your eye"—a reference to the way that God thinks of Israel according to Zechariah 2:7–9. "We thank you that you will never leave them or forsake them, in Jesus' name," she concluded.

The reference to Jesus in God's commitment to the Jewish people was more jarring to my ears than it had been to my eyes in reading about Christian Zionism. Perhaps no one else in the room was struck by the formulation. Rabbi Meister is a scholar and teacher of Christianity and has spent enough time among evangelicals to understand the love behind such language. I was seated toward the back of the hall so as not to draw attention to my tape recorder and the fact that I was writing in a notebook, but a man came over to speak with me. "Are you the rabbi?" he asked hopefully. "No, I'm writing a book on evangelical support for Israel," I replied and he seemed pleased. He explained that they'd invited the rabbi from a nearby synagogue to attend and hoped that I might be he. He welcomed me warmly anyway. The local rabbi never came.

Pastor Thomas was on his knees, his hands cradling his head on the floor, as others came forward to pray out. One young woman took the microphone and spoke of God's love for Jerusalem and Israel: "O Holy One of Israel, today we have felt your heart for your city and your land, for you are married to the land. We have heard the cries of Rachel weeping for her children," she said, citing an image that the prophet Jeremiah uses to symbolize grief over the exile of Israel, and Matthew 2:18 uses in describing the Slaughter of the Innocents.[16] "You have called them back from the north, south, east, and west," she said. "Give them hearts of flesh instead of hearts of stone," she pleaded, citing a prophecy by Ezekiel, sometimes interpreted as a wish that the Jews' hearts will be receptive when Christ returns, so that this time they won't reject him.[17] "Israel *will* be a praise in the earth, and they will eat the fruit," she went on, her voice becoming more fervent. "Father, you said it, and we believe it. Father, your son came as a babe the first time. But he's coming back as JUDAH'S LION!" she declared, her voice suddenly rising, and a shout went up from the congregation. Christ was born into humble circumstances and was the Prince of Peace in his first coming, she was saying, but he'll return as warrior to defeat Antichrist at the final battle in the end of time. "And Lord, we're so thankful for the Jewish people, that we're grafted in, that we're one, one new man in Messiah. Thank you, Lord!" Here, as Rabbi Meister had done, she was citing Paul's Epistle to the Romans, which says that the Gentiles are grafted onto the olive tree of the Chosen People. "The new man" was from Paul's Epistle to the Ephesians, in which he says that Gentiles and Israel are no longer distinct. Christ has abolished in his flesh Jewish law and ordinances, reconciling the Gentiles and Israel as one body, understood as the Church.[18] For Christians this is a beautiful concept of reconciliation and unity. Many Jews would have trouble appreciating the beauty in it, however.

A fourth woman came forward to pray that the Temple in Jerusalem would be rebuilt, that God's "biblical boundaries for Israel would be established, and that your shalom ['peace'] will be in the state of Israel." She was setting forth the preconditions for the Second Coming of Christ. Many Bible-believing Christians expect the messiah to return only when the Jews build the Third Temple and possess their entire biblical patrimony, including Judea and Samaria, the occupied territories of the West Bank. Many Israelis also want to keep those territories, which are precious to them for reasons of religion or security. But many others believe that holding onto all of the land will not secure the shalom for which this woman had prayed. Rather, it will engender continual strife with the Palestinians who live there. And building the Temple would almost certainly trigger a war, since it would be located on the Temple Mount, the site on which the Dome of the Rock sits.

Rodlyn Park rose again to ask God to send a fresh wind of revelation to the parts of the Church that are rising up against Israel, to mold and shape their hearts and impart the spirit of wisdom in them. This was a prayer to stop mainline Protestant denominations from pursuing plans to divest from companies that support Israel's occupation of the territories.

Pastor Thomas concluded the service. He confessed America's sin in turning its back on Jews who tried to flee Nazi German in 1939. "Lord, let us never do that again," he said. Then he repented the medieval Church's forced baptism of Jews "when it was totally against them, when this was a sacrilege to them. We know what we have done for almost 2,000 years. We need to call to be alongside the Jewish people. We need to lift up Jerusalem. Lord, we know that you are coming on the clouds. Lord, we know that you will enter the Golden Gate in Jerusalem." Here he made explicit why Jerusalem is so crucial to many evangelicals. It is the site to which Jesus will come when Christ returns, descending with the clouds in fulfillment of Daniel 7:13. "Lord, we know that you will raise up Jerusalem to be a jewel," said Pastor Thomas. "We know the significance to us, and to the Jews it has so much more. . . . You were with them in 1967. Lord, you go out before them in war." Here the congregation issued a cry of AMEN. "Lord," Thomas went on, "let them realize that the Church is with them, not behind them and not before them, but alongside of them. Lord, we just pray for peace, Lord, the shalom of Jerusalem."

Voices within Christian Zionism

These prayers and declarations represented a wide range of voices within Christian Zionism. Most Jews would find some of them entirely benign and supportive. Rodlyn Park's reference to being watchmen on the wall, standing in the gap to defend the Jewish people, certainly fits into that category. So does her rebuke of mainline churches' divestment programs. The young woman who prayed for God to transplant Jews' hearts of stone with hearts of flesh, however, was more ambiguous. It could have simply been a prayer for Jews to love God. More likely, though, it was a veiled hope for them to accept Christ—as her reference to the one new man, both Jew and Christian, firmly suggests.[19] Pastor Thomas's remorse for America's refusal to save Jews in 1939, and the medieval Church's harsh treatment of them, illustrated the sincere repentance of evangelicals for past injuries. His declaration that we are in the last days, however, and his allusion to Christ's coming on the clouds, were straight out of end-times theology. The woman who called for building the third Temple and establishing Israel in biblical borders reinforced that. She was expressing a powerful theological strain in Christian Zionism, a view of divine history that was developed less than 200 years ago. It has the awkward name "premillennial dispensationalism."

Premillenial Dispensationalism

Premillennial dispensationalism was conceived and disseminated in the midnineteenth century by John Nelson Darby, a one-time Anglican priest in the Church of Ireland. Darby adopted a "futurist" version of premillennialism, teaching that the Jews would return to their ancient homeland, where every biblical prophecy not already fulfilled by the time of the destruction of the Temple in A.D. 70 would come true for a modern Jewish state. Remarkably, he developed this theological program more than half a century before Theodor Herzl called for such a state in his book *Der Judenstaat* (*The Jewish State,* 1896) and over a hundred years before the actual establishment of modern Israel.

Reading scriptural narratives and prophecies as literally true, Darby divided salvation history into epochs, or "dispensations." Most dispensationalists believe that there are seven such periods. According to Cyrus Ignatius Scofield, whose Reference Bible did much to popularize Darby's theory, the first five dispensations are the Age of Innocence, until the Fall of Man; the Age of Conscience, between the Fall and Noah's Flood; the Age of Human Government, from Noah until the Tower of Babel; the Covenant or Abrahamic Age; and the Age of the Law, from Moses until the Pentecost. We are at the close of the sixth dispensation, the Church Age (also known as the Great Parenthesis). The final or Kingdom Age, during which the end-times will occur, is nearly upon us.

Darby's scheme is called *pre*millennial" because it drew on Scripture to predict the disastrous and miraculous final events of history that will unfold *before* the Millennium (Christ's thousand-year reign on earth, from Revelation 20). Believing Christians will be physically carried off into the clouds to be safe with Christ in an event called the Rapture, said Darby. Apostates and un-believers, including the Jews, will remain behind, and the Antichrist will rule for seven years, resulting in terrible tribulations on mankind. For the Jewish people, this period will be the "Time of Jacob's Trouble," spoken of in Jeremiah 30:7. The Antichrist will offer what appears to be peace to Israel and the Arabs will move the Dome of the Rock from the Temple Mount to a new Babylon. The Jews will then rebuild the Temple. But midway through the seven years, the Antichrist will demand to be worshipped as God, outlaw Jewish religious practices, and lead armies from the north, south, east, and west against Is-rael. Ultimately one-third of the Jewish people will convert to Christianity and spread the gospel. The rest will be killed. Christ and his raptured saints will break through the clouds and defeat the Antichrist in a battle at Armageddon, outside Jerusalem. He will cast Antichrist into a lake of fire, bind Satan, throw him into a bottomless pit, and judge the nations. Jesus will then rule over a Jewish kingdom with Jerusalem as its capital for 1,000 years, extending Jewish hegemony over the rest of the world. After that millennium has passed, Satan will be loosed and will launch another rebellion, which God will suppress. The last events will be the resurrection of the dead, Judgment Day, and the creation of a new heaven and a new earth.

Paul Boyer observes in *When Time Shall Be No More,* his important history of prophecy belief in modern America, that Darby's theological system con-tained few elements that were entirely new. Rudimentary divisions of divine history go at least as far back as the twelfth-century prophecy scholar Joachim of Fiore. Increase Mather wrote in 1669 that the Jews would return to their own land and establish "the most glorious nation in the whole world."[20] Mather and many others also spoke of a Rapture doctrine, though not by that name, since the Bible does not use the term. The concept is based on Paul's prophecy of the "catching away" of the faithful into midair:

> For the Lord himself will descend from heaven with a cry of command, with the archangel's call, and with the sound of the trumpet of God. And the dead in Christ will rise first; then we who are alive, who are

left, shall be caught up together with them in the clouds to meet the
Lord in the air; and so we shall be with the Lord. (1 Thessalonians 4:
16–17)

Darby, however, was unique in concluding that the Rapture would occur before
the seven-year tribulation. The Jews' central end-times role and the idea they
and Gentiles were on separate prophetic tracks were also distinctive and controversial aspects of dispensationalism.[21]

Darby popularized his theory through his writings and preaching tours,
including seven trips to the United States between 1862 and 1878. The timing
was propitious. Liberal theologians in America and Higher Criticism scholars in Europe were challenging the idea that the Bible is the literal word of
God, causing great distress to Bible-believing Christians. Embattled American
evangelicals welcomed Darby's emphasis on biblical literalism and prophecy.
Darby's focus on the Jews' return to Palestine, their centrality in the unfolding
of divine history, and their expected final acceptance of their messiah has had
a profound impact on generations of devout Protestants, particularly in the
United States. It spread through Bible conferences, Bible institutes, a network
of publications, and especially the *Scofield Reference Bible* of 1909. Scofield wove
Darby's dispensationalist doctrine into his commentary, which he printed on
the same page as the biblical text. By World War I, dispensationalism had
become nearly synonymous with fundamentalism and Pentecostalism. Today,
perhaps 10 percent of white American evangelicals, about five million people,
embrace Darby's ideas.[22] — just a wild guess

At the center of the dispensational system is the idea that the Jews would
establish their own state. Without that, there would be no Antichrist, no tribulation, no battle of Armageddon, and no Second Coming. "In short, everything
was riding on the Jews," Timothy P. Weber observes in *The Road to Armageddon*,
his foundational study of dispensationalism and Israel.[23]

The Restoration of the Jews

Darby dismissed theories that England was the new Israel. That idea dates to
the sixth century and appears in Bede's eighth-century *Ecclesiastical History of
the English People*.[24] Darby rejected, too, the expectation that the Millennium
would be set in America, as Jonathan Edwards and others had proposed. The
Puritans in New England were concerned to build a perfect Christian polity in
America. They referred to their own experience in the New World in biblical
language, as if they themselves were the new Israel. As a result, they were not
focused on the literal Zion in Palestine. Increase Mather (1639–1723) looked

forward to the Jews' conversion and restoration to Palestine as a prelude to Christ's return, and even called for the destruction of the Ottoman Empire in order to help that happen. But his goal was to build the kingdom of God in America. In the 1730s, Jonathan Edwards, the leader of the Great Awakening, argued that human perfection would usher in the Millennium. Then Christ would reappear. As the scholar of religion Yaakov Ariel notes, this optimistic "postmillennial" view, that human efforts could bring the millennial kingdom into existence *before* Christ's Second Coming, supported the notion of a Christian America as a redeemer nation. By the 1840s, the first strong premillennial influence reached America. William Miller and his followers believed that Christ would appear in 1843 and the millennial kingdom would follow. When that did not happen, Miller moved the date back a year. Twenty years later, some of his disappointed followers organized into the Seventh-Day Adventists. Miller's eschatology had no role for the Jews, whose importance, he thought, had ended with the birth of Jesus.

In England, by contrast, end-times beliefs issued in a very strong interest in the conversion of the Jews and their restoration to the Holy Land. There were, in fact, Christian proto-Zionists in England 300 years before modern Jewish Zionism emerged.

The availability of sixteenth-century English translations of the Bible, and the Protestant belief that authority rests in the Scriptures, not in exegesis by the Church Fathers, inspired some Protestants to read the Bible in new ways. Putting aside the Church's traditional amillennialism, which understands Revelation 20 figuratively, they read these verses literally and concluded that the Jews would convert to Christianity and be restored to the Promised Land. They did not advance this "restorationist" argument without risk. One of the first to express this view was the clergyman Frances Kett, who called for returning the Jews to Palestine in 1585. The Anglican Church declared his writing heretical and Kett was burned at the stake.[25] One of the early seventeenth-century restorationists, Sir Henry Finch, a legal officer of King James I, also suffered for his convictions. In 1621, Finch published *The World's Great Restauration, or Calling of the Jews and with them of all Nations and Kingdoms of the Earth to the Faith of Christ,* which proposed that Abraham's progeny should reclaim their biblical homeland. The book was understood at the time as calling for all Christian princes to acknowledge the supreme authority of the Jewish nation. That put Finch in an unenviable position at court. He was arrested and tried, and was released only after disavowing any challenge to the king's sovereignty.

By the 1640s, the restorationist movement had taken hold in England. Palestine was no longer a land of purely Christian associations but the once and future homeland of the Jews. Many Puritans no longer applied Old Testament narratives solely to themselves as the reembodied Israel. Rather, they now believed that the covenant remained in effect for the Hebrews' physical descendants. And the Jews' return to Zion was, for them, the necessary prelude to the coming of the Messiah.[26]

Curiously, these English beliefs may have influenced, and been influenced by, the Jewish false messiah Shabbatei Zvi. Zvi inspired hopes for national restoration when he declared himself the Messiah in Smyrna in 1665. Many Jewish communities, still shaken by massacres of Jews in eastern Europe in 1648, were overtaken by messianic fervor. Zvi's fame also spread among Christians in Holland, Italy, Germany, and England, where premillennialists paid close attention. Rumors about Zvi traveled as far as New England, where they impressed the clergyman John Davenport, an associate of Increase Mather who, like Mather, anticipated the restoration of the Jews. In 1666, however, the year in which some Christian writers expected the apocalypse, Zvi was arrested in Istanbul. Facing death, he chose to convert to Islam, devastating many of his followers.[27]

Sir Isaac Newton, who had a profound interest in Judaism, was, from the 1670s until his death in 1727, a premillennialist, a literal exegete of biblical prophecy, and an ardent advocate of the Jews' restoration to the Holy Land. Like most Christian Zionists today, Newton considered God's covenant with Abraham in Genesis to be permanent and irrevocable. Entering into a debate that still goes on, he rejected claims that the prophecies of the Jews' return from exile had already been fulfilled. Rather, he argued, the prophets foresaw two returns, one from Babylon, the other from the current diaspora. Newton based this "double return" of the Jews on Isaiah 11:11: "In that day the Lord will extend his hand yet a second time to recover the remnant which is left of his people." He believed that the Jews would convert to Christianity and return to the Holy Land prior to Armageddon, which, he calculated, would occur no earlier than the year 2060.[28]

English poets also addressed the restoration of the Jews long before the birth of modern Zionism. John Milton spoke in *Paradise Regained* (1671) of God's returning the repentant Jews' to their land in His own time:

> Yet he at length, time to himself best known,
> Rememb'ring Abraham, by some wondrous call
> May bring them back repentant and sincere,
> And at their passing cleave the Assyrian flood,
> While to their native land with joy they haste,

As the Red Sea and Jordan once he cleft,
When to the Promised Land their fathers passed;
To his due time and providence I leave them. (III. 433–40)

Alexander Pope depicted the Jews adorning the courts of a restored Jerusalem, and barbarous Gentiles worshipping in the third Temple, in "The Messiah" (1712), his versification of prophecies from Isaiah in the form of a Virgilian eclogue.[29]

English clergy and government officials were proto-Zionists, too. Joseph Priestly, an eighteenth-century clergyman and polymath (he co-discovered oxygen), believed in the restoration of the Jews to "Canaan." In the 1830s, as Darby and his associates were developing and promoting their dispensational ideas about the restoration of the Jews, Anthony Ashley Cooper, the lay leader of the evangelicals in Britain, tried to translate faith into political action. Ashley, the seventh earl of Shaftesbury, believed that the return of "God's ancient people" to Jerusalem would hasten the Second Coming, and he urged the English foreign secretary, Lord Palmerston, to facilitate it. In fact, the Zionist slogan "A land without a people for a people without a land" traces back to Shaftesbury. Though not a literal reader of the Bible himself, Palmerston had practical reasons to enable the Jews' return to Zion under British protection: to use them as a wedge into the region, to help prop up the collapsing Ottoman Empire, and to frustrate French and Egyptian ambitions regarding Palestine. Palmerston appointed the first Western vice consul in Jerusalem to protect its Jewish inhabitants. Then in 1840 he tried unsuccessfully to persuade the sultan that the Jewish people would bring wealth to the Turks, "promote the progress of civilization," and check the evil designs of Mehemet Ali, the ruler of Egypt and pretender to the Caliphate.[30]

Another biblical literalist and restorationist was the German-English William Hechler, who believed that the Jews' return to Zion and the Second Coming of Christ were imminent. As a boy, Hechler wrote, he "entertained an almost superstitious reverence for Jews" and sought to protect them. After the Russian pogroms of the early 1880s, he and Shaftesbury formed a committee to resettle Jewish refugees in Palestine. In 1893 Hechler published *The Restoration of the Jews to Palestine according to Prophecy,* in which he predicted that the Jews would possess the Holy Land within five years. In 1895 he became the chaplain in the British embassy in Vienna, where he introduced himself to Theodore Herzl, the founder of the modern Zionist movement.[31]

Herzl was not the first Jew in nineteenth-century Europe to propose Jewish emigration to Palestine. Starting in 1839, rabbis Judah Alkalai and Zvi Hirsch Kalischer each called for Jews to colonize the Holy Land. Contrary to Orthodox belief, the Jews did not need to wait for the Messiah to return to Zion, said Kalischer: they could do it themselves. Moses Hess, a German Jewish socialist who was inspired by Giuseppe Mazzini's attempts to unify Italy, called in 1862 for the Jews to fulfill their own national aspirations—in Palestine. Hess saw danger in the ethnic hostilities of Europe, especially German anti-Semitism. But it was in Russia that these fears were first realized, in 1881–82, in the pogroms and the "May Laws" that severely restricted Jewish rights. Some Russian Jews who had advocated secular enlightenment and cultural emancipation in a pluralistic society now looked to a different solution: departure for Palestine or the United States. Leo Pinsker, in his enormously influential book *Selbstemanzipation ("Auto-emancipation")* in 1882, asserted that the Jews would not have the respect of other nations until they had their own land—though he didn't think that it had to be Palestine. In any case, hundreds of thousands of Jews preferred to remain in Russia, hoping for more tolerant times.[32]

Herzl, for his part, was acutely sensitive to the insecurity of the emancipated European Jews. The last straw for him came when Alfred Dreyfus, a captain on the General Staff of the French army, was arrested in 1894 and convicted of a trumped-up charge of high treason. That, for Herzl, was a symbolic moment. Dreyfus was a Jew who was deeply concerned to be 100 percent French, but he was shamed nonetheless. Anti-Semitism seemed to Herzl to be on the ascent everywhere in Europe except England. He determined that the Jews must seize control of their fate by making a thoughtfully planned exodus from Europe.

Eager to advance Herzl's program for Jewish emigration to the Holy Land, Hechler arranged for him to meet with the Grand Duke of Baden, uncle to German Emperor Wilhelm. That led to an audience with the Kaiser, who, for a time, was very warm to Herzl's plan.[33] When the first Zionist congress met in 1897 in Basel, Hechler and a number of other Christians attended in a gesture of support. Herzl and the Zionists didn't take the Christians' millennialist motives seriously but appreciated the political value of their support. The Christian Zionists, for their part, were enthusiastic allies but were disappointed that Zionism was a secular movement.[34]

Veneration of the Bible, the Jews, and the Holy Land was also a factor in 1917 in the British government's issuing the Balfour Declaration, which supported a national home for the Jews in Palestine. David Lloyd George, the British prime minister at the time, said in his *Memoirs* that he had had practical motives for advancing the declaration: he supposed that American Jewish financiers were sufficiently influential to bring the United States into World War I on the side of the Allies and that Russian Jews could keep their country in the war.[35] Historian Barbara Tuchman dismissed those motives, arguing that British rulers' real reason for promising a Jewish homeland was that they intended to hold on to Palestine for its strategic value and they needed a high-minded justification. Tuchman also suspected that Lloyd George wrote the diary entry in order to conceal his private convictions, which, like Arthur James Balfour's, were biblical. Both he and Balfour certainly were influenced by their lifelong interest in the Holy Land and Judaism. Lloyd George wrote later of his natural admiration and sympathy for the Jews, and the fact that he was more familiar with the history of the Hebrews than of the English. Balfour referred to the Jews as "a great and suffering nation." His biographer said that he always spoke eagerly of his sympathy for Jewish philosophy and culture and of the immeasurable debt, shamefully repaid, that the Christian religion and civilization owe to Judaism.[36]

William E. Blackstone

Increasingly over the course of the nineteenth century, Americans advocated the Jews' return to their ancestral home. In 1819, for example, former president John Adams imagined a disciplined army of 100,000 Israelites conquering Palestine and establishing Judea as an independent nation. Methodists, Congregationalists, and Presbyterians embraced restorationism, though the more established Episcopalians and Unitarians did not. The fullest expression of this subject before the Civil War was by George Bush, a professor of Hebrew at New York University and a direct ancestor of the two presidents who bear his name. This George Bush wrote in 1844 that the Jews should reestablish their state in Palestine, thereby elevating themselves to a rank of honor among the nations. Like most American restorationists, though, he sought to accomplish this through prayer and "carnal inducements," not through political action.[37]

With the rise of dispensationalism in the United States in the last decades of the nineteenth century, American evangelicals become as intensely interested in the Jewish restoration to the Promised Land as their counterparts in Britain were.[38] American premillennialists were mainly passive in their support for Israel prior to 1948, though, with the conspicuous exception of William E. Blackstone. In 1891, Blackstone sent a memorial, or petition, to President Benjamin Harrison urging the restoration of the Jews to Palestine. More than 400 prominent Americans had signed it. He sent a second petition in 1916 to Woodrow Wilson. Though not a premillennialist, Wilson had grown up in an evangelical atmosphere and was a member of the Presbyterian Church, which endorsed Blackstone's proposal. Wilson spoke in favor of a Jewish home in Palestine at least twice, but only privately. American Zionists Louis Brandeis and Steven Wise said later that their success in winning Wilson's support owed to their appeal to his biblically based Christian faith. Brandeis and Wise welcomed Blackstone's contributions, and Brandeis actually called him the Father of Zionism, noting that his work antedated Herzl's. These leading American Zionists were not bothered by Blackstone's eschatology, with its catastrophic expectations for the Jews.[39] Several prominent American Jewish leaders and Israeli officials take precisely the same position today about evangelical end-times beliefs, as we shall see in Chapter 8.

Blackstone's efforts had no immediate results, but he added an important element to the American Christian Zionist narrative: that the United States has a mission to be the modern Cyrus, the Persian king who allowed the Jews to return to Jerusalem after the Babylonian exile. God has chosen America for this role because of its moral superiority to the rest of the world, according to Blackstone, and He will judge it according to how the United States carries out its task.[40] Evangelical supporters of Israel today, including some with close relationships with the Bush White House, still say the same, as we shall see in Chapter 2.

Between the wars, evangelical Zionists continued to be passionately interested in Jews, the Zionist movement, and the Jewish community in Palestine. They were often critical of Arab hostility toward the Zionist project, which some writers condemned as an attempt to block God's plans for the end-times, as many still do. Christian Zionists did not shape British policy on the Middle East, though. They may have had some influence, modifying it or balancing other views, but conservative evangelicals in Britain had weakened dramatically as a political force.[41] After 1925, American born-again Christians, for their part, largely withdrew from political and social contests. The founding of Israel in 1948 and the Six-Day War in 1967 contributed mightily to their reemergence in the public arena, however, especially in the United States.

Replacement Theology

Darby rejected the long-standing belief that God is finished with the Jewish people, that all of His promises of good to Israel have been transferred to the Church. Christian Zionists refer to that belief as "Replacement Theology" and they consider it a profound theological error. They believe that God's plan for the Jewish people is eternally valid and that to say otherwise is to assert that the Lord reneges on His promises.[42] Clarence H. Wagner, Jr., former international CEO of Bridges for Peace, one of the largest Christian Zionist organizations based in Israel, offers a classic repudiation of such "supersessionism." He points out that in Romans 11:17–23, the Gentiles are wild branches grafted onto the olive tree of Israel (the image to which Rabbi Meister referred at the Rend the Heavens conference). The tree, says Wagner, represents the covenants, promises, and hopes of Israel (Ephesians 2:12), rooted in the Messiah and fed by the sap of the Holy Spirit. Gentiles are told to remember that the olive tree holds them up, Wagner observes. He does not mention that, according to Romans, the Jews have been cut off from the tree because of their disbelief. Wagner does point out, though, that Gentiles should respect the natural branches, the Jews, who can be grafted back on again.

The New Testament references to Israel pertain to Israel, not to the Church, Wagner argues. They are literal, not figurative. The scriptural promises include the Gentiles, but they do not exclude the Jews. In Romans 11, a key chapter in this context, Paul says that the Jews are beloved for the sake of the Patriarchs, and that God's gifts and calling of Israel are irrevocable. Psalm 105:8–11 and Jeremiah 31:35–37 also speak of God's promises as everlasting. For the Christian Church to arrogate these promises to itself, as it has done since the second century A.D., is arrogant and self-centered, Wagner declares. The result, he says, has been centuries of anti-Semitism.[43]

When I asked Christian Zionist leaders in Israel and across the United States how George W. Bush, a Bible-believing, born-again Christian, could urge Israel to give up land that God promised to Abraham in Genesis, most of them offered a single explanation: he believes in Replacement Theology. That is a matter of debate, however.

2

❧❖❧

Promise and Prophecy,
Love and Remorse

The Bases of Evangelical Support for Israel

"I Will Bless Those Who Bless You"

It has been widely reported that evangelicals have a dangerous ulterior motive for backing Israel: the belief that the Jews' return to their biblical home will lead to their mass conversion or death and will hasten the Rapture and the Second Coming. The reality is far more complicated than that, however. Many evangelicals do embrace these dispensational expectations, but, according to the best estimate, the vast majority do not, as we shall see. Rather, Christian Zionists testify by their words and actions to a complex set of convictions and motivations that impel them to bless, support, and sometimes even love Israel and the Jewish people.

For very many born-again Christians, the chief biblical imperative to bless Israel is God's promise to Abraham in Genesis 12:3, which promises a reward for those who bless the Jews and punishment for those who curse them:

I will bless those who bless you and curse him who curses you.

This verse is by far the most prominent reason that evangelicals cite for their backing of the state of Israel. Every evangelical Zionist I spoke with, leaders and laity alike, from Jerusalem to Washington, D.C., to Midland, Texas, alluded to this promise of blessing for those who bless Israel. Cyrus Ignatius Scofield said in his note to this verse in his 1909 edition of the Scofield Reference Bible that this promise has been "wonderfully fulfilled in the history of the dispersion. It has invariably fared ill with the people who have persecuted the Jew—well with those who have protected him." Scofield added with confidence that the future will prove this principle even more remarkably. Many Christian Zionists today firmly believe that this has, in fact, come to pass.

Born-again Christians' support for Israel is often generous and heartfelt, but that is not to say that it is selfless. Jews who doubt evangelicals' sincerity or question their motives should consider that Christian Zionists' enthusiasm for Israel and the Jewish people is driven, in large measure, by self-interest. Genesis 12:3 is the central biblical foundation for that. The United States has been blessed, many evangelicals told me, solely because it has blessed Israel and the Jewish people. And they fear that if America should ever turn against Israel, God will do the same to the United States. "God has blessed America because America has blessed the Jew," said Jerry Falwell, invoking this verse in 1980. "If this nation wants her fields to remain white with grain, her scientific achievements to remain notable, and her freedom to remain intact, America must continue to stand with Israel."[1]

The point is just as potent for many evangelicals today, including some who advised George W. Bush and high officials in his administration. "I want God to bless America, not curse America," the Southern Baptist Convention's Richard Land told me in 2005. "I firmly believe that God blesses those who bless the Jews and curses those who curse them." Land, the president of the Southern Baptist Convention's Ethics and Religious Liberty Commission, is a highly influential public policy figure in Washington. He consulted every week with the Bush administration and had regular contact with Bush himself. Speaking with the perspective of a man who graduated magna cum laude in history at Princeton, then did his D. Phil. in theology at Oxford, Land observed that, when you consider our sin and our neo-pagan lifestyle, the United States isn't a nation that you'd pick to get the number one blessing in the world. We wouldn't even qualify for number two. But God has blessed us more than any other country, said Land. Just compare America in the twentieth century with Germany, or Russia, or Poland. God has bestowed this blessing because we've been the least anti-Semitic nation in the West and because we've supported Israel, he said. Harry Truman backed the establishment of the state in 1948, he noted. And Richard Nixon saved Israel during the Yom Kippur War in 1973 by sending it an emergency supply of weapons when attacks by Arab states placed it in existential danger. Land acknowledges that God has blessed the Arabs, too, through their progenitor, Ishmael. But the Lord's covenantal relationship is with the Jews through Isaac (Genesis 17:20–21). It is to them that he has given the land, and the United States must safeguard their claim to it. "I would be terrified for my country if we were at cross-purposes with the survival of the Jews in the Middle East in the land that God gave them," Land told me.[2]

Other Christian Zionist leaders, following Scofield, stress the curse that will fall on those who curse Israel. John Eidsmore, a legal scholar, wrote in his *God and Caesar* in 1984 that God has judged every world power that turned anti-Semitic: the Assyrians, the Babylonians, the Amalekites, the Phoenicians, the Philistines, and the Syrians. "If we turn anti-Israel," he warned, "God will judge us."[3] John Hagee, founder of the lobbying group Christians United for Israel, extended that list of the Jews' enemies. At the 2007 the American Israel Public Affairs Committee (AIPAC) policy conference in Washington, D.C., he asked what had become of those who had persecuted the Jewish people—the Pharaohs, the Babylonians, the Greeks, the Romans, the Ottoman Empire, and "that goose-stepping lunatic Adolf Hitler." Hagee's answer was graphic: they are all "footnotes in the bone yard of human history."[4]

Evangelical Zionists discover this curse in more recent circumstances as well. Jan Markell, a Christian of Jewish descent who speaks for Olive Tree Ministries in Maple Grove, Minnesota, in 2007, pointed to Tony Blair. The once-very popular British prime minister had lost much of his following in recent years, in large part because of his support of the Iraq war. Markell, however, attributed his decline to Blair's Middle East policy. "He thinks a Palestinian state, essentially forbidden in Joel 3, will cure the world's ills," said Markell. Leaders who ignore the Bible have no common sense or understanding of issues, she concluded.[5]

Christian Zionists trace the effects of Genesis 12:3 in Africa, too. Apostle Zilly Aggfey, an evangelical from Nigeria, lamented that the curse had fallen on his own country. He was one of 200 evangelicals from around the world who came to Israel in 2007 to celebrate the fortieth anniversary of the reunification of Jerusalem, a visit organized by the Knesset Christian Allies Caucus. Aggfey addressed the Knesset, saying that when Nigeria cut relations with Israel in 1973, its economy failed. Since restoring relations, however, it has revived economically. "Any nation that does not serve you will perish," Aggfey concluded. "African Christians would love to kiss the ground in Israel," he added. "They would love to kiss the feet of a Jew."[6]

Not every evangelical understands Genesis 12:3 to offer material blessing, or security, or personal success. David Parsons, the media director for the International Christian Embassy Jerusalem (ICEJ), says that the promise in Genesis 12:3 is not some special "prosperity powder" that Christians sprinkle on themselves by blessing Israel. Rather, Christians should bless the Jews because of what they have already received through them: the gift of eternal life. St. Paul says in Galatians 3:13–14 that everyone who hangs on a tree is cursed (as in Deuteronomy 21:23), Parsons notes. By suffering such a death, Christ willingly took on that curse, allowing the blessing of Abraham to come upon the Gentiles, he says. As a result, they "receive the promise of the spirit through faith." This, says Parsons, fulfills Jesus' own words, "Salvation is of the Jews" (John 4:22). And that, according to Paul, imposes an obligation on Christians to aid Israel financially: "If the Gentiles have come to share in their spiritual blessings, they ought also to be of service to them in material blessings" (Romans 15: 27). That is a principal mission of the ICEJ.[7]

Jews who favor an alliance with evangelicals emphasize Genesis 12:3 as the source of evangelical support for Israel. In fact, however, Christian Zionist beliefs comprise a complex system of scriptural mandate, historical justification, political conviction, and empathic connection. Much of it is founded on God's mystery, and on love.

God's Covenant Is with Abraham, Isaac,
and Jacob—*Not* with Ishmael

The high authority that evangelicals attribute to Scripture leads many of them to honor their common spiritual heritage with the Jewish people, and to prize the covenants and prophecies relating to Israel, as Robert Stearns does. God gave the Holy Land to Abraham, Isaac, and Jacob, the ancestors of the Jewish people, they affirm. But, like Richard Land, several prominent Christian Zionists emphatically note that He did *not* give it to Ishmael, Abraham's firstborn son, whom they take to be the ancestor of the modern Arabs.

Some evangelical leaders argue that there would be no Israeli-Arab conflict if not for Abraham's lack of faith, and his wife Sarah's. In fact, they say, there would be no Arabs. The Lord repeatedly promises Abraham a son in Genesis, but the patriarch is impatient, notes Franklin Graham, Billy's son and the president and CEO of both of the charity Samaritan's Purse and the Billy Graham Evangelistic Association. So Abraham and Sarah decide to give God some help. "Aren't we all prone to that?" Graham asks. Sarah has the brilliant idea to help God along by having Abraham father a child with her handmaid, Hagar, Graham wryly observes. Ishmael is the result. Modern Arabs trace their ancestry to him, says Graham, and the rivalry for the land is therefore a matter of cousin killing cousin. = half-brothers

The blood spilled in Israel is thus the result of Sarah's and Abraham's impatience and disbelief, says Graham. Then, he contends, the Israelites compounded the error by disobeying the Lord's command to make no covenants with the Canaanites (Judges 2:1–3). As a result, the descendants of Ishmael will be a thorn in your side, God tells His people. That thorn, Graham concludes, pricks the Jews to this day.[8] This is a standard Christian Zionist understanding of the Arab-Israeli conflict. Abraham's temporary lapse of faith led to 4,000 years of catastrophe for the Jews, says Hal Lindsey, whose *The Late Great Planet Earth*, the best-selling nonfiction book of the 1970s, popularized reading recent events in the Middle East through the lens of the Bible.[9]

Israel as God's Prophetic Clock

Many evangelicals support Israel because they believe that God's covenant with the Chosen People remains valid. They see these promises as eternal, inerrant, and literally true. Most compellingly, Christian Zionists believe that the scriptural prophecies that God will bring his people back to their land are coming to pass in our lifetime. They therefore see the founding of Israel in 1948 and the Israeli capture of East Jerusalem, Judea and Samaria on the West Bank, Gaza, and the Golan Heights in the 1967 Six-Day War as decisive turning points in history.

Jerry Falwell said that May 14, 1948, the day on which Israel declared its statehood, was the most important date since Jesus' ascension to heaven. (Behind his desk at Liberty University he kept a mounted page from the *Palestine Post*, dated May 16, 1948, with the banner headline, "STATE OF ISRAEL IS BORN.")[10] For several senior Christian Zionist leaders, that day changed their lives. Jack W. Hayford was one of them. The birth of the modern state of Israel was the pivotal moment for him, says Hayford. His pastor at the time, a dynamic Bible teacher, explained the prophetic passages that were being fulfilled, and Hayford marks that day as the start of his growth not only as a supporter of Israel but as a Christian leader.[11] He began ministering at the Church on the Way in Van Nuys, California, in 1969, and today is the president of the International Church of the Foursquare Gospel. He also oversees The Kings College and The Kings Seminary and has a worldwide teaching ministry.

For many devout Christians, the Israeli conquest of the old city of Jerusalem in 1967 also was a crucial event, marking the end of the "times of the Gentiles" that Jesus himself foretold (Luke 21:24). Jesus prophesied the history of the Jews in that verse: "They will fall by the edge of the sword, and be led captive among all nations; and Jerusalem will be trodden down by the Gentiles, until the times of the Gentiles are fulfilled."[12] As many evangelical Zionists understand it, this prediction spans nineteen centuries and more. It comprehends the rule over the city by a series of Gentile peoples, from the Romans in the second century to the Jordanians in the twentieth. With the return of the Jews to their land, however, the emergence of the Jewish state, and Israel's capture of Jerusalem, the time of the Gentiles has been completed. That brings history to the end of the age and to a new phase that will culminate in the "coming of the Son of Man." Pat Robertson is quite straightforward about the role that this prophecy played in his support for the Jewish state. In June 1967, as soon as he heard that war had broken out in the Middle East, he said, "Something just responded within me. I knew this had enormous significance, that we at CBN [the Christian Broadcasting Network] were linked with Israel. It had to do with the last times, and it had to do with the fulfillment of the prophecy that Jesus made when he said Jerusalem will be trodden under foot until the times of the Gentiles be fulfilled."[13]

Israel is thus God's prophetic clock, telling the hours and days until the advent of Christ. In the dispensationalist view, the clock had stopped but began to tick again with the birth of the State of Israel. With this in mind, Falwell called the existence of Israel "the single greatest sign indicating the imminent return of Jesus Christ."[14] John F. Walvoord, the president of Dallas Theological Seminary, called Israel's seizure of the old city of Jerusalem in 1967 "one of the most remarkable fulfillments of biblical prophecy since the destruction of Jerusalem in A.D. 70." Several authors argued in *Moody Monthly* that God had fought for Israel. In the Christian Zionist view, these events are enormously significant in moving divine history forward, but they are much more than that: they are empirical proof that biblical prophecy is true. L. Nelson Bell, who, along with his son-in-law, Billy Graham, founded *Christianity Today,* wrote in that journal that the Jews' possession of a united Jerusalem "gives the student of the Bible a thrill and a renewed faith in the accuracy and validity of the Bible."[15]

Indeed, the Six-Day War is specifically justified by Scripture, said one writer in the journal *Christian Life* in 1973.[16] The born-again Palestinian Walid Shoebat elaborated on that idea in 2006. Psalm 83, he said, speaks of a confederacy of Ishmaelites (Arabs, said Shoebat), inhabitants of Tyre (Lebanese), Philistines (Gazans/Palestinians, he said), and Assyrians (Syrians, Iraqis, and Turks). These peoples will attempt to cut Israel off from being a nation, the psalm tells us, but God will rebuke Israel's enemies so that they will be ashamed and will seek the name of the Lord. This, Shoebat said, actually happened in the 1967 war. In any case, it happened to Shoebat. He says the he was once a terrorist and a member of the Palestine Liberation Organization, but that he became a Christian while reading the Bible, "which had fallen from heaven on my arrogant head." "I changed from being a terrorist to being an ambassador for the coming Messiah."[17] He sought the name of the Lord.

In the eyes of Christian Zionists, the prophetic countdown proceeds and the hour is late. In September 2007, citing a report that Israel's Ehud Barak had offered joint control of the Temple Mount to Egypt, Jordan, and the Palestinian Authority, the Jerusalem-based organization Christian Friends of Israel responded incredulously: "Does he know what time it is?"[18]

Judgment

Some evangelicals cite another profoundly self-interested motive for supporting Israel: they believe that their treatment of the Jews will be God's principal standard for judging their souls at the close of time. The prominent Christian Zionist Derek Prince wrote in 1978 that the Lord will judge the nations as the prophet Joel foretold:

> For behold, in those days and at that time, when I restore the fortunes of Judah and Jerusalem, I will gather all the nations and bring them down to the valley of Jehoshaphat, and I will enter into judgment with them there, on account of my people and my heritage Israel, because they have scattered them among the nations, and have divided up my land. (Joel 3: 1–2)

God will condemn those who oppressed Israel or resisted his purposes for them and claimed jurisdiction over Israel's land, says Prince.[19]

John Hagee, one of the most active and influential Christian Zionists today, cites the same reason to bless the Jews. "Every Bible-believing Christian knows," says Hagee, "that when Jesus Christ returns to earth, the first thing that's going to happen is the Judgment of the Nations. The basis of that judgment is how did the gentile people treat Israel and how did they treat the Jewish people. If they are found guilty of anti-Semitism, they face the judgment of God."[20] Jim Sibley director of Criswell College's Pasche Institute of Jewish Studies in Dallas, makes the same case. The Old Testament prophets, he says, especially Zechariah and Isaiah, often speak of the coming judgment of the nations. And the Bible makes it clear that the basis of that judgment will be how concerned they were for the Jewish people, says Sibley. A Baptist who ministered to messianic believers in Israel for thirteen years, Sibley advocates evangelizing Jews. In fact, the Southern Baptist Convention appointed him as its chief missionary to the Jews.[21] But his beliefs about God's criteria for judging the world suggest that, like Hagee, he considers his primary duty to be supporting and defending the Jewish people.

Love

"It's almost embarrassing how respectful [evangelicals] are of God's Chosen People," says one prominent Jew who works with hundreds of Christian and Jewish pro-Israel groups.[22] But Christian Zionists' feelings for the Jewish people often go well beyond respect. Many Christian Zionists speak explicitly of a love for the Jews and Israel, a love that I thought I'd detected in Robert Stearns's face as he spoke to us at the Rend the Heavens conference. "It is not possible to say, 'I am a Christian' and not love the Jewish people," says Hagee. And the Bible teaches that love is not what you say but what you do, he adds, citing 1 John 3:18.[23]

God mysteriously planted this love, this "heart for Israel," in them, several evangelical leaders told me. This happened to some people without any apparent cause or preparation. Malcolm Hedding, executive director of the International Christian Embassy Jerusalem, had this feeling for Israel appear in his heart, for example, when he was a young man in South Africa. He'd had little previous exposure to Jews, and there wasn't much interest in Middle East affairs in his family, which he describes as very Victorian English. But God found him in the South African bush and gave him a heart for Israel.[24] Others came to care for Israel by reading *The Late Great Planet Earth,* as Ray Sanders, now the international director of Christian Friends of Israel, did in 1974.[25]

Other people needed no specific precipitating event. They somehow always knew that they would devote much of their lives to Israel. That was the case with Miriam Rodlyn Park, whom we met in Chapter 1. At fourteen she read *The Diary of Anne Frank.* Then, after living with a Jewish family for the last two years of high school, she was sure of her path. "I wasn't given to romantic fantasizing," she says. "I just knew deep down I'd be very much involved in protecting Jewish people." Her mother must have had a premonition about that: she gave her the Jewish name Miriam (Rodlyn goes by her middle name).[26]

The love that many evangelicals feel for Israel is inexplicable. "A wife asks her husband, 'Why do you love me?'" Pastor Glenn Plummer told me. "What's the right answer to that one? Whatever you say is wrong," he said. "There's no right answer. The same is true with my love for Israel." For Plummer, an African-American who came to Christ at the age of nineteen in Brooklyn while listening to a religious radio program, love for Israel came very gradually. "I never had any substantive relations with Jews at that time," he said. "The more I studied the Bible and preached, I used Israel as an illustration. It was a long process for me, though I had affinity to Jews because of my love for the Lord and the Bible." After his first trip to Israel in 1996, he began to feel a deep-seated passion to bring Jews there. Plummer is now the senior pastor of a nondenominational charismatic church in Detroit. He is also the former head of the National Religious Broadcasters Association, and founder and CEO of the Christian Television Network. His goal is to inspire love for Israel among American blacks. "Jews need to tell African-Americans, when you needed a friend, we fought for you, died with you," he said, speaking of the civil rights movement. "Now Israel needs a friend. Get in black people's faces. You can do that. I told the Knesset [the Israeli parliament] that."[27]

Unrequited love comes with heartache, though, and that can be true of love for Israel and the Jewish people. One Christian Zionist in Texas told me that he was dedicating his life to serving Jews, but that he and others "feel that our Jewish friends are tolerant of everyone but us." Rather than welcome the love he offers, this person said, Jews frequently express the fear that evangelicals secretly want to convert them. "They're like family. We fight more than other people," he noted sadly. This has taken a toll on him. "Nobody in his right mind would do this," he told me. I was used to hearing Jewish anxieties about evangelicals, but this gentle and dedicated man surprised me with a perspective I hadn't considered before. "Christians despise you because you're not proselytizing. Jews despise you because [they think] you are. It's so hard, so lonely. There's so much discouragement. If you didn't have this from God, there's no way you could stand up to this," he said.

Love need not be selfless, for Christian Zionists as for others. John Hagee cites the Gospel story of a Roman centurion who asks Jesus to heal his slave. The elders of the Jews tell Jesus, "He is worthy to have you do this for him, for he loves our nation, and he built us our synagogue" (Luke 7: 4–5). This Gentile did something practical to bless the Jewish people, Hagee points out, and therefore he deserved the blessing of God.[28] The obvious message is that the same applies to Christians today.

The loving gestures that Christian Zionists extend toward Israel include praying for the peace of Jerusalem (Psalm 122:6), as we saw in Chapter 1, and comforting the Israeli people, as God requires in Isaiah 40:1–2: "Comfort, comfort my people, says your God. Speak tenderly to Jerusalem, and cry to her that her warfare [or time of service] is ended, and that her iniquity is pardoned, that she has received from the Lord's hand double for all her sins." This is an important passage in motivating evangelical defense and support of Israel. It also inspires their philanthropy to the Jewish state, as does Paul's exhortation that Gentiles should share their material blessings with the Jews (Romans 15:27).

Gratitude

Many evangelicals acknowledge with gratitude the debt that they owe to Judaism and the Jewish people. Robert Stearns declares that he is indebted to the Jews for "the blessing of monotheism that was purchased with the blood of Jewish martyrdom." Hagee adds that, without the Jews, there would be no possibility of salvation for Christians. "Jesus Christ, a prominent rabbi from Nazareth, said, 'Salvation is of the Jews!'" Hagee notes (John 4:22). He points out that the Jewish people have given Christianity the Scriptures, the patriarchs, the prophets, Mary, Joseph, and Jesus, the twelve disciples, and the apostles. In return for these many gifts, Hagee declares, Christians should give practical support to the modern state of Israel, as Paul says in Romans 15.[29] This verse has become central to Christian Zionists, an important basis for the enormously generous amount of charity that they give to Israel every year. In 2006, for example, at the annual Night to Honor Israel at his Cornerstone Church in San Antonio, Texas, Hagee announced the John Hagee Ministries would donate $7 million to the Jewish state; in 2007, he gave Israel an additional $8 million to assist in immigration, absorption, and other philanthropic aid.[30]

Remorse

My evangelical informants repeatedly expressed their deep remorse for the Church's abuse of Jews in the name of Christ for nearly 2,000 years. Derek Prince traces the Church's "appalling record of anti-Semitism" from John Chrysostom through Martin Luther, then declares that "the Nazis merely reaped a harvest that the Church had sown." All Christians must accept our share of responsibility for Christian anti-Semitism, says Prince. He cites Pope John XXIII's little-known prayer of confession and repentance of 1965:

> We are conscious today that many, many centuries of blindness have cloaked our eyes so that we can no longer see the beauty of Thy chosen people, nor recognize in their faces the features of our privileged brethren.
>
> We realize that the mark of Cain stands upon our foreheads. Across the centuries our brother Abel has lain in the blood which we drew, or shed tears which we caused by forgetting Thy love.
>
> Forgive us for the curse we falsely attached to their name as Jew.
>
> Forgive us for crucifying Thee a second time in their flesh. For, O Lord, we know not what we did.[31]

A similar plea for forgiveness was expressed by the delegation of 200 evangelicals who came to Israel in 2007 to celebrate the fortieth anniversary of the reunification of Jerusalem. They brought with them a message of repentance for past Christian persecution of Jews and anti-Semitism. Pastor Pitts Evans of Virginia read it to the Knesset:

> On behalf of millions of Christians who love Israel and pray for her, we would like to repent before you for crimes committed against the Jewish people throughout history in the name of Christianity. We have sinned against God and against you.
>
> We have not lived according to the mandate given to us by the Scriptures; to love God with all our hearts and to love our fellow man as we love ourselves. May God grant you the ability to forgive us, and may we be brothers and sisters again.[32]

Some evangelicals, while accepting the guilt of Christian anti-Semitism, place the ultimate blame on Satan. In *Your People Shall Be My People,* Don Finto confesses that the Gentile Church not only failed to protect the Jews but also participated in their persecution. He points to Satan, the invisible but powerful opponent, as the source of this crime.[33] Other leading Christian Zionists also name the devil as the father of Arab and Muslim hatred of Jews, as we shall see in Chapter 5. Whatever its source may be, some evangelical leaders declare that unless they denounce this anti-Semitism, they are complicit in it. "Forgive us, Lord, that this hatred for your people continues to rise, *and so many of us remain silent,*" said a Bridges for Peace Prayer Focus following a story on increased acts of worldwide anti-Semitism in 2006 (emphasis mine). Robert Stearns's Eagles' Wings organization established its Watchmen on the Wall program specifically to teach Christian volunteers to denounce anti-Jewish acts and to serve as goodwill ambassadors for Israel. The training manual for this program begins by noting that the European Union reluctantly admitted in 2004 that "there is now widespread agreement that the present rise of Anti-Semitism in Europe is the most severe since World War II." But God is placing Watchmen on the Walls of Jerusalem, notes the manual, just as he promised in Isaiah 62:6–7. In the words of Isaiah, these watchmen "shall never be silent . . . until he establishes Jerusalem and makes it a praise in the earth." The first section of the manual reviews God's covenant with Israel, the Jewish roots of Christianity, and "The Miracle of Israel though the Eyes of [Jewish] History." It then offers a historical account of Christian persecution of the Jews that is far more detailed than most Jews ever learn. Each section of the manual is followed by a question and answer segment and a list of suggested readings.[34]

Christian Zionists' remorse is particularly focused on the Holocaust. Just as Robert Stearns openly lamented Lutheran Germany's unspeakable treatment of the Jews during the 1940s, other conservative Christians deeply repent of that horror. One senior evangelical leader was close to tears as she told me that the last thing many Jews saw before being killed and thrown into ditches on the eastern front was the cross—on the lapels of the German soldiers who were about to murder them.

Some evangelicals have come to feel this guilt and remorse only gradually. The prominent Christian Zionist Jack Hayford recalls how startled he was to discover, as he did in 1970, that Jews felt that the Holocaust had been perpetrated by Christians. Unlike Derek Prince, Hayford had considered it incomprehensible that Nazism could be equated with the word "Christian." This brought home to him how ignorant he had been of the death-dealing influence of Christians in the Crusades and the Holocaust, including the hands-off policies of the United States and the Vatican during World War II. "History, I found, had driven a spike into Jewish hearts and a wedge between God's ancient people and Christians at large," Hayford notes. That same year he made his first trip to Israel. These two experiences awakened his sensitivities and motivated him to be bold in supporting Israel and world Jewry, he says. Though he believes that the Holocaust was God's punishment of the Jews for turning away from Him (as in Deuteronomy 28), Hayford notes that "beyond the Law's judgments are the awe-inspiring promises of the prophets." He cites in particular Ezekiel's prophecy of the resurrection of God's Chosen and their return to their Land. This is laden with God's fullest heart of love for the Jews, says Hayford. Beyond the horror of the past is the God-given hope for the Jews' complete restoration and redemption, he says.[35] Hayford, who has visited Israel nearly three dozen times, sees Judaism as the spiritual foundation of Christianity. "A gentile who accepts the messiah joins the Jews," he said at the Jerusalem Prayer Banquet at the Beverly Hilton in Los Angeles in 2007. "So I see myself as Jewish spiritually," he noted. "I see myself as a gentile Jew."[36]

"The Jewish People Are Not Alone Any Longer"

Christian Zionists typically interweave these reasons for allying with Israel with political considerations. They especially cite the fact that Israel is a friendly democracy in a dangerous and hostile region, the front line against a terrorist enemy that also has the West in its sights, as we shall see in Chapter 4. For these evangelicals, politics and biblically based faith are inseparable. Indeed, they see current events in the Middle East not only as confirming and realizing the Word of God but as reiterating biblical events. "The ghost of Haman is alive in Ahmad[i]nejad," said Robert Stearns at the Jerusalem Prayer Banquet in Los Angeles. Stearns was warning that the genocidal plans of Haman, the Persian villain who tried to exterminate the Jews in the Book of Esther, are being revived in Ahmadinejad, the president of Iran (modern Persia). But evangelical Christians will stand with the Jews in this time of danger, Stearns declared. "The Jewish people are not alone any longer."[37]

Very many evangelicals also side with Israel for the simplest and, from their perspective, the most self-evident of reasons: because God does. Jack Hayford expresses this succinctly: "Every believer is charged to make Jews a priority in their value system because God has," he says. "Scripture speaks to us very clearly," Hayford adds. "We're dealing with the roots of everything that has to do with the revelation of God to humankind."[38]

There are other bases for their support that Christian Zionists mention less readily. One is the dispensational belief that the Jews' restoration to Israel will bring on the Second Coming. We shall examine this current manifestations of this view in Chapters 8 and 9.[39] Another, less well known aspect of Christian Zionists' beliefs is what many of them see as a conflict between God and the Judeo-Christian West, on the one hand, and Satan and Islam, on the other. Critics often dismiss evangelical expressions of this idea as isolated outbursts, reflections of religious extremism or personal craziness. We shall see in Chapter 5, however, that they are part of an integrated theology of cosmic war.

Modern Christian Zionism is informed, in large measure, by the evangelical faith from which it emerged. I therefore offer a brief overview of the history and character of evangelicalism in the next chapter before considering American evangelical views of Arabs and Muslims in Chapter 4.

3

The Evangelical Mosaic

Good News

Evangelical Christians are so individualistic and diverse that it's hard even to identify and count them, much less to define their theology or measure their political convictions definitively. There is no agreement about how many evangelicals there are in America, in part because there is no single comprehensive definition of who they are or what they believe. One should not think of evangelicalism as a single vessel majestically transporting a unified community of believers to political domination, social redemption, and eternal salvation. Rather, it is like a vast fleet of rowboats and boogie boards, each bearing an individual in search of an authentic personal experience with God.[1]

The word "evangelical" comes from the Greek noun *euangelion,* meaning "good news." The English word "gospel" is an exact translation of that phrase: *god spel* means "good news" in Old English. (Since it's not easy to say the sounds of *d, s,* and *p* together, the phrase was reduced over time to "gospel.") Evangelical religion has always focused on the gospel, the good news that Christ's sacrifice on the cross has made salvation available to mankind.

In the Middle Ages the word "evangelical" had various meanings. As the eminent church historian Mark A. Noll observes, it was used to designate the Christian message of salvation. Alternatively, the word also referred to the four Gospels (Matthew, Mark, Luke, and John), the entire New Testament, or the Old Testament book of Isaiah, in which Christian interpreters found prophecies of Christ. During the sixteenth century, the term came to be associated with the Protestant Reformation and became a virtual synonym for "Protestant." Evangelical Lutheran churches retain that meaning today.

Martin Luther's "evangelical" Christianity differed from the teachings of the Roman Catholic Church in several key respects. It came to stand for belief in salvation by faith alone (*sola fides*) rather than by good works. It defended the idea that Christ's death on the cross was sufficient in itself for salvation. This meant that people were not dependent on the mediation of the Church or the repetition of this sacrifice in the Catholic mass. It emphasized the supreme authority of the Bible alone (*sola scriptura*) as read by all believers, and the priesthood of all believers (rather than a class of priests).[2] The Protestant theologian Karl Barth elegantly defined evangelicalism as a faith "informed by the gospel of Jesus Christ as heard afresh in the 16th century Reformation by a direct return to Holy Scripture."[3]

Modern evangelicalism originated in a series of Protestant spiritual renewal movements in the middle third of the eighteenth century in England, Wales, Scotland, Ireland, and Britain's North American colonies. These were intense periods of response to gospel preaching and unusual efforts at godly living. The precipitating events were known in Britain as the Evangelical Revival and in America as the Great Awakening.[4]

Nineteenth- and Twentieth-Century Evangelical Views

Nineteenth-century British and American evangelicalism remained a single movement in many respects, though the American version was more socially dominant and culturally pervasive.[5] Evangelicalism in this period was conservative theologically but not necessarily politically. The evangelical William Wilberforce and his circle led the British antislavery movement, promoted prison reform, and sponsored charity schools. Evangelicals also supported national liberation movements, mainly concerning Christian minorities who sought independence from the Ottoman Empire. In addition, born-again Christians in the nineteenth and twentieth centuries led international reform campaigns, often supporting women's rights: they opposed suttee (the burning of widows) in India and foot-binding in China, and championed women's suffrage and female education in the Third World.[6]

Reverence for the Bible as the word of God, always important to the Puritans, was significant in shaping American cultural perspectives. It was particularly central in forming the battle lines against two new theories that were imported from Europe in the nineteenth century: Higher Criticism of the

Bible and Darwinian evolution. Both of these theories posited historical patterns that directly challenged Judeo-Christian core beliefs. Higher Criticism, or "source criticism," analyzed the literary strands of the Bible to argue that the text consists of distinct strata that were added and edited over time. This approach, developed chiefly by German scholars, challenged the bedrock Jewish and Christian conviction that God alone authored the Scriptures. It also ran directly contrary to a main current of American historiography by reading the Bible through the prism of history. American writers, by contrast, tended to do the opposite, interpreting history through the lens of Scripture.[7]

Many American evangelicals did, however, welcome another European theory that was popularized in the United States, starting at almost precisely the same time as source criticism and evolution: premillennial dispensationalism. Like Darwinism, this new theory traced historical events to understand how they led to the present. And like the Higher Criticism, it scoured the Scriptures to find previously unnoticed patterns and connections. Unlike them, however, this approach affirmed the literal truth of Scripture and God's authorship of events, as we saw in Chapter 1. By identifying discrete historical epochs as a series of fresh starts, this belief accorded with the American tendency to view experience as consisting of new departures.[8] And by placing Israel and the Jews at the vortex of climactic world events, it helped set the stage for the current popular American support for the Jewish state, as we shall see.

Evangelicalism and Fundamentalism

American fundamentalism was born of these contests of belief about natural history and Scripture, and of resistance to cultural changes that many Christians regarded as spiritually degrading. One common paradigm is that fundamentalism represents an attempt by true believers to resist assaults on their faith and social values. The distinguished historian of religion Martin E. Marty identifies a pattern in which fundamentalism typically emerges in any culture: a constituency with a conservative or traditional point of view feels threatened to the core by "modernity." (No modernist group has ever turned fundamentalist.) The perceived danger may be different in different times and contexts, but it always involves the undercutting of deeply felt values. The threat becomes especially urgent when modernist signals reach one's children.[9]

The word "fundamentalism" derives from a series of pamphlets called *The Fundamentals: A Testimony of Truth*. Written by American and British theologians, they were a grassroots response to the liberalism of elite seminaries and churches. From 1910 to 1915 three million of these pamphlets were distributed free of charge to Protestant pastors, evangelists, missionaries, YMCA secretaries, and others, with the intention of halting the erosion of fundamental Protestant beliefs: the inerrancy of the Bible; God's direct creation of the world *ex nihilo;* the authenticity of miracles, the Virgin Birth, the Crucifixion, and the bodily Resurrection; the doctrine that Jesus died to redeem man's sins; and, for some believers, Christ's imminent return to judge and rule the world. In 1920, a conservative Baptist editor added *-ist* to "Fundamental," inventing the word "fundamentalist" to describe people who were prepared to do "battle royal" for the religious principles expressed in *The Fundamentals.* Although not all early fundamentalists were premillennialists, about half of the American contributors to the pamphlets were, including C. I. Scofield, editor of the reference Bible that contained the commentary of choice for American premillennialists.[10]

The Scopes "Monkey" Trial

By the 1920s, "evangelical" had become a designation without clear meaning, used by theological liberals and conservatives alike.[11] "Fundamentalism," by contrast, was now a broad generic term for conservatives from major Protestant denominations and revivalists who militantly opposed modernism and liberalism in the churches and society.

The Scopes "Monkey" trial in 1925 is often represented as the pivotal event in which modernism, championed by H. L. Mencken and Clarence Darrow, discredited the fundamentalist biblical view of the world and shamed those who opposed the teaching of natural selection. In many ways, though, the trial represented a defeat for modernism. Tennessee's anti-evolution law stood for forty-two more years and publishers all over the county purged Darwinism from high school textbooks. In addition, the trial seemed to end the possibility of wedding progressive politics to evangelical moralism, as William Jennings Bryan, the prosecutor in the case, had tried to do in his career.[12] The division between religious liberalism and conservatism now became a chasm. Theological liberals gained control of the mainline denominations in the North, and the fundamentalists became more fixed in their convictions, and more separatist. Protestant fundamentalists withdrew to their own churches and Bible colleges, and founded radio ministries, publishing houses, mission agencies, and other constituents of an alternative religious infrastructure. The fundamentalist subculture thrived. Yet it remained beyond the view of many triumphalist liberal thinkers for decades. This degree of separatism ultimately became a principal distinction between fundamentalists and the people who now referred to themselves as evangelical.[13]

Billy Graham and the New Evangelicals

In the 1940s and later, evangelicalism came to represent a deliberate attempt by moderate fundamentalists to break away from the separatist, oppositional, and anti-intellectual faith in which they'd been raised.[14] In 1949, Billy Graham, a young preacher associated with the Youth for Christ movement, made headlines with the spectacular success of his revivalist tent meetings in Los Angeles. He became the leader of the "new evangelicals," who tempered the militancy of their fundamentalist background and engaged with society in order to transform it through the gospel.[15]

Those who now called themselves fundamentalists advocated a strict separation from secular culture, a change from the meaning of the term prior to the 1920s. They also wanted to keep themselves pure of what they considered to be God-forbidden fellowship with false Christian teachers of unscriptural doctrines. Evangelicals, by contrast, formed a broad coalition with other theological conservatives. George M. Marsden, one of the most distinguished scholars of fundamentalism, notes that some evangelicals tended to be more militantly conservative, or "fundamentalistic," than others. His shorthand definition of a fundamentalist (or a fundamentalistic evangelical) is "an evangelical who is angry about something."[16]

Marty observes that fundamentalists are first and foremost oppositionist. They recognize the corrosive force of the "acids of modernity," which they experience as a threat. They then fight back to reclaim the world for God. Marty notes that one expression of this is that fundamentalists are antihermeneutical: they deny that symbols are multivocal, that readers' presuppositions color interpretations, and that understanding of the whole determines the rendering of each part. Protestant fundamentalists believe, rather, that ordinary people making ordinary use of their senses can make sense of the Bible and the world. Nineteenth-century Protestants thus became self-confident about their purchase on the truth. Another aspect of fundamentalists' oppositionism, says Marty, is that they deny that many different contentions can all be legitimate. They conflate that view with relativism, which they reject. They also oppose developmental and progressive understandings of history, endorsing instead millennialism, in which the end of events is already known.[17]

The Religious Right

Ironically, fundamentalists, who sought for half a century to isolate themselves from popular culture, have found themselves compelled to take an active part in politics in the last three decades. In withdrawing from the secular world, they had hoped to avoid the contamination of political and social contests. Jerry Falwell, in his 1965 sermon "Ministers and Marchers," called on the church to preach the word, not to "reform the externals." Preachers, he declared, are called to be soul winners, not politicians. By the late 1970s, however, Falwell and others on the religious right, comprising fundamentalists, fundamentalistic militants, Catholics, and Mormons, shifted radically, from quietism to political activism.[18] There were a number of reasons for that. The cultural revolution of the 1960s and 1970s posed a serious threat to traditional concepts of family and sexuality. The anti–Vietnam War movement angered many people who wanted to defend Western values and simple patriotism. It also provoked those who saw Satan working through godless Communism. Supreme Court decisions to remove Bible reading and prayer from public schools, give women the unrestricted right to abortion, and relax constraints on pornography also moved fundamentalists to engage in political debate.

Randall Balmer, a scholar of religion at Barnard College, offers a darker account of the political emergence of the religious right, however. He says that conservative Christians were activated in the 1970s by a desire to defend racist admissions policies at private Christian schools. They came to focus on abortion only later. Balmer charges that evangelicals have abandoned the nineteenth-century spirit of their movement, of fighting for the disenfranchised and championing abolition, women's suffrage, and universal education.[19]

Three Evangelical Camps

When analyzing religious, political, and social views, survey experts often don't distinguish between evangelicals and fundamentalists, or between those groups and Pentecostals and charismatics (who emphasize the gifts of the Holy Spirit, especially speaking in tongues, faith healing, and prophecy). John Green, the eminent demographer of American religion and politics, speaks of evangelicals as a general, inclusive group. But he notes that, according to polling data, there are three camps among them. The largest group consists of traditionalists, who comprised 12.6 percent of all Americans in 2004. They maintain orthodox religious beliefs in the face of social change and are the main constituents of the religious right. Many of them are adherents of figures like Robertson and, until his death, Falwell. Seventy percent of traditionalists identified as Republicans. Ninety-three percent opposed evolution, and 77 percent believed that the world will end in a battle between Christ and the Antichrist at Armageddon.

The next largest camp consists of centrists, who made up 10.8 percent of the American population in 2004. They are represented by leaders like Rick Warren. Author of *Purpose-Driven Life,* which has sold thirty million copies, Warren is the founder of Saddleback Church in Lake Forest, California, where 22,000 people worship each week. Though theologically and socially conservative, he avoids politics and focuses enormous effort on fighting AIDS and poverty in Africa. Nationwide in 2004, under half (47%) of centrist evangelicals were Republicans, 57 percent opposed evolution, and 53 percent expected Armageddon.[20]

Increasingly, the traditionalist and centrist camps have clashed over whether to expand their interests to address issues such as global warming. Richard Cizik, vice president of governmental affairs for the National Association of Evangelicals (NAE), for example, opposes abortion and gay marriage but also calls on evangelicals to adopt a much broader range of concerns. "Are we going to be the Religious Right theocrats, ideologues of sex?" he asks. Or are evangelicals going to pursue "God's agenda," including care for the poor and HIV/AIDS victims in Africa? That more inclusive view involves a commitment to "creation care" (including steps to arrest global warming), human rights, economic justice, and remedies for hunger around the world, says Cizik. Evangelicals will advance a human-rights biblical agenda no matter how much social conservatives like James Dobson, founder of Focus on the Family, urge them to stick to traditional marriage and abortion, Cizik declares bluntly. And he exhorts young evangelicals to heed both science and Scripture (Psalm 24:1) to become "Earth protectors," defying the traditionalist view that global warming is, in Falwell's words, "a satanic distraction."[21] Ted Haggard, then-president of the NAE, noted in 2005 that this wide range of concerns is actually scriptural. "The Bible is not about two or three issues," he said, adding that it is possible to be a Bible-believer and a liberal.[22]

The smallest of the three groups, representing less than 3 percent of the American population, consists of modernist evangelicals. Leaders like Jim Wallis, author of *God's Politics,* represent many people in the modernist camp. Wallis's *Sojourner's* newsletter advocates a comparatively liberal politics and carries articles critical of Israel. He argues that the Christian right's political views are almost the opposite of the true meaning of Christianity. "How did the faith of Jesus come to be known as pro-rich, pro-war, and only pro-American?" Wallis asks. For him, the religious right distorts the biblical vision of social justice by focusing only on sexual and cultural issues. He seeks to rally evangelicals to questions of poverty, the environment, and what he considers the unjust war in Iraq.[23] As early as 1973 Wallis and other progressive evangelicals had called for an organized born-again movement against poverty, racism, sexism, and violence, but for decades they wandered in the political wilderness.[24] They are currently receiving much more attention in the media. In 2004, modernists constituted 11 percent of evangelicals, and more of them were Democrats than Republicans (44% to 30%). Only 10 percent of modernists opposed teaching evolution and 29 percent expected the final battle at Armageddon. These evangelicals also reported lower levels of church attendance than did those in the other camps.

Although the press typically cites Robertson as a main spokesman for evangelicals, as they did Falwell until his death, the centrists and modernists together make up the majority of American evangelical Christians. Another measure, by the Pew Research Center, found in 2006 that 20 percent of white evangelicals considered themselves to be members of the religious right and 7 percent affiliated with the religious left, while most identified with neither.[25]

This taxonomy is important in understanding the concealed fracture lines in evangelical positions. Traditionalists, for example, are the most ardent evangelical supporters of Israel over the Palestinians. Interestingly, biblical literalists across religious traditions tend to share the same political views. Differences about policy virtually disappear among Catholics, evangelicals, and mainline Protestants who read the Bible as literally true.[26]

Three Characteristics of Evangelicalism

Scholars often cite three irreducible characteristics of evangelicalism. One is experiencing spiritual rebirth, which involves submitting oneself to the authority of Christ and accepting that one is saved solely because of faith in him. This is in accordance with John 3:3, in which Jesus says, "Truly, truly, I say to you, unless one is born anew, he cannot see the kingdom of God." This verse is the epicenter of the biblical message for born-again Christians, as the writer Mark Lilla puts it. When considered along with verse 16 in the same chapter: "For God so loved the world that he gave his only Son, that whoever believes in him should not perish but have eternal life," it captures the essence of evangelical theology.[27] The actual experience of being reborn can vary with the individual, though the Holy Spirit "readies the heart" in advance. Often a person confronts painful emotions, then turns to God, who meets him or her at the point of need and "strangely warms the heart," in the words of John Wesley.

The second characteristic is belief in the high authority of the Bible. Though interpretations of Scripture can vary, evangelicals typically accept Holy Scripture as the actual word of God.

The third defining aspect of evangelicalism is sharing one's faith. The spiritually reborn Christian may witness to the Gospel with spoken testimony or by doing service for God, including missionary work or charitable activities. It may involve modeling a good life, or "lifestyle evangelism." A 2005 survey found, in fact, that while fewer than half of white born-again Americans shared their faith with others through oral witness, three-quarters reported practicing lifestyle evangelism.[28] This is particularly congenial to the major Christian Zionist groups, since Israeli officials work with them only if they refrain from overt attempts to proselytize. For Robert Stearns, leader of a pro-Israel evangelical organization called Eagles' Wings, it means defending and valuing Jews and Israel without attempting to spread the Good News to them. He cites an admonition frequently attributed to St. Francis of Assisi: "Preach the Gospel always, and when necessary use words."[29]

David Bebbington offers an often-cited perspective on the same set of beliefs, emphasizing four essential convictions in evangelicalism: Christ's atonement for mankind on the cross; an eagerness to learn from the Bible as the guide and source of all ultimate truth; conversion, the belief that lives need to be changed; and activism rooted in zeal for the gospel, the idea that spiritual rebirth should result in some form of service for God. As Philip Yancy points out, under this overarching definition, Roman Catholics, mainline Protestants, and Orthodox can call themselves evangelical, and many happily do.[30]

The common element that underlies all of these qualities of evangelicalism is transformation—of the individual's heart and life, then of the world in the light of biblical values. Evangelicalism is all about change and movement, internal and external. When George W. Bush said in a debate of Republican presidential candidates in 2000 that Jesus was his favorite philosopher because "he changed my heart," conservative Christians knew exactly what he meant. Evangelicals are called to be action-oriented, a people on the move. The Holy Spirit summons them to go forth and save others in the same way that the first believers who made up the "church" in the New Testament were called. Indeed, the Greek word *ekklesia,* usually translated as "church," can be rendered as a "called-out assembly." Many evangelicals still consider themselves to be people who have been called out.[31] The early church was characterized by a globe-changing passion, said Carl F. H. Henry. "A Christianity without a passion to turn the world upside down is not reflective of apostolic Christianity."[32]

These shared convictions, as Noll says, have never been a tidy or precise guide to identifying evangelical Christians. Rather, they are like a spiritual river that runs through different denominations, including mainline Protestant and Roman Catholic churches. It passes through stand-alone churches and nondenominational megachurches, voluntary societies, and personal networks.

These emphases are fluid, shifting with the time and place, but they do provide an underlying coherence among believers.[33]

A Theological Free-For-All

For evangelical Christians, the church may be a central spiritual and social locus, but it is not the instrument of salvation. The Holy Spirit is. One is redeemed not through sacraments but through a wholly individual experience with the Spirit.

As Randall Balmer, the Barnard scholar, notes, evangelicalism is virtually a theological free-for-all. Each person's convictions are shaped by his or her own interpretation of Scripture, his or her local church and pastor, and the devotional materials he or she uses.[34] Many evangelicals aren't interested in doctrine. For them, feeling is believing, and faith is far more important than religion, which they associate with discord, says Alan Wolfe in *The Transformation of American Religion*. One minister categorized his church as "Heinz 57," reflecting the many varieties of belief found there. The great cathedral-like megachurches also resist doctrine, says Wolfe. Their pastors tend to think of their Christianity as postdenominational and try to convey a few core beliefs rather than a coherent set of specific doctrines.[35]

Evangelical theology isn't uniform because evangelicals aren't motivated by theology but by pragmatism, Dr. Jim Denison, the senior pastor of Park Cities Baptist Church in Dallas, told me. Once a person has found faith in Christ, his job is to help pass it on to the world. This is the Great Commission with which Jesus charged his followers in Matthew 28:19–20:

> Go therefore and make disciples of all nations, baptizing them in the name of the Father and of the Son and of the Holy Spirit, teaching them to observe all that I have commanded you.

"That is the heartbeat of evangelicals," Denison said. "It's certainly my heartbeat." Whatever theological perspective is helpful to fulfill that charge is acceptable, he added, and that's why evangelical beliefs and practices are so various.

Billy Graham, Denison pointed out, is the stereotypical evangelical. "He's brilliant, but he never went to seminary and he's not theologically sophisticated. He's trying to be practical. He wants to bring people to faith in Christ." Prominent evangelical preachers like Rick Warren, Charles Stanley, Joel Osteen, and Bill Hybels are also more practical than theological. "It doesn't mean that we're un-theological, but it's not the primary reason we're evangelicals,"

Denison told me. Evangelical sermons typically deal with pragmatic issues, he noted: "How to help your marriage, how to help you raise your kid, how to deal with your money. We are pragmatic to a fault."[36] That impulse toward pragmatism is a surprisingly important factor in evangelical support for Israel, as we shall see.

Unexpected Convictions

Just as evangelicals' paths to faith are varied, their social and political convictions are diverse. They generally try to make sense of their culture through the lens of their theologically conservative beliefs, but their conclusions are far from uniform. "You think that you Jews disagree with each other," one Christian Zionist leader in Texas said to me. "That's nothing compared to us!"

Evangelicals often don't fit the template of opinion that the press attributes to them, and sometimes they hold very surprising convictions. Former secretary of state Condoleezza Rice, for example, an intensely religious born-again daughter and granddaughter of ministers, supports a woman's right to abortion. She describes herself as a "pro-choice evangelical," a category that would confound most white conservative Christians.[37]

Another startling example: Pat Robertson approves the use of condoms and even abortion when the circumstances warrant it! Evangelical leaders are often pragmatic and this, for Robertson, is a matter of pragmatism over principle. Many conservative Christians disagree vehemently. They argue that sex education should stress abstinence and fidelity rather than birth control. Robertson defies the type, though. His charitable group, Operation Blessing, includes "the responsible use of condoms" in its AIDS education program in Africa. What's more, Robertson joined with modernist evangelicals Tony Campolo and Jim Wallis in signing a Global Fund letter endorsing the distribution of condoms to prostitutes! Dobson, by contrast, forcefully criticized this Global Fund policy, saying that it "legalized prostitution and all kinds of wickedness around the world."[38]

Even more remarkably, Robertson also has defended abortion when the situation requires it. Though he opposes abortion as a matter of conviction, he said in 2001 that he understands China's one-child-per-family policy, which in effect mandates that form of birth control. "They've got 1.2 billion people and they don't know what to do," Robertson said on CNN's *Wolf Blitzer Reports*. "If every family over there was allowed to have three or four children, the population would be completely unsustainable." "Won't your critics on the right be saying that Pat Robertson is justifying abortions in China?" Blitzer asked him.

(Indeed, one conservative critic said that Robertson was losing a screw, advancing a glorified abortion-for-convenience argument.) But Robertson stood by his point: that the Chinese government has to take action to prevent overpopulation, large-scale unemployment, and political instability.[39]

A third surprising illustration: Falwell said that he would vote for a Muslim for president. Evangelical leaders express broad distrust of Islam and many Christian Zionists warn that Muslims are conducting a religious war against God and the West, as we shall see in Chapter 5. After 9/11, Falwell himself denounced the Prophet Mohammed as a terrorist. But five years later he said that he would have no problem voting for a Muslim. The candidate would have to take the right position on terrorism, Israel's right to exist, and fiscal and social issues, of course.[40]

Ted Haggard provides another example of unexpected convictions, one ultimately colored by personal disgrace. Haggard was the founder and senior pastor of the 11,000-member New Life megachurch in Colorado Springs, Colorado. He is theologically conservative, a charismatic, spirit-filled Christian. On the question of Israel, though, Pastor Ted took a surprisingly heterodox theological position. Exploding the stereotype that all evangelicals fiercely oppose Israel's giving away an inch of its biblical inheritance in the West Bank, Haggard told Prime Minister Ariel Sharon in 2004 that Israel's security fence should not cut into Palestinian areas! "I told him walls work, but it's got to be on your own land," said Haggard.[41] Evangelicals' beliefs about Israel are surprisingly various, reflecting their faith and their politics, as Haggard's did in this case. Indeed, dozens of prominent evangelicals, including some leaders of the NAE, call on Israel to withdraw from the West Bank, as we shall see.

Another issue about which Haggard showed atypical convictions was gay rights. Despite the NAE's uncompromising stand on the subject, Pastor Ted displayed unusual tolerance. Like James Dobson, his friend and neighbor in Colorado Springs, Haggard publicly rebuked homosexuality and backed an amendment on the 2006 Colorado ballot defining marriage as a union between a man and a woman. But Pastor Ted did not oppose Colorado's Referendum 1, which would have given same-sex couples legal rights and benefits.[42] And, remarkably, he applauded a 2003 Supreme Court ruling that struck down a Texas antisodomy law. "Two consenting adults in a bedroom is not really the role of the state," he said. Moreover, when other local churches threatened to withdraw from an Easter event at New Life because a choir from a mostly homosexual church had been invited, Haggard refused to exclude the gay group.[43] At the time, his views seemed surprisingly liberal. In retrospect, it's easy to say that Pastor Ted's unusual inclusiveness came from a secret sympathy or identification with homosexuals. In November 2006, a male prostitute revealed that

Haggard had paid for sex with him and for methamphetamine over a period of three years. Pastor Ted resigned as president of the NAE. Soon afterward, the board of overseers of New Life Church dismissed him.

Ted Haggard's fall was an embarrassment to the evangelical movement in general, to the NAE, and to the Bush administration, which immediately tried to distance itself from him. (A White House spokesman falsely stated that Pastor Ted had not been a regular participant in weekly conference calls with evangelical leaders.) Evangelicals know better than most, however, that unwanted impulses persist in a fallen world. "What else is new?" said Dobson of his friend's disgrace. "We're flawed. Go back to the greatest men in the Bible. Look at King David. He killed a man to get his wife for sexual purposes. He repented. He said, 'I've sinned before God.' "[44] "Classic Christianity has always had a negative view of human nature," explained Michael Cromartie, vice president at the Ethics and Public Policy Center. The underlying belief is that people are frail and broken. "I'm not surprised by vice. I'm surprised by virtue," said Cromartie, who is evangelical himself. But, he noted, if people confess their wrongdoing, there is a saving grace that can release fallen humanity from guilt, shame, and sin. "That is why the gospel is called good news," he said.[45]

Heterodoxy among the Devout

There can be a tremendous gap between the views of conservative Christian leaders and those of ordinary evangelical Americans. This has been true from the earliest days of evangelicalism. Wesleyan professor Henry Abelove observes in *The Evangelist of Desire* that what John Wesley taught in the eighteenth century was not necessarily what Methodists learned.[46] Similarly, there is a distance today between pastors and their flock on several key items of faith. For example, more than two out of three born-again or evangelical Christians believe that a good person who isn't of their religious faith can get into heaven. That appears to defy Jesus' teaching in John 14:6: "No one comes to the Father but by me." As Steven Waldman, the editor of *Beliefnet,* said, that's pretty amazing, considering that it contradicts what they are most likely to hear their pastors say in church.[47] What's more, although 84 percent of evangelicals affirmed in 2004 that salvation is only by faith in Christ, in another survey that year, 80 percent of them said that Jews can go to heaven![48] Billy Graham, incidentally, is sympathetic to the heterodox position on salvation. He has preached all of his life that Jesus is the only way to heaven, but he won't say that God closes the door to Jews and other non-Christians. "I think he loves everybody regardless of what label they have," says Graham.[49]

Despite the extreme diversity of their faith, evangelical Christians share one conviction, Pastor Jim Denison told me: that lost people need Jesus. This belief, he says, is the only thing that Baptists from his church have in common with all of the other evangelicals from different denominations in local churches. The Billy Graham crusade in Dallas in 2002 brought together a broad variety of evangelicals, Denison recalled, and there was only one conviction that all of them shared: lost people need Jesus.[50]

4

⥜⥈⥜

The Arab and Muslim Enemy

Historian of religion Mark Noll criticizes classic dispensationalism for having promoted a supernaturalism that failed to attend to the reality of the world. Its adherents looked to the Bible to explain events and conditions without analyzing the actual conditions and events for themselves, says Noll.[1] No one can say that about modern Christian Zionists. Their Web sites, e-mails, publications, and broadcasts are filled with current detail about the Middle East, always as seen from a profoundly conservative perspective. Christian Zionists rarely cite scriptural reasons alone for their support of the Jewish state. Rather, their commitment to Israel is typically founded on a marriage between religion and geopolitics.

Nearly every evangelical supporter of Israel I spoke with joined his biblical and political views to reach two related conclusions: that God has given the Jews eternal ownership of the entire biblical land of Israel and that Arabs and other Muslims are determined to sabotage that divine covenant. A number of prominent Christian Zionists see Muslim opposition in a larger and even more threatening context: they warn that Islamic extremists, and perhaps all Muslims, intend to subdue not only Israel but Jews and Christians everywhere. They do not see political Islam as driven by Israel's occupation of the West Bank or American Middle East policies. As a result, they are certain that the Israeli-Arab conflict cannot be ameliorated through compromise, which they dismiss as appeasement. Rather, this is a clash of religions and cultures, in their view. Convinced that Islamists seek nothing less than worldwide Muslim domination, many evangelicals believe that Israel is fighting not only for its own existence but for the survival of the West. The Jewish state, for them, is the front line in the global war against Islamic fascism.

"'Land for Peace' Is a Cruel Chimera"

Their perception of the Arab-Israeli conflict leads Christian Zionists into a philosophical paradox. When it comes to Iraq, evangelicals tend to be the most confirmed political idealists in America: more than any other religious or ethnic group, they have supported the goal of transforming the region by spreading freedom and democracy, even by force. They hold the opposite philosophy with regard to the Israeli-Palestinian conflict, however. In that respect, Christian Zionists tend to be confirmed political realists, insisting that the Palestinian people cannot be transformed. The Palestinians will never tolerate a Jewish state, they say. Planting democracy among them is pointless, since they would only create a terrorist state dedicated to annihilating Israel.

In virtually every Web site and newsletter on the subject, Christian Zionists express the core belief that conceding territory will not bring Israel peace. The Palestinians do not seek two states side by side, they say, only the phased destruction of the Jewish state. (In 2007, 82% of American Jews agreed that this is the Arabs' true goal and seven of every ten Israeli Jews said that the Palestinians would destroy Israel if they could).[2] Jack Kinsella, in his *Christian Intelligence Digest*, for example, spelled out the steps of the Palestine Liberation Organization's (PLO) Phased Plan for the Destruction of Israel, adopted in 1974:

1. Through "armed struggle" (i.e., terrorism), to establish an independent combatant national authority over any land that is "liberated" from Israeli rule.
2. To continue the struggle against Israel, using the territory of the national authority as a base of operations.
3. To provoke an all-out war in which Israel's Arab neighbors destroy it completely.[3]

When the late Yasser Arafat spoke in English, he renounced terrorism and accepted the principle of a two-state solution to the Middle East conflict, but no Christian Zionist I spoke with ever trusted that. Becky Brimmer, international president of Bridges for Peace, told me shortly before Arafat's death, for example, that she believed him when he told audiences in Arabic that a Palestinian state would be the first step in the destruction of Israel.[4]

Hal Lindsey, in his book *The Everlasting Hatred: The Roots of Jihad,* refers to the Palestinian approach as the "Quraysh Strategy." It is based, says Lindsey, on the actions of the prophet Mohammed, who signed a ten-year peace treaty with the Quraysh tribe, his enemies in Mecca. Within a year, he annihilated them and captured Mecca, Lindsey observes. Arafat, speaking in a Johannesburg, South Africa, mosque in 1994, likened his signing of the Oslo Peace Accords the previous year to Mohammed's agreement with the Quraysh, notes Lindsey. Arafat then called for jihad to liberate Jerusalem. That incensed Israel's prime minister, Yitzhak Rabin, though it did not end the peace process. Faisal Husseini, Arafat's representative in Jerusalem, whom many Israelis considered a moderate, confirmed before his death in 2001 that Arafat was indeed using such a strategy. As Lindsey correctly points out, Husseini told an Egyptian journal that the Oslo Accords were a Trojan horse, a deception aimed at getting inside the walls of Jerusalem. The Palestinians, Lindsey concludes, clearly consider the Oslo framework and all other political agreements with Israel to be temporary steps toward their ultimate goal—taking all of historic Palestine from the Jews.[5]

Pat Robertson summed up the case against the Palestinians in a fiery speech at the Herzliya Conference in Israel in December 2003, when he told Israeli leaders and scholars,

> I hardly find it necessary to remind this audience of the stated objectives of Yasser Arafat, the PLO, Hamas, Hezbollah, and Islamic Jihad. Their goal is not peace, but the final destruction of the State of Israel. At no time do they, or their allies in the Muslim world, acknowledge the sovereignty of Israel over even one square inch of territory in the Middle East. If a Palestinian State is created in the heart of Israel . . . the ability of the State of Israel to defend itself will be fatally compromised. The slogan "land for peace" is a cruel chimera. The Sinai was given up. Did that bring lasting peace? No. Southern Lebanon was given up. Did that bring lasting peace? No. Instead Hezbollah rode tanks to the border of Israel shouting, "On to Jerusalem!." . . . Arafat was brought up at the knees of the man who yearned to finish the work of Adolf Hitler. How can any realist truly believe that this killer and his associates can become trusted partners for peace?

Robertson appealed to his Israeli audience not to surrender territory in the illusory hope of achieving peace. "Please don't commit national suicide," he implored them. "It is very hard for your friends to support you, if you make a conscious decision to destroy yourselves. . . . Be strong! Be strong!"[6]

"Yasser Arafat in a Suit"

Many evangelical leaders have no more faith in the Palestinian Authority's dem-ocratically elected president, Mahmoud Abbas, than they did in Arafat, despite the fact that Abbas has denounced terrorism and declared his willingness to rec-ognize Israel. The Bush administration expressed its support for Abbas, which it renewed after Hamas seized control of the Gaza strip in June 2007. American officials then considered it urgent to support Abbas as the comparatively mod-erate hope for a negotiated peace settlement and a viable Palestinian state. But Bridges for Peace, one of the major Christian Zionist groups in Israel, dismisses the Palestinian president as "Yasser Arafat in a suit." Bridges cited reports that a member of Abbas's Fatah party called his leader's recognition of Israel's right to exist a "political calculation." Fatah plans to flood the Jewish state with mil-lions of Palestinians, the Palestinian source said. Any other strategy would lead to civil war. Bridges followed this story with a passage from Psalms declaring God's derision of such deceit among the "nations" (peoples other than Israel):

> Why do the nations conspire, and the peoples plot in vain?
> The kings of the earth set themselves,
> And the rulers take counsel together,
> Against the Lord and his anointed, saying,
> "Let us burst their bonds asunder,
> And cast their cords from us."
> He who sits in the heavens laughs;
> The lord has them in derision.[7]

In 2007, Bridges asked its readers to pray "that the world will realize the true nature of Abbas, who speaks with a forked tongue to achieve the goals of his terrorist organization."[8]

After Hamas took control of Gaza, Bridges dismissed Bush's and Olmert's plans to bolster Abbas as insanity, which it defined as "doing the same thing over and over while expecting different results."[9] Christian Friends of Israel (CFI), another of the major evangelical Zionist groups in Israel, asked its read-ers to "pray that Israelis would see the futility of trying to appease the enemy by giving up their heritage for a bowl of stew." In saying that, it urged Israel to remain Israel, the name that Jacob took after wrestling with an angel (Genesis 32). It should not become Esau, Jacob's brother, who despised his birthright and sold it for bread and pottage (Genesis 25:29–34).[10] Gary Bauer, a candidate for president of the United States in 2000 who now leads the Washington-based group American Values, derided the Bush administration, the European

Union, and Israel for thinking that supporting "Holocaust denier Mahmoud Abbas" and his "Palestinian mafia" is the way to peace.[11] An informal poll by Yechiel Eckstein's International Fellowship of Christians and Jews in the summer of 2007 suggested that this feeling was widespread among Christian Zionists. Eighty-five percent of Eckstein's pro-Israel evangelical readers who responded said that "Fatah has blood on its hands—Israel and the U.S. should not support it under any circumstances."[12] In the fall of 2007, several Christian Zionist newsletters carried a report that appeared to confirm Abbas's duplicity: at the same time that the Palestinian leader was calling in English for progress in an upcoming peace conference in Annapolis, Maryland, the report said, Palestinian Authority TV was repeatedly playing a song in Arabic that promised the destruction of Israel.

Abbas would be assassinated if he even tried to achieve a Palestinian state, adds Jan Willem van der Hoeven, the head of the International Christian Zionist Center in Jerusalem. Fanatic Islamists would kill any one who wants to make peace with Israel, he says. The same Muslim extremists who murdered Anwar Sadat in 1981, and who now were destroying George W. Bush's dream of Western democracy in Iraq, will bring all peace efforts with Israel to a very bloody stop, says van der Hoeven—"all to Israel's pain and possible destruction."[13]

There is no compromise or concession Israel can make that will end the fighting, says Bauer. He argues that "the Islamofascists do not want peace with Israel or even a piece of Israel. They don't want a 'two-state' solution, where Israel is allowed to exist at all; they want a 'one-state' solution, where all 'Palestine' is governed by Shari'a [Islamic] law. They want to see the Islamic flag flying over Jerusalem. And their hatred won't be appeased until the last Jew has been driven out of Israel."[14] The ardent Christian Zionist John Hagee agrees. "There is no hope for peace between Israel and the Palestinians because Hamas and Hezbollah have covenants calling for the destruction of Israel," he warned in 2007. "They are terrorists sworn to the death of the Jews, so any attempt to make peace with them is a farce."[15]

Christian Zionists' political positions generally comport with their faith. Their representation of modern Arab savagery and duplicity is consistent with scriptural passages that prohibited biblical Hebrews from making agreements with Arabs, including Exodus 34:12: "Take heed to yourself, lest you make a covenant with the inhabitants of the land whither you go, lest it become a snare in the midst of you." Christian Friends of Israel cited this verse and juxtaposed it to 2 Corinthians 6:15: "What accord has Christ with Belial? Or what has a believer in common with an unbeliever?"[16] By quoting this latter passage to refer to the Palestinians, CFI implicitly linked Islam to the devil. That is a familiar evangelical view, as we shall see in Chapter 5.

The Election Of Hamas, January 2006

Several leading Christian Zionists, like other conservative supporters of Israel, have argued that the stunning upset victory of the Islamist group Hamas in the Palestinian Legislative Council elections of January 2006 revealed the Arabs' true murderous intentions. Hal Lindsey made that case forcefully: "The so-called 'moderate Islamic majority' that allegedly exists within the Palestinian population cast their ballots for Hamas—knowing full well that the existence of Hamas is dedicated to but one singular purpose: the destruction of Israel and the eradication of the Jewish population from the Middle East."[17] Gary Bauer said in one of his daily e-mails to supporters that even if Hamas officials promised to accept Israel's existence, their words would be empty. They would say that only to get aid from the West. From the moment it was conceived, said Bauer, Hamas has excelled at only one thing—killing Jews. He drew attention to a gruesome video on the Hamas Web site in which a suicide terrorist says, "My message to the loathed Jews is there is no God but Allah. We will chase you everywhere. We are a nation that drinks blood, and we know that there is no blood better than the blood of the Jews."[18]

Several Christian Zionists leaders see all Islamic terrorists and many or all Muslims as part of a murderous organic whole. "In the heart of the Muslim Arab lies no fertile ground for peace," charged Stan Goodenough, an avidly pro-Israel evangelical, in the Christian Zionist online news service *Jerusalem Newswire*. Goodenough likened Israel's enemies to a boa constrictor whose three crushing concentric circles surround the little Jewish state. The innermost circle consists of the Arab citizens of Israel, who, according to Goodenough, are aligning with Hamas. Next is Hamas itself, "that uncompromising gang of murderers and their supporters—those 'ordinary' Arabs U.S. Secretary of State Condoleezza Rice *still* insists want to live in peace with Israel." The outermost coil of this malevolent snake is "the unstable and arrogant Ayatollah-run Iran." All of these enemies of Israel constitute a single, venomous organism, said Goodenough.[19] Intentionally or not, he was adapting and paraphrasing the Hamas charter, which says, "The liberation of Palestine is bound to three circles: the Palestinian circle, the Arab circle, and the Islamic circle. Each of these circles has its role in the struggle against Zionism."[20]

In 2006, several Israeli and American officials did see a growing alliance of convenience among these groups, if not a unifying bond based on faith. They warned that the cutoff of Western aid to the Hamas-led government would drive it into the arms of Iran. By late that year, Avi Dichter, Israel's minister of public security, concluded that Hezbollah was Iran's northern wing vis-à-vis Israel and Hamas had become its southern wing. Some moderate Arab states, too, saw Hamas, an offshoot of the Muslim Brotherhood, as part of a global Islamic movement that is challenging Arab governments.[21] Some Christian Zionists welcomed Hamas's victory in one respect, however: it provided moral clarity. The West may have fooled itself into thinking that Arafat wanted lasting peace, but that was a deception, they said. The Palestinians' true intentions were now out in the open.

A number of observers argued, by contrast, that Hamas's election victory did not reflect a majority of popular support. Many Palestinians who are not radical Islamists voted to punish the ruling Fatah party for its venality and incompetence. "The reign of plunder and arrogance that Fatah imposed during the years of its primacy . . . gave Hamas its power and room for maneuver," said Fouad Ajami, author of *The Dream Palace of the Arabs*.[22] In the end, it was hopelessness that led the Palestinians to vote for Hamas, added James D. Wolfensohn, the former Middle East envoy of the Quartet (the U.S., Russia, the European Union, and the UN). The Palestinians were extremely optimistic after Israel removed its settlements from the Gaza Strip in 2005, he said, but they descended into despair when the border terminals were closed, turning Gaza into a prison. On top of that, they resented the Fatah leadership's embezzlement and graft. Employment stood at 50 percent in Gaza, yet Fatah officials drove through refugee camps in Mercedes, built luxury homes for themselves, and created private armies.[23]

Moreover, Fatah conducted an inept electoral campaign. Its candidates ran against each other, splitting the vote, while Hamas was disciplined. As a result, although Hamas got only 41 percent of the votes, it swept most of the races. Hamas also was helped by the popularity and organizational strength of its network of efficient and honest social service providers. "Hamas was building schools and kindergartens and clinics while the PLO was building casinos and villas for its leaders," said the Israeli-Arab journalist Khaled Abu Toameh, speaking of the Fatah-controlled Palestinian Liberation Organization. "Hamas is in power today because of Arafat and Abbas."[24]

Abbas was weak and tentative and had failed to reform Fatah after Arafat's death. But Israel bore some responsibility for Fatah's defeat as well. Sharon had weakened Fatah and Abbas by disengaging from the Gaza Strip unilaterally, declaring that Israel had no one with whom to negotiate. That robbed Abbas of a victory. And it allowed Hamas to claim that it had driven Israel out of Gaza by force, which was more than years of negotiations had accomplished. Still, Palestinians expressed a clear preference for Fatah and a distrust of Hamas's competence and veracity.[25] A majority (57%) said that they supported a two-state solution, not the destruction of Israel.[26]

To Christian Zionists, however, what mattered was that the Palestinians had chosen a murderous band of Islamofascists to represent them. Many Israelis and others agreed that the Palestinian vote was in fact an endorsement of Hamas's intent to destroy the Jewish state.

"First the Saturday People, Then the Sunday People"

Especially since 9/11, many conservative religious Americans, and many others as well, have come to associate Islamic suicide bombers in Israel with Al Qaeda's attacks on American targets. When Bush asked Karl Rove in the spring of 2002 what "our people" think of the Israeli-Palestinian conflict, Rove replied, "They think it's part of your war on terror."[27] That is true of many supporters of Israel, regardless of their religious persuasion. Several evangelical leaders say that if Israel falls to the terrorists, the United States will too.

In that respect, Christian Zionist leaders now ascribe to Islamists the theological status that they attributed to the Soviet Union before its collapse. Conservative Christians previously had declared that it was Russia that would have to deal with Israel before attacking the United States. Tim LaHaye, for example, said in 1984 that "Israel is the Achilles heel to the Soviets' design for world supremacy. Before they can suppress the world with their totalitarian ideology they must first knock out the United States. And to do that, they must first remove Israel." As long as the Israeli Air Force has nuclear weapons, said LaHaye, Russia will not attack the United States.[28] Arab rulers, the "kings of the south" (Daniel 11:4–45), were expected to join Russia in the final assault on Israel, but they were mere allies of the Soviets. The rise of Ayatollah Khomeini in Iran in 1979 brought new attention to the Muslim threat. The Iraqi invasion of Kuwait in 1990 quickened interest in dispensationalism, and sales of Hal Lindsey's 1970 book, *The Late Great Planet Earth*, spiked by 83 percent. Dispensationalists expected Saddam Hussein to rebuild Babylon so that Christ would return and destroy it.[29] Al Qaeda's attacks on the United States on September 11, 2001, then established Arabs as the principal threat to the West as well as Israel.

The NAE's Richard Cizik says explicitly, "Evangelicals have substituted Islam for the Soviet Union. The Muslims have become the modern-day equivalent of the Evil Empire."[30] Mark Noll doubts that radical Islam excites the same degree of animus among evangelicals that communism did, but it certainly seems to in leaders of the religious right, including many Christian Zionists. Paul Weyrich, a founder of the Christian right, predicted in 2007 that radical Islam would be *the* motivating issue in the 2008 presidential election, if Christian voters could be educated to appreciate the danger that it truly represents. Pat Robertson agreed. Islamic extremists are a worse threat than the Russians ever were, said Robertson, declaring that "the blood lust of Islamic terrorists" was the overriding issue in the 2008 election.[31] Many Christian Zionist leaders warn that the Muslim world's expansionist program has taken up where the Soviets' left off, with theology as the driving force. Radical Islamists' true goal, they say, is worldwide domination over Christians as well as Jews. Evangelical leaders sometimes cite a graffito attributed to Hamas, "First the Saturday people, then the Sunday people": the terrorists intend first to wipe out the Jews, who keep the Sabbath on Saturday, then the Christians, who honor it on Sunday.[32]

Seeing world events through the prism of faith, many evangelicals recognize that fundamentalist Islamists do the same. This leads them to the conviction that although conflicts and terrorist acts may seem isolated, and though Islamist groups may be distinct, the danger is unified and global: it is organized around a shared religious vision and expressed in common tactics. George W. Bush reached similar conclusions. The difference is that he attributed this to Muslim extremists while defending Islam as a faith. Many Christian Zionist leaders, by contrast, see the perils posed by Hezbollah, Hamas, Al Qaeda, and Iran as a single expression of the threat inherent in Islam itself. Western nations have been blind to this, they argue.

The Christian Zionist Jack Kinsella has repeatedly warned that Muslims are bent on seizing control of the United States and Europe. He says of Muslims, "From the point of view of the enemy, this is a spiritual war between the forces of Islam and the 'People of the Book.' . . . It isn't a military war in any traditional sense, since the battle is less about material conquest than it is about spiritual conquest. (The jihad's goal is the conquest of the West by conversion to Islam.)" The failure to see this spiritual dimension to the conflict, he warns, is the West's Achilles' heel.[33]

Many evangelical leaders warn that Muslim extremists intend to establish a worldwide Islamic caliphate. James Dobson's Focus on the Family's Web site endorsed that view by carrying a link in 2006 to an article called "The War Is Over; the Jihad Isn't." Written by Robert Spencer, the author of *The Politically Incorrect Guide to Islam (and the Crusades)*, this article argues that Muslim militants all over the globe are committing murder to restore the caliphate. Under classic Islamic law, says Spencer, the caliph has the responsibility to wage war on Jews, Christians, and Zoroastrians. The war will continue until these nonbelievers either submit to Islam or accept dhimmi status—a protected but inferior social position that requires them to pay a poll tax (*jizya*). He cites radical Islamists around the world who state a common ambition: to make jihad against all who resist Islam and to eliminate all un-Islamic governments.[34]

Pastor Reza Safa, a self-described "fanatical Muslim" whose heart was changed by Jesus, warned in 1996 that Muslims intend to conquer Europe, though not through force of arms or conversion. Rather, massive Muslim immigration to the West would amount to a peaceful invasion, accomplishing what military aggression in earlier centuries had failed to do. In many areas, he said, there are more Muslims than Christian denominational groups. Mosques are rising all over England. Muslims believe that if they can win London to Islam, it will not be hard to capture all of Western Europe, he said. The means were different from the terrorism that evangelical leaders would come to fear in later years, but for Safa, the Muslim goal was the same: world domination.[35] Nine years later, Robert Stearns cited this same danger, as we have seen.

Evangelicals believe, however, that they have an indomitable ally who will lead them to final victory over the Muslim threat: Almighty God. Christian Friends of Israel (CFI) notes the danger that Arabs and other Muslims pose but declares that the Lord will emerge triumphant. A CFI weekly update in March 2006 noted,

> Adherents of Islam boast that they will rule the world. The arrogant Islamists in Iran and Syria threaten not only the demise of Israel but also the United States. They do not take into account that the true and living God, the God of Abraham, Isaac, and Jacob, has already made his plans. God's word is a sharp two-edged sword that has already pierced the great dragon who is now in his death throes.

This article appeared under the title "The Fall of Islam."[36]

From the conservative Christian perspective, Hamas's and Hezbollah's attacks on Israel in the summer of 2006 illustrated and clarified the peril about which Christian Zionists had been warning for years. The Israel Defense Forces (IDF) did not achieve their goals in that war, failing to drive back or destroy Hezbollah. Afterward, CFI's Carolyn Jacobson warned that Muslims were much more zealous to conquer the world for Islam because they believed that Hezbollah had won. She asked readers to pray that God "will rise up and fight for His people and bring down the arrogance of Islam." Jacobson also chastised Bush for praising Islam during the Muslim holiday of Ramadan in October 2006. Hosting his sixth annual Iftar dinner at the White House to mark the end of a day of fasting for Muslims, Bush said that Islam brings "hope and comfort to more than a billion people around the world." Jacobson followed this story with a prayer: "Pray for President Bush who has surely heard of the dangers of Islam. Pray that he would be shaken out of his pride of being a peace maker." She did not mention that Bush's guests included Muslims from nations that were helping to prosecute the war on terror.[37]

In May 2006, the Kansas-based Unity Coalition for Israel (UCI), a network of 200 groups, most of whom are evangelical and the rest Jewish, carried a story on a new e-book called *The Islamic Conquest of Europe 2020.* The blurb for the book says, "The Islamic tide of history is sweeping across the world like an unstoppable Tsunami! If you are one of the more than one billion Muslims in the world than [*sic*] you will love this book. If you are a Christian, Jew or Hindu you can prepare for your conversion to Islam . . . or your funeral!"[38] Two weeks later, the UCI reprinted a column by Brigitte Gabriel, a Lebanese Christian, warning that Hamas, Islamic Jihad, Hezbollah, and the Islamic Brotherhood are now working in the West to sabotage it. "Their goal is to destroy our world in an Islamic Jihad, forcing those who survive to be Dhimmi—subjected and despised ones." It's barbarism versus civilization, said Gabriel. It's democracy versus dictatorship and good versus evil.[39]

That same week, Bridges for Peace reported an ominous threat by a Hamas leader: "We will rule the nations. By Allah's will, the USA will be conquered. Israel will be conquered. Rome and Britain will be conquered. . . . Just as the Jews ran from Gaza, the Americans will run from Iraq and Afghanistan, and the Russians will run from Chechnya, and the Indian will run from Kashmir, and our children will be released from Guantanimo." The Hamas speaker warned that this will not happen by peaceful means but by the sword and the gun. Bridges followed this story with a prayer that recalled Pat Robertson's and Gary Bauer's sounding of the alarm: "Pray that the world will begin to take Islam's exposed plans seriously and guard effectively against their agenda." One year later, in May 2007, Bridges quoted the acting speaker of the Palestinian Authority's Legislative Council, who declared Israel a cancerous lump in the heart of the Arab Nation. In a broadcast on Palestinian television from a packed mosque, this official called Muslims "the masters of the world" and declared that "America and Israel will be annihilated, Allah willing." Jews and Americans are "cowards who are eager for life, while we are eager for death for the sake of Allah," he said. This confirmed Christian Zionists' direst charges against the Palestinians and Muslims in general. Bridges followed the story with a call for Christians to respond vigorously—with prayer: "The demons of hell are all too glad to fulfill the prayers that come from wicked lips. We must rise up and pound heaven's doors to counter every curse spoken from evil men."[40]

Hamas's Al Aqsa TV channel has attempted to indoctrinate Palestinian children in the goal of world conquest, according to a column in the Christian edition of the *Jerusalem Post* in 2007. Hamas television had used a Mickey Mouse-like figure named Farfur to teach children to hate and resist Israelis. In the column,

David Parsons, media relations officer for the International Christian Embassy Jerusalem, warned that Hamas's intention was even more threatening than that. He interviewed Itamar Marcus, the director of the Palestinian Media Watch monitoring agency, who noted that the message of the children's program was that Muslims will rule over everyone, Christians as well as Jews. This "Mickey Mouse program is not just anti-American, anti-Jewish, and anti- Israel," Marcus said. "It's actually teaching a very virulent Islamic supremacist ideology."[41] In April 2008, Hamas TV showed a puppet of a Palestinian boy telling a President Bush puppet (dressed in army fatigues and boxing gloves) that the White House had been converted to a mosque and that the infidel Bush was too impure the enter. The child then killed Bush with the "sword of Islam." Bridges for Peace reported this and followed it with the prayer that "the world will see that Islamic fundamentalists have a world agenda and their target is not simply Israel and the Jewish people."[42]

Christian Zionists are not alone in this view. Former Israeli prime minister Benjamin Netanyahu agrees that destroying Israel is merely the first step for Islamic extremists intent on global domination. Hezbollah is an Iranian army division fighting a war to achieve Iran's goal of recreating a Muslim empire, he says.[43] At the other side of the Muslim religious divide from Hezbollah, Ayman Al-Zawahiri, Osama bin Laden's number two man, who is Sunni, also confirmed many of these claims. During Israel's attack on Hezbollah in the summer of 2006, Al-Zawahiri proclaimed to Muslims everywhere, "All the world is a battlefield open in front of us." The war with Israel, he declared "is a jihad for the sake of Allah." The jihad will last, he vowed, until Islam prevails from Spain to Iraq. Gary Bauer immediately quoted from this speech in his American Values e-newsletter, declaring that the jihad is against free and civilized societies.[44]

Bauer points out that Hamas is committed to a world in which all of Europe and the United States will live under Islamofascism. He notes that Khaled Meshal, the Damascus-based leader of the military wing of Hamas, has said so explicitly. Muslims will achieve global domination, Meshal declared. "The nation of Islam will sit at the throne of the world. . . . Muhammed is gaining victory in Palestine [and] Iraq. . . . The Arab and Islamic nation is rising and awakening. . . . Tomorrow we will lead the world."[45] The Islamofascists want the United States to abandon Israel and retreat from the Middle East, leaving them in control of that vital region, says Bauer. But only a fool would believe that would satisfy them, he warns. "Having achieved their goal of ethnically cleansing the Middle East, they would turn their fury against 'infidels' everywhere, plunging the world into another dark age." He concludes that Western civilization remains at war against a very determined enemy.[46]

Bauer elaborated on this in July 2006, when terrorists bombed commuter trains in Mumbai, India. Within days, Hamas attacked Israel from Gaza in the south and Hezbollah attacked from Lebanon in the north, in both cases killing and abducting IDF (Israel Defense Forces) soldiers. That triggered the Second Lebanon War. "Whether it's bombings in Bombay [Mumbai], missile launches in North Korea, Hamas and Hezbollah attacking Israel, or terrorists in Baghdad," said Bauer, "the common thread is the war being waged against all of civilization by Islamofascism." Noting that Lee Hamilton, co-chairman of the 9/11 Commission, had said that the September 11 hijackers' motives were opaque, Bauer offered a crystal-clear response: the hijackers' motive "isn't something we have to guess at. Osama bin Laden and his ilk have been painfully honest. We are 'infidels' in their minds, and we must either convert or die."[47]

Bernard Lewis lends historical weight to the claim that attacks on Israel are merely one stage in a worldwide struggle. He notes that from an early date, Muslim law has obliged followers to wage war on unbelievers until all mankind either embraces Islam or submits to the authority of the Muslim state.[48] Israeli historian Benny Morris carries that into the present. Although Islamists prefer to speak only of liberating Iraq, Afghanistan, and Palestine, says Morris, "in fact they are united in wishing the extirpation of all Western influence ('pollution,' in their jargon) from the sacred Islamic lands, stretching from Pakistan to the Atlantic Ocean." And their goals go further. Morris notes that it is a basic tenet of Islam that any land conquered by Muslims remains perpetually sacred Islamic land (*Dar Al Islam*). Beyond that, the rest of the world must be conquered or converted to Islam. That is what the Islamists want, says Morris: global domination under Allah. They see the world as in constant conflict between the forces of darkness (the West) and light (Islam), with the forces of light certain to win.[49] This, of course, is a mirror image of the evangelical belief that good and evil are in conflict in the world, and that good, represented by Christians and Jews, will ultimately prevail.

"One Size Does Not Fit All"

A number of experts on terrorism and religion disagree with these representations of the Islamists' motives and goals, and of Islam itself. Some leading scholars of terrorism see most attacks by different militant groups not as a unified Islamic conspiracy but as disconnected events. Gregory F. Treverton, former vice chairman of the National Intelligence Council, says of the various terrorist organizations, "One size does not fit all": disparate groups are not part of a single movement driven by their radical faith. The University of Chicago's Robert A. Pape concurs. In his book *Dying to Win: The Strategic Logic of Suicide Terrorism,* Pape observes that 95 percent of terrorist attacks worldwide have been local actions intended to drive out foreign combat troops. He concludes that speaking of global Islamic terrorism overplays religion and underestimates political objectives.[50] The 9/11 Commission lent support to that conclusion in 2004. The Commission, which was charged with examining what happened and why during the terrorist attacks on September 11, 2001, found that while some of the hijackers were orthodox Muslims, others were not. Some even drank or used drugs, despite Islamic proscriptions. The terrorists were united not by faith but by outrage at the United States, according to an FBI official familiar with the case. The terrorists sympathized with the Palestinians and with people who oppose repressive regimes in the Middle East, and they focused their anger on the United States because of its Mideast policies.[51] Olivier Roy, a French terrorism expert, adds, "The Europeans don't buy the concept of global terrorism as a strategic and political idea." In keeping with this view, one Hamas member of the Palestinian government accused the United States of trying to put Hamas and Hezbollah in a single basket and to present it to the world as the image of terror.[52]

Moreover, many religion experts say that the claim that Islam seeks world domination misrepresents the mainstream of that faith. Christian Zionists generally cite the threats and boasts of extremists from Hamas, Al Qaeda, Hezbollah, and Iran. But many scholars of Islam say that it is bizarre to assert that these fundamentalists' distortions of their religion are normative belief. One can't condemn an entire faith because of its extremes, notes John Esposito, the founding director of the Center for Muslim-Christian Understanding at Georgetown University. To believe that Al Qaeda or Hamas represents Islam would be like claiming that the Ku Klux Klan speaks for Christianity, says Esposito. It would be analogous, he adds, to declaring that Baruch Goldstein represented mainstream Judaism—a reference to the far-right-wing American who murdered twenty-nine Muslims as they prayed in the Tomb of the Patriarchs in Hebron in 1994.[53] "Terrorists can attempt to hijack Islam and the doctrine of jihad," says Esposito, "but that is no more legitimate than Christian or Jewish extremists committing their acts of terrorism in their own unholy wars."[54]

Martin Marty makes a similar point about Robert Spencer and other anti-Muslim sources whom Christian Zionists often cite. These critics of Islam read the Qur'an and other Islamic texts the same way that Muslim extremists read the genocidal passages in the Old Testament books of Joshua and Judges, says Marty: they focus on extremes that do not represent the mainstream of the faith today. Such critics of Islam are simplistic and unambiguous in declaring that it is not a religion of peace, does not respect human rights, and is not compatible with Western pluralism, Marty argues. "The fact that so many Spencers (and their analogues in militant Islam) are in positions of power suggests how difficult it will be for any measures short of war to be enacted," he concludes.[55]

Islam does not require mass conversions, adds Esposito. There is no such expectation in the Qur'an or other early sacred Islamic texts. Evangelicals who claim that it is at the heart of the religion are citing radical voices, not normative Islam, he says. Muslim caliphs of old did use conversion as an excuse to justify imperial expansion, Esposito observes. They claimed that conquest would be a way to call all people to God, just as Christians did. Some extreme Muslims still make this claim today, Esposito notes, but he says that Bernard Lewis is simply wrong to suggest that it is part of mainstream Islam.[56] Nor do most Muslims aim to conquer the world to establish a caliphate that will put all mankind under Shari'a law, says Esposito.

A World Public Opinion poll released in 2007 showed that large majorities in Morocco, Egypt, and Pakistan do, in fact, want to unify all Islamic countries into a caliphate. They don't necessarily want to achieve it through violent means, though.[57] But extremists in Hamas and Al Qaeda do, and American religious and social conservatives are paying very close attention to that.

World War III

In the run-up to the American midterm elections of 2006, prominent conservative political figures said that they considered the conflict with radical Islam to constitute nothing less than a world war. Appearing on *Meet the Press* in July 2006 as Israel went to war with Hezbollah, Newt Gingrich, former Republican Speaker of the House, put the alliance between Iran, Syria, Hamas, and Hezbollah in a larger context of recent terrorist activity: the British home secretary's report that there were 1,200 terrorists in Britain; seven people in Miami videotaped pledging allegiance to Al Qaeda; eighteen Muslims in Canada caught with explosives, threatening to bomb the Canadian Parliament and behead the prime minister; and planning by groups in three different countries to destroy the tunnels of New York City. "We are in the early stages of what I would describe as the third world war," said Gingrich.[58] Senator John McCain (R-Arizona), who was seeking the Republican nomination for president, agreed that World War III has begun. So did Bill Bennett, secretary of education under Ronald Reagan and national drug czar under George H. W. Bush. Then-senator Rick Santorum (R-Pennsylvania) said the same.

Leading Christian Zionists also declared that a world war with jihadi extremists was underway. Christian Friends of Israeli Communities, which encourages American evangelical empathy and financial support for Jewish settlements in the occupied territories, added that the war actually started on September 11, 2001. Bridges for Peace concurred, asking its readers to pray for the world to recognize that the battles with Hezbollah and Hamas are not just Israel's problem but part of a global conflict.[59] James Dobson, founder of Focus on the Family, struck a similar note. World War III has started, and no one seems to know it, Dobson declared in 2006 at three rallies urging evangelicals to vote for Republicans in the midterm elections. Pat Robertson, who, in an act of courage, visited northern Israel in August 2006 as Hezbollah rockets were falling there, saw that war as part of this worldwide conflict. The Jewish state is waging the war against Islamofascism for all of us, he said. "They are fighting for the United States, they are fighting for Western Europe, they are fighting for freedom-loving people everywhere."[60]

From this perspective, the Israelis are the advance forces in the war on terror, as Robert Stearns had told me. "Israel is the last firewall between Islamic terrorists and America," declared Mike Evans, founder of the Jerusalem Prayer Team. "Events in Israel will not stay in Israel. Sooner or later, America will face the same kinds of devastating attacks that we see there." Exhorting his readers to support the Jewish state, Evans cited the story of Esther, who delivered the Jews from annihilation in ancient Persia. He quoted a passage from the biblical Book of Esther that for many evangelicals contains a severe warning to those who do not act to save the Jews:

> For if you keep silence at such a time as this, relief and deliverance will rise for the Jews from another quarter, but you and your father's house will perish. And who knows whether you have not come to the kingdom for such a time as this? (Esther 4:14).

Evangelicals often cite this verse. It provides a theological explanation for their rise to political influence in perilous times, and inspires them to use their power to support good against evil.[61] This passage has acquired additional resonance because of the antagonism of the current president of Iran (ancient Persia) toward Israel and the West. Many Christian Zionists consider him a new Haman (the evil vizier in the Esther story) or a second Hitler, as we shall see.

Some prominent dispensationalists go beyond warnings of world war. The incursions by Hamas and Hezbollah in July 2006 and Israel's response, said Jerry Falwell, may well be signs of the approaching end of time. "It is apparent that the present day events in the Holy Land may very well serve as a prelude or forerunner of the future Battle of Armageddon and the glorious return of

Jesus Christ," he wrote in his "Falwell Confidential" weekly e-newsletter.[62] Hal Lindsey cited Scripture and recent events to document this. He had received intelligence that Russia had signed a defense pact with Iran and Syria, Lindsey revealed. He concluded that recent events were setting up the prophecy in Ezekiel 38–39 that Russia will lead Persia (modern Iran) in the first battle of the war of Armageddon. Since Ezekiel says nothing about Syria, Lindsey turned to Isaiah, chapter 17, which prophesies that Damascus will become a heap of ruins. Putting these biblical texts together, Lindsey predicted that Syria will launch biochemical weapons or dirty radioactive bombs at Israel, or will provide them to terrorists. Jerusalem will respond by nuking Syria. Terrified, the world will then embrace the Antichrist, leading to the final worldwide conflagration, as in the dispensational understanding of Scripture.[63]

A lot of people evidently wondered if the end-times really have begun: in July 2006, as Israel's war with Hezbollah raged, a quarter of a million people visited the Rapture Index Web site (www.raptureready.com), which offers updated measurements of catastrophic events that may portend the end of time. That was up from 180,000 in June. Pat Robertson demurred, however. Lecturing on the *700 Club* about the parallels between Ezekiel and Israel's conflict with Hezbollah, he asked, "Is this what precedes the coming of the Lord? I don't think so." It wasn't the end yet.[64]

A "Shorthand Interpretation of Reality"

The American politicians' talk of world war discomfited Israeli leaders of both the political left and right. "They are completely disconnected from what is going on here," said a Knesset member from the far-left Meretz Party. "They haven't learned anything and they don't understand anything," said a member from Labor. Even the extreme right-wing religious nationalist leader Benny Elon, who maintains perhaps the closest ties to the American religious right of any Israeli politician, disagreed with the claims about world war. Such comments originated, he speculated, with the staunch Christian Zionist John Hagee's 2006 book, *Jerusalem Countdown*.[65]

Thomas Pickering, former U.S. ambassador to Israel, Russia, and the United Nations, says that calling the current conflict World War III is a bad mistake, "a rapid, facile, miscellaneous shorthand interpretation of reality." To lump the Shia and Sunni radicals together as a single adversary encompassing the whole of Islam represents sloppy phrasing or bad analysis, he says. The Shia and the Sunni extremists pursue their own interests, notes Pickering. Each tries to negate, destroy, minimize, or ignore the interests of the other. "There is little rational basis for linking unlike political forces, unlike religious forces, because they have a common penchant for extremism," he says. Bin Laden would like us to make the mistake of turning our war on terrorism into a war on Islam. But it is dishonest to say that Al Qaeda and the ayatollahs in Iran share a common goal of establishing a caliphate, says Pickering.[66]

Some foreign policy experts argue that it would make more sense to make use of enemies' differences rather than treat them as a single entity. Dividing opponents and exploiting local alienation against them have been key elements in successful campaigns against terrorists in the past. Indeed, Harvard professor Samuel Huntington, who popularized the notion of a clash of civilizations with the Muslim world, argues that Washington should take advantage of the tremendous divisions within Muslim society. The United States, he says, should calm tensions with Muslims by accommodating the specific interests of segments of that world.[67] Fareed Zakaria, editor of *Newsweek International*, adds, "Rather than speaking of a single worldwide movement—which absurdly lumps together Chechen separatists in Russia, Pakistani-backed militants in India, Shiite warlords in Lebanon and Sunni jihadists in Egypt—we should be emphasizing that all these groups are distinct, with differing agendas, enemies and friends. That robs them of their claim to represent Islam."[68] Yale professor Ian Shapiro points out that the diversity of hostile Islamist states and groups today creates tensions and competition among them, lending itself to a policy of containment. Shapiro notes that that George Kennan, who formulated the policy of containing the Soviet Union in the late 1940s, similarly advised identifying and exploiting the rifts among opponents.[69]

Predictions of a Terrorist World War

The idea that the conflict with Islamic terrorists is a world war actually dates back at least to 1992, when the Count de Marenches, a longtime head of French intelligence, spoke of this struggle as World War IV. (The third global war, in his view, had been the Cold War with the Soviet Union.) The next world war, he predicted, will be a terrorist war. There may be large battles, but the world's intelligence services will play a critical role, combating small, deadly units of terrorists camouflaged among immigrant populations in northern cities.[70] Eliot A. Cohen, an influential neoconservative scholar at Johns Hopkins, revived this concept shortly after 9/11 in a *Wall Street Journal* opinion piece titled "World War IV: Let's Call This Conflict What It Is." James Woolsey, a former head of the Central Intelligence Agency (CIA), said in 2002 that America is indeed in a world war in which it faces three enemies: first, the Islamist Shia clerics of Iran, who have been at war with the United States since 1979, when Iranian radicals seized the U.S. embassy in Tehran; second, the fascist Ba'athists in Syria and (until 2003) in Iraq, who have been at war with the West for over a decade; and third, Islamist Sunnis, including Al Qaeda. These extremist Muslims focused on their "near enemies," the rulers of Egypt and Saudi Arabia, until the mid-1990s, said Woolsey. Then they began to concentrate on Crusaders (Christians) and Jews.[71] The idea that the contest between radical Islam and the West is a world war was subsequently adopted by others, including Christian Zionists. One of them is John Hagee.

Jerusalem Countdown

Hagee said in his 2006 book *Jerusalem Countdown* that on 9/11 Americans woke up to the fact that the third world war is underway. Worse is yet to come, he warned: Islam's highest goal is a holy war against the United States (the great Satan) and Israel (the small Satan). Hagee noted that Iranian president Mahmoud Ahmadinejad has stated his intention to wipe Israel off the map and has promised that Islam will strike down the United States as well. Iran's drive to develop nuclear weapons, and Ahmadinejad's declared willingness to transfer nuclear know-how to other Islamic nations, have made this threat urgent and extreme, Hagee observed. The West cannot allow so dangerous a nation to achieve nuclear power, he argued, and only America and Israel have the power to stop it. "We are on a countdown to a crisis," he said, a conclusion with which it seemed hard to find fault at that moment.

Critics accuse Hagee of wanting the United States and Israel to attack Iran in order to hasten the end-times. One claimed that Hagee prays for Armageddon. Far from cheerleading for the final confrontation, however, Hagee tried in *Jerusalem Countdown* to arouse the world to prevent it. The West has to stop Tehran before it achieves its ambitions, he warned. "There isn't very much time to get it right. The stakes are high and failure is not an option." At the same time, though, Hagee considers it certain that if Israel takes out Iran's nuclear facilities, a vast pan-Arabic Islamic army will attack the Jewish state. That could trigger the global war predicted in Ezekiel 38–39, with Russia leading the invasion that ends in the battle of Armageddon, he says.[72]

Hagee neither invents nor misrepresents evidence about the Iranian military threat. Rather, he presents the worst possible case, documenting his claims meticulously. His sources include Netanyahu, who told him that Iran was working on missiles capable of hitting London, New York, and Jerusalem. Western civilization would be crushed in an hour if Iran were to strike those three cities with nuclear weapons, Hagee responded. He notes a published report that a former consultant to the Federal Bureau of Investigation believes that least seven teams of Islamist terrorists with nuclear devices are now in the United States. They could use suitcase nuclear bombs, Hagee warns. He also cites another report that rogue states have the ability to use an electronic magnetic pulse to halt all electricity in the United States for months or years.[73]

Hagee's sense of urgent peril is consistent with dispensationalism's deeply pessimistic, prophecy-based expectation of catastrophe. Critics consider it needlessly alarmist and provocative, a distortion of the actual peril. There have been times when such a view has been vindicated, though. A lot of evangelicals clearly understood the Holocaust as it was happening, for example, when the *New York Times,* and many Jews, were blind to the true dimensions of its horror.[74] Many Christian Zionists believe that the threat to the Jews and the West is mounting again, and that they have been sent for such a time as this.

"Eighty Million Evangelicals at the Gates of the White House Cheering" and a New Intelligence Estimate

Some of these dangers are real but probably not as immediate as Hagee says. By 2006, North Korea had sold missiles to Iran with a range of over 1,500 miles and was preparing to test missiles capable of reaching the United States. By all public accounts, none has yet been developed, however.[75] Iran has test-fired missiles suitable for carrying nuclear weapons with a range of 1,240 miles, capable of hitting Israel. There is debate within Israel, though, about how much of a threat these weapons would pose. Both Tzipi Livni, Israel's foreign minister, and Efraim Halevy, the former chief of the Mossad, said that a nuclear Iran would not be an existential danger to Israel.[76] Moreover, in a stunning reversal of a 2005 National Intelligence Estimate (NIE), American intelligence agencies determined with "high confidence" in late 2007 that Tehran had shut down its nuclear weapons program four years earlier. The new NIE also judged with "moderate confidence" that the program remained frozen, and that Iran would not have enough fissile material for a nuclear weapon until 2010–15. Bush officials were still skeptical of Iran's intentions, however. And former Mideast negotiator Dennis Ross pointed out that weaponizing is comparatively easy; Tehran could put it on hold for a while without compromising its ultimate goal. The hard part of becoming a nuclear power is the enrichment of uranium and plutonium, said Ross, and Iran was going full speed ahead on both.

The NIE had diverted attention from that crucial point, he concluded.[77] Israeli defense minister Ehud Barak asserted that Iran probably had restarted its weapons research anyway.[78] Senior Israeli intelligence analysts added that for them, the point of no return was not when Iran actually had fissile material but when it attained the potential to produce enough of it to make a bomb. That was likely to happen by 2009, they said.[79] Israelis who favored a preemptive strike on Iran knew that the window of political opportunity was closing quickly, too: the Bush administration would leave office in January 2009. The next president might be far less understanding.

Jerry Falwell had said of Iran, "The day Israel takes out the weapons of those barbarians, there will be eighty million evangelicals at the gates of the White House cheering." President Bush will be cheering too, said Falwell.[80] But more moderate voices urged Jerusalem and Washington to let internal reform ameliorate the government in Tehran. Azar Nafisi, for example, author of *Reading Lolita in Tehran* and lecturer at Johns Hopkins' School of Advanced International Studies, urges Western governments to choose a path between the extremes of appeasement and belligerence. "The notion that Iran will be subdued into compliance with a handful of precision-guided missiles is as dangerous and fanciful as the belief that an invaded Iraq would serve as a model of enlightened democracy," says Nafisi.[81] Others argued that the United States could influence Iran by diplomacy. They noted that Tehran had offered in 2003 to end its support for Hamas, turn Hezbollah into a solely political organization, and agree to the 2002 Saudi peace initiative if Washington recognized Iran's security interests in the region and ended its attempts to isolate it. They argued that it was still possible for Iran to adopt a "Malaysian profile" toward Israel, refraining from direct confrontation with the Jewish state while not officially recognizing it.[82]

Still, Falwell and Hagee were not alone in their exhortation to Israel to strike before Iran does. Robert Baer, an ex-CIA agent, warned that Ahmadinejad and his Revolutionary Guard colleagues are capable of making a bomb and launching it at Israel. "They're apocalyptic Shias. If you're sitting in Tel Aviv and you believe they've got nukes and missiles, you've got to take them out. These guys are nuts and there's no reason to back off."[83] After the 2007 NIE's startling reassessment, Baer cautioned that Iran is a black hole. The Iranians could build a bomb and the West wouldn't know about it until they tested it, he said. The good news, Baer noted, is that for the moment, Armageddon had been postponed.[84]

Bernard Lewis confirmed that Iran's leaders are poised for an imminent global war. They think apocalyptically and are preparing their people for general destruction, said Lewis. Ahmadinejad and his followers clearly believe that the terminal struggle is already well advanced, he warned. Schoolbooks tell young Iranians to be ready for the final worldwide conflict with the evil enemy, the United States. Eleventh-grade textbooks quote the late Ayatollah Khomeini's vow that if the infidel Western nations stand against Islam, Iran will annihilate all of them. If large numbers of Muslims are killed, so be it. The official Iranian view, said Lewis, is that "Allah will know his own" and will reward them in heaven while the infidels go to hell.[85]

Hezbollah is similarly indoctrinating children with radical Shia beliefs, including the need to wage a final battle against "evil." According to documents that Israeli forces found in Lebanon during their invasion in 2006, Hezbollah runs a youth program called the Imam Mahdi Scouts, which has trained 42,000 young Lebanese, aged ten to fifteen, in the principles of the Iranian revolution and the personal glorification of Ayatollah Khamenei. This program includes a summer camp, which offers sports, social programs, and military training.[86]

The Islamists and Hitler: Feeding a Crocodile

Christian Friends of Israel laments that the IDF's disappointing showing against Hezbollah in the war of July and August 2006 left the entire West vulnerable, as did Israel's withdrawals from Lebanon and Gaza and the apparent failure of the American effort in Iraq. Muslim militants around the globe now believe that the free world has grown soft and can be defeated, said a CFI newsletter. It asked its readers to pray that God would humble the proud and haughty Sheik Sayyed Hassan Nasrallah, the leader of Hezbollah, and cited Isaiah 10:33–34: "The lofty will be brought low . . . and Lebanon with its majestic trees will fall."[87]

Several American religious and political conservatives, advocating an aggressive response to the Iranian and Arab peril, take Winston Churchill as their model. They particularly admire his dogged determination in warning of the approaching danger of Nazi Germany in the 1930s. Like him, they name what they see as the coming fascist threat and they disdain attempts to appease it. Discussing a foiled terrorist plot in 2006, Gary Bauer quoted one of Churchill's classic lines: "An appeaser is one who feeds a crocodile, hoping it will eat him last." (A few days later, Defense Secretary Donald Rumsfeld used the same quip.) Bauer also has cited Churchill's words rallying the British people against Adolf Hitler: "You ask, what is our aim? I can answer in one word: It is victory, victory at all costs, victory in spite of all terror, victory, however long and hard the road may be; for without victory, there is no survival." Bauer is far from the only evangelical who reveres Churchill. James Dobson is so devoted to the late

English prime minister that the largest painting in his Colorado Springs office is not of Christ but of Sir Winston. (Dobson's wife didn't want him to buy it because she was afraid he would put it in their bedroom!)[88] George W. Bush also regards Churchill as a heroic role model and keeps a stern-looking bust of him in the Oval Office. "He watches my every move," Bush joked.[89]

Bauer considers the Islamist threat today to be equivalent to the danger posed by the Nazis in the 1930s, and equally impossible to appease through compromise. Hagee says the same. In 2007 he received standing ovations at AIPAC's annual policy conference in Washington when he succinctly reiterated language that had become current among Christian Zionists: "It is 1938; Iran is Germany and Ahmadinejad is the new Hitler." Hagee warned that the "misguided souls of Europe . . . the political brothel that is now the United Nations, and sadly even our own State Department will try once again to turn Israel into crocodile food." But Israel is not the problem, he said. The problem is radical Islam's "bloodthirsty embrace of a theocratic dictatorship"[90]

Some Israeli and American former officials and commentators also evoke the Nazi threat in describing the present conflict with Islamic terrorists. Netanyahu says that, in Ahmadinejad, Israel is confronted by an enemy of the sort the Jewish people have not faced since Hitler. The conflict is not about territory but about Islam's goal of eradicating the Jewish state, he says, a statement that agrees perfectly with the warnings of Michael Evans and other Christian Zionists. Jihadist Muslims intend to perpetrate a second Holocaust, says Netanyahu. In fact, Ahmadinejad presents an even more serious threat than Hitler did, Netanyahu adds: Hitler lost the war because he could not develop nuclear weapons, but Ahmadinejad is on the verge of accomplishing that.[91] General Moshe Ya'alon, former IDF Chief of Staff, also compares the current threat to that of Hitler's Germany. He praises Israelis who are willing to take the battle to Iran and Syria in order to win World War III. When Ahmadinejad threatens to wipe Israel off the map, he means to destroy the West, says Ya'alon, a charge that echoes those made by Christian Zionists.[92] William Kristol, editor of the *Weekly Standard,* has repeatedly compared the rise of Islamism in Iran to that of Nazism in Germany. Though he acknowledges that Hamas is a branch of the Sunni Muslim Brotherhood, and therefore at odds with Shia Iran, he warns that alliances of convenience are nonetheless dangerous, as Hitler's accord with Stalin was.[93] "We had no problem understanding that Nazism and fascism were evil racist empires," added then-senator Rick Santorum in 2006. "We must now bring the same clarity to the war against Islamic fascism." It is the great test of this generation, he declared.[94] Such claims are not unprecedented, incidentally. In 1990, President George H. W. Bush likened Saddam Hussein to

Hitler. He said later that he caught hell for that comparison, but that he still felt that it was appropriate.[95]

George W. Bush and World War III

One proponent of the idea that World War III has begun is George W. Bush, who sees the Islamist threat much as the Christian Zionists do and has used the same language to describe it. Bush has taken pains to note that the battle is not with the "great religion" of Islam, which he has called a religion of peace, but with terrorists. Yet in describing the goals of radical Islamists, Bush repeatedly has spoken in terms identical to Bauer's, Hagee's, and Robertson's. Addressing the National Endowment for Democracy in October 2005, Bush warned that militants practicing a clear and focused ideology of Islamofascism seek to establish "a radical Islamic empire that spans from Spain to Indonesia." They are a loose network rather than an army under a unified command, he observed, but they have a common ideology and vision for the world. Against such an enemy, Bush said, the West can never accept anything less than complete victory.[96] In March 2006 he warned that we face "a global enemy." Terrorists who bomb mosques in Iraq share a hateful ideology with those who attacked the United States on 9/11, blew up commuters in London and Madrid, and murdered tourists in Bali, workers in Riyadh, and wedding guests in Jordan. In May he spoke of the struggle against these terrorists as World War III.[97] Today's terrorists, the president told the American Legion national convention in Salt Lake City later that month, are "successors to Fascists, to Nazis, to Communists and other totalitarians of the twentieth century." Whether they strike at the World Trade Center, in Baghdad, over the Atlantic, or in Israel, they constitute a worldwide network of radicals. The battle against their dark, totalitarian ideology "is the decisive ideological struggle of the 21st century."[98] In September 2006 Bush added that the Al Qaeda charter states that "there will be continuing enmity until everyone believes in Allah." The Iranian Shia extremists, for their part, are learning from the Sunni ones, he said, and like them, have clear aims: to drive America out of the region, destroy Israel, and dominate the broader Middle East. Ahmadinejad has called on the West to bow down before the greatness of Iran and surrender, the president noted. Bush acknowledged that the Shia and Sunni extremists are distinct groups. He argued, though, that they represent "different faces of the same threat. They draw inspiration from difference sources, but both seek to impose a dark vision of violent Islamic radicalism across the Middle East." As in World War II and the Cold War, the president concluded, freedom is in a global contest with the forces of darkness and tyranny.[99]

In October 2007, Bush warned that a nuclear-armed Iran *could* lead to World War III. One to two months before he made that statement, intelligence officials had told him about new indications that Iran had halted its nuclear weapons program in 2003.[100] Bush remained convinced, though, that Iran was, is, and will be a threat.

A Mirror Image

Many Muslims see events as an almost exactly opposite mirror image of these claims. The massive Israeli attack on Hezbollah in 2006, which devastated much of Lebanon, seemed to them to substantiate Osama bin Laden's charge that the West, with Israel as its proxy, had declared war on Islam. That is a legal justification for jihad. It is also, of course, the inverse of the worldview expressed by religious and political conservatives in the West, who believe that Muslim extremists have declared war on them. But American support of Israel, the invasions of Afghanistan and Iraq, ridicule of the prophet Mohammed in Danish cartoons, and harshly critical statements by Jerry Falwell and other evangelical leaders all persuaded many people in the Muslim world that Islam was under attack.

Leaders in Tehran saw Israel's battles with Hezbollah as a stage of a wider war: the United States' confrontation with Iran. Vali Nasr, a professor at the U.S. Naval Postgraduate School who briefed President Bush, noted that Tehran interpreted every hostile move against Hezbollah as part of a larger campaign against Iran. It prepared for the coming showdown by sending more sophisticated weapons to Hezbollah.[101] From the mullahs' perspective, the West had embarked on a world war. The American occupation of Afghanistan and Iraq has inevitably created a siege mentality in Ahmadinejad's government, notes Yale professor Ian Shapiro.[102] Khalid al-Dakhil, a King Saud University professor, confirms that. "There is no way to avoid the fact that the U.S., with its Western allies, is occupying Iraq and Afghanistan," he says. "Israel is occupying the Palestinian territories in Gaza and the West Bank. So, there is a truth in how the militant groups put the issue here."[103]

The Syrians, too, fear Israeli attack. One reason they built up Hezbollah was to prevent an Israeli drive across Lebanon's Bekaa Valley, said Martin Indyk, a former U.S. ambassador to Israel who is now the director of the Saban Center for Middle East Policy.[104] To complete the mirror image, Ayatollah Ali Khamenei, the supreme leader of Iran, predicted that the Bush administration's aggression in Iraq will be stopped, as Hitler's was in World War II.[105]

Muslim perceptions of pro-Israeli evangelicals also create a symmetrical but inverse reflection of the Christians' charges against them. Speaking at a graduation ceremony in 2002, Sheik Nasrallah said that Christian Zionists intend to redraw the political map of the world.[106] *The American Muslim* journal ran an article in 2006 that saw in Christian fundamentalism many of the same dangers that evangelical leaders see in Islam. George Bush's foreign policy, said the author, was shaped by the Christian fundamentalists' agenda of global conquest. Since they see Jesus alone as the path to salvation, the article added, Christian Zionists want to bring the entire world to heel before him, by force or conversion. Bush's Christian commitment "is a vengeful, hate-driven creed rooted in the notion of the triumphalist Church that desperately seeks to subjugate the entire world and expand the borders of Christendom to the ends of the earth." This is the equal and opposite reflection of the conservative evangelical charge against Islam. The author added that Muslim anti-Western sentiments do not stem from barbarity or hostility to freedom but from the brutality of Western imperialism. Christian Zionism, he contended, is a call for global war—again, the mirror image of the accusations made against Islam. It is based, the article concluded, on a tribal Jewish version of God, the claim that all other faiths are false, and the expectation that a grand world war will soon erupt.[107] Extending the inversion of accusations, Ghassan Rubeiz, an Arab-American sociologist who writes for the *Christian Science Monitor*, added that if jihad is defined as war in the name of God, then the right-wing evangelical movement is hyper-jihadist.[108]

Both Christian and Shia fundamentalists anticipate a final conflict in which their own faith will triumph, as we shall see. The contrast could not be starker. And yet Thomas Pickering laments the ironic parallels between these views. "Each one is ready for a cataclysm to justify its existence and ratify its success," Pickering observes. And each scenario involves the massive suffering and destruction of Jews.[109] He is referring to the dispensational end-times scenario in which Jews will accept Christ or die, and to the Shia belief that the vanished twelfth imam, the Mahdi, will return at the end of days and dispense justice, punishing evil states, especially Israel. In fact, many Christian Zionist leaders have a more nuanced eschatology than is generally thought, and most Iranian Shia do not believe in the imminent return of the Hidden Imam, as we shall see.

5

❧❀☙

The War with Islam as a Faith

An Ancient Enmity

Just as evangelicals' political support for Israel comports with their religious convictions, so too is their opposition to Israel's enemies embedded in theology. It is an ancient enmity, rooted in deep spiritual conflict. The struggle, for Christian Zionists, goes beyond terrorism and the wars between Israel and its Arab and Muslim neighbors, and is even more than a clash of civilizations. It is a contest between God and Allah: the Lord God of Judaism and Christianity versus what they view as the dubious supernatural being that Muslims worship. For many evangelical Zionists, this is the divine conflict behind the earthly hostilities in the Middle East. It is the other half of the picture, complementing their scripturally based alliance with the Jewish state.

Several of the most prominent American evangelicals have denounced not just Islamic radicals but Islam itself and the prophet Mohammed. After September 11, 2001, Franklin Graham, the son of Billy Graham, called Islam a "very evil and wicked religion." Jerry Falwell, on *60 Minutes*, denounced Mohammed as a terrorist. Jerry Vines, former president of the Southern Baptist Convention, called Islam's founder a "demon-possessed pedophile," and Pat Robertson called Mohammed a robber and a brigand. These were not random outbursts. They were expressions of a theology of cosmic war.

Christian Zionists are prominent among those who contend that Islam demands world domination, as we saw in the previous chapter. In many instances, though, they go further, claiming that Islam is inherently violent and even demonic. In 2002, Robertson stated on the *700 Club* that Muslims want to coexist only until they can control, dominate, and, if necessary, destroy. "Islam, at its core, teaches violence," he added in 2005. "It's there in the Qur'an in clear, bold statements."[1] In 2006, after watching a news segment on the *700 Club* about Muslim riots in Europe over cartoons satirizing the prophet Mohammed, Robertson declared that the Muslims were in the thrall of the devil. "These people are crazed fanatics, and I want to say it now: I believe it's motivated by demonic power," said Robertson. "It is satanic and it's time we recognize what we're dealing with."[2] Soon thereafter, Robertson called Islam "a bloody, bloody, brutal type of religion." Noting that Mohammed called for the execution of nonbelievers who refused to accept Islam, and that today, Muslims who convert to another faith are executed, Robertson declared, "Islam is not a religion of peace. Islam means submission. Submission to the Quran, to Muhammad. . . . And the penalty of not submitting is death." In 2007, on the *700 Club*, he went still further, saying that Islam is not a religion at all but a global political movement bent on dominating the world.[3] Muslims around the world were offended by Robertson's comments and very many evangelicals were embarrassed. A lot of people dismissed him as impolitic or crazy. But each of these assertions was rooted in a conservative Christian theology that sees Islam as inherently violent and threatening.

Robertson has denounced Allah as a pagan deity, the moon god Hubal.[4] Asked about this later, Ted Haggard, then-president of the National Association of Evangelicals (NAE), laughed and said, "No one pays me enough to explain Pat Robertson's comments. We all have to pray for Pat Robertson."[5] But Robertson is far from the only evangelical leader who has referred to Allah as the moon god. This charge appeared in the 1996 book *Inside Islam* by Pastor Reza F. Safa, an Iranian Shia Muslim who converted to evangelical Christianity. Pastor Reza, who is now based in Tulsa, Oklahoma, noted similarities between modern Islam and the worship of the god Baal in Phoenicia and Canaan. In pre-Islamic times, adherents of Allah worshipped the sun, the moon, and the stars, Reza observed.

The suggestion that Islam derived from an ancient astral religion has made an impression on several evangelical leaders. At the 2003 convention of the National Religious Broadcasters, Islam was denounced as a "pagan religion."[6] Walid Shoebat, a self-proclaimed former Muslim PLO terrorist who became a born-again Christian and developed a heart for Israel, wrote in 2005 that Islam is a revival of a Babylonian religion in which the moon god is one of 360 idols. This god became synonymous with al-Ilah, Shoebat says. Jack Kinsella repeated this in his online *Christian Intelligence Digest*, noting that the moon god was "coincidentally ALSO named Allah." Pre-Islamic worship of this god involved bowing in prayer toward Mecca several times a day and making a pilgrimage to Mecca, just as Muslims do today, he noted. The symbol of the moon religion was the crescent moon, which remains the symbolic image of Islam. Thus, says Kinsella, for then-President Bush to equate Allah with God betrayed "an almost breathtaking ignorance of Islam."[7] Robert Stearns's Eagles' Wings, the New York state–based Christian Zionist organization that works closely with the Israeli consulate in Manhattan, makes the same point. Its "Watchmen on the Wall" brochure, a detailed training manual for evangelicals who want to pray for and defend Israel, cites archaeological evidence that Allah was the pre-Islamic moon god. "Muhammad decided that Allah was not only the greatest god but the only god," it says. The Eagles' Wings manual interprets this as duplicity: "Muhammad thus attempted to have it both ways. To the pagans, he said that he still believed in the Moon-god Allah. To the Jews and the Christians, he said that Allah was their God too." But Muhammad did not fool the Jews and Christians, the manual observes. They realized that this was not biblical monotheism but rather a revival of the ancient moon god cult.[8]

"My God Was Bigger Than His"

Some conservative Christians claim that Allah is a devil or a false or evil deity. In 2003, C. Peter Wagner, a former professor at Fuller Theological Seminary, wrote that "one billion Muslims worship a high-ranking demon who has gone by the name of 'Allah' since long before Mohammed was born."[9] In the same year, Lieutenant General William G. "Jerry" Boykin made international headlines for his public statement that Allah is an idol. A devout evangelical, Boykin had declared that, since George W. Bush was not elected by a majority of voters in 2000, he must have been appointed by God. General Boykin has also made it clear that he takes his orders directly from the Lord. In January 2003, in a Daytona Beach, Florida, church, he told the story of an Islamic extremist in Mogadishu, Somalia, who boasted that the Americans would never catch him. "Allah will protect me," the militant declared. "Well, you know what?" Boykin told the congregation, "I knew that my God was bigger than his. I knew that my God was a real God and his was an idol." The militant later was captured. In June 2003, Defense Secretary Donald Rumsfeld nominated Boykin for a third star and named him deputy undersecretary of Defense for intelligence, a new position with a formidable charge: to track down Osama bin Laden, Saddam Hussein, and former Afghani leader Mullah Omar. The next day, Boykin told a church congregation in Oregon that extremist leaders hate Americans "because we're a Christian nation. . . . The battle we're in is a spiritual battle. Satan wants to destroy this nation." Bush had asserted that the war on terrorism is neither a war against Islam nor a clash of civilizations, and he had distanced himself from Falwell's and Robertson's statements about Islam. But he did not publicly rebuke General Boykin. Nor did Rumsfeld. Many Muslims were disturbed by what seemed to be tacit approval of Boykin. They were similarly disconcerted when the Defense Department invited Franklin Graham to hold a Good Friday service at the Pentagon that April, despite his disparaging remarks about Islam.[10]

Jan Willem van der Hoeven, a founder of the International Christian Embassy Jerusalem (ICEJ), cited the words of a leading Islamic extremist to prove that Allah has nothing whatsoever to do with the God of the Bible. Abdel Aziz Rantisi, who briefly led Hamas, said that Allah has declared war on Prime Minister Sharon and President Bush. This means that Allah has declared war on Israel, God's chosen ones, said van der Hoeven. And that proves that Allah is not God, he concluded. Rather, he is "another deity, one who drinks blood as water, who loves *jihad* and terror, and promises virgins in his so-called paradise to those who kill Jews—the more Jews the better." This "evil, bloodthirsty 'god'" has, like the biblical Amalek, made war against the only true God and his elected people, van der Hoeven observed. The muezzins may shout out that *Allah hu ahbar*—"our Allah is greater," he added, but "the God of Israel remains infinitely greater." Rantisi was killed by an Israeli missile in a targeted assassination in April 2004.[11]

The NAE has called on Christian leaders to moderate their anti-Islamic statements and has rejected anti-Muslim propaganda.[12] But this does not imply recognition that Muslims and Christians share the same deity. "I'd never, ever promote the idea that Jews and Christians worship the same God as Muslims," Ted Haggard, then the NAE president, told me in 2006. Though he doesn't agree with Pat Robertson that Muslims worship the moon god, neither does Pastor Ted believe that Allah is the God who revealed himself to Abraham, Isaac, and Jacob. Rather, Haggard expresses a view that is compatible with that of his friend and colleague C. Peter Wagner—that Allah is a high-ranking demon. There are many spirit-beings, Pastor Ted told me, including angels and demons who masquerade as the Lord. But there is only one Almighty creator of the universe. "God is a personality," and this personality is very different from that of the spirit-being that spoke to Mohammed, said Haggard.[13] "The Christian God encourages freedom, love, forgiveness, prosperity and health," he noted. "The Muslim god appears to value the opposite." Like many other evangelical leaders, Pastor Ted fears Islamic ambitions to dominate the world, and he supports efforts to convert Muslims to Christianity. He saw the tsunami that devastated Indonesia in 2005 as a God-given occasion to bring people to Christ. Indonesia was "the number one exporter of radical Islam," said Haggard. "That's not a judgment. It's an opportunity," he said.[14]

Pastor Reza Safa made similar points ten years earlier about the character differences between the Christian and Muslim deities. There is a vast gap of nature and personality between God and Allah, Safa said in *Inside Islam*. He cited 1 John 4:3: "Every spirit that does not confess Jesus is not of God. This is the spirit of the Antichrist." Since Islam denies Jesus' divinity, it was born of that antichrist spirit, Safa contended. And that, he concluded, makes Muhammad a false prophet and Islam a false religion. "I believe Islam is Satan's weapon to oppose God," Safa declared. The spirit that raised Islam has three objectives, he said: to challenge Christ, to hinder the end-time world revival, and to oppose the Jewish people and take over their God-given land. Islam has always been inherently violent, he added: it has left a fingerprint of blood on every page of its history.[15]

Franklin Graham also believes that God and Allah are wholly distinct. In 2006 he stood by his earlier description of Islam as evil, saying that the God that he worships tells him to love his enemy, to give him food when he's hungry and water when he's thirsty, not to kill him. Billy Graham doesn't share his son's opinion of Islam, incidentally. He knows many wonderful Muslims whom he loves greatly, he says, and he thinks that Americans should learn more about Islam.[16]

Hal Lindsey and the Pope

Many evangelical leaders stress brutality as a defining quality of Islam. In this view, Muslims are violent not merely for political reasons but because of the aggression and severity of their faith. The West has been trying to convince itself that Islam is a religion like Unitarianism, or Buddhism, or Christianity, chides Hal Lindsey, author of *The Late Great Planet Earth*. But Islam's version of the Great Commission is to make war on all nonbelievers until they accept Islam, Lindsey says. Osama bin Laden made this clear during the campaign in Afghanistan when he declared that he had been ordered to fight all men until they say, "There is no God but Allah," Lindsey adds. Citing the story of two Fox News journalists who converted to Islam under threat of death at the hands of a Palestinian group that had kidnapped them in 2006, Lindsey observed, "Jesus didn't tell Christians to come to him at the point of a gun."[17]

Lindsey found further proof of violence at the heart of Islam when Muslims rioted in September 2006 after Pope Benedict XVI delivered a scholarly address at the University of Regensberg. In his talk, Benedict cited the Byzantine Emperor Manuel II Paleologus, who claimed to have spoken of the evil of Islam in a dialogue with a Muslim in 1391–92. Mohammed spread Islam by the sword, said the emperor, and God is not pleased by blood. This is an ancient accusation. Christians since the seventh century have attacked Islam as a religion propagated by violence. But this claim was peripheral to the pope's main point in the speech: that Catholicism has achieved a happy blending of faith, based on Scripture, and Hellenic reason, founded on Greek philosophy. Jews and Muslims, by contrast, lean too much toward obedience to God's law, so their beliefs are less rational than those of Christians. This is a curious assertion. In fact, Islam was heavily influenced by Greek philosophy (just as many Jewish thinkers have revered the rationalist Moses Maimonides).[18] It was medieval Arabs who preserved classical texts that Christendom had lost and transmitted them to the West. As the late Yale University scholar Dorothee Metlitzki observed, the Arabs "were the true representatives of classical knowledge and the giants on whose shoulders Latin science and philosophy had to be placed." In comparison to Muslim civilization in the eleventh century, the Christian world seemed infantile, barbaric, and provincial, Metlitzki concluded.[19] Moreover, the princes of the Catholic Church today might be circumspect about criticizing any other religion for propagating faith by force, given the history of Christian violence, including crusades, inquisitions, and coerced conversions.

But that wasn't what prompted the fury of the Muslims' response. Rather, they took Benedict's allusion to the medieval emperor's insult as representing the pope's own views. There were protests across the Islamic world, some of them violent. Palestinians with guns and firebombs attacked seven churches in the West Bank and Gaza Strip. In Somalia, a religious leader urged Muslims to hunt down the pope and kill him, and an elderly Catholic nun was shot to death in what may have been a related incident. In Britain, at a rally outside Westminster Cathedral, a Muslim leader demanded capital punishment for Benedict. Muslims burned the pope in effigy and attacked a church in Basra, Iraq. Several Iraqi extremist groups threatened to kill all of the nation's Christians unless the pope apologized.[20]

These outbursts proved his point about Muslims, Lindsey declared. They launched this wave of violence to show that Islam is not a violent religion, he observed sardonically.[21] Bridges for Peace (BFP), one of the three main Christian Zionist organizations in Jerusalem, offered further evidence. Its online Israel News Update noted that Muslim religious leaders in the Gaza Strip warned the pope to accept Islam if he wanted to ever live in peace again. A Palestinian group threatened to kill all Christians in Gaza, BFP reported, and an Iraqi militant group associated with Al Qaeda threatened attacks on the "worshippers of the cross." This Iraqi group, the Mujahideen Shura Council, told Christians, "You have no other choice but Islam or death. We shall break the cross and spill the wine."[22] Sheik Abu Saqer, a prominent preacher in Gaza, said that "this little racist pope" was the spiritual leader of "the Crusader ideology." All true believers know that Islam must rule all relations, said the sheik. "The only dialogue we will accept is when all other religions agree to convert to Islam." Ayman Al-Zawahiri, bin Laden's chief deputy, called for the pope and all Christians to become Muslims and repudiate the Trinity and the crucifixion.[23]

An Unfavorable View of Islam

Evangelicals in general, and particularly their elites, have a broadly negative attitude toward Muslims and the Islamic faith. White evangelicals are far more disapproving of Muslims than any other religious group in America is, but even they are not as negative about Muslims as their born-again leaders are.[24] Seventy-seven percent of evangelical leaders hold an unfavorable view of Islam, according to a 2002 poll. Ninety-seven percent said that it is important or very important to evangelize Muslims in the United States and abroad. Seven in ten evangelical leaders said that Islam is a religion of violence. Forty-five percent believed that "the war against terrorism is a war between the West and Islam," and only 10 percent agreed with President Bush's declaration that Islam is a religion of peace. Nearly eight of every ten born-again leaders disagreed when Bush said that Muslims and Christians pray to the same God.[25]

"Why *wouldn't* evangelical leaders hold an unfavorable view of Islam?" Richard Land asked me emphatically. "*I* hold an unfavorable view of Islam!" Islam is a different religion from Christianity, with a different God, argued Land, who is the president of the Southern Baptist Convention's public policy arm in Washington, D.C. It is an erroneous religion in that it teaches that Allah is not the father of Jesus Christ, Land told me. When President Bush said that Muslims, Christians, and Jews worship the same God, he was speaking from a deep moral conviction, but he was wrong, Land argued. "He's the commander in chief, not the theologian in chief." Bush was mistaken, too, to say Islam is a religion of peace, he added. That comment was more a wish than a fact, said Land. Still, the SBC official cautioned against confusing all of Islam with jihadism. "Islam is like Christianity: it's a many-splintered thing. There are many expressions of Islam, and some of them kill other Muslims." The biggest problem with Islam, he added, is that it never went through a Reformation, which led in the West to modernity and the conviction that you don't kill people with whom you disagree. As a result, Islam includes violent elements, as Christianity has in the past. Islam is a very normal religious expression for the twelfth century, Land concluded.[26]

"God Loves Arabs as Well as Jews"

Some other evangelical leaders declare that the Lord still cares for the children of Ishmael. "God loves Arabs as well as Jews," said John Walvoord, the former president of the Dallas Theological Seminary, in 1989. But His promises to Abraham and his descendants through Isaac are unalterable, Walvoord declared. Those who resist that are "fighting the Bible." Jerry Falwell forcefully denied that people who are pro-Israel are anti-Arab. "The God of the Bible is pro-people!" he declared in 2006, citing the biblical story of Jonah. "Where did God send him?" asked Falwell. "To Nineveh, capital of the Assyrian Empire, which today includes a number of Arab nations."[27]

Robert Stearns, the leader of Eagles' Wings, also observes that God loves Muslims. "God loves everyone," he told me. Islam is not salvific and it's not the truth, he said. Still, he respects it. Islam as a religion is not a danger, he added, but radical, violent political Islamists are. "Extreme Islam is the modern face of evil, and it has to be resisted," Robert said. Gary Bauer agrees that not all Muslims are enemies of the West, though he notes that a significant number of them intend to "kill the infidel" or die trying. In 2007 he showered praise on former Pakistani prime minister Benazir Bhutto for being angered by what Islamic extremists were doing in the name of her faith. "This is not the Islam I was taught," he quoted Bhutto as saying. Noting hints that she was preparing to return to her country to fight against Islamofascists, even if it meant her death, Bauer declared, "May she inspire others to be just as courageous!"[28] When Bhutto was assassinated in Pakistan in December 2007, Bauer lamented that the "dark forces of Islamofascism" had taken her life. "It is difficult for the civilized mind to comprehend the extent to which the Islamic world is immersed in a culture of death," he said.[29]

Bridges for Peace, too, sees the difference between politicized Islamic extremists and other Arabs. In its *News Update and Prayer Focus* in July 2006, BFP carried a prayer implicitly acknowledging that not all Muslims are the enemies of Western culture: "Pray that the Arab world will strongly resist the radical terrorists in their midst." The same news update depicted Islamic radicals, however, as the enemies of God whom the Lord will incinerate. Following a story on how Sheik Sayyed Hassan Nasrallah, the leader of Hezbollah, challenged Israel and the United States to bring on World War III, BFP cited a warning from Psalm 21:

> Your hand will find out all your enemies; your right hand will find out those who hate you. You will make them as a blazing oven when you

appear. The LORD will swallow them up in his wrath; and fire will consume them.[30]

Violence in the Qur'an

Not every evangelical leader distinguishes among Muslim groups or the branches of Islam. A number of them caution that so-called moderate Muslims are no different from the radical fundamentalists: they all pose a danger to the West. The late Ed McAteer, a godfather of the modern Christian Zionist movement, once said that no matter how much good fortune Arabs receive, they will never know peace. They cannot bear to see any Jew in the Holy Land, he contended, because they have a fire in their souls.[31] Franklin Graham, despite the fact that he felt compelled to apologize for calling Islam a "wicked, violent religion," said on Fox News Network's *Hannity and Colmes* in 2002 that terrorism is mainstream in Islam. "It's not just a handful of extremists. If you buy the Qur'an, read it for yourself, and it's in there," said Graham. "The violence that it preaches is there."[32]

Some evangelical leaders exhort people in the West not to deceive themselves about how dangerous Muslims really are. Commenting in 2006 on a report that Al Qaeda plans to conquer Iraq and neighboring Arab states, then to destroy Israel, Pat Robertson warned that the West is not listening to what Muslims are saying. Like other Christian Zionists, and like Bush, Rumsfeld, and other political conservatives, Robertson likened the Islamist threat to that posed by the Nazis in the 1930s: "If we had listened to what Hitler said in *Mein Kampf*, the West might have been prepared, and World War II would have been averted." Similarly, said Robertson, "We are not listening to what these guys say"—not only the radical Islamists but Muslims in general. "Well, you'd better believe them, and we'd better be prepared."[33] In August 2006, following Israel's war with Hezbollah, Robertson asked, are Islamic extremists an aberration from the teachings of the Qur'an? "I'm not sure they are." Then he added that Osama bin Laden may be one of the true disciples of the Qur'an because he follows it word for word. Citing the enmity that Wahhabi mullahs preach in mosques, Robertson concluded, "Islam is not a religion of peace. No way."[34]

Noting that "the hatred and rage of Islam flares up over incidental matters," Christian Friends of Israel warned that it is a very big deception to distinguish moderate from fanatic Islam. Islam is not moderate, said CFI's Carolyn Jacobson in a Watchman's Prayer Letter in 2006. "It is deadly serious about ruling the world and eliminating those who are against it." The solution is conversion to Christianity, she said. "Pray that the foundations of Islam would crumble," Jacobson urged in 2007, adding the wish that "more and more Muslims would come to a saving knowledge of Jesus Christ."[35]

Hal Lindsey charges that Western leaders don't understand that the only true expression of Islam is fundamentalism. "It is time for the world to wake up," he says. President Bush and his cabinet need to open their eyes to the fact that Muslims understand only one language: "overwhelming power and the will to use it." When fundamentalist Muslims see kindness and compromise, he warns, they take it as a sign that it is time to move in for the kill.[36]

An article on the Focus on the Family Web site declared that the line between political Islam and moderate Islam is disturbingly thin. James Dobson, founder of that organization, concedes that not all Muslims are violent. But with 1.2 billion Muslims in the world, he notes, "a small percentage of a big number is a very big number."[37] And John Hagee argues that Islamic terrorists are not fanatics—they are devout followers of Mohammed who are doing exactly what the Qur'an teaches: making war on everyone who doesn't accept Islam. "Islam not only *condones* violence; it *commands* it," says Hagee. To illustrate that, he cites Qur'anic verses, including Surah 9:5: "Fight and slay the Pagans [Christians and Jews, notes Hagee] wherever you find them, and seize them, beleaguer them, and lie in wait for them in every stratagem." As further proof, he quotes Harvard professor Samuel Huntington's *Clash of Civilizations:* "Some Westerners, including President Bill Clinton, have argued that the West does not have problems with Islam, but only with violent Islamic extremists. Fourteen hundred years of history demonstrate otherwise."[38]

Huntington's point is not that all Muslims are religious extremists. (Hagee, too, acknowledges that there are many peace-loving Muslims.) Rather, he notes a mix of factors that heightened hostility between Islam and the West in the twentieth century, including the West's effort to universalize its values and institutions at the same time that the Islamic Resurgence had renewed Muslims' confidence in the superiority of their own civilization. "The underlying problem for the West is not Islamic fundamentalism," says Huntington. "It is Islam, a different civilization whose people are convinced of the superiority of their culture and are obsessed with the inferiority of their power." The problem for Islam, he continues, is the West, whose people believe that their own culture is superior, and that their power obliges them to extend it across the world. Those, he says, are the basic ingredients of the clash of civilizations. Muslims fear and resent Western power and the decadent influence of Western culture but also find it seductive, says Huntington.[39] This is an extension of a long history of confrontation and tension with the West.

A History of Conflict

Spiritual conflict with Islam has a long lineage in Christian thought. Bernard Lewis, the dean of Western scholars of Islam, points out that the two faiths are natural opponents, largely because they have so much in common. Of all the religions in the world, Lewis notes, only these two believe that their truths are both universal and exclusive. Adherents of each faith believe that they bear God's final message and that it is their duty to bring it to the rest of mankind. Beyond that, many on both sides are convinced that the world is in the final stage of a millennial struggle. These parallels in heritage, self-perception, and aspiration inevitably lead to hostility, Lewis argues, and that is the real clash of civilizations. The Dome of the Rock in Jerusalem symbolizes this conflict. Built in the seventh century in the style of early Christian churches, it bears an inscription specifically intended to rebuke the Christian faith: God does not beget; that is, He has no Son. The caliph who built the mosque was sending a message to Christians, Lewis observes: "Your religion is superseded; your time has passed; move over; we are taking over the world."[40]

This enmity between the religions continued through the Crusades, the fall of Byzantium, and Ferdinand and Isabella's reconquest of Spain in 1492. For almost a thousand years, Islam threatened to conquer Christian Europe, both through invasion and through conversion and assimilation. Most of the first Muslims in lands west of Iran and Arabia were converts from Christianity. North Africa, Egypt, Syria, and Iraq had been Christian, and Europeans feared the same fate would befall them.[41] Charles Kimball, author of *When Religion Becomes Evil,* contends that this spiritual contest has left a permanent scar. "Islam is the only religion that has ever threatened the existence of Christianity," he observes. "That is deeply woven in our subconscious, into Western literature and culture."[42] For centuries, Islam, variously represented by Saladin, the "Grand Turk," or the Ottoman Empire, was associated with the forces of darkness. In medieval folk eschatology, Muslims (and Jews) were Antichrist's demonic agents. Mohammed and Islam were identified with Antichrist or Gog. Joachim of Fiore, for example, told Richard the Lion-Hearted in the late twelfth century that Saladin was the Antichrist and that Richard would defeat him.[43]

Unveiling Islam

In America, hostility to Islam traces back at least to Jonathan Edwards, a grand-father of modern evangelicalism. According to Edwards, there is some truth in the Qur'an, but Islam as a whole is demonic.[44] In recent decades, evangelical leaders and writers have focused on the idea that Islam rejects central Jewish and Christian beliefs. In his influential 1978 book, *Promised Land,* the late Derek Prince, an Eton- and Cambridge-educated student of Bible prophecy and radio show host, noted that Islam denies that Isaac was the chosen son of Abraham, that God can have a son, and that Jesus died on the cross. "If Jesus was a true prophet, then Mohammed was a false prophet," Prince concluded.[45]

Evangelical leaders often rely on Ergun Mehmet Caner as the source of their statements about Islam. Indeed, Jerry Vines drew on Caner when he denounced Mohammed.[46] A Muslim who became a born-again Christian as a young man, Caner is now professor of theology and church history and president of the seminary at Jerry Falwell's Liberty University. He and his brother Emir Fethi Caner elaborate on the distinctions between God and Allah in their book, *Unveiling Islam,* which reportedly has sold over 100,000 copies.[47] Unlike God, Allah does not comprise the three persons of the Trinity, they note in the book; he has no Son; he is neither the vicarious Redeemer and atoning Lamb of God, as Christ is, nor a loving, involved Father. Instead, he is a distant sovereign and judge. Mohammed knew the story of Christ and rejected it, the Caners point out. They add that, according to Muslim scholars, the Bible is not inerrant but is instead corrupt. Islam teaches that Paul and his companions altered Christ's message. Moreover, in Islamic belief, Jesus was not crucified. Instead, Allah raised him to himself. Jesus will reappear to defeat Antichrist and will then confess Islam, kill all pigs, break all crosses, and establish righteousness for a thousand years. In Islamic belief, Jesus never intended for anyone to worship him or to identify him with God, the Caners add. The Qur'an states emphatically that Abraham was not a Jew, they note, and that Mohammed saw followers of Moses and Christ as children of Satan.[48]

Christian Zionist leaders cite other definitive differences between Christianity and Islam as well. David Parsons, media director of the International Christian Embassy Jerusalem (ICEJ), argues that one crucial distinction is the concept of martyrdom. The Islamic martyr actively seeks death while attempting to murder others, says Parsons. The Christian martyr, by contrast, accepts death passively, if that is required to sanctify the name of the Lord. "Islam mandates the hatred and killing of those outside the faith," Parsons argues. "How then can anyone say we all worship the same God?"[49]

Another profound distinction is that Muslims anticipate the final victory of Islam over Judaism, says Walid Shoebat, the self-identifed PLO terrorist who became a born-again Christian. Shoebat cites the words of the prophet Mohammed describing the slaughter of the Jews at the end of time:

> The day of judgment shall not pass until the tribes of Islam defeat the tribes of Israel. Then the trees and stones will cry out: "There is a Jew hiding behind me. Come O Muslim, come O slave of Allah, come and kill him, until not one male Jew is left."

Hamas cites this text in its charter, declaring that it represents the promise of Allah.[50]

It is easy to see why many evangelical leaders rebuke Islam. For them, the followers of Allah are an affront to the true faith, devoted to a false revelation and obdurately hostile to God's Chosen People.

The Arab-Israeli Conflict: "A Contest over Whether or Not the Word of God Is True"

The real origin of the Arab-Israeli conflict, according to many Christian Zionist writers, does not reside in nationalist or economic factors but in the opposing spiritual forces. In 1931, following the violent Arab riots in Palestine of two years earlier, an editorial in the *Moody Bible Institute Monthly* wrote off Arab resistance to the Zionist enterprise as futile rebelliousness against God's plan.[51] After the establishment of the Jewish state in 1948, much Western prophecy writing assumed that the Arabs would join with Russia in the final days and invade Israel in the service of the Antichrist. Derek Prince argued in 1978 that Muslims, the followers of a false prophet, are the enemies not only of Israel but also of Christianity and God Himself.[52] John Hagee made a corollary claim in his 1996 book, *Beginning of the End:* Muslims believe that they will overcome the Jews because their theology insists that it will triumph over every other faith. "If the Arabs do not eventually defeat Israel in combat, Muhammad lied, the Koran is in error, and Allah is not the true God," said Hagee, echoing Derek Prince.[53] On the floor of the United States Senate in 2002, Senator James Inhofe (R-Oklahoma) made a similar point. Listing seven reasons why the West Bank rightfully belongs to the Jewish state, Inhofe concluded that the conflict "is a contest over whether or not the word of God is true."[54] In 2003, Pat Robertson told the prestigious Herzliya Conference in Israel that the confrontation with the Arabs is not about money or ancient customs versus modernity. "No," said

Robertson, "the struggle is whether Hubal, the Moon God of Mecca, known as Allah, is supreme, or whether the Judeo-Christian Jehovah God of the Bible is supreme."[55]

In February 2006, Hal Lindsey said that the conflict is not a clash of civilizations. It is a spiritual war pitting Christians and Jews against the forces of Islam. Speaking of "the almost impenetrable blindness caused by Islam over those born into it," Lindsey said that radical Islam silences nonviolent Muslims, denies every tenet of Christianity, and seeks to destroy the United States.[56]

Christian Zionists are not alone in this conviction. Former Israeli prime minister Ariel Sharon believed that Arab enmity toward Israel is rooted in Islam itself. It is more than the anger of an injured people, Sharon thought, and so is different from the antagonism between the Koreans and the Japanese or the French and the Germans. Asked why, Sharon replied simply, "Look at the Qur'an." David Chanoff, who co-wrote Sharon's autobiography, *Warrior*, understands the former prime minister's response to mean that in Islamic belief, Allah despises the Jews because of their hostility to Mohammed. Arabs traditionally have seen Jews as cowardly and feckless. That such a people should reestablish itself, defeat Arab armies in successive wars, and lay claim to Jerusalem, Islam's third holiest city, was an intolerable rebuke to the beliefs of devout Muslims. Knowing this, Sharon dedicated his life to establishing Israel's claim to the land beyond any challenge. He determined to make it clear to the Arabs that their assaults would come at too high a cost. In the end they would have no choice but to recognize Israel. This helped establish Israel's national character of toughness and determination.[57]

Testimony in the Knesset in 2007 appeared to support the claim that, for at least some Muslim authorities, the contest with Israel is a conflict of religious, not national interests. According to Palestinian Media Watch, new schoolbooks in use in East Jerusalem were for the first time inculcating the lesson that the hostilities with Israel are not over land and cannot be resolved by partition. Rather, the twelfth-grade texts taught that the conflict is existential and cannot be ended through compromise. The books, which were written by officials appointed by the supposedly moderate Fatah (not the more extremist Hamas), asserted that it is a religious duty to pursue Israel's destruction. Hal Lindsey quickly cited this as "hard evidence that there is no such thing as a 'peace-seeking Muslim Palestinian.'" Also in 2007, Mahmoud A-Zahar of Hamas, a former foreign minister of the Palestinian Authority, confirmed that recognizing Israel would contradict the Qur'an. Hamas, he declared, remained dedicated to the principle that all of Palestine is Muslim land.[58] Surveying the political landscape in 2008, Israeli historian Benny Morris concluded that the Muslim leaders who were riding high were all true believers in this cause: Hamas' Ismail Haniyeh and Khaled Meshal, Hezbollah's Nasrallah, and Iran's Ahmadinejad all believed that the struggle to eliminate the "Zionist entity" from the sacred soil of the Middle East is not merely a national conflict but a religious crusade in accordance with Allah's command.[59]

Anti-Semitism, Satan, and the Arabs

Bible teachers became increasingly attentive to the perils they saw in Islam after the oil crisis of 1973. John F. Walvoord expressed this concern in *Armageddon, Oil, and the Middle East,* which sold 750,000 copies.[60] In 1984, Jerry Falwell warned that Islamic fundamentalism was one of the most dangerous movements on earth. Still, he did not consider Islam to be inherently anti-Semitic. Hatred of Jews, he said, "is not the product of Christianity or any other religion for that matter"—thus implicitly absolving Islam. Rather, Satan is the author of anti-Semitism, said Falwell. The devil hates God. Therefore he hates the Jewish people, who represent God's sovereignty, grace, and love. That, said Falwell, is why Satan worked through the pharaohs, the Caesars, and Hitler to try to destroy the Jews. John Hagee elaborates on the theology of cosmic conflict and hatred of the Jewish people. Satan hates the Jews, he says, because they produced the Word of God and the Son of God, who broke Satan's hold over humanity. Anti-Semitism, Hagee says, is a demonic spirit conceived in the bowels of hell to take revenge on the Jews for bringing God's light to humanity.[61]

The devil knows that in God's providential plan "all Israel will be saved" (Romans 11:26), says the passionate Christian Zionist Don Finto, who argues that Jesus will not return until the Jews are in Jerusalem to welcome him (Matthew 23:39). But Satan calculates that none of this can happen if the Jews cease to exist or if they lose their religious identity. That, says Finto, is why the deceiver has misled the Church into persecuting the Jews. It is why Satan, the fiend, has sought to annihilate God's people. The devil has tried to delay their return to the Holy Land as well because God's plans will be delayed until the Jews "come home." The Church, in its historical hostility to the Jews, has thus been a pawn in the hands of her enemy, Finto declares.[62] Hal Lindsey adds that because the Lord has chosen the Jewish people to redeem the world, they have become the prime targets of the devil. The prophet Isaiah declares that Israel is a light to the Gentiles, the source of God's salvation to all nations (Isaiah 49:6). But, says Lindsey, "a malevolent spiritual force" has tried to subvert that divine plan by inspiring the mindless slaughter of Jews in every century, up until today.[63] "Kill the Jew and you kill God and his purpose in the world," says Malcolm Hedding, executive director of the ICEJ. "This is the sinister plan that lurks in the hearts of men and drives the powers of darkness." That, Hedding concludes, is the root of anti-Semitism.[64]

Many Christian Zionists take this to the next logical step, declaring that Muslims have become Satan's army in this ancient struggle. God has a plan for Israel that will result in the salvation of all believers. They warn, however, that the Muslim nations endanger God's design by striving to annihilate the Jewish state. More than one evangelical leader told me that Satan inspired the Holocaust in the hope of frustrating God's plan to redeem the world through the Jews. The devil is trying to do the same thing now through the Arabs and Muslims, they said.[65]

Walid Shoebat says explicitly that the Arab-Israeli conflict is an extension of the Holocaust. In 1993, Shoebat undertook a close reading of the Bible in an effort to persuade his wife to convert to Islam. Instead, he found Jesus. "I changed from being a terrorist to being an ambassador for the coming of the Messiah," he said. He soon discovered that everything he had been taught about Jews was a lie, he said later. A lifelong Holocaust denier, he studied Jewish history and realized that not only had the Holocaust happened, it had never ended. Rather, the Arabs were attempting to finish the job that Hitler had begun. "Simply put, the survivors had decided to go home and defend themselves, while mobs all around call on them to open their windows and doors so they can be killed and raped again and again and again," Shoebat observed.[66]

Derek Prince explicitly states that Satan is the driving force behind this Arab hostility to Jews. The Palestinian conflict with Israel is Satan's attempt to frustrate God's plan. In establishing their control over Jerusalem, the Jews have advanced God's wishes and dealt a blow to the devil, Prince observes. "Satan realizes that his kingdom is being threatened as never before, and he is fighting back with every weapon and tactic he can muster," he declares. "It is vital that God's people do not succumb to Satan's tactics."[67] That is to say, Christians and Jews must unite to keep the Land of Israel—and especially Jerusalem—in Jewish hands. Christian Zionist writer Stan Goodenough applies that lesson to the Temple Mount in particular. Satan is savvier than many Christians and Jews and he knows the Bible pretty well, Goodenough warns. The devil knows the central role that hill will play in God's redemption plan for the world, and so he has the Temple Mount in his sights. If he can use the UN to entrench Arabs there, says Goodenough, he can delay or even prevent the coming of Christ, "the One he dreads."[68]

Televangelist Benny Hinn, a Palestinian born in Jaffa who is now an evangelical famous for faith healing, described the opposing sides with simple clarity in an appearance in Dallas in 2002. The conflict is not between Arabs and Jews, said Hinn. "It's a war between God and the devil."[69] Jack Hayford says the same. Arab animosity is driven not only by political causes but also by "spiritual powers that will not be satisfied until Israel ceases to exist," he says. These forces are just as hostile to Christian believers as to Israel and they cannot be overthrown politically, Hayford declares. The only way to break them is by intercessory prayer.[70]

Mike Evans actually sees this demon-inspired enmity as good news in a way. "We have two opponents," he said in his Jerusalem Prayer Team e-newsletter in 2007: "the irreconcilable wing of Islam and the evil power that inspires it." Evans found comfort in this, for two reasons. First, the hostility of Islamists is confirmation that the Bible is true, he declared. There is no better proof that the devil does exist, as Scripture says, than the fact that those following his agenda—i.e., Muslim extremists—seek first to destroy the Jews, then the Christians, Evans concluded. Second, he saw this as the greatest opportunity in history to "confront the source of all evil" by defeating Satan's Islamic agents. If we fail, however, the results will be catastrophic, Evans warned.[71]

The ICEJ's Hedding finds this cosmic conflict symbolized in Genesis 15. In that chapter, Abraham sacrifices animals and birds to mark God's covenantal promise that the Chosen People will inherit the land. Birds of prey descend on the offering and Abraham drives them away. These vultures symbolize the power of darkness, which eternally attempts to destroy the Jewish people, says Hedding. "Since Israel is central to God's plan for humanity, the only way vultures can resist His will is to attack the Jews," he notes. Their trail of blood begins in Egypt and their footprints are seen in Herod, Titus, the Crusaders, Hitler, Arafat, Hamas, Hezbollah, and the current president of Iran. Just as Abraham, with God's help, drove off the birds of prey, Christians who love God must do the same today, Hedding declares. The vultures have sworn to destroy first the Saturday people (the Jews), then the Sunday people (Christians), he says, repeating the familiar Christian Zionist warning.[72] To resist these Arab and Muslim foes is thus both a sacred calling and a matter of self-defense.

Dispensationalists see this in the context of the end-times. The insoluble problems of the world, especially those in the Middle East, says Hal Lindsey, will lead people to rush under the spell of the Antichrist. Working through Satan's power, he will appear to usher in a period of peace and prosperity, inspiring a global delirium of hope. After three and a half years, though, he will sit in the Holy of Holies in the rebuilt Temple and declare himself to be God. Christ will send the Second Rider on the Red Horse of the Apocalypse with a great sword, which Lindsey interprets as weapons of mass destruction. Iran will lead the Muslim Confederacy and Russia to attack Israel. Many Israelites will be awakened to faith in the true Messiah, Jesus Christ, during the holocaust that follows, says Lindsey.[73]

Hezbollah: Satan's Hand at Work

The founder of the Christian Zionist Eagles' Wings Ministry, Robert Stearns, saw Satan's hand at work during Israel's war with Hezbollah in the summer of 2006 and its aftermath. Hezbollah and its supporters revealed a new layer of "the enemy's" sinister strategy in the global contention between light and darkness, Stearns said. The fact that Muslim troops would be included in the UN peacekeeping force in Lebanon along the Israeli border was a further sign of the devil's plan. "We desperately need to see with the Lord's eyes the realities of our day," Robert said, and he called for people like the sons of Issachar in 1 Chronicles 12:32, who understood the times and knew what to do. In citing that biblical chapter, Robert was exhorting his followers to be a spiritual army in the service of the Lord. In the scriptural text, the warriors of Israel, "like an army of God," rally to King David, who in that context is often seen as a type of the Messiah. Robert called on his army of God to gather in New Jersey at the time of the Jewish New Year for seventy-two hours of nonstop prayer and worship, to declare God's word and pray for the defeat of Satan's plan.[74]

One week later, Robert issued a dramatic summons: he called his supporters in Eagles' Wings to battle "under the banner and with the blessing" of Christians United for Israel and Pastor John Hagee. Iranian president Mahmoud Ahmadinejad, Hezbollah's chief patron, was coming to address the United Nations. Malcolm Hoenlein, executive vice chairman of the Conference of Presidents of Major Jewish Organizations, was organizing an emergency protest, and Robert was determined to show support. He called on his Eagles' Wings followers to participate, describing the planned protest as a battle between the Lord's army and the enemy, Satan. He reminded them that he had often said that the day would arrive when he would have to mobilize thousands of Watchmen on the Wall quickly. "That time has come," Robert declared. "That time is now. I am asking you to skip work. I am asking you to skip school. I am asking you to bring your children," Robert exhorted them. "Bring your Bibles, your shofars, your tambourines, and your praise." It was no accident that, months in advance, Eagles' Wings had scheduled this three-day prayer session in the New York City region at exactly this time, Robert noted. His spiritual warriors would be ready for Satan's agent. "The enemy has overplayed his hand. The enemy is coming, and the Lord's army will meet him, prepared. The battle, and the victory, belongs to the Lord." In calling the prayer meeting, Robert implied, he had been unknowingly following a divine plan to stand with Israel in confronting its eternal foe.

Evangelical leaders rallied their followers around the country to attend the protest. Gary Bauer urged his 100,000 readers to go there on buses provided by the Conference of Presidents. Thirty-five thousand Jews and Christians attended the hastily organized rally, many of them blowing rams' horns. Hundreds of Christians, some from as far away as Michigan and California, carried signs saying "Christians United for Israel." The speakers included Hoenlein, Nobel laureate Eli Wiesel, Harvard law professor Alan Dershowitz, and Diana Hagee, John's wife. "The enemies of Israel are the enemies of America," Mrs. Hagee declared. "They are the enemies of life, liberty, and the pursuit of happiness. Our enemies have drawn the battle lines, and if that line be drawn, draw it around Christians and Jews, for we are one and we are united."[75]

One year later, in September 2007, Ahmadinejad was scheduled to return to New York to address the UN, and Eagles' Wings exhorted their "praying warriors and watchmen" to rally again in protest against "this monster." The Iranian president had been given a platform to spread his anti-Semitism and his genocidal fantasies about Jews, said an Eagles' Wings Prayer Update. "AS CHRISTIAN WATCHMEN IN THIS HOUR, WE CANNOT LET THIS ATROCITY GO UNCHALLENGED AND UNCONTESTED!" Eagles' Wings called on their followers to stand with the Jewish people at the UN and say with one voice, "Never again! . . . Not on our watch!"[76] Meanwhile, Yechiel Eckstein urged evangelical members of his International Fellowship of Christians and Jews to attend the rally, and Mike Evans asked his Jerusalem Prayer Team readers to sign a petition to protest the decision to allow Ahmadinejad into the country.[77]

Willingness to Die for Israel

For Christian Zionists, the ultimate outcome of the cosmic contest, and Israel's role in it, are not in doubt, but the conflict on the ground is unfair: Israel is a small but heroic David forced to confront the huge, fierce Goliath of the Arabs and other Muslims. Israel has had to endure "hostile neighbors, five wars, terrorism, inflation, media misrepresentation, economic boycott," wrote Derek Prince in 1978. He described Israel as a tiny state of five million Jews surrounded by 150 million hostile Arabs with standing armies of one million men. There is one inescapable fact, Prince concluded: Israel's survival is at stake.[78] This was undoubtedly important to Robert Stearns in declaring his willingness to die for Israel.

Robert is hardly the only conservative Christian supporter of Israel who would lay down his life for the Jewish state. "We all would," one respected senior evangelical leader told me without a moment's hesitation. We were speaking in a cafeteria at the United Nations in New York, where she was so well known that the staff all recognized her pleasantly. A number of prominent Christian Zionists have been threatened repeatedly because of their support for Israel, she said. One received a threat on his grandson's life. I knew that John Hagee's life had been threatened when he announced his first event to honor Israel in San Antonio and that someone then shot out the windows of his station wagon in his driveway. An Iranian cleric issued a fatwa in 2002 saying that Falwell was a "mercenary and must be killed" following Falwell's charge on *60 Minutes* that Mohammed was a terrorist.[79] Threats make Christian Zionists cautious about security but don't deter them, my informant told me. She was a veteran member of the movement. She has had access to the White House, especially under Republican presidents, since the time of Ronald Reagan and met with Prime Ministers Shamir, Netanyahu, and Sharon often over the years. Her group has donated millions of dollars to Israel, especially to settlements on the West Bank. In 1996 they rented the entire Mount of Olives in Jerusalem to celebrate the three-thousandth birthday of King David, she told me. She gave me an insiders' perspective of the personal commitments and sacrifices that the prominent Christian Zionists make, things that aren't reported in the press. She's received threats, too, and wants no public credit for what she does in any case. I agreed not to name her in this book. When she appears, I'll call her Faith.

Mahmoud Ahmadinejad

Especially in recent years, prominent Christian Zionists have focused on Iran as a principal threat to Israel and the West. As always, this comports with their theology. Ezekiel 38:5 specifically names Persia (Iran) as an ally of Gog, enemy of Israel. All agree, the Scofield Bible declares, that Gog's kingdom is Russia, which, with Persia and other allies, will make a last mad attempt to exterminate the remnant of Israel in Jerusalem at the end of days. In 1979, with the Islamic revolution in Iran, prophecy writers argued that this prediction was coming true: the Ayatollah Khomeini was a forerunner of the Antichrist.[80]

By 2006, Iran's president Mahmoud Ahmadinejad had become a central villain in the Christian Zionist worldview. His denial of the Holocaust, his explicit threats against the state of Israel, and his apparent drive to develop a nuclear weapon deeply alarmed many people in Israel and the West. Evangelicals were particularly disturbed by this, and by his eschatology. Ahmadinejad may actually embrace radical religious beliefs of the kind sometimes attributed to George W. Bush, except that the Iranian leader's convictions are the Shia mirror image of Christian end-times views. Ahmadinejad has openly declared that he has been in touch with God, a charge sometimes leveled at Bush. Moreover, Ahmadinejad says, God has assured him that he will win in his conflict with global evil, by which he means Israel and the United States.[81]

Curiously, Ahmadinejad attempted to bring Bush to Islam. In an eighteen-page personal letter, he tried to enlist the American president in the service of the prophets, citing convictions that he supposed he and Bush shared. Two of these could not have been more divisive, however: the Islamic teaching that Jesus was a prophet (not God), and the Shia belief in a final day of judgment. Ahmadinejad seemed not to realize that he would offend Bush or any other believing Christian by denying the divinity of Christ. And by alluding to "the divine rule of the righteous on earth" on the Last Day, he invoked Shia eschatology, a point of profound theological difference with Christianity.[82]

The Hidden Imam

Ideologues around Ahmadinejad see the creation of Iran's Islamic Republic as paving the way for the imminent return of the Mahdi, the twelfth, or hidden, imam. Shia Muslims believe that in A.D. 939, God withdrew the twelfth in the line of imams from the world, placing him in a state of occultation, or hiddenness. Many Shia believe that his "second coming" will occur in an end-times scenario that parallels the dispensational expectation of the apocalypse and the Millennium. Chaos, global battle between good and evil, and pestilence (recalling the Tribulations) will precede the Mahdi's arrival. He will kill the Dajjal, or anti-Mahdi, (similar to the Antichrist). According to "The World toward Illumination," a series of essays on an Iranian government Web site, the Twelfth Imam will return at Mecca (as dispensationalists believe that Jesus will return to Jerusalem) and all of Arabia will submit to him. The Mahdi will then triumph over his enemies in Iraq and establish his global government in a mosque in the Iraqi city of Kufa. The "prophet Jesus" (who is not God) will appear as his lieutenant. A blissful period of justice and prosperity will ensue (paralleling the premillennial expectation of Christ's thousand-year rule), which, the Web site specifies, will be marked by an astounding growth of science and technology as well as economic prosperity. All injustices will disappear—including, one may assume, American hegemony and Israeli power.[83]

Not all Shia Muslims embrace this theology. Some believe that they should pave the way for the Mahdi by creating a just order themselves (recalling the postmillennial view popular in America in earlier times). Others live in expectation of these final events, however, and, like conservative Christians, they look more urgently for signs of the times during periods of crisis. The rallying cry of Muktada al-Sadr's followers in Iraq, for example, is "Hasten the coming of the Mahdi."[84]

Eight institutes in Iran are now studying and disseminating information about the Mahdi's return and trying to speed it. One, the Bright Future Institute, employs a staff of 160 and maintains a Web site (www.bfnews.ir). There is also a new messiah telephone hotline that updates the indications of the Mahdi's imminent return (recalling the evangelical Rapture Index, discussed in Chapter 4). In 2002, signs began to appear in Tehran declaring, "He is coming." The Iranian cabinet has earmarked $17 million for the mosque at Jamkaran, which, tradition holds, the Mahdi himself ordered to be built. Shiite faithful drop written prayers into a well adjacent to this mosque (just as Jews place written prayers in the cracks of the Western Wall in Jerusalem). Pilgrims say that their prayers were answered after they came to the mosque forty nights in a row.[85]

Some senior religious authorities and journals in Iran have accused Ahmadinejad of spreading religious superficiality and superstition, and of politicizing belief in the Mahdi.[86] Only 20 percent of Iranians subscribe to the "Mahdaviat" belief in the hidden imam's imminent return. Ahmadinejad may be one of them, however. He is said to be associated with a semisecret ultrareligious Shia group called the Hojjatieh society, whose members assert that only the Mahdi can establish an Islamic state (much as many ultra-orthodox Jews challenge the legitimacy of a Jewish state until the messiah establishes it). They also are said to believe that they can hasten the Mahdi's return by creating chaos on earth. The late Ayatollah Khomeini disbanded political parties in Iran largely to curb the movement's influence, but for years members of the Hojjatieh society reportedly have held positions in the Iranian parliament and government. In 2005, the head of Ahmadinejad's office denied that the society had any connection to the government. Shortly thereafter, however, Ahmadinejad chose a prominent Hojjatieh figure, Ayatollah Taqi Mesbah-Yazdi, as his spiritual mentor. Mesbah-Yazdi, a hard-line fundamentalist cleric from the Iranian holy city of Qom, is known as "Professor Crocodile" for his support of strict Islamic rule and the use of violence against opponents. He reportedly claimed that the Mahdi was preparing to return during the Iran-Iraq war, but that Ayatollah Khomeini spoiled that by agreeing to end the war in 1988. Mezbah-Yazdi also is said to have ruled that Islamic law permits the use of nuclear weapons.

Ahmadinejad believes that government policy should be directed to hastening the Mahdi's return and he has instructed his cabinet to sign an oath of loyalty to the Twelfth Imam. In April 2008, he declared that the Mahdi was directing his government's policies, a claim for which senior Iranian clerics rebuked him.[87] "I have no doubt at all, and my Iranian friends and informants are unanimous about this, that Ahmadinejad means what he says," Bernard Lewis observes. "He really means it, he really believes it, and that makes him all the more dangerous." Lewis adds that Muslims generally believe that they can expedite the coming of the final struggle, and the final victory.[88]

In an appearance at the UN General Assembly in September 2005, Ahmadinejad made his convictions plain, calling on God to hasten the emergence of "the promised one." The Iranian president's theology accounts for his hardline policies, according to the political editor of Iran's conservative *Resalat* newspaper. He added that Ahmadinejad thinks he has a religious mission to bring the messiah (a charge sometimes made against Bush).[89]

Christian Zionists and the Mahdi

Christian Zionists have repeatedly pointed out the messianic underpinnings of Ahmadinejad's actions. Joseph Farah, a Christian journalist of Arab descent, said that Ahmadinejad, in his own words, sees his main mission as to "pave the path for the glorious reappearance of the Imam Mahdi, may Allah hasten his reappearance." "All Iran is buzzing about the Mahdi," Farah added.[90] Gary Bauer warned that the Iranians may find the urge to destroy Israel with a nuclear weapon irresistible, since they believe that this will hasten the Hidden Imam's return. Bauer quoted Ayatollah Ibrahim Amini, a professor at the Religious Learning Center in Qom, who said that the soldiers of the Mahdi will kill any Jew or Christian who persists in disbelief. "It seems unlikely that this catastrophe can be avoided," said Amini. "Warfare and bloodshed are inevitable."[91]

Hal Lindsey associates the Mahdi with the Antichrist. Citing a recent Egyptian book that attempts to reconcile Islamic belief with Christian scripture, Lindsey notes that Muslims consider the Mahdi to be the first of the Four Horsemen of the Apocalypse. He is the rider on a white horse in Revelation 6:2:

And I saw, and behold, a white horse, and its rider had a bow; and a crown was given to him, and he went out conquering and to conquer.

According to Christian interpretation of this verse, however, the rider on the white horse is the Antichrist, says Lindsey.[92] Jan Markell, speaking for the conservative Christian Olive Tree Ministries in Maple Grove, Minnesota, says that Satan is actually the source of the belief in the fake messiah, the Mahdi. "The enemy is having a field day with the Muslims getting them to believe a lie," says Markell, a Jew who came to Jesus under the ministry of Jewish evangelist Hyman Appelman.[93]

Mike Evans, founder of evangelical Jerusalem Prayer Team, was provoked by Ahmadinejad's reference to "the Prophet Jesus Christ" in his UN address. "It is quite easy to see that from his perspective, this is a religious war. He is telling Christians that Jesus Christ is not the Third Person of the Trinity," Evans wrote in his group's online newsletter. Evans added that the Iranian president, in longing for the Hidden Imam, "the perfect human being," was calling on Muslims to usher him in through violence and martyrdom. Evans cautioned, as Bauer did, that the Iranian president's faith in this Islamic end-times paradigm is so strong that he may go to apocalyptic lengths, including a nuclear attack on Israel or America, to prompt the Mahdi's return. Like other Christian Zionists, Evans associates the Iranian threat with devil worship. In spring 2006, speaking of the danger from Tehran, he urged his readers to "pray that the powers of hell would be bound in Jesus' name and that God would intervene in Satan's evil plans." Four months later he warned that Ahmadinejad sent his letter to Bush as a prelude to a strike on the United States. According to Islamic fascism, said Evans, Ahmadinejad was obliged to first invite the president to convert to Islam. Evans developed this case in his book, *Showdown with Nuclear Iran,* which, he told his readers, "is the most important book, I believe, you will ever read, other than the Bible." It could help save America and Israel from a nuclear holocaust, he noted.[94]

Christian Friends of Israel, pointing out in its online newsletter that Ahmadinejad "is very sincere, deceived, and dangerous," has repeatedly linked Islam to the devil. It specifically associated Islam with the story of Satan's rebellion against God, then asked its readers to pray that the Church will wake up to the fact that "the god of this world masquerading as Allah (God) is in a rage for 'he knows his time is short.'" The "god of this world" is the devil (2 Corinthians 4:4). The remainder of the quote adapts Revelation 12, the chapter that describes Satan's war against God—except that it substitutes the name "Allah" for the biblical words "the devil."[95] CFI's Carolyn Jacobson later observed that God will turn the evil of the Muslims to his own purposes. Noting that Muslim rulers believe they can hasten the return of the Mahdi by creating chaos, Jacobson concluded that, ironically, God is using them to fulfill His own plans: since Jesus will return in times of chaos, the Lord is letting the Muslims create the atmosphere in which that will happen.[96]

Bridges for Peace, leaving no doubt about how God will treat the Iranian president, followed a story about him with a promise of vengeance from Psalm 11:5–6: "The Lord tests the righteous and the wicked, and his soul hates him that loves violence. On the wicked He will rain coals of fire and brimstone." This recalled the organization's expectation that God's fire will devour Ahmadinejad's close ally, Hezbollah's leader Nasrallah. The Bridges newsletter later added, "Praise God that it is a Jewish Messiah and not an Iranian Mahdi who will reign over the earth one day." Pat Robertson, for his part, gets right to the point in assessing Ahmadinejad's beliefs: "People like that are fanatics, they are crazy," says Robertson (using language sometimes directed at himself).[97]

The Politics of Bellicosity

Some experts on Iran believe, however, that Ahmadinejad's claims and threats are political gestures as well as theological pronouncements. Vali Nasr, author of *The Shia Revival,* says there is little evidence in Shia eschatology or Ahmadinejad's rhetoric that he is gunning for Armageddon. The Iranian president's bellicosity is intended, at least in part, to position Iran as a regional leader. By expressing belligerence toward Israel and the West, he is choosing themes that unite Arabs and Iranians, Sunnis and Shia. This gives him the aura of a Third World champion, a new Gamal Abdel Nasser.[98] Said Arjomand, an expert on Islamic apocalypticism and the author of *The Shadow of God and the Hidden Imam,* offers a corollary analysis. Ahmadinejad's focus on the Mahdi is not intended to bring on the end-times, says Arjomand. He adds that the Iranian president has no thought of spreading chaos to facilitate the hidden Imam's return. Rather, Ahmadinejad is trying to boost his position vis-à-vis Ayatollah Khamenei, the Supreme Leader, says Arjomand. By turning attention to the Mahdi, Ahmadinejad is reminding the Iranian people that the Twelfth Imam is the true ruler and that Khamenei is just standing in for him until his return. As for Ahmadinejad's calls for the destruction of Israel, Arjomand believes that he obviously means them. But, like Nasr, he argues that the Iranian president takes this stand partly to enhance his popularity in the Arab and Muslim world. Ahmadinejad's denial of the Holocaust serves the same purpose.[99]

Millions of Iranians evidently do not share Ahmadinejad's skepticism about the Holocaust, incidentally. In the fall of 2007, they were glued to their television sets every Monday night to watch the wildly popular "Zero Degree Turn," which recounted the story of an Iranian-Palestinian Muslim who saved a French Jewish woman and her family during the Holocaust. The show was based on the life of an Iranian diplomat in Paris who rescued over a thousand European Jews by forging Iranian passports. It was the most lavish and expensive production ever aired by the Islamic republic's state-owned television.[100] Trita Parsi, author of *Treacherous Alliance—The Secret Dealings of Israel, Iran and the US,* cites "Zero Degree Turn" as one piece of evidence that Israel and the United States should look past Iran's "deliberately misleading hyperbole." They should attend instead to its pragmatists, who do not think apocalyptically, says Parsi.[101]

Despite his bluster and threats, Ahmadinejad has very limited power, say analysts in Iran. As president, he is in charge of the civil government, managing the budget and making appointments to local and regional positions. His broader influence derives chiefly from support by Khamenei, backing by the Basiji militia and elements of the Revolutionary Guard, and the opprobrium of the West. That Western animus enhances his status at home and in the Middle East.[102]

Ahmadinejad does seem to believe that the Holocaust is a Zionist falsification of history. He was indoctrinated in this view earlier in his life as a member of the Revolutionary Guards and he championed it as a student leader. Ahmadinejad did not actually threaten another Holocaust, however. He was quoting Ayatollah Khomeini's threat of years earlier, which was not against the Jewish people but against the Israeli government. Ahmadinejad's statement was, "The Imam said this regime occupying Jerusalem must vanish from the page of time."[103]

"Disengenuously Distorting the Facts"

The charge that mainstream Islam is inherently violent is a distortion, notes John Esposito, the Georgetown University scholar. It takes Qur'anic and other Islamic religious texts out of context while ignoring warlike passages in the Old Testament, he says. The Qur'an does speak of warfare, but it is against enemies who attacked Muslims, Esposito observes. That is true of Surah 9:5, the passage that, according to John Hagee, calls on Muslims to slaughter Jews and Christians. In reality, this text exhorts Muslims to fight "unbelievers," who were Meccan pagans, not people today, notes Esposito. Moreover, at the end of passages that call for battle, the Qur'an requires Muslims to stop fighting if their enemy does, a fact that Christian Zionists don't mention, he observes. All three of the Abrahamic world religions—Judaism, Christianity, and Islam—have a warrior side. But evangelicals disingenuously distort that fact, Esposito argues, by citing New Testament commandments to love one's neighbor while saying nothing about Old Testament strictures to kill the enemy's women and children.

Eric Yoffie, president of the Union for Reform Judaism, agrees that violence and suicide bombing do not have deep Qur'anic roots. At a conference of Chicago's Islamic Society of North America (ISNA) in 2007, he denounced Pat Robertson and Franklin Graham by name, declaring that the time has come to stand up to religious leaders who make vicious attacks against Islam and demonize Muslims, exploiting fear. The claim that fanaticism and intolerance are fundamental to Islam is the product of huge and profound ignorance, Yoffie asserted. Islam is far removed from the perverse distortions of the terrorists who claim to speak in its name, he said. Yoffie acknowledged that the Hebrew Bible, like the Qur'an, contains passages that appear to promote violence and offend ethical sensibilities. He exhorted the moderate majorities of Jews, Christians, and Muslims to denounce the fanatic minorities among them who find in those sacred texts a vengeful, hateful God. "To all those who desecrate God's name by using religion to justify killing and terror, let us say together, enough," Yoffie declared.[104] Some Jewish leaders immediately insisted that Yoffie had chosen the wrong audience: the ISNA, the largest Muslim umbrella group in North America, was an unindicted co-conspirator in the trial of the Holy Land Foundation, a Texas-based Muslim charity that Justice Department officials accused of providing "blood money" for suicide bombings. Yoffie observed that leaders of the ISNA had denounced terrorism. The ISNA itself stated that it rejects all terrorist acts, including those by Hamas or any other group that claims Islam as its inspiration.[105]

Scholars of Islam say that historically, Muslims have never taken the gruesome passage that Shoebat and Hamas cite, in which the stones and trees call on Muslims to slay Jews, as an actual exhortation to murder. This passage is not in the Qur'an. It is from a collection of hadith, traditions concerning the words and deeds of Mohammed. This particular passage comes from one of the most authoritative of those collections, but experts note that Islamic religious leaders do not consider it to be part of their normative faith. Moreover, it applies to the end-times, not today. Extremist Muslims may convert it into an obligation to kill Jews at random, but the classical tradition emphatically militates against that.[106]

Muslim religious authorities have not taken a uniform position on whether terrorism violates Islamic law and tradition. Bin Laden, al-Zawahiri, and other Islamic radicals have cited Shari'a reasoning to justify their acts of "resistance." They argue that when publicly constituted leaders do not resist the oppression of Muslims, individuals and groups are obliged to do so, and they may strike without distinguishing between civilian and military targets. According to experts on Shari'a, necessity "makes forbidden things permitted." There has been debate about this among Muslim authorities, though most Islamic critics of "martyrdom operations" by Al Qaeda and Hamas focus on pragmatic considerations rather than on legitimacy.[107]

Several prominent Muslim clerics and scholars declare, however, that radicals have distorted Islam, which is a religion of justice and peace, not violence. Sheikh Ali Gomaa, the grand mufti of Egypt, considers suicide bombers to be ignorant extremists who are outside of Islamic tradition. One of the highest-ranking Muslim clerics in the world, Gomaa explicitly criticizes Wahhabism, the fundamentalist official doctrine of Saudi Arabia. He says that Muslim fundamentalism honors an imagined past rather than an Islamic future, and he forcefully repudiates violent jihad as a form of warfare that seeks to destroy peace. Muslims throughout history and around the world have rejected that as barbaric, says Gomaa in his article "The Meaning of Jihad in Islam." Rather, jihad is multivalent, much as the word "crusade" is. The Prophet Mohammed spoke of the greater jihad, "the jihad of the soul," by which he meant the spiritual exercise of confronting one's lower impulses. Jihad can involve opposing aggression and alleviating tyranny but not committing aggression, which Allah does not love (Qur'an 2:190). Suicide bombing is specifically against Islam, Gomaa adds, because the Qur'an does not permit suicide. It also absolutely forbids attacking civilians, he observes, adding that there can be no excuse for the terrorist crimes committed in New York, Spain, and London.[108] Gomaa is conspicuously silent in the article about killing civilians in Israel, however. He does not condemn extremist Muslims who justify attacks on Israeli women and children as self-defense against aggression and tyranny. And he has issued statements supporting Hezbollah as a resistance movement.[109]

Religious jihad is outside of the norm for Islam and must be authorized by the highest relevant political authority, adds Abduallah al-Askar, professor of history at King Saud University in Riyadh, Saudi Arabia's premier university. "Islam does not accept the justifications voiced today by terrorists," he says categorically. Al-Askar adds that unauthorized jihad is murder and terrorism, one of the worst crimes that any Muslim can commit. Authorization is required, he says, even when the potential suicide bomber is fighting against "illegal occupation and state terrorism by a harsh occupying force"—a clear condemnation of Israel.[110]

Prominent Muslim clerics have defined defensive jihad broadly, however, saying that it includes resistance to oppression anywhere it exists. In keeping with that, Hamas officials assert that its attacks are not terrorism but acts of resistance against Israeli injustice and aggression. As for the prohibition against self-murder, militant Palestinians do not see suicide bombing in that context. They consider it, instead, to be self-sacrifice in the cause of their people's freedom. And they justify killing Jewish women and children on the grounds that both male and female Israelis serve in the army.[111] Esposito points out, though, that suicide bombing and the slaughter of civilians have opened deep cleavages in the Muslim world, even within Hamas.[112]

It might surprise many evangelical leaders to learn that most Muslims share their apprehension about Islamic extremism. According to a 2006 Pew

Research Center poll, large majorities in Muslim states are concerned about the rise of Islamic extremists, as are the overwhelming number of Muslims living in Europe. Relatively few of these Muslims said that they support Al Qaeda or trust Osama bin Laden.[113] Also in 2006, however, a significant 13 percent minority of Britain's 1.6 million Muslims regarded the four men who carried out the London tube bombings of July 7, 2005, as martyrs, and 16 percent said they would be indifferent if a relative joined Al Qaeda.[114] A University of Maryland poll released in April 2007 revealed that 88 percent of Egyptians and approximately two-thirds of Moroccans and Indonesians believe that Islam opposes violence of the kind that bin Laden's group employs. Still, 38 percent of the people surveyed shared many of Al Qaeda's attitudes toward the United States. And from 4 percent to 7 percent of Moroccans, Egyptians, Pakistanis, and Indonesians approved of attacks on civilians in the United States. These are small percentages but they represent large numbers of people.[115]

As for the charge that Allah is not God, Esposito points out that the Qur'an is very clear on this point: Mohammed said in his early teaching that Islam is a reform movement reclaiming, in his view, the God of Abraham. Arabs prior to the time of Mohammed had many gods and their high deity was called Allah. But Islam appropriated that divine name for the God of the Christians and Jews. Christian Arabs still refer to God as Allah.[116] The Qur'an itself (39:4) indicates that the pagans used the name Allah to describe a supreme deity. It was common to all pre-Islamic Arab tribes, and when they gathered, they used it in a more universal sense: al-Ilah ("the-god") became Allah ("the God"). That may be linked to the fact that the Meccans, under the influence of Jews and Christians, seem to have been moving toward monotheism in any case. The Qur'an repeatedly points out that the pagan gods are figments of the imagination, "empty names." Allah alone can create and destroy, and control fate—"*La ilaha illa'llah*": "There is no god but Allah." Only Allah is all-knowing, the divine creator simultaneously transcendent and immanent. By the same logic, the Qur'an derides the Christian idea that God could have a son. Mohammad also denounced the crucifixion as a Jewish calumny. The Qur'an accused Jews and Christians of having distorted or neglected God's revelation to them (Qur'an 2:70, 75).[117]

Pre-Islamic rituals do, in fact, persist in Islam, as some evangelical Christian critics assert. Mohammad wanted to root his faith, and the social justice that is its spiritual foundation, in Arab culture. To accomplish that, he retained traditions, including the pilgrimage to Mecca known as the *hajj*. Customs at the Kabah, the cube-shaped granite shrine in Mecca that is the holiest site in Islam, were ancient even in Mohammad's day and he sought no disruption of these practices.[118] That does not make Islam a form of paganism. Rather, it infused old ritual forms with new meaning.

Evangelicals and Muslims Reach Out to Each Other

As is true of so many things about evangelicals, there is no single consensus view of Islam. Some conservative Christians engage in dialogue with Muslim leaders and recognize the perspectives they share, including devotion to their sacred scriptures, opposition to homosexuality, antagonism to the coarsening of popular Western entertainment, and concern about current sexual mores.[119] Evangelical author Philip Yancey adds, "The very things we resist in Islam, some Christians find tempting. We, too, seek political power and a legal code that reflects revealed morality. We, too, share a concern about raising our children in a climate of moral decadence. We, too, tend to see others (including Muslims) as a stereotyped community, rather than individuals."[120]

Richard Cizik, vice president for governmental affairs for the NAE, is active in building connections to moderate Muslims. In 2005, he met with Islamic party leaders in Morocco and told them, "Gentlemen, we are two sides of the same coin." Moroccan Muslims who maintained a dialogue with Cizik have taken dramatic steps to enhance religious moderation: they helped mobilize more than a million of their countrymen to rally in Casablanca against radical Islamic terrorism. They also helped organize the World Congress of Rabbis and Imams for Peace in Brussels in 2005 and in Seville in 2006. Within Morocco, King Mohammed VI is encouraging modernity and moderation, building mosques while halting the slide toward fundamentalism.[121]

The National Prayer Breakfast in Washington, which is funded by an evangelical Christian group, has also reached out to moderate Muslims. In February 2006, Jordan's King Abdullah II was a featured speaker at the Breakfast. He advanced a temperate, mainstream vision of Islam, telling the largely evangelical audience, "Nothing would please the extremists more than for terrorist events to advance the idea of a clash of civilizations" between the Judeo-Christian West and the Islamic world. Cizik lamented, "The stereotype we have of Muslims is as bad, I would suggest, as some Muslims have of us."[122]

Interestingly, the organization that sponsors the National Prayer Breakfasts, a secretive elite fundamentalist group called "the Fellowship" or "the Family," eschews the hostility to Muslims that conservative Christian leaders so often express. It is led by Douglas Coe. A friend to a succession of world leaders, Coe has been close to more American presidents than perhaps anyone else, including Billy Graham. Sometimes called the "stealth Billy Graham," Coe was included in *Time* magazine's list of the twenty-five most influential American evangelicals in 2005. D. Michael Lindsay, a Rice University scholar, points out that members of the Fellowship work quietly to promote social change internationally, using faith-based diplomacy to address conflicts. Coe and his associates sometimes travel with members of Congress and reportedly played a backstage role in the diplomatic success of the Camp David Accords between Israel and Egypt in 1978. President Ronald Reagan, speaking at the annual Prayer Breakfast in 1985, noted that because of the Fellowship, "political figures who are old enemies are meeting with each other in a spirit of peace and brotherhood."[123] The journalist Jeff Sharlet shows, however, that the group also has befriended ruthless dictators. "I don't take positions," said Coe. "The only thing I do is bring people together."[124]

Leaders from the Muslim world often attend the Breakfasts and Arafat was a speaker at one. The Fellowship has, in fact, one of the most amicable relationships with Islam of any evangelical group.[125] This is consistent with their faith. Unlike many Christian Zionists, the Fellowship's core members do not see Muslims as the enemy of God's plan for Israel. Rather, Sharlet observes that these leaders consider God' covenant with the Jews to be broken.[126] That is certainly not true of some of the most visible members of the group, however, including Senators Sam Brownback and James Inhofe.

Small but influential groups of evangelicals and Arabs made gestures toward mutual accommodation in 2007. It began in February at the U.S.-Islamic World Forum in Doha, Qatar, where four born-again leaders shocked Muslim and American diplomats by saying that they favored a Palestinian state.[127] Five months later, a delegation of fourteen evangelicals attended a remarkable lunch with Arab diplomats at the home of the Egyptian ambassador in Washington. Among them was Gordon Robertson, who had expressed a more nuanced view of Islam than had his father, Pat, and a willingness to be educated about it.[128] Jonathan Falwell, Jerry's son, also was there, along with Ralph Reed and other prominent born-again leaders. The evangelicals, two of whom are of Arab descent, assured the ambassadors from Algeria, Morocco, Libya, Kuwait, and other Arab nations that their love for Arabs was just as important to them as their love for Israel. The diplomats, for their part, told the Christians that not all Muslims are terrorists.

Each side wanted something. The evangelicals sought more freedom for Christians to practice their faith and to evangelize in Arab states. The diplomats wanted to explore the possibility of connecting with a new generation of born-again Americans and to win sympathy for the Palestinian cause in a group that they had seen as implacable opponents. Neither achieved its main goals. The Christians did not get a commitment to greater religious freedom in the Arab world, though one of the ambassadors said his nation was trying to head in that direction. Nor did Jonathan Falwell, who had taken over his father's ministry after Jerry's death six weeks earlier, get the response he hoped for when he asked the Arabs to denounce Islamist violence. Many evangelicals

repudiate fellow Christians who attack abortion clinics, Falwell noted. But he
got no assurance that the Arabs would rebuke their own extremists. The Arabs,
for their part, failed to drive a wedge between the evangelicals and Israel. When
they asked for a more balanced approach to the Palestinian problem, Reed, the
former executive director of the Christian Coalition, replied that evangelicals'
support for the Jewish state comes from the Scriptures. It is therefore largely
nonnegotiable, he told them. But the evangelicals did say that God loves everyone, including Arabs, and Reed added that he would love to build more positive relationships with them.

The meeting had been organized by Benny Hinn, a Palestinian Christian who has attracted huge crowds to his revival meetings and faith-healing
campaigns and has held such events in Jordan, Dubai, and the United Arab
Emirates. Hinn is on very friendly terms with the Arab diplomats and he pro-
nounced the event extremely productive. "We've had our arm around Israel for
years," he told the ambassadors. "It is time for us to put our other arm around
you." Cizik, who also participated in the meeting, echoed King Abdullah's
words at the National Prayer Breakfast the year before: "We want to make sure
that Samuel Huntington's projections of a 'Conflict of Civilizations' doesn't
occur," he told the participants. That would only serve the cause of terrorists
like Osama bin Laden, he noted. Evangelicals and Muslims need to summon
the moral imagination and biblical wisdom to see their way through the current difficult relations, Cizik declared, adding, "It could well be the most important thing we set our minds to at this time in history." Cizik was pleased by
the initiative. The younger evangelicals are more diplomatic than their fathers'
generation, he said, "more willing to acknowledge that the words they use can
be incendiary." Hinn asked him to arrange the next gathering, a larger meeting in fall 2007. One senior member of the Bush administration was privately
enthusiastic about an evangelical-Muslim rapprochement. Even John Hagee
was willing to say "Hooray and Hallelujah"—as long as the Arabs recognized
Israel's right to exist and agreed to desist from terrorism.[129] Those were not
reasonable expectations of this dialogue, though.

Evangelical Support for a Palestinian State

Liberal Israelis do not welcome the Christian Zionist view of cosmic conflict
with Islam. "If it's a war of my God against your God, there can be no one who
wins it," says Rabbi Michael Melchior, a Member of Knesset who descends
from a dynasty of Danish rabbis. "There can be no solution." And what of the
idea that a Judeo-Christian coalition will wipe out Islam or be annihilated by

it? "I think it's insane," says Melchior.[130] Many socially progressive evangelicals similarly do not want a clash with Muslims. They do not demonize them and, in fact, they often sympathize profoundly with the Palestinians. Fifty-eight of them sent a letter to George W. Bush in 2002, asking him to employ an "even-handed policy toward Israeli and Palestinian leadership." Acutely sensitive to the suffering of the Palestinians under Israeli occupation, these prominent born-again figures called for justice consistent with the exhortations of the Hebrew prophets.[131]

Five years later, many of the same people wrote to Bush again, asserting that large numbers of evangelical Christians support a Palestinian state. In this letter, which was published in the *New York Times* in July 2007, thirty-four born-again Christian leaders urged the president to proceed confidently and forthrightly with the peace initiative he had just proposed. They argued that blessing Israel and the Jews, in accordance with Genesis 12:3, can mean criticizing them in order to promote genuine peace for both Israelis and Palestinians.[132] One of the signatories was David Neff, the editor of *Christianity Today,* which ran an editorial elaborating on that reading. It affirmed the desire to bless Israel, as in Genesis 12:3, but in a way that reproached Christian Zionism. The biblical verse, said the writer, "is often misused as a warm affirmation of anything done for the expansion of Israel's influence or borders." But true love is sometimes tough love, said the column. Genuine love "asks not only about the extent of Israel's land, but also about its national character." To bless Israel can mean to reject the notion of a Greater Israel that encompasses the occupied territories, said the writer. That dream comes at too high a price, the editorial concluded.[133]

"This group is in no way anti-Israel," said Ronald J. Sider, speaking of the evangelicals who helped draft the letter to Bush in 2007. "But we want a solution that is viable." Sider was one of the four born-again leaders who surprised Muslim and American diplomats by favoring a Palestinian state at the U.S.-Islamic World Forum in Doha, Qatar. It was there that he and his colleagues got the idea to write the letter. Bob Roberts, a pastor who was with him in Qatar, said that the letter exemplified "Christian charity and caring for the underdog." God loves the Jews, but he loves the Palestinians too, said Roberts.[134] They planned to have the letter translated into Arabic and disseminated in the Middle East and Europe.

The pro–two-state letter set off a melee between evangelical camps. Prominent Christian Zionists immediately rebuked the initiative. Pat Robertson called it unbiblical and appallingly naive, in view of Hamas's militancy and Fatah's corruption. General Jim Hutchens, an official of Hagee's Christians United for Israel lobby (CUFI), declared that the signers of the letter are supersessionists: they believe that the Church has replaced Israel in God's divine economy.[135] Hagee himself added that Bible-believing Christians will scoff at the letter. CUFI hand-delivered its own letter to the White House, signed by Hagee and fifty other CUFI pastors and activists, declaring that land-for-peace is a failed policy that has led to nothing but war.[136] Timothy P. Weber, the author of *On the Road to Armageddon: How Evangelicals Became Israel's Best Friend,* put Hagee's position in a religious context. The dispensationalists have parlayed a minority theological position into a major political voice, he said. Joel C. Hunter, one of the signers of the letter published in the *Times,* rebuked Christian Zionists for saying that Israel can do no wrong. "There are many more evangelicals who are really open and seek justice for both sides," said Hunter, who resigned as president of the Christian Coalition in 2006 when its board refused to put "compassion issues" like global warming and world poverty on its agenda.[137]

Some centrist and modernist evangelicals criticize the Israeli occupation of the West Bank and urge Jerusalem to trade land for peace, as we shall see in the next chapter. In that respect, they are closer to liberal mainline Protestants than to most conservative born-again Christians.

A Muslim Mirror Image

Conservative evangelical and Islamic leaders often fear each other in similar ways. Each associates the other with the devil, emphasizing the irrationality and urgency of the threat to which the other's faith gives birth. In a mirror-image inversion of the Christian Zionist view, Muslim leaders accuse evangelicals of being in league with Satan and seeking to hasten the coming of the Messiah. "The World toward Illumination," the series of discussions about the Mahdi on the Iranian government Web site, charges that Christian Zionists are obsessed with the end of time. Their fascination has been accelerated, according to the site, by "the highly suspicious 9/11 events" (an allusion to the widespread belief in Islamic countries that the Americans or the Israelis, not Arabs, perpetrated the 9/11 terrorist attacks). Evangelicals have determined the date of the Second Coming, the site mistakenly declares, and it falsely claims that Pat Robertson predicted that the Messiah would return in 2007. The Web site denounces Christian Zionists as a group of oppressors trying to dominate the world, precisely mirroring evangelical fears about the Islamists. Evangelicals are followers of Satan, guilty of political greed, says the site. These Christians, it charges, superstitiously divide mankind into good and evil, as can be clearly seen in the remarks of George W. Bush. No one knows the date of the Mahdi's return, says the Iranian site.[138] Citing this Web site, Joel C. Rosenberg, an American Jew who found Jesus, reversed the point of the article, questioning whether Ahmadinejad is planning a messianic war to annihilate Israel by the end of Iran's calendar year on March 20, 2007.[139]

These mirrored animosities and fears appear in Sunni sources as well. Ahmed al-Tamimi, an official of the Palestinian Authority's Religious Judicial Council, reportedly has attacked Christian Zionists for having "adopted Satan as God." The devil "drives their crazy nature," he alleged.[140] Sheikh Kamal Hatib, vice chairman of the Islamic Movement, charged that "crazy" Christian support of Israel is based on the belief that Israel's existence "hastens the arrival of the Messiah. Allah Forbid!"[141]

In the mutual enmity between religiously conservative Christians and Muslims, each side sees in the other a profound threat to its deepest convictions and yearnings. Each views the other as its own negation. And neither sees the possibility of common ground, but rather regards the other as the devil's agent.[142]

6

⚜

Criticisms of Christian Zionism

One of conservative Christians' main political accomplishments in the last eighty years has been to broaden popular American support for almost unrestricted backing of Israel. Even evangelicals who reject dispensational end-times scenarios often continue to believe that God loves the Jewish people and that Israel is central to His plan for salvation.[1] Especially when Israel has been in distress, these American Christians have expressed this view forcefully, as we shall see in Chapter 10. Many critics of Christian Zionism argue, though, that this support is misconceived or comes at too high a price. There are four principal charges: First, that Christians support aliyah (Jewish emigration to Israel) mainly because it speeds the Rapture, the battle of Armageddon, the mass conversion or death of the Jews, and Christ's Millennial kingdom. Second, that evangelicals' true motive is to convert the Jews. Third, that Christian Zionist theology distorts Christianity: that it misunderstands biblical covenants and ignores the scriptural emphasis on doing justice, relieving suffering, and showing compassion to the oppressed, who, in this view, are the Palestinians. The fourth major criticism is that the evangelical Zionists are allied with extreme right-wing Israeli politicians in opposing any exchange of land for peace. That, says the writer Gershom Gorenberg, poses a greater danger to the Jewish state than terrorism does. "As frightening as Palestinian terror is," says Gorenberg, "it does not threaten Israel's existence." But Palestinian demographics do, he argues, as long as Israel holds on to all of the land from the Mediterranean to the Jordan, as evangelical supporters urge it to do.[2]

We shall consider these criticisms here and in the next three chapters.

Mythic Players in the Final Drama

Dispensationalism enhanced the conviction that the Jewish people are the apple of God's eye, set aside for the Lord's blessing. Critics are disturbed, though, by the idea that Jews are not human beings in this perspective but scripturally inspired archetypes, and that disaster awaits those who don't accept Jesus. Historian of religion Mark Noll observes that dispensationalism is thus a two-edged sword: it is anti-Semitic and philo-Semitic at the same time.[3] Paul Boyer, in *When Time Shall Be No More,* questions whether Israel should accept support predicated on the ultimate destruction of the Jewish people, which he describes in graphic language: "Contemplating the river of Jewish blood oozing its crimson way through these 'theological abstractions,'" Boyer cautions, "one may well ask whether turning a blind eye to one of premillennialism's core doctrines is not a very high price to pay for the premillennialists' admittedly enthusiastic backing of Israel."[4] Grace Halsell, in *Prophecy and Politics,* says that dispensationalism reduces Jews to abstract entities, mere pawns in the scheme of salvation.[5] Gorenberg, in *End of Days,* his landmark study of the Christian and Jewish religious right's apocalyptic beliefs, similarly argues that dispensationalists love the Jews not as real people but as mythic players in the impending final drama of history. "This is incredibly dangerous to Israel," says Gorenberg. "They're not interested in the survival of the State of Israel. They are interested in the Rapture. . . . We are merely actors in their dreams."[6] Karen Armstrong, in *The Battle for God,* is even more damning of dispensationalism: "At the same time as Protestant fundamentalists celebrated the birth of the new Israel, they were cultivating fantasies of final genocide at the end of time," she says. "The Jewish state had come into existence purely to further a Christian fulfillment. The Jews' fate in the Last Days is uniquely grim, since they are doomed to suffer whether or not they accept Christ." Armstrong adds darkly of dispensationalists, "Their literal reading of highly selected passages of the Bible had encouraged them to absorb the Godless genocidal tendencies of modernity."[7] Max Blumenthal, a journalist whose work has appeared in *The Nation,* also evokes the Holocaust, saying that Christian Zionists' professed support for Israel "is really an insidious attempt to fatten up the Jews like a Thanksgiving turkey before sticking them in the oven."[8] Gerald R. McDermott, professor of religion at Roanoke College in Salem, Virginia, and a Christian Zionist himself, confesses that "some of us have . . . supported Israel out of love for our own politico-theological agendas more than real concern for the Jews." The press has repeated this charge so often that very many Jews and others believe it implicitly. In fact, when asked about the basis of his claim, McDermott said that he heard it from Jewish friends![9] These are valid criticisms of dispensational doctrine. In practice, however, many evangelicals show unexpected nuance, humility, and diversity in their eschatology. And many dedicated born-again supporters of Israel have only the most general expectations of the end-times, as we shall see.

Evangelizing the Jews

The second major accusation is that Christian Zionists have a hidden agenda: to convert the Jews. Timothy P. Weber, for example, charges that born-again Christians support the Jewish state in order to preserve it until the end-times, when the Jews will convert or die. That, he contends, is why evangelicals contribute to groups like Yechiel Eckstein's International Fellowship of Christians and Jews (IFCJ). Over 400,000 evangelicals give money to the IFCJ to underwrite Jewish emigration to Israel and social services in the Jewish state. Many of them do that at a genuine personal sacrifice. Weber charges that their true motive, though, remains conversionist and that they give to fulfill biblical prophecies about the Jews and Israel. The rabbi has obviously learned to look the other way about this, he says.[10] Eckstein himself vigorously disputes that, as we shall see. But American Jews maintain a deep suspicion that this is the real motive behind evangelical Zionists' support for Israel.

Jews are understandably offended when someone tells them that their faith is incomplete or that they're going to hell. That feeling is exacerbated by their vibrant historical memory of discrimination, prejudice, and extermination because of their Jewish faith or identity. This came to the fore in the United States in 1973, when 140 Christian denominations agreed to cooperate in a nationwide evangelizing effort aimed at Jews as well as other nonbelievers. Jews felt insulted and vulnerable, fearing that this campaign, which was called Key '73, would provoke anti-Semitism. Rabbi Solomon S. Bernards, director of the Department of Inter-religious Cooperation of the B'nai B'rith Anti-Defamation League, expressed Jews' extreme discomfort at being targets for conversion. The long Jewish experience with Christian evangelism, said Bernards, "has been and continues to be extremely painful and sorrow-laden." The Gospels record the early Christians' frustration at the Jews' resistance, and the charges the Christians laid against them: "blindness, stubbornness, demonic perverseness, unredeemed decadence, corruption and degeneracy." Rabbi Marc Tanenbaum of the American Jewish Committee called Key '73 an assault on the honor and truth of Judaism. It created an opening for renewed anti-Semitism, he warned. Carl F. H. Henry, editor of *Christianity Today,* the journal that had first conceived of the national evangelizing program, dismissed such fears as fantasy. But the United Church of Christ; the United Presbyterian Church, USA; the Episcopal Church; and even the NAE refused to participate in Key '73, and most commentators considered it a failure. Four years later, the World Council of Churches, the umbrella organization of Protestant Churches worldwide, urgently repudiated proselytizing Jews.[11]

American Jews remain anxious about anti-Semitism today, to a degree that is out of proportion to reality. This is true to such an extent that Jewish social scientists speak of a "perception gap" between Jews' sensibilities and their actual circumstances. Jews have a sense of vulnerability that is out of sync with their actual degree of political empowerment in the United States.[12] Interestingly, the same is true of evangelicals, though some top officials of major American Jewish organizations find that incredible. In any case, Jews' response to past Christian hostility is deep and visceral, as Elliott Abrams points out in his 1997 book, *Faith or Fear*. Abrams, who became deputy national security adviser in the George W. Bush administration, notes that Christian attitudes toward Jews and Judaism have gone through an epochal shift toward acceptance and understanding. "A two-thousand year-old war against Judaism is being called off," he observes. But this has been amazingly underreported and so has made little impression on American Jews, who, he says, continue to believe that evangelicals are likely to be anti-Semites. Anti-Christian bias seems to be the only form of prejudice that American Jews consider respectable, Abrams charges.[13] These feelings of past injury, present vulnerability, and continuing threat only intensify many Jews' feeling of being attacked when Christians try to evangelize them. Jewish community leaders argue that conversion means the loss of a Jew to his people, which they find abhorrent after the murder of so many Jews in the twentieth century. "There are barely 14 million Jews left alive on this planet. In 1933, that number was 15.3 million. Leave us alone," wrote an analyst for the *Jerusalem Post* in an article titled "Why 'Jews for Jesus' Is Evil."[14]

Not one of the evangelical leaders and pastors I talked to tried to convert me overtly, though a few said that they hoped I would find my Messiah, and there was no doubt Whom they had in mind. Evangelizing is the heartbeat of evangelicalism, after all. The major Christian Zionist organizations officially disclaim any intention of targeting Jews for conversion, but other evangelical groups don't. The Southern Baptist Convention makes a special point of proselytizing Jews and supporting Messianic Jewish groups (Jews who have found Jesus but retain Jewish traditions). In 1996, it adopted a resolution pledging to direct its energies to proclaiming the Gospel to the Jews. The theologically conservative Lutheran Church-Missouri Synod and the pentecostal Assemblies of God have special departments that target Jews for conversion. Billy Graham has expressed disapproval of missionary efforts that single out Jews, but his view has not prevailed. Evangelicals are, in fact, the primary backers of Messianic Jewish organizations, supporting their evangelizing in the United States and abroad. Jews for Jesus, the best known of these groups, reported $17 million in revenue in 2005, most of it from private donors.[15]

Individual evangelical churches and ministries also aim to bring Jews to faith in Jesus. Chuck Smith, the longtime pastor of Calvary Chapel in Costa Mesa, California, for example, is associated with efforts to convert Israeli Jews, especially new immigrants from the former Soviet Union (FSU). Pastor Chuck is a revered figure: he was the father of the Jesus Movement that brought hippies, surfers, and others from the 1960s counterculture to Christ; and he has been the inspiration for over 600 Calvary Chapel churches across America and a hundred abroad.[16] He also fits the stereotype of Christian Zionists that Jews have come to know and distrust. Pastor Chuck is an ardent supporter of Israel. He reads the *Jerusalem Post* regularly, warns in his sermons when Washington's policies seem to take an anti-Israel turn, and keeps a menorah on his church altar, as other Calvary Chapel pastors do. He frequently travels to Israel, where he often meets with government officials.[17] At the same time, he is a dispensationalist who anticipates the end of days. In fact, Smith once funded an attempt to X-ray the Temple Mount, thinking that if one could find the tablets of the lost Ark, it might inspire the Israelis to build the Third Temple.[18] And Pastor Chuck supports missionary efforts in Israel. In 1990, Pastor Bradley Antolovich was "sent out from Calvary Chapel of Costa Mesa" to Israel. Antolovich's mission was to minister among Russian Jews, who were then arriving in a massive aliyah. Jews from the former Soviet Union, Pastor Bradley explains, "are the most open group in Israel to the Gospel." By late 1991, in fact, hundreds of new immigrants from the former Soviet Union had found Jesus and two new congregations of Russian-speaking Messianic Jews had opened, in Haifa and Jerusalem. In 1996, with Chuck Smith's blessing, Antolovich says, he started Calvary Chapel of Jerusalem, "seeking to bring the Word of God and the truth of Yeshua the Messiah to the Jewish people here in Israel." According to the Calvary Chapel of Costa Mesa Web site, Bradley's ministry provides new immigrants with furniture, clothing, and food while encouraging them to be part of the Calvary Chapel Jerusalem fellowship.[19] It is illegal in Israel to offer material inducements for conversion. Perhaps Pastor Bradley provides these gifts as a humanitarian gesture, independent of his ministering to the Russian Jews' spiritual needs.

The Israeli law restricting missionizing is almost never enforced anyway. Israeli leaders know that they are receiving enthusiastic support from the very people whose activity those laws would limit, and they have accepted compromises that allow these efforts to continue. This hasn't particularly bothered them, since they believe that the evangelizing won't succeed.[20] Rabbi Ron Kronish, the director of the Interreligious Coordinating Council in Israel, argues, in fact, that there are virtually no Christian missionaries in Israel and evangelizing poses absolutely no threat to Jewish identity.[21] The chief rabbinate of Israel disagrees vehemently, as we shall see.

Jews for Jesus and other Christian Jewish groups in Israel have become especially effective in missionizing, often with financial support from foreign evangelicals. A 1999 survey among Messianic congregations indicated that there were some 6,000 Messianic Jews in Israel, though one Jewish anti-missionary group claimed that there were 20,000. The actual number today is probably somewhere in between. There may be as many as 4,000 missionaries in Israel, and Messianic Judaism is perhaps the fastest-growing religious movement in the country.[22] More than a hundred Messianic congregations and fellowships in Israel reach out to Sabras (native-born Israelis) and Jewish immigrants but also welcome Jews who converted to Christianity in the former Soviet Union, Ethiopia, or other countries, then made aliyah. Messianic congregations, most of which are evangelical, have learned to use the Internet or mail to bring the Gospel to Israelis.[23]

Many evangelicals believe that Jews can find Yeshua (the Hebrew name of Jesus) while keeping their Jewish identity, with all of their customs and beliefs intact. Especially since the Six-Day War, missionaries have emphasized that Judaism and Christianity are not incompatible. When a Jew finds Christ, they say, he affirms his attachment to Israel and Judaism, rather than abdicating it. This view was championed in the 1970s by Moishe Rosen, founder of Jews for Jesus.[24] Rosen deeply impressed evangelicals by arguing that Messianic Jews are not lost as Jews but completed or fulfilled. Messianic Jews observe Shabbat on Saturdays, read from the Torah, keep Jewish holidays, and wear shawls to pray. They call themselves *maaminim* (believers), not converts, *Yehudim* (Jews), not *Notzrim* (Christians).[25] In many cases they call their places of worship synagogues, not churches, though a number of Messianic fellowships in Israel meet in church facilities. Almost all such congregations in Israel observe Jewish holidays, which they understand to have their fulfillment in Jesus. They normally celebrate communion on Shabbat, in some cases during Passover or other Jewish holy days. Many of the active participants in Messianic fellowships are immigrants from the former Soviet Union and Ethiopia, including a number of Ethiopian Christians who arrived during Operation Moses in 1984–85.[26]

Jewish leaders have condemned the Messianic Jewish movement. In 1981, Rabbi Tanenbaum, while empathizing with Christian Jews who wish to maintain a cultural link with their people, said that they have forsaken Judaism and made a mockery of Jewish rituals. Elie Wiesel, the great Jewish writer about the Holocaust, calls Jews for Jesus hypocrites who do not have the courage to declare that they have repudiated their people. "They exploit weakness, ignorance, and unhappiness" in attracting young Jewish people, he charges.[27] Israelis, despite their dislike of evangelizing, have become increasingly tolerant of Messianic Jews, however. A poll in 1988 showed that most of them (78%) felt that Jewish Christians should enjoy the right of citizenship if they participate in the life of the community.[28] Israeli officials, while tolerating missionizing, are far from sympathetic, and Orthodox Jews are openly hostile to it. Traditionally, Rabbi David Rosen of the American Jewish Committee in Jerusalem observes, Jews have considered conversion to Christianity to be an act of betrayal.[29] Israel's Law of Return, which grants every Jew the right to live as a citizen in Israel, specifically excludes those who have willingly converted to another religion.

To support Israel while seeking to convert Jews is "to couple a caress with a stab in the back," says Gorenberg.[30] Several of the leaders of the major Christian Zionist groups respect these sensitivities. Robert Stearns of Eagles' Wings, for example, strictly avoids proselytizing. Robert himself told me very honestly, though, that he hopes that Jews will find Christ. "The best thing that ever happened in my life," he said, "is I met and had a spiritual encounter with a Jew named Jesus. That gave me purpose, a connection to God, and peace. I want that for everyone, to feel the unconditional love I've received because of my relationship with him." Robert's evangelicalism defines him, he said, and determines his role: to spread the Good News. "I'm not gonna sit here and tell you, Steve, that as a Christian, an evangelical Christian, that I don't hope for everybody to know about Jesus," he told me. "And everybody includes you, and everybody includes the Jewish people. But I'm gonna be very upfront with you about that. I'm also gonna say, if we never agree on who he is, if we never see the situation the same way, my commitment and support of you as my elder brother, as the Jewish people, is unconditional." Robert recognizes that his Jewish friends can be committed to their own spiritual journey. Both can have the mission of *tikkun olam* (Hebrew for "repairing the world"), he notes, reconciling God and man and making the world a better place. "I live in the hyphen of Judeo-Christian values," he said.[31]

David Neff, the editor of *Christianity Today*, explains that, for evangelicals, "helping Israel and sharing our spiritual understandings with Jews are two forms of the same familial love." Neff thinks of Jews and evangelical Christians as estranged cousins. Both descend from Abraham—the Jews biologically, the Christians spiritually. Evangelicals live out this sense of relatedness more often in their spiritual imagination than in real life, Neff concedes, but he argues that they still share their beliefs as cousins, not enemies. And the deepest conviction that they have to share is that every member of the human race is lost to sin, with a fundamental proclivity to self-love. That is the bad news of evangelicalism, says Neff, and it applies to everyone. But so does the good news, that there is a cure: rescue from sin's guilt and power through Christ. Evangelicals urge this on their Jewish cousins, he says, just as naturally as they hope for the security of Israel and for justice and peace in the Middle East.[32]

The major Christian Zionist groups in Israel similarly believe that Jews need to find Jesus. In view of Israeli sensibilities, however, these organizations say that they focus instead on defending and assisting Israel and the Jewish people.[33] Not all evangelicals, and not all pastors in smaller ministries, are as publicly sensitive. Nor are all televangelists. Pat Robertson wrote in 1990 that he was pleased that many Israelis were willing to talk about Jesus and receive Christ as Messiah. He was frustrated and sad, though, about most Jews' "obstinate denial" of the obvious truth that Jesus fulfilled every messianic prophecy.[34] In October 2004, Robertson traveled to Jerusalem to celebrate the Feast of Tabernacles, the Christian event that coincides with Succoth, and declared that the Jews need to cry out for their Messiah. "I've met wonderful Jews in Siberia, Brazil, the United States, here in Jerusalem who are all saying, 'Yes, Jesus, you are our Messiah,'" he said. The International Christian Embassy Jerusalem, which sponsors the event, chose not to distribute tapes of this speech to the press. David Parsons, the ICEJ's media officer, commented that Robertson's views "are off." The late Yuri Shtern, then–co-chair of the Knesset Christian Allies Caucus, declared that he was very upset with the televangelist.[35] Robertson declares that he treats Jews like everybody else, by which he means that he hopes they will be saved through faith in Christ. That could take place in the end-times, he says. "Just think what would happen if God Almighty would appear on the Mount of Olives, with all His angels. What do you think the Jewish people would do? They would fall on their knees and worship Him. It wouldn't be a question of forced conversion."[36]

Jerry Falwell, too, believed that Christians should evangelize Jews. In 1980 he declared that the Jews "are spiritually blind and desperately in need of their Messiah and Savior."[37] Over the years, he personally led many Jews to Christ, he said, and a number of them became members of his Thomas Road Baptist Church in Lynchburg, Virginia. In 2004 he endorsed the missionary efforts of Jews for Jesus.[38] It is especially important to convert Jews and all other nonbelievers now that the end is near, he suggested in 2006, as Israel and Hezbollah attacked each other. "With the world on the brink of pandemonium," he said, "it is our responsibility to point people—no matter their heritage, ethnicity or religion—to the one and only solution, Jesus Christ. May we work while it is yet day, for the night approaches when no man can work" (John 9:4).[39]

"You Can't Silence Us"

Israeli officials will deal with evangelical groups only if they forgo evangelizing. The Knesset Christian Allies Caucus, founded in 2004 to enhance relations between Israel and its Christian supporters, also condemns efforts to convert Jews. In 2007, the American author and radio show host Janet Parshall, one of the most skilled and articulate evangelical advocates for Israel, withdrew from a planned Woman's Summit in Jerusalem for precisely that reason: she insisted on her right to share the Gospel. The Caucus, which sponsored the Women's Summit, comprises thirteen members of the Knesset from across the political spectrum. They hold monthly meetings in the Israeli parliament with Christian Zionist guests and organize pro-Israel meetings at home and abroad. They are very vigilant against working with anyone who attempts to convert Jews, says Josh Reinstein, the young director of the Caucus. Parshall saw that as self-serving. She believed that Israel should not say, "We'll take your aid, your support and your tourist dollars, but we won't take your Jesus." Christians shouldn't have "to choose between the cross or Israel," Parshall declared. "We have to tell them, as a friend, [that] you can't do that. You can't silence us."[40]

A special committee of the Israeli Chief Rabbinate felt that the Christian Allies Caucus wasn't strict enough, however. Two of the three rabbis on the committee determined that Bridges for Peace and the Christian Embassy, which were participating in the Women's Summit, violate Torah thought and law. The rabbis acknowledged that Christian Zionist groups are helpful: "They make tremendous efforts and support us all over, and are even more right-wing than we are in some ways, and they help us with Bush," said one. The rabbis' finding was consistent, though, with the late Rabbi Yosef Soloveitchik's contention that Jewish-Christian theological dialogue is wrong (though social and political cooperation is fine).[41] In the end, the rabbinic committee concluded, these Christian Zionist groups have only one goal: to convert Jews. Bringing Christian and Jewish women together to study Jewish-Christian values and the Jewish foundations of Christianity, the rabbis said, is actually part of a long-term campaign to blur the differences between the religions in order to bring Jews to Jesus. They were particularly distressed by what they called "the terrible phenomenon of Messianic Jews wreaking havoc and destruction in Israel by trying to bring Jesus as messiah into Israel."[42]

Many evangelicals certainly do hope for such a spiritual "blurring." That would fulfill Paul's declaration in Galatians 3:28 that "There is neither Jew nor Greek . . . you are all one in Christ Jesus." Paul adds in Ephesians that Christ has broken down the dividing wall of hostility between Gentile and Jew, creating "one new man."[43] From this faith perspective, Jews who accept Jesus embody that new man. That's why many evangelical leaders prize and honor them.[44] Jews may see this as anti-Semitism, disrespecting the inherent value and completeness of their faith. In fact, the underlying dynamics are the opposite: a desire to merge rather than isolate and exclude, along with an idealization of the Jew as chosen, blessed, and the source of blessing. Christians who adopt Jewish rituals also seek to merge, from the opposite direction.

This does not prove the rabbis' assertion that evangelicals engage in religious dialogue solely to convert Jews. Many of them seek understanding. But very many evangelicals do see evangelism as a major purpose of interfaith conversation. Shortly after the rabbinic decision, *Christianity Today* polled its readers about the true purpose of interreligious dialogue about faith. Nearly two in three said that its intent is to evangelize. The majority said that they hoped to gain understanding as well.[45] The Christian Zionist groups in Jerusalem have disavowed missionizing, however, as we have seen.

The rabbinic decision about the Women's Summit was accompanied by charges that Bridges for Peace and other Christian Zionist groups were quietly funding Messianic Jewish churches and ministries. Bridges also was accused of having signed a nonmissionizing pledge with a loophole: born-again signatories to the pledge promised not to alienate Jews from their tradition and community, but they did not specifically renounce evangelizing. Since many evangelicals believe that Jews can accept Jesus while remaining fully Jewish, they can justify converting Jews without technically violating the terms of the pledge.[46] Rebecca Brimmer, international director of Bridges, did not respond to repeated invitations to comment on these charges, leaving open the possibility that they have some basis in truth.[47] But Benny Elon, the chairman of the Christian Allies Caucus, declared that the rabbis were misinformed. The conference went ahead as planned, without Parshall.

The rabbis continued to press their case, however. Four months later, the Chief Rabbinate forbade Jews from participating in the International Christian Embassy's twenty-eighth annual Feast of Tabernacles parade in Jerusalem. This Feast was expected to attract thousands of evangelicals from over ninety countries, many of whom would process through the capital in colorful native costumes, waving flags. The march was billed as the largest single tourism event of the year. The Feast would infuse up to $18 million into the local economy, according to the Christian Allies Caucus.[48] The Rabbinate's Committee for the Prevention of the Spread of Missionary Work determined, however, that some participants in the Feast were actively missionizing Jews. "Those who fear for their souls should distance themselves," the committee warned.[49]

The Christian Embassy objected forcefully to the rabbis' accusations. "The ICEJ has never conducted any missionary programs in Israel and we clearly instruct our Feast pilgrims against such activity during their stay here," said Malcolm Hedding, the group's executive director. Citing Isaiah's prophecy that the sons of foreigners would build up the walls of Jerusalem (60:10–14), Hedding noted, "We see ourselves as those friendly Gentiles promised in Scripture."[50] "We have to be wary of missionary activity," he added.[51]

When the Feast of Tabernacles arrived, 60,000 to 80,000 people, including 8,000 evangelicals, attended the parade in Jerusalem. El Al pilots, soldiers, postal workers, and other Israeli Jews walked through the streets of Jerusalem alongside born-again Christians while the Police Band kept the rhythm.[52] They either had never heard about the rabbinic prohibition or they ignored it.

The rabbis were right in one respect, though: some participants in the Feast did actively want to evangelize Jews. That was not surprising. Cognizant of Jewish sensibilities, the ICEJ, like other Christian Zionist organizations, has pledged not to proselytize.[53] But it has not agreed to dissociate itself from people who do. That would cut the organization off from all the Christian Zionists who wish to bless and support the Jewish people spiritually, in their view, as well as materially—by saving their souls as well as their bodies.

Indeed, the Christian Embassy embraces prominent advocates of Messianic Judaism and has arranged for them to speak at its Feast celebrations. In 2004, the ICEJ invited Don Finto, a passionate backer of Jewish Christian congregations in Israel, to deliver the opening plenum address. That was the same event at which Robertson attracted such attention for declaring that Jews are accepting Jesus.[54] Among the principal speakers at the 2007 Feast was Pastor Jack Hayford, president of the Foursquare Church denomination, which represents over four million Pentecostal worshippers in 37,000 churches in 142 countries. Hayford, seventy-two, is among the most influential evangelicals today and one of the most prominent Christian Zionists. He has visited Israel thirty-five times and calls himself a "gentile Jew."[55] He is co-founder, with Robert Stearns, of the International Day of Prayer for the Peace of Jerusalem, and he says that if the Israelis need soldiers, he and his Pentecostal congregants will fight side by side with them.[56] Pastor Jack is also a firm advocate of bringing the Jewish people to Christ. In July 2007, for example, two months before the Feast, he had a series of Israeli Messianic Jews speak at the Foursquare Church's international convention in Jerusalem. They described the struggles they faced in sharing Christ with Jews in Israel, and they asked the 3,000 delegates to pray that the gospel will break through in the Jewish state, especially in Jerusalem.[57] Hayford said, in fact, that one of his principal goals for the convention was to discern the challenges that the Messianic community in Israel faces in ministering the gospel.[58]

The International Christian Embassy, in addition to featuring speakers who hope to bring Jews to Christ, has been accused of accommodating and promoting evangelizing efforts themselves. At the Christian Embassy's 1999 Feast of Tabernacles celebration, half a dozen booths reportedly promoted missionizing Israelis. A laptop slideshow by the Holyland Ministries showed evangelizers giving bread to hungry immigrants from the former Soviet Union while engaging them in Christian prayer. "We can't cut ourselves off from the body of believers," explained the Christian Embassy's media officer, David Parsons. The ICEJ had compromised, he said, allowing missionary groups to leave materials available to pick up in the booths, as long as no one actively handed them out.[59] In 2004 the Orthodox counter-missionary group Yad L'Achim claimed to have repeatedly caught ICEJ members assisting missionary attempts to convert Jews.[60] In 2007, the Christian Embassy was accused, along with Bridges for Peace, of covertly funding missionary groups.[61]

Asked about these charges, Hedding told me that his organization has never done anything covertly and has never funded missionizing of Jews. In one case, the ICEJ did support a Messianic group in Jaffa that was helping destitute Arab children. He was criticized for that, but to do otherwise would have been a denial of Jesus, Hedding said.[62] He affirms that the call to missionize the world, including the Jewish world, is a major tenet of evangelicals' biblical faith, For pro-Israel evangelicals to reject that call would totally discredit them. So how do they proclaim the Good News without offending Jews? By confirming that everything that Christian Zionists do is compelled by the love of Jesus in them, says Hedding. His organization will not proselytize, he points out, but they will share their faith if Jews ask about it.[63] Parsons adds that the Christian Embassy recognizes that others are called to "the ministry of confrontation on an individual level." He notes that the ICEJ never signed the anti-missionizing pledge. Bridges for Peace hadn't either, to the best of his knowledge. The Knesset Christian Allies Caucus, despite its avowed vigilance on the question of missionizing, does not make the pledge a requirement, he says.[64] The nonevangelizing pledge was a political sham in any case. In 1998, the Netanyahu government, indebted to Christian Zionist groups in the West, accepted the statement in lieu of passing strict anti-missionary legislation. The Christian groups that signed it were not trying to convert Jews anyway, observes Yaakov Ariel in his authoritative study, *Evangelizing the Chosen People.* Messianic Jews, Jehovah's Witnesses, and other groups that do actively evangelize refused to sign.[65]

Christian Zionists' yearning for Jews to find Christ is so strong that it sometimes breaks through. Ray Sanders, international director of the Jerusalem-based Christian Friends of Israel (CFI), says explicitly that his organization does not attempt to convert Jews. "We believe that Jesus is the promised Messiah for the Jewish people," Sanders told me, "but redemption is God's responsibility. Only God can draw people to Himself."[66] The organization's Web site states that their stand alongside Israel is not contingent on the Jews' accepting Christ.[67] But CFI is hopeful. A Christian CFI writer named Carolyn Jacobson declared in a 2006 Watchman's Prayer Letter that "the hearts of the Jewish people are beginning to open to hear the good news of his salvation and redemption."[68] Jacobson also noted that "aliyah and the salvation of the Jewish people are the most important items on our prayer list." The reason is that "the salvation of Israel is linked to God's promise to bring back the Jewish people to His Land." Jacobson cited Ezekiel 36:24–26, in which God says the he will sprinkle clean water on his people, cleanse them, then take away their heart of stone and re-place it with a heart of flesh. She clearly had in mind the Jews' softening so they will accept Jesus, since she next cited Zechariah 12:10, which says that the inhabitants of Jerusalem will see "Him '*whom they pierced.*'"[69] Jacobson capital-izes the word "Him" to denote Christ. She also italicizes "*whom they pierced*" for emphasis, making the point of her prayer certain: that the Jews of the world, after immigrating to Israel, will come to know Christ, who was pierced during the Crucifixion. The Scofield Study Bible interprets Zechariah 12:10 in pre-cisely that way and relates it to the events following the battle of Armageddon. Though Christian Friends of Israel may not proselytize, it does ask its member to pray that the Jewish people will return to Israel and become Christian as the end-times commence. CFI prays for Muslims to find salvation in Jesus too. In September 2007, in a prayer update marking the Jewish High Holy Days and the Muslim holiday of Ramadan, Jacobson asked readers to pray "that God will send Holy Spirit revelations to the Jewish and Muslim people at this time and that a harvest of souls will be gathered into his barns."[70]

Your People Shall Be My People

Dispensationalists initially expected the Jews to find Christ before returning to Israel. The historical reality led their heirs to accept that the conversion would come later, however. The ingathering of the Jewish people is now, for many born-again Christians, the prelude to that conversion, which is a precondition of Christ's return. Don Finto cites the biblical necessity of Jews' finding Yeshua as their Messiah prior to the Second Coming. In Matthew 23:38–39, he notes, Jesus tells the Jewish leaders in Jerusalem that he will return only when they are ready to bless his coming. That means that a significant number of Jews will be in the land and will have accepted Christ *before* he returns, says Finto in his book *Your People Shall Be My People.*[71] He therefore celebrates Messianic Jewish congregations in Israel—the same groups whom the committee of the Chief Rabbinate denounced with horror. These converts' presence is a start, from Finto's perspective. When enough Jews in Israel have accepted Christ, the scene will be set for the end-times.

Even organizations that officially avoid proselytizing seem to sympathize with Finto's beliefs. Surprisingly, Robert Stearns's Eagles' Wings carried an ad for *Your People Shall Be My People* in 2006. And a new organization called Christian-Zionism.org. did the same in 2007. Christian-Zionism.org. is sponsored by a consortium of evangelical Zionist groups, including several that publicly disavow attempts to convert Jews, such as Bridges for Peace, Christian Friends of Israel, Christians United for Israel (CUFI), Eagles' Wings, and the Christian Embassy. Leading participants in the organization include two Jews who actively work with evangelicals, David Brog of CUFI and Esther Levens of the Unity Coalition for Israel. Yet Christian-Zionism.org. listed Finto's book as a notable publication in its introductory e-mail to readers.[72] This may be because *Your People Shall Be My People* contains an impassioned appreciation of Judaism as the root of Christianity, grief for the suffering of the Jews, repudiation of Replacement Theology, and unconditional love, blessing, and support for Israel and the Jewish people.

"Fatal Criticisms" of Christian Zionist Theology

A third kind of attack rebukes Christian Zionists' understanding of God's relationship with Israel. Liberal mainline Protestants leaders can be passionate about that, but some of the most forceful of these challenges have come from fellow evangelicals. Several of them attack Christian Zionism directly, disputing its foundational theological convictions. Others rebuke it indirectly, by challenging Israel's claim to the occupied territories, and even its right to exist.

Wheaton College professor Gary M. Burge, for example, offers what he calls "fatal criticisms" of the theological framework of Christian Zionism. The New Testament makes it clear, says Burge, that Christians are the children of Abraham and heirs to God's promises to Israel. Moreover, says Burge, the covenantal promises to the Jews are conditional: "Their blessings are revoked when there is faithlessness. The Babylonian exile is the best example of this."[73]

Christian Zionists reject the first point, the idea that God's promises to the Jews are transferred to Christians. They consider this "Replacement Theology" to have been a principal source of the Church's historical persecution of the Jews. It is, for evangelical supporters of Israel, a profound doctrinal error for which they remain deeply remorseful, as we have seen. A number of Christian Zionist leaders suppose that George W. Bush subscribes to this doctrine, which, they believe, explains how he could favor giving away parts of the Holy Land as the basis for a Palestinian state. But the truth, these evangelicals say, is that God's covenants with the Jewish people are eternal. If He reneges on his promises to the Jews, what would prevent Him from doing the same to Christians?

The same issue is at the heart of Burge's second theological challenge, that God's commitments are conditioned on just behavior. Donald E. Wagner, professor of religion and Middle Eastern studies at North Park University in Chicago, for example, cites biblical authority for that argument. God offered the land to Israel not as an everlasting possession but as a conditional loan, says Wagner. The Holy Land is thus a place to live "in return for services rendered," including doing justice and caring for others. By biblical standards, Israel cannot have the land and also oppress the poor, Wagner argues. The restatement of the covenant in Deuteronomy 27–30, he notes, makes it clear that the Hebrews will lose the land if they are not faithful to God's will, as, in fact, they did, falling to the Assyrians, then the Babylonians. Wagner adds that dispensationalists shift the terms of the Jews' obligations away from obedience to God. They focus instead, he says, on supernatural signs of the coming of the Millennium, such as the Jews' occupying the land. Christian and Jewish Zionists thus commit idolatry, he concludes: they elevate the land above the covenantal relationship with God. Wagner argues that "neither the Jews nor the Palestinians can claim ownership of the land by divine right." Instead, they should both be caretakers, and God will judge them based on how they treat each other. He understands Genesis 12:3 to require Jews to be a blessing to others. Only then, he says, will they truly be the people of God.

In that respect, Wagner accuses Israel of sin. He cites a PLO official named Zughdi Terzi who deeply moved him and other Christians in 1979 by likening the modern Israelis to the biblical King Ahab. That evil ruler illegally seized the vineyard of a peasant named Naboth in 1 Kings 21, just as the Israelis have done to Palestinians, razing 400 of their villages to the ground since 1948, said Terzi. Elijah confronted Ahab for doing that, as modern Elijahs should do to Israel, said the PLO spokesman. Wagner comments approvingly that though most Americans would dismiss Terzi as a terrorist, he spoke the truth in love and justice, like a prophet.

Wagner also recounts the painful story of Abuna Chacour, a Palestinian Christian cleric whose family was expelled from their home in 1948. They were permitted by the Israeli High Court to return to their village four years later, only to watch the Israeli army demolish it in an illegal and unauthorized action. Wagner concludes that this illustrates the "old Zionist strategy": from the beginning, he says, the Jews took the land inch by inch, seizing it from a defenseless population.[74] Wagner draws a grim analogy between Israel and a dangerous vine that nearly destroyed the flower garden of his home. "The killer vine had literally surrounded the base of each rose bush and had extensively reproduced itself through a massive network of nodules," he says. Wagner compares that to "the past one hundred-year process of Zionist occupation of Palestine. The weeds and vines had moved in to take over the land and disrupt both the flowers and vegetables that had been the previous dwellers."[75]

Richard Mouw, president of the Fuller Theological Seminary, declares that it is entirely appropriate for Christians to criticize the Jewish state as the prophets did whenever the people were guilty of injustice. "The prophets knew that God would never bless Israel unless that nation conformed to God's standards of justice and righteousness," says Mouw.[76] In July 2002, he joined Wagner, Burge, and fifty-five other evangelical leaders in spelling out Israel's moral failings. In a letter to George W. Bush, they abhorred the Palestinian suicide bombings of the previous twenty-two months but also urged the president to vigorously oppose specific Israeli acts of injustice,

> including the continued unlawful and degrading Israeli settlement movement. The theft of Palestinian land and the destruction of Palestinian homes and fields is surely one of the major causes of the strife that has resulted in terrorism and the loss of so many Israeli and Palestinian lives. The continued Israeli military occupation that daily humiliates ordinary Palestinians is also having disastrous effects on the Israeli soul.[77]

The modernist evangelical leader Jim Wallis, author of *God's Politics,* also faults Israel for its treatment of the Palestinians, and conservative Christians for condoning that behavior. Wallis traveled to Israel in 2004 to attend a conference organized by the Sabeel Ecumenical Liberation Theology Center, a Palestinian Christian group about which we shall see more shortly. On that trip, Wallis says, he saw that Israeli settlements in the West Bank and Gaza "are aggressive forays into Palestinian territory by people who believe that God has given them all the land." The settlements make peace more difficult, he says, adding that "this was the intent of the policy from the beginning."[78] Palestinians told him stories showing that Israeli soldiers were in the territories not to keep peace or protect Palestinians but only to safeguard the settlements. "Control the roads, control movement, control the daily life of the entire Palestinian population—that's the consequence of the settlement policy," he says. Though

Wallis denounces Arab terrorism, he concludes that the Israelis use those violent acts to justify massive, disproportionate retaliation, which can also be called terrorism. "The more I saw, the more it reminded me of apartheid in South Africa," he says. Wallis specifically rebukes what he calls the "simplistic 'we are right and they are wrong' theology" of the Christian right and the Bush administration. Such a belief system limits the opportunity for self-reflection and correction, and leads to dehumanization of the other, Wallis observes.[79]

Jimmy Carter, the first avowedly born-again American president, also likens Israeli policy to apartheid, though he concedes that Israel's policy is driven by the acquisition of land, not racism. Carter charges that Israel's "colonization" of Palestine is the preeminent obstacle to peace. The Israelis are seizing more and more land for their settlements, which divide Palestine into fragments, he adds. And, he says, Israeli occupying forces have become increasingly oppressive, depriving Palestinians of basic rights.[80] Carter considers the security fence and wall that Israel is constructing to be a prison. It is being built entirely within Palestinian territory, confiscating land and water sources, says the former president. It cuts Palestinian communities off from one another and it encircles the West Bank. The barrier, says Carter, is more an "imprisonment wall" than a security fence. It leaves the Palestinians completely enclosed, with no chance for a viable state, he argues.[81] Carter particularly blames Christian Zionists for supporting the growth of Israeli settlements and connecting highways on Palestinian territory. "Strong pressure from the religious right has been a major factor in America's quiescent acceptance" of this policy, he says.[82]

Like Burge and Wagner, Carter raises the possibility that God will punish Israel. Commenting on the way that secular Israelis ignore the Mosaic law, the former president points out that, in the Bible, "Israel was punished whenever the leaders turned away from devout worship of God." He recalls asking then-prime minister Golda Meir if that worried her. There were Orthodox Jews who could assume that responsibility, she replied.[83]

"The Jews Are the Victims of Injustice, Not the Perpetrators"

Christian Zionists reject the claim that the Abrahamic covenant is conditional. The late John F. Walvoord, president of the Dallas Theological Seminary from 1952 to 1986, invoked the doctrines of unconditional election and divine grace, in which God blesses those who are unworthy. "God makes promises which depend on Himself and His grace, not on human faithfulness," said Walvoord. It is true that, in the Bible, an individual Israelite would qualify for personal blessing by virtue of his obedience to God, and when the Jews were disobedient, they were taken away into captivity, he noted. But the current exile is the final dispersion, said Walvoord. There will not be another. And the ultimate fulfillment of the covenant with Abraham has never been in doubt, he declared.[84] That is an article of faith among dispensationalists. The Jews, all of them, "shall return to remain, no more to go out," as William E. Blackstone, the most active of nineteenth-century American Christian Zionists, said in 1898, citing prophecies from Amos, Ezekiel, and Isaiah. "They shall be exalted and dwell safely, and the Gentile nations shall flow unto them."[85]

Moreover, many Christian Zionists argue passionately that the Israelis are not at fault in their conflict with the Palestinians. The Jews are the victims of injustice, not the perpetrators, they say. These evangelicals deeply regret the long history of persecution of the Jewish people and are profoundly sympathetic to Israelis' having to endure terrorism now. The Palestinians seek the destruction of Israel, say many Christian Zionists. If the terrorists laid down their arms, there would be peace; if the Israelis did, there would be a massacre. Fully endorsing the official Israeli perspective, they say that the checkpoints and other security restrictions in Judea and Samaria (the West Bank) are saving lives by preventing infiltration by armed terrorists. So is the security fence, which, they say, has reduced suicide bombings in Israel dramatically. Yechiel Eckstein, writing to evangelical members of the International Fellowship of Christians and Jews in 2005, conceded that the fence does inconvenience Palestinians. "But we must keep our priorities straight," he said, expressing a view that many of his evangelical readers share. The fence has stopped hundreds of terrorist attacks on Israelis, Eckstein observed. "How can anyone justify placing Palestinian convenience before Israeli lives?" Every state has the duty to protect its citizens, Eckstein noted. And the implication that Israel bears any resemblance to apartheid-era South Africa is repugnant, he said.[86]

In the conservative evangelical understanding, it is the Arabs who are unjust, duplicitous, and deserving of divine punishment. From this perspective, in fact, the Palestinians are serving Satan's purpose by undermining God's plan for salvation. In this view, the Arabs may have deceived the Europeans and the mainline churches in America but not evangelical supporters of the Jewish state. For them, Israelis are courageous and strong allies in the war on terror. Far from wanting to restrict the Israeli Defense Forces' actions on the West Bank, or asking Jerusalem to remove checkpoints or take down the separation fence, these evangelicals want Israel to have a free hand to root out terrorist infrastructures.

What's more, it is unfair for Wagner, Burge, and others on the evangelical left to use biblical prophets to attack the modern state of Israel, says Rabbi Yehiel Poupko. These evangelicals employ the same scriptural texts against Jews that the Church used for 2,000 years, argues Poupko, who is the Judaic scholar at the Jewish Federation of Metropolitan Chicago. Christian critics transfer these biblical verses to Israel but don't apply the same standards against France, or Luxemburg, or Nigeria, he charges. That is theological anti-Semitism, Poupko observes. "Israel is a government like any other, but you don't treat it that way. When you use elements of the *adversus Judaeos* tradition," he says, referring to Church anti-Jewish polemics, "you have an agenda."[87] Poupko is particularly offended by Donald Wagner's portrayal of Israel as a killer vine. That grotesque description of Zionism, the national liberation movement of the Jewish people, recalls the metaphor system of the Nazis, says Poupko. "We all know what happens when a group of people is described as a cancer or a vermin," he points out. "'A massive network of nodules' indeed!" Poupko declares.[88]

Poupko, historian of religion Martin Marty, and a small group of other Jews and mainline Protestants met for three years to develop a model for interfaith discussion about Israel. They recognized the pain of all peoples in the Middle East. They acknowledged that Christians often do hold Israel to a higher standard than they do undemocratic nations but they noted that this demonstrates their respect for the Jewish state, their concern for human rights, and their higher hopes for Israel. In a clear rebuke to many evangelical supporters of Israel, they declared that only a biblical prophet can know God's intent for any given event, and that prophecy ceased t2600 years ago. The group also noted that most Jews (unlike evangelicals) have never attributed theological significance to Zionism. At the same time, the participants reproached critics who resuscitate Christian medieval anti-Jewish motifs or modern anti-Semitic notions in their attacks on Israel.[89]

"Modern Israel Is Not the Fulfillment of Prophecy"

Another critique that goes to the heart of Christian Zionist principles is the charge that modern Israel is not the fulfillment of prophecy. That criticism appeared even before the birth of the state—for example, in a letter sent to the editors of the *Moody Bible Institute Monthly* in 1931. The author, one "F.M.B.," asserted that Mosaic law applied only until the coming of Christ. The Old Testament Israelites' work then ceased and the Holy Land was no longer the exclusive site of worship. "Future worship is neither on the hill in Samaria nor in Jerusalem, but wherever the Omnipresent Lord is known and loved," said the writer. There are many holy cities, he added, but only one New Jerusalem. The editors, writing against the background of British steps to limit Jewish immigration to Mandatory Palestine, gave a dispensationalist response. God has ordained the reestablishment of the Jewish state, not for the Jews' sake alone but for the world's, they declared. "He is going to be known and loved in Jerusalem by the people who once rejected and caused him to be crucified," they predicted, and cited Psalm 2:6: "I have set my king on Zion, my holy hill." There is only one holy city, Jerusalem, the editors affirmed, and God has arranged for it to exist without impinging on the New Jerusalem that will come down from heaven.[90]

Donald Wagner makes the case that the Bible, particularly the New Testament, does not predict or justify the existence of the modern state of Israel. He affirms that the Jews are neither replaced nor rejected, as Paul says in Romans 9:11. Wagner appears quite willing, through, to consider the dissolution of the Jewish state. He concedes that Jews need security. But that does not necessitate a nation-state, certainly not at the cost of another people's suffering, Wagner declares. He cites the eminent British evangelical leader John R. W. Stott to the effect that the secular state of Israel does not fulfill Old Testament prophecies, which promise that the Jews will return to the land in faith. Moreover, according to Stott, the New Testament does not confirm the Old Testament promises about the land. Wagner agrees. What Christian Zionists fail to note, he observes, is that the New Testament says nothing about restoring Israel to the land. Even Luke 21:24, in which Jesus predicts that Jerusalem will be trodden down until the times of the Gentiles are over, does not mention the Jews' return to the land, he says. Wagner cites Stott's assertion that the Old Testament promises are fulfilled in Christ and Christians in any case. The true Israel today, Stott observed, is neither Jews nor Israelis, but all believers in the Messiah. Indeed, Stott declared, "political Zionism and Christian Zionism are biblically anathema to the Christian faith"![91]

David Parsons, the International Christian Embassy spokesman, refutes these points on biblical grounds. Psalm 105:8–12, he notes, confirms God's bequest of Canaan to Israel for a thousand generations.[92] The New Testament confirms the land component of the Abrahamic Covenant, Parsons adds. The martyr Stephen, in his dying sermon in Acts 7:5, says that God gave the land to Abraham's descendants even before Abraham had a child.[93] Parsons agrees that the Mosaic covenant places conditions on Israel's right to enjoy possession of the land, but loss of domicile does not mean loss of ownership, he says (Leviticus: 26:44–46). This, he contends, is the central flaw in Donald Wagner's approach and that of other critics of Christian Zionism: they maintain that Israel has been divested of its title to the land. But this is contrary to the Bible, says Parsons, arguing that "Both the people and the land of Israel were chosen for the purpose of world redemption." Even when the prophets speak of exilic judgment, he notes, they also voice the hope of return, as in

Isaiah: "For a brief moment I forsook you, but with great compassion I will gather you" (54:7). Jesus himself affirms the land promise, Parsons observes, since all references to promises made to the fathers necessarily include the land. He refutes Stott's argument by citing Ezekiel 36 and Jeremiah 31, which state that Israel will return to the land in unbelief, and then, in a separate phase, will come back to the Lord spiritually, says Parsons. In Ezekiel 36:24–26, for example, the Lord promises to gather the Israelites from the nations, bring them back to their own land, and cleanse them. He will remove their heart of stone and give them a heart of flesh.[94] Christian Zionists cite that verse often, as we have seen. It signifies the Jews' renewed openness to faith, though faith in Whom is a question about which evangelicals and Jews do not necessarily agree.

The Sabeel Ecumenical Liberation Theology Center

Among the most quietly effective opponents of Christian Zionism and Israeli policies is an Arab Christian organization called the Sabeel Ecumenical Liberation Theology Center, which is headquartered in Jerusalem. Beneath the radar of the mainstream American media, Sabeel officials have passionately urged mainline Christian denominations in the West to oppose Israeli policies and encouraged them to divest economically from the Jewish state. Sabeel also has conducted a theological war against Christian Zionists. Sabeel's founder and director, Naim Ateek, a Palestinian Anglican priest, calls Christian Zionism a heresy. It is, he declares, the dark side of the Bible, perhaps the most dangerous distortion of Scriptures today. "Due to their faulty theology," says Ateek, evangelical supporters of Israel "are unwittingly and unconsciously contributing to the oppression and killing of many innocent Palestinians by Israel." Jesus himself warned that this would happen, he asserts, quoting John 16:2–3 as his proof-text: "Indeed, the hour is coming when whoever kills you will think he is offering service to God." Christian Zionist theology defaces and disfigures God and Christianity, Ateek declares.[95]

Ateek specifically rejects the evangelical focus on God's promise to bless those who bless Abraham in Genesis 12:3. He dismisses the verse as "a primitive form of nationalism," adding, "Such pronouncements attributed to tribal gods were not uncommon in the ancient world." Christians who quote this Old Testament passage contradict the teachings of Jesus because they are not working for peace or reconciliation, says Ateek. In any case, he points out, the verse doesn't mention Jews. Since Ishmael and Isaac were both children of Abraham, he argues, the blessing applies to both and to their offspring.[96]

Christian Zionists, like religious Jews, are emphatic, however, that God blessed Isaac and established his everlasting covenant with him and his descendants, *not* with Ishmael. God told Abraham, "Through Isaac shall your descendants be named" (Genesis 17:19–21, 21:12). It is a common evangelical argument, as we have seen, that while Isaac was the chosen son, Ishmael was the product of Abraham and Sarah's impatience and lack of faith. Curiously, Ateek's suggestion that Genesis 12:3 is a survival of paganism mirrors Christian Zionist claims about Islam as a religion.

Ateek speaks of peace, justice, and reconciliation in accordance with Christ's teachings. In taking this stand, he has had an important impact on many socially liberal Christians, including modernist evangelicals. Jim Wallis calls him "one of the most articulate voices for justice and peace in the Middle East . . . both a pastoral and prophetic leader in the midst of the present conflict."[97] But in his zeal to defend his people, Ateek has resuscitated centuries-old anti-Semitic diatribes against Jews. In a Christmas Message in the year 2000, during the violence of the second, or Al Aqsa, Intifada (uprising), Ateek referred to Israeli officials as "modern day 'Herods.'" In so doing, he evoked Herod the Great, the evil ruler responsible for the Slaughter of the Innocents—who, according to this analogy, are the Palestinians. In 2001 Ateek spoke of Israel's military responses to terrorist attacks as a "crucifixion system." "Jesus is on the cross again with thousands of crucified Palestinians around him," he said. "Palestine has become one huge Golgotha." In these agonized expressions of grief for his people, Ateek revived medieval charges that Jews are baby-killers and deicides.[98] Christians who support the Jewish state are, in his view, endorsing the acts of "oppressors and warmongers." Ateek goes beyond disputing Israel's policies and challenges its legitimacy as a state. He acknowledges Israel's need to exist, but not its right to do so. He even raises the possibility that the Jews will leave Israel for the West or "other countries in the Middle East."[99]

Ateek also criticizes evangelical Zionist hermeneutics. Christian Zionism, he told the General Synod of the United Church of Christ in 2003, makes an elaborate jigsaw puzzle of the Bible.[100] That is a valid assessment. Connecting texts from different biblical books to arrive at a unified vision is hardly unique to dispensationalism, however. Rather, that approach has a long lineage in Jewish and Christian thought. Rabbinic interpretation of the Torah (the "Midrash") freely drew connections among diverse biblical texts.[101] Early Christian writers also created theological mosaics, sometimes joining Scripture to other sources. The story of Lucifer's rebellion against God and his fall from heaven, for example, was a conflation of Old and New Testament passages with apocryphal texts.[102]

Other critics rebuke Christian Zionists for reading biblical prophecy as a literal forecasts of events. Donald Wagner says that the basic hermeneutical method of dispensationalism is projecting Old and New Testament texts onto the future. But God does not ask us to use the Bible to predict the future, he says. Rather, we should trust in Him and live the gospel of the kingdom every day. Moreover, in the New Testament, the land, the Temple, Jerusalem, and future promises are all understood allegorically or spiritually, says Wagner.[103] Jonathan Kuttab, a member of the Sabeel board, also challenges the dispensational use of prophecy. "Is prophecy a form of fortune telling, and predictions about current national and international affairs?" he asks. "Is it a predictor of the end-times, and a method for identifying which political powers or movements today are evil, or constitute an antichrist?" Kuttab's own understanding of the prophetic books would be uncongenial to most Bible-believing evangelicals, however: prophecy, he suggests, is not an account of the future but instead a call to repentance.[104] Dispensationalists, by contrast, apply literal interpretation to all Scripture, including prophecy. To read much of the Bible literally but then allegorize or spiritualize prophecy is inconsistent, they argue. After all, they say, the Old Testament prophecies of Christ's first coming were all fulfilled literally. That confirms the validity of a literalist approach, for them.[105]

Kuttab also declares that the Lord is not tribal and territorially based but is instead the sacrificial God who loves the whole world. That is a central issue in Palestinian liberation theology and a critical rebuke to Christian Zionism. Liberation theologians deplore the particularism of the Old Testament, in which God selects one people, Israel, as His own. They stress instead the universalism of the New Testament.[106] Evangelicals agree that God loves everyone, but a defining aspect of Christian Zionism is that He made a unique covenant with Israel, His Chosen People. His choice was tribal. For very many evangelical, that is the whole point.

Kuttub then moves on to the heart of his indictment, the politics of Christian Zionism. The movement is "crassly simplistic and unabashedly biased," he says.[107] It is certainly true that evangelical Zionists accept and champion the religious nationalist Israeli perspective. In making that choice, they simplify the complex, competing, and mutually contradictory Jewish and Palestinian narratives. Sabeel's account of history is incomplete and partisan, too, however. "The Jerusalem Sabeel Document," which is labeled "Principles for a Just Peace in Palestine-Israel," lists among its complaints, for example, that Israel "acquired by force 77 percent of the land of Palestine in 1948, approximately 20 percent more than the United Nations had allotted." The document doesn't mention that the Jews actually accepted the UN partition plan. It was Arabs who rejected it and invaded Israel to destroy the fledgling Jewish state, losing land in the process.

Ateek and his colleagues are, understandably, Palestinian nationalists. He believes that Zionism was conceived in sin, ignoring the rights of the Arab inhabitants of the land. He says explicitly that Zionists incarnate the spiritual hosts of wickedness against which Christians are called to struggle (Ephesians 6:12–13).[108] Justice, for Ateek and his associates at Sabeel, comprises the maximal Arab demands, short of calling for the annihilation of Israel.[109] For Christian Zionists, politics comports with theology. For Sabeel, theology comports with politics.

Ateek, like Halsell and other critics of Israel, accuses Zionism of negating the Palestinians. In his view, Jewish and Christian Zionists portray Arabs in the most derogatory and denigrating light.[110] Yale University scholar Adam Gregerman argues, however, that Palestinian liberation theology does exactly the same thing in reverse: it removes the Jewish people from their own story and rejects any interpretation of the Bible that emphasizes God's faithfulness to His people. It taps into deep wells of historical anti-Judaism and anti-Semitism, applying old anti-Jewish images in new settings, says Gregerman. Liberation theologians demonize Jews, he argues. They suggest the worst possible explanations for Israelis' behavior, representing them as "irreligious, violent, malevolent, selfish, and indifferent to the suffering of non-Jews."[111]

"Challenging Christian Zionism"

In the spring of 2004, the Sabeel Center hosted an international conference in Jerusalem called "Challenging Christian Zionism" to rebuke evangelical support for Israel. Six hundred and forty Bible scholars, religious leaders, and peace activists from thirty-two countries attended. Among the speakers was Catholic theologian Rosemary Ruether. Thirty years earlier, she had published *Faith and Fratricide: The Theological Roots of Anti-Semitism,* a comprehensive study of the Christian *adversus Judaeos* tradition. But Ruether has since become an outspoken critic of Israel and its evangelical allies. From 1990 on, she has been involved in the movement to develop a Palestine liberation theology, a theology of the oppressed. She has been active in Sabeel since its inception. Ruether challenges the religious, political, and ethical bases of Christian Zionist belief and Israeli policy. The concept that Israel has an a priori right to exist, she says, is a religious myth based on a tribalist God's relationship with a single people.[112] She questions what sort of God would mandate taking land away from its residents, and she challenges a belief system that renders a conquered people invisible. The modern Palestinians are being ethnically cleansed, as the ancient Canaanites were, Ruether says. Israel's treatment of the Palestinian people, she concludes, has been "an endlessly worsening crime."[113] At the 2004 Sabeel conference, Ruether denounced Christian Zionism as an enormously dangerous belief, specifically repudiating its use of the "language of apocalyptic warfare and messianic nationalism." Other speakers concurred. Stephen Sizer, author of *Christian Zionism: Road-map to Armageddon?* made the blanket statement that Christian Zionism is the most powerful and destructive force in America. It shapes U.S. Middle East policy and incites hatred for Muslims, he declared. Sizer also accused leading evangelical Zionist groups of pursuing a plan to evangelize Jews. Barbara Rossing, author of *The Rapture Exposed,* dismissed dispensational eschatology as bad theology. Ateek himself declared that Christian Zionism identifies the Gospel with an "ideology of empire, colonialism, and militarism."[114]

Ateek's words were included in the official conference statement:

> The Christian Zionist programme provides a worldview where the Gospel is identified with the ideology of empire, colonialism, and militarism. In its extreme form, it places an emphasis on apocalyptic events leading to the end of history rather than living Christ's love and justice today. . . .We categorically reject Christian Zionist doctrines as a false teaching that undermines the biblical message of love, mercy, and justice. . . .
>
> We reject the heretical teachings of Christian Zionism that facilitate and support these extremist policies as they advance a form of racial exclusivity and perpetual war. . . .
>
> Rather than condemn the world to the doom of Armageddon we call upon everyone to liberate themselves from ideologies of militarism and occupation and instead to pursue the healing of the world. We call upon Christians in churches on every continent to prayerfully remember the suffering of the Palestinian and Israeli people, both of whom are victims of policies of occupation and militarism.[115]

Sympathy Straitened by Conviction

The Sabeel statement's reference to the Israeli people as victims along with the Palestinians raises the crucial question of compassion, or its absence, which is an unspoken subtext of much of the Middle East debate. Jonathan Kuttab, the Sabeel board member, accuses Christian Zionism of being "oblivious to the suffering of non-Jews."[116] The Sabeel statement thus demonstrates that the conference participants, by contrast, are compassionate toward Jews as well as Arabs.

Ateek and his colleagues do extend gestures of compassion for their opponents. At the conference, for example, the participants spoke the name of each victim of the violence, Israelis as well as Arabs.[117] Sabeel also expresses sorrow over the suffering of the Jews in the Holocaust, though it insists that Palestinians should not be punished for what happened in Europe.

There are limits to this compassion, however, as is typically true in conflicts. In his essay "Suicide Bombers: What Is Theologically and Morally Wrong with Suicide Bombings?" Ateek's empathy for Palestinian bombers is far more palpable than it is for their Jewish victims. Though he denounces such attacks as crimes against God and man, Ateek speaks movingly of the bombers' willingness to make "the supreme sacrifice" for their faith and their homeland. Humiliated by the Israeli occupation, these young people have lost the ability to dream of a better life, he says, so they dream of revenge. He presents in particular the case of a young Palestinian named Abdel Baset Odeh. Ateek tells us that Odeh felt that the Israeli authorities ruined his life when they prevented him from crossing from the West Bank into Jordan to get married. The Shin Bet (Israeli domestic intelligence) then asked to speak with Odeh, but, he refused, suspecting that they wanted him to become an informer. "His future plans . . . shattered by the Israeli army, he turned to suicide bombing," Ateek notes, with evident compassion for the bomber and blame for Israel. "His father attributed his son's action to humiliation and a broken heart."[118] In March 2002, Abdel Baset Odeh blew up a Passover seder in Netanya, killing thirty people and wounding 140. The consequences were profound: the brutality and scale of the attack outraged Israelis and provoked Ariel Sharon to launch a massive military assault on terrorist strongholds on the West Bank. The ferocity of the fighting prompted George W. Bush to demand that Israel withdraw, which, in turn, aroused Christian Zionists to rally in fervent support of Israel, as we shall see in Chapter 10.

Christian Zionists' compassion for the suffering of the Jews is heartfelt and deep, as Ateek's is for the Palestinians. These evangelicals' sympathy for Arabs is often straitened by conviction, however, as Sabeel's is for Jews. Another important limiting factor is the fear and anger that each side feels, which can subdue or extinguish empathy. I asked Martin Hoffman, author of *Empathy and Moral Development: Implications for Caring and Justice,* why genuine empathy so often flows in only one direction—in this case toward the Israelis or the Arabs but very rarely toward both. Interestingly, Hoffman said that psychologists have not addressed the failure of empathy in such circumstances. Studies do suggest that empathy is inborn and natural, and that circumstances can turn it off. In the course of our conversation we concluded that empathy is impossible when one feels confronted by a threatening evil.[119] The urgency of the threat, either to oneself or to a group that one empathizes with, can govern the limits of compassion. Empathy, then, is typically the province of the secure rather than the threatened, the victor rather than the victim. That is consistent with recent psychological studies indicating that fostering a sense of security, even in an experimental environment, results in increased compassion and altruism.[120] In Israel and the occupied territories, however, insecurity, distrust, and a deep sense of injustice ally with religious conviction to obviate compassion for the other.

Most Israeli Jews, living in the shadow of the Holocaust, experience the Arab and Muslim threat as existential. Many of their evangelical allies view it as cosmic, as we have seen. Vicious anti-Semitism in the Arab and Muslim media persuades many Israelis that the Arab states and Iran are implacably hostile. Faced with Muslim leaders' Holocaust denials and threats to wipe out the "Zionist entity," the large majority of Israeli Jews believes that their enemies would drive them into the sea if they could.

From the Palestinian perspective, by contrast, the conflict with Israel is a story of pure one-sided victimization. The Palestinian narrative is one of dispossession and injustice in which the powerful Israelis have illegally exploited and oppressed a helpless people. Edward Said, perhaps the most brilliant exponent of the Palestinian viewpoint, expressed this in a simple observation: "There is still a victim and a victimizer," he said, and the Palestinians are the victim. Said dismissed any consideration of "Israeli psychological security, which if they don't have now, they never will."[121] With so much at stake, and such a twinned sense of victimization, empathy for the other is a lot to ask.

In her study of the origin of Satan, Princeton professor of religion Elaine Pagels notes that, in the view of some social scientists and anthropologists, many people divide the world into binary oppositions. It is a matter of "we" and "they," in which "we" equals human and "they" nonhuman. From the beginning, she observes, Israelite tradition did precisely that, defining "us" in ethnic, political, and religious terms as "the people of God," as against "them," the alien enemies of Israel. In Genesis, Ishmael, the progenitor of the Arab people, is a son of Abraham, but he is not one of "us," notes Pagels. Rather, he is a violent inferior. An angel predicts that Ishmael will be "a wild ass of a man, his hand against every man and every man's hand against him" (Genesis 16:12).[122]

Much of the history of Jewish-Christian relations has been tragically shaped by a similar us versus them dichotomy in which compassion has failed entirely. Many Christian Zionists deeply regret that history today, but the same is not always true of their view of Muslims, as we have seen. Critics charge that born-again Zionists are blind to the plight of Arabs, including Arab Christians. Grace Halsell stresses that point in *Prophecy and Politics,* noting that Jerry Falwell's tours of Israel in the 1980s ignored and essentially negated the Christians who were all around the tourist routes.[123] In *The Rapture Exposed,* Rossing goes further, quoting a claim by Ateek that dispensationalists don't even acknowledge that Palestinian Christians exist. "They call us cultural Christians only," says Ateek.[124] Weber takes a more balanced position on the question of evangelicals' attitude toward Palestinian Christians. He notes that most American evangelicals do not have much in common with them, since the majority of Palestinian Christians belong to one of the Eastern Orthodox churches. Moreover, evangelicals do not engage in ecumenical enterprises like the Middle East Council of Churches. He concludes, however, that, since dispensationalism does not leave much room for Palestinian believers, "dispensationalists do not have to pay them any mind."[125]

Christian Zionist Sympathy with the Palestinians

Contrary to reports, evangelical Zionists often do sympathize with the Palestinians to a surprising extent, as long as it is compatible with their convictions.[126] Sometimes this comes from unexpected sources, such as Tim LaHaye, who has had enormous success popularizing dispensational motifs in his *Left Behind* novels. LaHaye wrote in 1984 that the Israelis had not always respected the human rights of the Arabs. If they become inhumane, said LaHaye, the United States would have to reevaluate its policies toward Israel.[127] Improbable as it seems from a post-9/11 perspective, Pat Robertson made an even stronger case in 1990, indicting Israel and sympathizing with the suffering of the Palestinians! Writing as the first Intifada was under way, Robertson accused the Israeli military of using excessive force in subduing stone-throwing Palestinian rioters, "far beyond any recognized or acceptable norms of crowd control." Israeli security forces had broken bones in deliberate attempts to maim Palestinians as painfully as possible, said Robertson. Israeli officials, he added, had shown contempt for Arabs. They had bulldozed their homes, put them in virtual concentration camps in the Negev without filing charges, deported them, and harassed drivers with Palestinian plates. Robertson went so far as to assert that Israel was practicing a type of apartheid! He did not link Arabs to Satan or accuse them of seeking world domination, as he did after 9/11. Muslims had not yet supplanted the Soviets as the agents of evil, and Robertson's relations with Jews were often acrimonious at that point. He did assert the dispensational conviction that Jerusalem must remain a Jewish city, though. And he affirmed the fundamental Christian Zionist tenet that "so long as this nation has any concern for God's favor, we cannot turn our backs on Israel."[128]

Franklin Graham, who gained notoriety after 9/11 when he called Islam a "very evil and wicked religion," nonetheless expressed sympathy for the suffering of the Palestinians in 2002. He lamented that "hundreds of thousands of Palestinian Arabs have been displaced and, tragically, they have ended up in refugee camps scattered throughout the Middle East. From these camps of misery and despair come many of the terrorists and suicide bombers today," he observed. But the question remains, said Graham, to whom does the land belong? God leaves no doubt that He owns the Holy Land, Graham noted. He alone can dispose of it, and He has given it to Abraham, Isaac, and Jacob. Jews and Arabs can coexist harmoniously in Israel, Graham added, and for him, that ends the debate.[129]

Christian Zionists reject hatred of any people, said the heads of the three major evangelical Zionist organizations in Israel in a joint statement that they called "The Jerusalem Declaration of Christian Zionism." They believe that God loves all people equally, they added, but He has chosen the Jews to bring redemption to mankind.[130] Richard Booker, founding director of the Institute of Hebraic-Christian Studies in Texas, emphasizes compassion for Arabs while making a similar theological argument. "Christian Zionist support for Israel does not mean that we are anti-Arab," he says. "It is just the opposite. We desire that the Arab people find the fullest blessings of the Almighty. We know that the Lord loves all people the same and so should we. But we also recognize that the God of the Bible has different plans and purposes for different people groups." The Arabs will only receive the full measure of God's blessing when they acknowledge His covenant with the Jews, says Booker. "Until then, we pray and work for the peace of Jerusalem."[131]

Robert Stearns's Eagles' Wings expresses exceptional empathy toward Palestinians in its "Watchmen on the Wall" training manual. This detailed compilation includes a section titled "How to Pray for Arabs: Crying Out for Ishmael," which was written by Arab evangelical Christians, among others. It begins with the standard Christian Zionist understanding of the origin of the Arab-Israeli conflict: Abraham expelled Ishmael, the father of the Arab people, engendering his envy toward Isaac and the strife that still rages in Israel. The manual then expresses compassion for the Palestinians, asking Christians to "see the tragedy and injustice that the Arabs have also suffered during the long years of conflict with Israel." One day, it hopes, the sons of Isaac (the Jews) will confess with a breaking heart and repent what they have done to their half-brother. Eagles' Wings urges evangelicals to pray in particular for

Arab Christians. It asks God to heal the emotional wounds and social injustices that the Israelis or the Church have inflicted on Arab believers. The traditional Christian Zionist critique of Islam and impulse to evangelize also appear, though. The Eagles' Wings authors ask for prayers that the "spiritual darkness of Islam and its propaganda be lifted" and that Muslim zeal for Islam should be translated into "a passionate pursuit of the Lord Jesus Christ."[132]

Other Christian Zionists also convey sympathy in ways that confirm the truth of their own beliefs. The ICEJ's David Parsons, for example, wants Muslims to support Israel for their own benefit. "If you hate and curse the Jewish people, you're gonna be cursed," he said in 1998. "We'd like to see this lifted from them."[133] Evangelicals implore God to bestow mercy on the Palestinians by showing them the evil of struggling against His plan for Israel or by bringing them to Christ. In June 2007, Bridges for Peace reported on a planned suicide bombing in Israel by two Palestinian mothers, one of them pregnant with her ninth child. Bridges followed the story with this prayer: "May God extend His great mercy to the Palestinian people by sending them a revelation of the truth of their situation"—that is, that they are choosing evil when they should be choosing life. In the same week, Christian Friends of Israel, another Zionist organization in Jerusalem, noted that Hamas had seized control of Gaza by force. CFI asked its readers to pray for the Palestinian people, who are in a desperate situation. It also asked Christians to pray that the truth of the gospel will reach the Palestinians' hearts.[134]

7

⚜

"It's My Land and Keep Your Hands off of It"

Christian Zionists and the Israeli Right Wing

The fourth main charge against Christian Zionists is that their insistence that Israel keep all of Jerusalem and the occupied territories makes them natural allies of the Israeli far right. "The Christian fundamentalists were vehemently opposed to the peace process," says Itamar Rabinovich, Israel's ambassador to the United States under Labor prime ministers Yitzhak Rabin and Shimon Peres from 1993 to 1996. "They believed that the land belonged to Israel as a matter of divine right. So they immediately became part of the campaign by the Israeli right to undermine the peace process."[1] Likud prime ministers Menachem Begin and Benjamin Netanyahu cultivated particularly close relations with evangelicals. So did Ariel Sharon until late 2003, when he disclosed his policy of disengagement from Gaza. From that point on, many evangelicals felt betrayed by him—and by George W. Bush, who supported this policy.

Their stand against territorial concessions allies Christian Zionists with Jewish religious nationalists in particular. Both groups are Messianic, though in very distinct ways. Inspired by Rabbi Zvi Yehudah Kook, this faction of Jews believes that the Messianic age has begun and that the secular state of Israel is the Kingdom of God. Despite the radical differences in their Messianism, these Christians and Jews share the belief that Redemption will come only when the Jews settle the whole Land of Israel. Israeli governments initially encouraged establishing settlements in the occupied territories for security reasons, but the Kookists' goal was to advance the Redemption. The settlement process thrived under Likud governments, though Labor politicians supported it too. Even the dovish Shimon Peres initially supported the settlements.[2] And many in the general Israeli public admired the settlers' rejuvenation of the original Zionist ethic of settling the land and establishing political facts on the ground. Sharon was the chief proponent of the settlements. Then in 2005 he oversaw the removal of thousands of settlers he had previously encouraged.

Gershom Gorenberg shows in *End of Days* that the Christian and Jewish religious right also have a common interest in building the Third Temple, which, to both, is a precondition of the coming of the Messiah. There is an obstacle, however: the Dome of the Rock and the Al-Aqsa mosque occupy the Temple Mount, the site where Jews believe the Second Temple stood. The possibility that radical Jews or Christians will try to destroy the mosque and the shrine is extremely worrying to Israeli authorities. As Grace Halsell points out, such an act might well trigger a war. Still, she reports hearing Israeli settlers, members of the religious nationalist Gush Emunim ("Bloc of the Faithful"), openly discussing plans to destroy the Muslim holy structures on the Temple Mount. And if that led to an apocalyptic war? So be it, one of them told her. Israel would win and expel the Arabs.[3]

Menachem Begin and Christians

The Christian Zionist alliance with right-wing Israeli politicians is usually traced back to Menachem Begin, who was elected prime minister in 1977, largely with the backing of religious Israelis. The rise to power of the religious right in Israel at that time was part of a worldwide pattern in which religion acquired a new political potency. In 1976, Jimmy Carter, an evangelical, was elected president of the United States, defeating Jerry Ford, who also called himself a born-again Christian.[4] In 1977 Mohammed Zia ul-Haq came to power in Pakistan, initiating an Islamic revival in that country. In 1979 the Islamic revolution took place in Iran. In the same year in the United States, Jerry Falwell and other fundamentalists established the Moral Majority and, at about the same time, evangelicals began to forge a political connection with conservative Roman Catholics to oppose abortion. Ralph Reed says that the return to orthodoxy among pro-life Catholics at that time (especially under the influence of the new pope, John Paul II), combined with the Southern Baptist Convention's turn toward religious conservatism, were perhaps the most important changes in American religious life in the previous fifty years. John Paul II also took an active political role in Poland, allying with the *Solidarnosc* (Solidarity) trade union movement that undid Communism in that country. And Catholicism played a crucial part in the Sandinista uprising in Nicaragua and other political conflicts in Latin America. In India, a Hindu-inspired national-ist movement also emerged. During the 1980s virtually every serious political conflict in the world involved resurgent fundamentalism, liberation theology, or some other religious influence.[5] Begin complicated that factor in the Middle East equation by forming alliances with Christians: evangelicals in the West, and Maronites in Lebanon.

Commentators sometimes say that it was Begin who first solicited Ameri-can Christian Zionist support for Israel. One version of this story is that this was the result of divinely guided events—or entirely fortuitous circumstances, depending on your perspective. In May of 1977, Begin suffered a heart attack and came under the care of Dr. Larry Samuels, a professor of nuclear medicine at Hadassah Hospital in Jerusalem. An evangelical from Illinois, Samuels had asked God for direction in his life and had received "a very clear calling to come to Jerusalem," he said later. He arrived in Israel in 1976. Knowing no one but obeying the calling of the Lord, he made his way to Hadassah Hospital. One year later, Samuels found himself treating Begin medically. He took that op-portunity to inform the new prime minister of evangelical support for Israel and the Jewish people. "You know, I think you have more supporters among evangelical Christians in North America than you have Jews supporting Israel," Samuels told him. He recalled that Begin was very excited about that and replied, "We sure need that—how can we tap that reservoir of support?" According to this account, Begin thus inaugurated Israel's fateful alliance with evangelical Christians.

Samuels, for his part, formed a network of Christians living in Israel, many of whom traveled abroad to speak to Christian groups in support of the Jewish state. When thirteen nations, protesting Israel's annexation of East Jerusalem, moved their embassies from Jerusalem to Tel Aviv in 1980, Samuels and other Christians joined with Jan Willem van der Hoeven to establish the Interna-tional Christian Embassy Jerusalem (ICEJ).[6] It is now one of the two largest Christian Zionist organizations in Israel. It provides philanthropic services, helps thousands of Jews make aliyah, and, in its own words, displays "lov-ing comfort" for and solidarity with Israel. The ICEJ also sponsors the annual celebration of the Feast of Tabernacles, corresponding to the Jewish holiday Succoth. Among the Israeli officials who have warmly welcomed evangelical visitors during the Feast was Teddy Kollek, the longtime mayor of Jerusalem. "You have come to the mountain of the Lord," Kollek declared at one ICEJ conference in Jerusalem in the mid-1980s. "The Christian Embassy gives us all strength and courage," he told them. Noting that these evangelicals had come despite widespread fears of terrorism, the mayor added, "You all deserve a medal!"[7] Thousands of Christians now travel to Jerusalem each year at Succoth for a conference and the Jerusalem March, in which they process through the streets in colorful native costume.[8]

Begin's longtime friend, adviser, and biographer Harry Hurwitz gives a totally different account of the genesis of Begin's friendship with evangelicals, however. After Begin was elected in 1977, he dispatched Hurwitz to the United States, where he addressed a large Christian conference in Houston. Hurwitz explained why it was important to back the Jewish state and left with a letter of support from the delegates and leaders. Begin asked him how many Christians the letter represented. Eleven million, Hurwitz replied! Begin consulted with his staff, and from that point on, he was ready to reach out to American evangelicals.

Despite these competing foundational stories about Begin's courtship of Christian Zionists, he is often named as the source of their alliance with Israel. On his death in 1992, the Evangelical Christian Zionist Congress of America issued an open letter declaring that Begin's unconditional friendship "forged the first visible bonding of the people of Israel with their Biblical allies."[9]

Yona Malachy

In reality, however, it was not Begin who initiated the evangelical alliance with the Jewish state. Israeli officials had identified Christian Zionist support and sought to develop it decades before he took power. W. A. Criswell, the beloved pastor of First Baptist Church of Dallas and two-term president of the Southern Baptist Convention, traveled to Israel in the early 1950s and met with Prime Minister David Ben-Gurion. On his return to Texas, Criswell preached that the Jews' return to Israel fulfills biblical prophesy and he remained an ardent supporter of Israel for over forty years.[10] Ben-Gurion received Oral Roberts in Israel in 1959 (he may not have known that Roberts evangelized Jews).[11] Ben-Gurion also actively encouraged Pentecostals to hold their World Conference of Pentecostal Churches in Jerusalem in 1961. The prime minister's office helped to organize the conference and had a State medal minted for each of the 2,589 delegates. The Ministry of Religious Affairs published a special issue of its journal *Christian News from Israel,* which was a forerunner of the many newsletters, journals, and bulletins from Israel that now reach Christian readers in the West. Ben-Gurion himself sent written greetings to the conference, declaring that "today we are privileged to see the fulfillment of the prophecy and promise of the Bible." Interestingly, not one of the Pentecostal speakers mentioned eschatology. They didn't want to offend their Israeli hosts.[12]

By the 1960s, the Ministry of Religious Affairs had opened a Department of Christian Affairs to deal with Christian leaders and visitors, and to study evangelical support for the Jewish state. In 1967, two months after the Six-Day War, the ministry sent Yona Malachy, a young Polish-born scholar with a Ph.D. from the Sorbonne, to the United States. His assignment was to research Christian attitudes toward Israel. The religion scholar Yaakov Ariel charges that as recently as the mid-1980s, the Israeli Foreign Ministry official in charge of liaison with Christian churches was completely ignorant of the distinction between conservative and mainline Protestant churches and that Israeli officials still do not fully comprehend Christian Zionist beliefs about the Jewish state.[13] If so, they need only read Malachy's conclusions.

An expert on Christian eschatology, Malachy received a warm welcome from American Christian Zionists. During his travels in the United States, he made a study of Christian denominations, sorting out which stood with Israel and which were critical.[14] He also urged evangelicals to publicly declare their support for the Jewish state. In a visit to Biola College (formerly the Bible Institute of Los Angeles), Malachy thanked the faculty for backing Israel during the recent war but asked for a tangible expression of their support. In response, Biola issued "A Proclamation Concerning Israel and the Nations," which noted that Satan, the archenemy of God's intentions, had attacked Israel throughout its history. It went on to say,

> Untaught and unholy men have unwittingly cooperated with the devil in this. It is our conviction that the true people of God should not be found in league with those who oppose the will and work of God for Israel.[15]

Malachy became assistant director of Israel's Department of Christian Affairs in the Ministry of Religious Affairs in 1968 and served as editor of the ministry's *Christian News from Israel*. Malachy died young, in 1972, but the Institute for Contemporary Jewry at Hebrew University edited the manuscript of his study of the Christian Zionist movement. In 1977, about the time that Begin came into office, it was published as *American Fundamentalism and Israel: The Relation of Fundamentalist Churches to Zionism and the State of Israel*.[16]

The Jerusalem Conference on Bible Prophecy

Premillennialists' interest in Israel increased dramatically after the Six-Day War, and Israeli officials encouraged this friendship. Many evangelicals believed that God had fought alongside Israel in its dramatically quick victory—in stark contrast to the United States' quagmire in Vietnam. Ben-Gurion, maintaining his connection with Christian Zionists after retiring from office, addressed a group of 1,400 Christians at the Jerusalem Conference on Bible Prophecy in 1971. Its organizer, a Pennsylvania minister named Gaylord Briley, promoted the conference as "a ringside seat at the second coming." Undeterred by this overtly Christian theology, the Israeli government provided the Jerusalem convention center free of charge as the conference site. Ben-Gurion was the highlight of the event, welcoming the participants and stressing that Israel is the land of the Bible. The former prime minister evidently remained fascinated by Christian Zionism until his death. When he died in 1973, Hal Lindsey's *The Late Great Planet Earth* was on his reading table.[17]

This Bible prophecy conference helped spur the large-scale evangelical tourism of Israel, which remains crucial to the Israeli economy today. The Israeli Ministry of Tourism brought hundreds of evangelical pastors to the Jewish state at no charge. A number of them, deeply impressed by the experience, started their own Holy Land tours. In 1981, Begin personally convinced David Lewis, an Assemblies of God pastor from Missouri, to open his own travel agency to promote Holy Land tours. Some of these group visits, including those led by Chuck Smith, founder of the Calvary Chapel movement, included mass baptisms of American Christians in the shallow waters of the Jordan River.[18] (Israelis joke that there is more history in the Jordan than there is water.)

As liberal Protestant support for Israel eroded following the Israeli Defense Forces' capture of the West Bank in 196, Jerusalem increasingly sought to develop its ties with evangelicals. Unlike many mainline Protestants, who began to see the Israelis as occupiers and the Palestinians as victims, many conservative Christians were enthusiastic about the occupation. Paul Boyer says that Israelis privately ridiculed the premillennialists' interpretations of Bible prophecy but recognized the importance of their support. In any case, in the 1970s and 1980s the Israeli government gave the red carpet treatment to Holy Land tours led by American pastors, including televangelist Oral Roberts. After one trip, Roberts exulted over the spiritual significance of events in Israel, which, he said, "leaps in my blood like a flame. God's ancient people are carving out an empire," he declared and did not hesitate to link this to the Second Coming of Jesus Christ. Top Israeli officials, including Defense Minister Moshe Arens, gave briefings to the tourists. Prime Minister Begin himself met a delegation of sixty American evangelical leaders on one occasion and discussed Ezekiel 38 and other Bible prophecies in individual meetings with pastors.[19] At least once, he hosted the Reverend Lewis and his wife at his home.[20]

Falwell and Begin

A serious Bible scholar and a romantic nationalist, Begin reportedly believed that anyone who reads and believes the Bible cannot be a bad person.[21] So it is little wonder that he liked evangelicals from the start. Zev Chafets, who was appointed director of the Israeli Government Press Office in 1977, says that Begin enjoyed swapping Old Testament quotes with Christians. And, like Christian Zionists, Begin believed that the Bible gives the Holy Land to the Jews eternally. One day the singer Johnny Cash, who loved Bible history, visited Begin, along with his wife, June Carter. The two American singers had just seen Masada, the fortress overlooking the Dead Sea where Jewish Zealots had resisted the Romans until, in a supreme act of defiance, they had committed mass suicide in A.D. 73. When Begin learned that his guests had just come from there, he startled them by slamming his hand on his desk and declaring, "Masada will never fall again!"[22]

Begin soon developed close ties to Jerry Falwell, who had become one of Israel's most stalwart Christian friends. Falwell hadn't always loved Israel and the Jews. He was, by his own admission, a redneck bigot as a young man. He became a Christian in 1952 and began to read the Bible intensively. From that time on, he says, the hatred and prejudice was flushed out of his system. He became increasingly committed to Israel and the Jewish people, internalizing the suffering that the Jews had experienced for thousands of years in the name of Christianity. In 1957, when enemies attacked his Thomas Road Baptist Church in Lynchburg, Virginia, it was local Jews who underwrote the renovation of the church, reinforcing his philo-Semitism. After the Six-Day War, support for the Jewish people and Israel became an obsession for Falwell. He made his first trip to Israel in the late 1960s and was deeply impressed, but he was shocked to realize that "the most important piece of real estate in the world is also one of the tiniest." He came to feel that Israel's destiny is the most crucial international issue in the world.[23]

When Falwell established the Moral Majority, becoming a power in the Republican Party, Begin saw how useful his support could be. The Israeli leader had no problem with the first three of the four principles on which this organization was funded: opposition to abortion (never a political issue for Begin), support of the family, and a strong American military. The fourth point, support for Israel, was all that Begin needed to see Falwell's value. Several commentators have reported that the Israeli leader gave Falwell a private jet to show his appreciation, but that is a myth. Begin did give him access and friendship, however. In 1980 he gave Falwell the prestigious Jabotinsky

Award—an act that Rabbi Alexander Schindler, the head of Reform Judaism, condemned, calling right-wing evangelicals "a danger to the Jews of the U.S."[24] Begin reportedly felt a strong enough alliance with Falwell to ask him in 1981 not to oppose the reelection of Senator Edward Kennedy the following year. Begin had become concerned after the 1980 elections, when the Moral Majority claimed credit for defeating three liberal senators who were also staunch allies of Israel, Jacob Javits, Frank Church, and Birch Bayh. Kennedy was one of the Senate's most reliable supporters of Israel and Begin did want to lose him.[25] The day after Israel bombed Iraq's nuclear facility at Osirak in 1982, Begin called Falwell to ask his help in shaping public opinion in the United States.

Falwell maintained a connection with every Israeli prime minister after Begin. He tried to help Yitzhak Shamir when George H. W. Bush pressed him to halt expansion of settlements in the West Bank, and he stood up for Benjamin Netanyahu when Bill Clinton pushed him to fulfill the terms of the Oslo agreement. Netanyahu called Falwell from Jerusalem in 1998 to say that Clinton had summoned him to Washington, D.C. On short notice, Falwell and Voices United for Israel arranged for 1,500 evangelicals to welcome Netanyahu at the Mayflower Hotel.[26] This display of popular Christian support for Netanyahu's government was intended to send a message to the American president. "It was all planned by Netanyahu as an affront to Mr. Clinton," said Falwell. Falwell promised Netanyahu that evening that he would mobilize 200,000 conservative Christian pastors across the United States to oppose handing any part of the West Bank over to the Palestinians. John Hagee made the same point as he roused the crowd by chanting, "Not one inch!"[27] The next day, Clinton confronted Netanyahu about this defiant snub, but, according to Falwell, in the middle of the meeting, an aide came in and informed him that the story had broken about his improper relationship with the young White House intern Monica Lewinsky. "Clinton had to save himself," Falwell recalled later, "so he terminated the demands" to relinquish territory in the West Bank.[28]

Falwell and other Christian Zionists developed ties with Ariel Sharon and Ehud Olmert as well. But the bridges they built are not limited to conservative prime ministers. (After Sharon and Olmert championed withdrawal from Palestinian territories, the question of who qualified as a conservative became problematic in any case.) Conservative Christian leaders also have a relationship with Ehud Barak. As prime minister, Barak offered part of Jerusalem to Arafat in a peace deal, which was anathema to most Christian Zionists. Yet he is listed as a faculty member of Pat Robertson's Regent University.[29]

"Empire, Colonialism, and Militarism"

Critics charge that dispensationalists and others who read the Bible literally hold that for Christ to return, the Jews must possess the entire land that God gave to Abraham. The result, according to this line of argument, is that conservative Christians oppose any pragmatic compromise between Israel and the Palestinians that is based on the exchange of land for peace. In "The Jerusalem Declaration on Christian Zionism" in 2006, the Latin Patriarch and the heads of three other Churches in Jerusalem offered an extreme expression of this criticism. They denounced Christian Zionism for embracing the Zionist "ideology of empire, colonialism and militarism." Christian Zionists, they declared, perpetuate policies of racial exclusivity and perpetual war, occupation, and militarism. "We categorically reject Christian Zionist doctrines as false teaching," they said. If these charges sound familiar, it is because most of them were taken verbatim from the Sabeel conference statement of two years earlier, cited in Chapter 6.

The heads of the major Christian Zionist organizations in Israel—Bridges for Peace, the International Christian Embassy Jerusalem, and Christian Friends of Israel—responded that this attack was inflammatory, unbalanced, and one-sided. "It totally ignores the jihadist goals of the Hamas government, and turns a blind eye to terrorism perpetuated by this regime," they said.[30] It is certainly true, however, that many evangelicals urge Israel not to give up land for peace. Moreover, their religious convictions have led some of the most prominent Christian supporters of Israel to threaten that God's vengeance will fall on anyone who tries to give back covenant land.

Christian Zionists have repeatedly warned that the Land of Israel belongs to God, not to man, and that He will punish anyone who tries to divide it. Speaking in October 2004 in Jerusalem, Pat Robertson affirmed that Israel is part of God's providential plan. Islam, on the other hand, wants "to destroy Israel and take the land from the Jews and give East Jerusalem to Yasser Arafat. I see that as Satan's plan to prevent the return of Jesus Christ, the Lord," Robertson said, adding, "God says, 'I'm going to judge those who carve up the West Bank and the Gaza Strip. It's my land and keep your hands off it."[31]

In his 2006 book, *Jerusalem Countdown,* John Hagee similarly warns of God's vengeance when he denounces the Roadmap for Peace (a phased plan toward Middle East peace devised by the Quartet: the United States, the European Union, the Soviet Union, and the United Nations). The Roadmap, Hagee contends, is an ill-conceived document that violates the Word of God. He cites

Joel 3:2, in which God says that he will gather all nations (including America, Hagee points out) in the valley of Jehoshaphat and pass judgment on them for dividing up his land, Israel. "When America forced Israel to give up Gaza, it was clearly violating Joel 3:2," Hagee declares (though he doesn't prove that the United States played such a role). "It's time for our national leaders in Washington to stop this madness," says Hagee.[32] Christian Zionists similarly deplore Prime Minister Ehud Olmert's "convergence" or "realignment" plan for unilaterally withdrawing from 95 percent of the West Bank.

The Dutch evangelical pastor Jan Willem van der Hoeven, a longtime resident of Israel and a founder of the International Christian Embassy Jerusalem, also declares that God will punish land-for-peace initiatives. "God has warned you repeatedly not to do this evil to your people and nation," says van der Hoeven. "He has even warned that he will severely judge the nations who advocate such a path"—an explicit threat to the United States and the rest of the Quartet. In 2006, van der Hoeven poured scorn on Olmert's rationale that withdrawal from the territories was necessary to maintain Israel's character as both democratic and Jewish. The real problem, van der Hoeven argued, is abortion. If Israelis had not terminated two million pregnancies since the founding of the state, there would be no demographic threat. "Go ahead," he said sarcastically, "give in to the pressures of a world that will in any case not fight for your survival." If the Israelis divided the land, van der Hoeven warned ominously, they would see what the divine answer will be.[33]

The American televangelist Perry Stone cites the prophet Zechariah to support the same argument. Zechariah speaks of the "apple of God's eye" (which Stone takes to refer to Jerusalem) and says that God will shake his hand against any nation that comes against it (Zechariah 2:8–9). "Leave Jerusalem alone," Stone exhorted the Bush administration on his ministry's Web site in 2007. America's leaders should "get their finger out of God's eye."[34]

Pat Robertson and Ariel Sharon

The natural conclusion of this religious logic is that God has already been punishing Israeli leaders who have sought to return land won in 1967 and the Americans who have urged them on. Early in 2006, Pat Robertson attracted a firestorm of criticism when he made this claim about Ariel Sharon. With sorrow and compassion, Robertson declared that God had inflicted a massive and disabling stroke on Sharon for withdrawing from Gaza and some settlements in the West Bank. Robertson then took this one step further. The assassination in 1995 of Israeli Prime Minister Yitzhak Rabin, he added, was "the same thing": God had used a young Israeli student named Yigal Amir to kill Rabin for signing the Oslo Accords, which envisioned a Palestinian state on covenant land, and for shaking Arafat's hand at the White House.[35]

Comments like these accelerated Robertson's loss of respect among fellow evangelicals, a decline that had been under way for years. He had reached the apex of his influence in the late 1980s and 1990s. He ran for the Republican nomination for president in 1988 and achieved significant political influence by founding the Christian Coalition in 1989. A 1995 *Time Magazine* cover story called Ralph Reed, the executive director of that organization, "the right hand of God" and credited the Christian Coalition with helping to engineer the "Republican revolution" in 1994. The Christian Coalition, said *Time,* had provided the winning margin for roughly half of the Republicans' fifty-two new congressmen and a sizable number of the nine new GOP senators were the organization's candidates. In the 1996 campaign, Robertson's group continued to have an impact on national politics, sending out 45 million voter guides.[36] Following Bob Dole's failed presidential run in that year and Reed's resignation in 1997, though, membership in the organization dropped. In 1999, the IRS denied it tax-exempt status. The Christian Coalition fell into debt and creditors filed lawsuits against it. Robertson resigned as its president in 2000.

Robertson has retained high visibility, however, in large part through his television program, the *700 Club,* for which he claims an audience of 18 million.[37] In keeping with his charismatic brand of evangelicalism, which embraces prophecy as one of the gifts of the Holy Spirit, Robertson believes that God speaks to him directly "all the time" and that he knows God's mind in some events. On the show, he ad-libs comments and shares revelations from God. That, combined with his disinhibited penchant for reckless candor, has added up to increasingly frequent notoriety—especially after his declaration that God played a role in 9/11 and his call for the assassination of Hugo Chavez, the president of Venezuela. His critics have always thought that he was out of his mind, but in recent years a lot of evangelicals have come to think so too, the journalist Zev Chafets observes.[38]

In early 2006, when he attributed Sharon's stroke to God, some of the most prominent evangelical leaders in the country rebuked Robertson, pointing out that he does not represent all conservative Christians. The Southern Baptist Convention's Richard Land said that Robertson speaks for "an ever diminishing number of evangelicals, and with each episode like this the rate of diminishment increases." Ted Haggard said that Robertson no more speaks for evangelicals than Dr. Phil does for psychologists.[39] Jim Wallis added that Robertson is a theocrat who gets his religion from the "twisted theologies of an American brand of right-wing fundamentalism."[40] The elites were not alone in disowning Robertson. "The vast majority of the evangelical center and progressives—which is to say more than half of evangelicals—are regularly embarrassed by Jerry Falwell and Pat Robertson," says Ron Sider, author of *The Scandal of the Evangelical Conscience.*[41] Born-again intellectual and former Watergate felon Chuck Colson also has gone on record rebuking Robertson: "I shudder every time I hear triumphalist statements by Christian leaders because they feed such fears." In a 2006 *Beliefnet* poll, half of white evangelicals gave Falwell an unfavorable rating and almost as many (46%) didn't like Robertson.[42] The press still confers on Robertson a level of importance that exceeds his actual influence, though. "The only person who takes Pat Robertson seriously is Tim Russert," says Michael Cromartie, vice president of the Ethics and Public Policy think tank in Washington, D.C., speaking of the host of NBC's *Meet the Press.*[43] After Robertson's comment about Sharon's stroke, the Israeli Ministry of Tourism declared that it would do no further business with him. That jeopardized a plan to build a $50–60 million Christian Heritage Center in the Galilee, though Chafets notes that the Center was only in the talking stage anyway and there were no other investors. In reality, Israeli officials weren't too shocked by Robertson's comments. Sharon's potential political heirs simply felt the need to defend his good name—though Sharon himself always was amused by right-wing Israeli rabbis who had said similar things for years. He probably would not have been particularly offended by Robertson's statement, says Chafets.[44]

What wasn't sufficiently reported in press accounts of this story was the deep personal commitment to Israel that Robertson has demonstrated for more than three decades, ever since 1974, when he vowed on the Mount of Olives to be a faithful friend of the Jewish state. Rabbi Yechiel Eckstein, founder of the International Fellowship of Christians and Jews, is convinced that evangelical support for Israel would not be as broad as it is if not for Robertson. "He and Jerry Falwell were the first to really stand up," Eckstein recalled. They signed a protest of the Reagan administration's sale of AWAC warplanes to Saudi Arabia, which Billy Graham declined to sign." Because of them, Christian support for Israel went from a tendency to a movement, Eckstein observed.[45]

My senior evangelical source, Faith, who knows Robertson well, told me one expression of his love for Israel that few people know about: Robertson feels that he should never turn down any opportunity to support Israel, whatever the personal cost. On one occasion, he was invited to a prayer breakfast at the Israeli embassy in Washington on the day that his wife was having surgery. Robertson was inwardly torn about attending, but he felt obliged to come, and he spoke forcefully at the event. He asked Faith to pray with him about his decision.

Israeli and Jewish American leaders have gone out of their way to show their appreciation of Robertson's commitment, both publicly and privately.

In 2001, the newly elected prime minister Ariel Sharon gave him the Jabotinsky award in recognition of his service to Israel. The following year, the Zionist Organization of America honored him with its State of Israel Friendship Award.[46] On a more personal occasion, Israeli officials flocked to a birthday party for Robertson at the King David Hotel in Jerusalem. Faith told me that Sharon was supposed to attend but had to decline because there were two bus bombings that morning. One of the evangelical Christians at the party was astounded by how many leaders did come, though. Israeli officials try not to congregate in any one place because of the fear of a terrorist attack, but a crowd of them showed up for Robertson's party. "It's a good thing they don't know who's in this room," she said of the terrorists.[47]

In a note to Sharon's sons, Robertson apologized for the insensitivity of his remarks about their father's illness. Israeli officials didn't forgive him immediately, though, and Christian organizations continued to distance themselves from him. *Christianity Today* editorialized that Israel should never have included Robertson in its plans for the Galilee project in the first place. "He has manipulated too many similar projects to his own personal financial ends," said the evangelical journal. "Israel tourism's breaking ties with him is healthy for Israeli politics and for the future of evangelical relations with Israel."[48]

Robertson retains tremendous influence and affection, however. Pastors of all Protestant denominations, asked to name the most trusted spokesperson for Christianity in 2004, ranked him tenth.[49] Many evangelicals just wish that he would be more politic. And less than two months after declaring, "We will do no business with him," the Israeli tourism ministry announced that it had engaged Robertson to appear in ads on the 700 *Club* in which he would personally appeal to evangelicals to visit Israel.[50]

In August 2006, as Hezbollah rained missiles on northern Israel, Robertson traveled there in a display of personal courage and support for the Jewish state. Prime Minister Olmert not only met with him in Jerusalem but joined hands with him as they prayed together for victory in Lebanon—despite the fact that Olmert is resolutely secular and highly cynical.[51] Tourism Minister Isaac Herzog declared that there was no longer any ambivalence about partnering with Robertson. Tourism in Israel, which is a mainstay of the state's economy, had fallen 40 percent below expectations for 2006. The Jewish state needed Robertson's help to win back evangelical visitors. In 2007 the Ministry of Tourism resumed negotiations with evangelical leaders on constructing the Christian Heritage Center. The Israelis ostensibly continued to exclude Robertson from the project, but they were working with Michael Little, the president of Robertson's Christian Broadcasting Network. "Nuts or not, Robertson is a man with his own university, an army of lawyers, and a million viewers a day," Chafets observes. The Israelis know that he's a good man to have on their side.[52]

"The Fist of God?"

The notoriety that has attended his comments did not dissuade Robertson from issuing yet another provocative warning in early 2007: that Olmert's government was moving toward national suicide by allowing the United States to push it toward establishing a Palestinian state.[53] Robertson could hardly say otherwise, believing as he does in the sanctity of the land and in the divine retribution that will follow if Israel appeases its Arab enemies. He is far from being the only one to believe that God punishes those who seek to divide the Holy Land. In 2002, on a segment of *60 Minutes* called "Zion's Christian Soldiers," Kay Arthur said of Rabin's assassination, "No person dies accidentally." Arthur, who has trained over 25,000 pastors and seminarians in Bible study and written over a hundred books, with more than five million copies in print, added, "I think that God did not want that Oslo Accord to go through." (On the same program, Jerry Falwell said that Mohammed was a terrorist.)[54] Hal Lindsey, whose *Late Great Planet Earth* galvanized evangelical understanding of Middle East events in the light of prophecy, stated a similar view in an online commentary. God has punished every Israeli leader who gave land to Muslim usurpers, said Lindsey. He cited in particular Begin, "who gave away the Sinai [and] resigned in disgrace in 1983," as well as Rabin and Sharon. Lindsey expresses his great fear for the United States and its leaders if they continue to push Israel toward a two-state solution. "God will judge the United States," he warns. "We will fall overnight."[55]

In August 2005, a number of evangelicals and Jews in Israel and the United States declared that God had sent Hurricane Katrina to devastate much of New Orleans and the surrounding area in order to punish America for supporting Israel's withdrawal of Jews from the settlements in Gaza. The Christian Zionist online news service *Jerusalem Newswire* ran an editorial headlined "Katrina—The Fist of God?" which said,

> For six days thousands of weeping people were pulled and carried from their homes. "While this was taking place, a small tropical depression was forming near the Bahamas . . . That small depression had turned into a frightening fiend . . . Is this some sort of bizarre coincidence? Not for those who believe in the God of the Bible . . . The Bible talks

about Him shaking his fist over bodies of water and striking them. While the "disengagement" plan was purportedly the brainchild of Israeli Prime Minister Ariel Sharon, the United States of America has for more than a decade been the chief sponsor and propeller of a diplomatic process that has dangerously weakened Israel . . . the Sharon disengagement plan was something that was forced on Israel, primarily by the United States.[56]

The Jerusalem-based Christian Friends of Israel said something similar in its e-mail update two days later: "We know that God only disciplines his own. Perhaps there are enough good men left in the United States that God thinks it worthwhile to send an occasional reminder not to tamper with the Land that He calls His own."[57] Jane Hansen noted that both 9/11 and Katrina happened in the Hebrew month of Elul, the time of repentance leading up to Yom Kippur. Could God be calling on Americans to turn back to him, wondered Hansen, who is the president of Aglow International, a worldwide transdenominational organization of evangelical Christian women.[58]

Seen from that faith perspective, Hurricane Katrina was not the only sign of God's anger over the withdrawal from Gaza. In March 2006, when bird flu was discovered in Israel, the *Jerusalem Newswire* cited three biblical precedents in which God sent illness or plague to punish the Israelites for their transgressions. Secular liberalism blinds most Israelis to the fact that the Lord punishes sin, the author argued.[59] For people who have a biblical view of the world, though, God's actions in defense of the Jews' scriptural patrimony are manifest. Indeed, Bill Koenig, a White House correspondent, has documented the consequences (i.e., curses) that occur whenever American presidents press Israel to divide covenant land. In his book *Eye to Eye: Facing the Consequences of Dividing Israel,* Koenig lists ninety-two record-setting catastrophes and terrorist events from 1991 to 2001 that struck the United States and the Jewish state within twenty-four hours of Israel's being pressured in this way.[60] In 2007, Koenig added, major natural disasters occurred in America after four of the six visits that Secretary of State Rice made to Israel on peace missions.[61] Bush's faith is genuine, Koenig told me in an interview, but God will punish him, too, for urging Israel to give up land. "The Lord showed me that someday President Bush will know the consequences of what he's done," he said. "The land is not to be divided."[62]

Opponents of this view say that by taking so obdurate a stand on any territorial compromise, "allies" like Robertson, Arthur, Lindsey, and Koenig effectively foreclose any possibility of peace in the Middle East. Instead, there will only be perpetual conflict. In the dispensational end-times scenario, the whole matter will be resolved by the Second Coming, and not before. But for people who yearn for Israel to have security now, this represents a potentially serious roadblock. It placed many leaders of the Christian right at odds with the Israeli policy of withdrawing from the Gaza Strip and parts of the West Bank. A few of the American Jewish leaders I interviewed put it bluntly: the evangelicals, they said, are prepared to fight to the last Jew. In fact, however, Christian Zionist leaders are unexpectedly flexible about this, both theologically and politically. They are surprisingly varied in their eschatology. And, as we shall see in the next chapter, they are far more pragmatic and accommodating in their posture toward Israel than their dire public threats and warnings would suggest. That is something that both the Bush administration and Ariel Sharon confirmed for themselves.

Pulsa Denura

Religious Zionist Israelis also see divine agency behind the misfortunes that have befallen leaders who chose to offer land for peace. Former chief rabbi Mordechai Eliyahu, the spiritual mentor of the National Religious Party, declared in 2006 that the land of Israel itself had struck down a long list of leaders who had proposed territorial concessions. The land, said Eliyahu, had performed a kabbalistic curse, a *pulsa denura* (Aramaic for "lash of fire"), against them. Any prime minister who carries out another disengagement, he warned, "may be disengaged from this world." Eliyahu's threat was chilling in view of reports that *pulsa denura* ceremonies were performed against Yitzhak Rabin shortly before he was assassinated in 1995 and against Ariel Sharon in July 2005, five months before his first stroke. Rabbi Eliyahu specifically denied that men could invoke such a curse, however. Only *Eretz Yisrael,* the land of Israel, could do so, he said. Eliyahu added that Kadima, the party founded by Ariel Sharon and subsequently headed by Olmert, was led by sinners who had divided the land and so "betrayed the entire nation."[63] The belief that God avenges men's attempts to divide the land is not restricted to these few rabbis. In 2007, one in every four religious and ultra-orthodox Jews in Israel believed that Sharon's illness was a punishment from heaven. An offshoot of the Chabad movement declared that every leader who perpetrated "the crime of disengagement" from Gaza would also be punished by God.[64]

Radical Muslims also saw a divine hand in Sharon's stroke, though for very different reasons. Sheik Raed Salah said in September 2006 that Allah had punished Sharon for allegedly planning to break into the Al Aqsa mosque.

Salah, the head of the northern faction of the Islamic Movement, told a crowd of 50,000 at that group's annual rally that Allah similarly punished American President Bill Clinton and Israeli President Moshe Katsav. Both of them wanted to divide sovereignty of the mosque between Jews and Muslims, said the sheik, so Allah afflicted them with charges of sexual misbehavior. Muslims will retain control of the mosque and Jerusalem will be the capital of the new caliphate, vowed Salah, who served three years in an Israeli prison for aiding terrorism by funneling money to Hamas.[65]

8

❧❈❧

God's Timetable

Theologically Speaking, "So What?"

The claim that all Christian Zionists adamantly demand that Israel keep every inch of its biblical territory is vastly overstated. So is the charge that they are yearning for the Jews to convert or die at the end of time. In fact, Many Israeli officials and American Jewish community leaders dismiss these concerns with a joke (actually, it's the same joke in every case). And many of the most prominent evangelical supporters of Israel, despite their uncompromising public declarations, acknowledge that they will respect the right of the democratically elected Israeli government to give up land in the hope of gaining peace. They may think that such policies are suicidal and inimical to God's plan, but they'll accept them. As always, their politics comports with their theology.

This has been widely misunderstood, even among well-informed observers. Leon Wieseltier, the often-brilliant literary editor of *The New Republic,* for example, calls the alliance between Christian Zionists and Jews "a grim comedy of mutual condescension." Evangelicals offer their support before they convert or kill the Jews, he says, and the Jews accept them as allies while believing that their eschatology is nonsense. "This is a fine example of the political exploitation of religion," Wieseltier concludes.[1] There is, of course, no evangelical plot to kill Jews. Classic dispensationalism does expect Jews to accept Jesus or die in the last days, but many Christian Zionists today disavow that belie, as we shall see. And while there is widespread popular concern about evangelicals' motives for backing Israel, many Israeli officials and American Jewish leaders are actually quite comfortable accepting their support. Not one whom I interviewed expressed contempt for Christian eschatology. Certainly very many Jews do. But the Jewish American and Israeli officials I talked with simply weren't worried about it. The more politically conservative among them welcome the Christian Zionists' political views, which agree with their own.

As early as 1981, Rabbi Marc Tannenbaum, then-director of interreligious affairs for the American Jewish Committee, said that it would be self-destructive for Jews to turn aside evangelicals' support because of their eschatology. The Moral Majority's intentions may not be pure, he observed, but for the sake of heaven, "the effects can be pure." The following year, Nathan Perlmutter, then-director of the Anti-Defamation League, said that he wasn't concerned about dispensationalists' end-times beliefs.[2] The same attitude prevails among many Israeli government officials and Jewish organizational leaders today. Every one of them I spoke with had the same response to the dispensational end-times scenario: essentially, "So what?" "I say to evangelicals, when the Messiah comes, we'll ask him if it's the first time or the second," a top official at the Israeli consulate in New York told me. "If he says it's the first time, you'll apologize to me. If it's the second, I'll apologize to you." This joke dates back more than fifty years. The great Israeli writer Amos Oz recalls his grandmother's saying it to him when he was a child, in the 1940s or early 1950s. "You'll see," she told him. "Christians believe that the Messiah was here once and he will certainly return one day. The Jews maintain that he is yet to come. Over this . . . over this, there has been so much anger, persecution, bloodshed, hatred. . . . Why can't everyone simply wait and see? If the Messiah comes, saying 'Hello, it's nice to see you again,' the Jews will have to concede. If, on the other hand, the Messiah comes, saying, 'How do you do, it is very nice meeting you,' the entire Christian world will have to apologize to the Jews." Until then, she told young Amos, we should just live and let live.[3] Jewish leaders have been telling this joke for decades and I heard half a dozen versions of it. Many of them understand that Christians may be motivated by apocalyptic end-times beliefs, but they use diplomatic good humor to shrug off any insult or threat. Rabbi Yechiel Eckstein, who speaks to evangelical listeners with clarity and candor, also told this story at a conference that his International Fellowship of Christians and Jews organized in Washington, D.C., in September 2005. He added a twist, though. Knowing his mixed audience and the sensitivity of this matter, Eckstein said that when the Messiah is asked at a press conference at the end of time if it's his first coming or his second, being the Prince of Peace, he'll answer, "No comment."[4]

Malcolm Hoenlein also considers the whole end-times issue unthreatening. The executive vice chairman of the Conference of Presidents of Major Jewish

Organizations, Hoenlein represents the organized American Jewish community to the White House, the other branches of U.S. government, and the American public. As we sat in his small office on Third Avenue in New York, its walls and shelves filled with memorabilia of his association with presidents and prime ministers, Hoenlein pointed out that his collection also includes mementos of Christian support for Israel. In his view, Jews who fear evangelicals are actually anxious about their own religious identity. "The problem is that people aren't secure enough in their Judaism," Hoenlein said. "That's why they feel threatened by what the evangelicals represent." He appreciates Christian support for Israel and spoke that day with special warmth of John Hagee, who had just announced his new pro-Zionist lobby, Christians United for Israel. Hoenlein is keenly aware of the range of views among conservative Christians and the delicate complexity of accepting their support, however. "We need as many friends as we can get," he told me, "but you don't make common cause because somebody happens to share a view with you. We can differ on other issues with respect, appreciate what we can do together, and establish the conditions for a dialogue. We do it with Jesse Jackson and others. Why can't we do it with them?" And the end-of-days scenario? "At the end of time we'll worry about it," he remarked.[5]

Abe Foxman, the current national director of the Anti-Defamation League, says essentially the same thing. Foxman has never hesitated to do battle with anyone who demeans Jews or tries to tear down the wall between church and state. In 1994, in fact, Foxman's organization issued *The Religious Right: The Assault on Tolerance and Pluralism in America,* a book-length critique of conservative Christians' attempt to break down church-state separation. This report gave particular attention to Pat Robertson. Though noting his support for Israel, the ADL accused Robertson of scapegoating and even threatening Jews. The report specifically rebuked him for suggesting that Jews were trying to de-Christianize the United States.[6] Foxman has no problem with evangelical backing for Israel based on end-times theology, though—as long as it's offered with no quid pro quo. If their support came with conditions, such as expecting Jews to be silent while they attempt to Christianize America, "I'd say, '*Gey gesunterheyt*'" (Yiddish for "Go in good health," i.e., "I'm done with you!"), Foxman told me. But he has often pointed out that there are no strings when Christians champion Israel out of religious conviction, including eschatology. A lot of American politicians support Israel to get money and votes, Foxman observed. Evangelicals do it because of faith. "That's okay and this isn't?" he asked, with a little Jewish twist in his syntax.[7] "We must manage our relationship with the Christian right with care and vigilance," Foxman cautions. On the other hand, "When you are in danger and someone offers you help, you don't question the purity of their motives. You just accept the help." As for Christians who are motivated to hasten the advent of Christ, Foxman offers a variant of the familiar refrain: "I figure that when the Messiah comes we can ask whether he—or she—has been here before and settle the question once and for all."[8]

Elliott Abrams, deputy national security adviser in the White House, has said for years that Jews should accept Christian backing for Israel. In his book *Faith or Fear: How Jews Can Survive in a Christian America* Abrams asks, if most Jews support Israel for religious reasons, why shouldn't Christians have the same privilege? "Many Jews argue that evangelicals favor Jewish control of the Holy Land because they see it as a step toward the messianic era when Jesus returns, and therefore as a means to an end inimical to Judaism," he notes. "But the support itself is surely no less valuable or authentic."[9]

God's Mystery and Land for Peace

In fact, many evangelicals' end-of-days beliefs are neither uniform nor rigid, and their faith doesn't necessarily lead to inflexible political convictions about Israel. Several factors moderate Christian Zionists' eschatology. One is that for many evangelicals, premillennial end-time views are not core doctrines. Ted Haggard says in his book *Primary Purpose,* for example, that most eschatology, including pre-Tribulation Rapture theology, is only a deduction; it is far less certain than a core belief.[10] Nor do all conservative Christians link biblical prophecy to events in Israel today. Not even all Christian Zionists do that. Billy Graham, for example, acknowledges that at one time he tried to force prophetic passages to correspond to events in the Middle East. "But I came to see that this was not wise or necessary," says Graham.[11]

Another important factor is that even evangelicals who accept prophetic claims may abandon those that are not central to their beliefs.[12] This allows political pragmatism—and even the most controversial evangelical leaders often are pragmatists.

One more key fact is that pious Christians frequently disagree about eschatology. As one Baptist minister said jokingly, evangelicals are all "pan-millennialists": they believe that everything will pan out in the end.[13] Many born-again Christians have only a very vague notion of Israel's role in the final days, and even among evangelical elites there is remarkable diversity and nuance in their beliefs. That, in turn, allows flexibility about the principle of land-for peace. Indeed, though it flies in the face of the common stereotype, 52 percent of evangelical leaders are in favor of a Palestinian state on land that God promised to Abraham, as long as it doesn't threaten Israel! That may surprise people who fear born-again Christians' obduracy on the question of covenant land. But the explanation, says the University of Akron's John Green, is simple: They want to see peace in the Middle East.[14]

Even when evangelicals do share a common understanding of the final events, they inevitably concede that the mystery of God's providence may confound their expectations. Robert Stearns, the leader of Eagles' Wings, is representative. In an interview, I asked what he was thinking that night at the Rend the Heavens conference in New Jersey when he praised then-prime minister Sharon's courage in determining to withdraw from Gaza, as we saw in Chapter 1. Robert explained, "God is not on my timetable. God sees the end from the beginning. What seems contrary to my understanding of promises doesn't mean that's how things will play out in twenty years." In the long term, God's covenants are true, he said, and asked, "Who am I to know God's intentions?" We must be peacemakers, Robert told me, but quickly added, "I don't think you're going to get peace for land. The educational system in Palestine leads only to hatred. . . . But the decision has been made. Let's do our best to make sure people keep their commitments."[15] Several evangelical pastors and other Christian leaders in the United States and Jerusalem say very similar things. The key principle, as always, is that their political views accord with their faith.[16]

The Bush Administration Assessed Evangelical Convictions

The Bush administration took these evangelical religious-political convictions into account before declaring U.S. policy. A high White House official asked the Southern Baptist Convention's Richard Land, for example, how Southern Baptist voters would react if the United States supported Israel's disengagement from Gaza. Land replied that if the democratically elected government of Israel decides of its own volition to give back territory for peace, most evangelicals will respect that. This political assessment is consistent with Land's own eschatology, which holds that Israel won't have possession of all of the covenant land until the second advent of Christ. Until that time, he says, "Our understanding is that Jews will be in the land in great numbers. But nothing requires Jews to be in control of all of the land." As a result, he would be comfortable with a two-state solution.[17] In fact, Land said in 2003, "Nothing could be more secure for Israel than creating a viable, self-sustaining Palestinian state that agrees to live in peace and agrees to suppress terrorism." Most evangelicals agree with that, he notes. That is why the most popular president ever, for them, was George W. Bush, the first president to make a two-state solution American Middle East policy.[18]

Startling as it may seem, Pat Robertson reportedly gave the White House comparable advice: Republicans would not lose many evangelical votes if Bush encouraged Israel to give up parts of the West Bank.[19] His public declarations, as always, warned of catastrophe if Israel ever yielded on that. In early 2006 Robertson implicitly attributed Ariel's Sharon's stroke to the disengagement from Gaza, as we have seen. That August, as Robertson visited Israel during the second Lebanon war, he remained strongly opposed to giving land for peace. He called Ehud Olmert's plan to withdraw from most of the West Bank "an absolute disaster." And yet Robertson was flexible about how he would respond if Israel carried out the plan. "I don't think the holy God is going to be happy about someone giving up his land," he observed. "But that would be between Mr. Olmert and his God. It isn't for me to say." It's up to the Israelis as a free society to determine their own actions, he said.[20]

Jerry Falwell adopted a similar posture for decades. "I am quite content to see Israel possess all the territory from the Jordan to the Mediterranean Sea," he said in 1984. But, he added, "If Israel desires to give up part of her land to her neighbors, that is her business."[21] Over twenty years later he took precisely the same position about Sharon's withdrawal from Gaza. "I trust Israeli leaders to know what they're doing," Falwell noted. That fits with his religious conviction that Christ's Second Coming probably won't happen anytime soon. There will be time enough for Israel to recover its biblical patrimony before Christ returns.[22]

Senator James Inhofe also acknowledges that Israel should be free to cede land for peace, however ill-advised he thought that was. Critics of Christian Zionism often cite Inhofe's March 2002 Senate speech as an extreme formulation of the religious and other reasons that Israel should keep the West Bank. And, in fact, the Oklahoma senator did list "Because God said so" as the most important reason to hold on to the land. But even he prefaced his comments with the statement, "If this is something that Israel wants to do, it is their business to do it."[23]

Ted Haggard's Advice to Ariel Sharon

Ted Haggard, then-president of the NAE, gave Sharon a similar assurance in 2004. Sharon asked him if evangelicals would abandon Israel if it disengaged from Gaza. No, Haggard replied. "We all have an undergirding theology that's supportive even when portions of us are unhappy at specific things you may do." Most conservative evangelicals will be upset and angered by the Disengagement, Haggard told him. But within nine months they'll be supportive again.

Sharon then asked him how evangelicals felt about Israel's pulling back from Judea and Samaria in the West Bank in order to build a separation fence on the Palestinian side of the 1967 border. As it happens, the prime minister asked him this on July 9, a few hours after the International Court of Justice in The Hague had ruled that the 437-mile Israeli barrier is illegal. "We are a law-and-order people," Pastor Ted told him, "but you have your citizens being blown up." A bus had exploded in front of Haggard's hotel. "There were poor people in those buses," he recalled later. "Arab body parts were mixed with Jewish body parts in that explosion." The barrier would reduce the number of such attacks by preventing Palestinian terrorists from infiltrating from the West Bank. So he encouraged Sharon to build the wall because walls work, a pragmatic rather than a theological reason. "Until there is a partner to negotiate with, I don't know that there's any choice but to have a wall," Pastor Ted said.

As for leaving covenant land on the Palestinian side of the barrier, Haggard told Sharon that not once since God established the borders of Israel have the Jewish people controlled all of the land that God promised them. In that sense, Israel was already in disobedience. "If you're going to have biblical borders," he told the Israeli leader, "then go take them." Since Israel didn't seize all of the covenant land, though, it should be free to adjust its existing borders. He offered an analogy, "If you're committing adultery, you're committing adultery. It doesn't matter if you're committing adultery a little." (The irony in Pastor Ted's rebuking adultery was not apparent until two years later, when he resigned from the NAE amid charges that he had paid a gay prostitute for sex.)

Sharon then asked Haggard to explain why he thought it was okay to give the land back or to take it. The American replied that he didn't think there was a biblical exhortation about that, but he had a very practical concern, which again had nothing to do with theology: part of the problem, he said, was that we call the land "occupied territory." "Just think, if we called Texas 'occupied territory,'" Pastor Ted told the Israeli leader. "There would be constant struggles between the U.S. and Mexico. So we call it the United States of America. We took it. We own it. We've defended it. That's what you need to do. So you need to give the occupied territory back or annex it. Take it." As long as the land was considered Palestinian property, though, he urged Sharon not to build the wall on it. That would cause constant problems. Instead, the wall should adhere to the internationally recognized 1967 borders. He also advised the prime minister to secretly promise his Arab neighbors that Israel would never invade them; Sharon should warn them, though, that if they ever attacked and Israel secured land, it would keep it forever. Pastor Ted stressed to me later that he would never have said any of these things without being asked. It's not the role of American evangelicals to tell the elected government of Israel what to do, he said, or to tell the State Department how to deal with Israel. "It's only our role to answer questions when asked."

Haggard's liberality on the issue of the land derives from his theology, or at least agrees with it. As he told Sharon, Israel needn't hold on to borders that are currently not biblical. There was another consideration inherent in his advice to the Israeli leader, however, one that I didn't expect: unlike many evangelicals, Pastor Ted does not support Israel because of his end-time beliefs. Rather, he backs it chiefly for geopolitical reasons, because the Jewish state is a bastion of democracy and an ally. He blesses and advocates for Israel, but he believes that the Jewish people all over the world are in fact the Israel of which the Bible speaks. "Israel is Israel even if the state of Israel did not exist," he told me. "I hope that Israel is there for the next five hundred years," he said. But if there were no Jewish state, that wouldn't affect Haggard's beliefs about the Second Coming, because Israel would still exist, in the Jewish people. His backing for the Israeli state does have spiritual dynamics, he said. He is strongly influenced by Genesis 12:3, but that promise of blessing, he believes, refers to all of the Jewish people around the globe. "Since Israel is the only nation with a Jewish majority, that triggers the Genesis blessing for Israel," he said. "I am a Christian Zionist. But I am not a Christian Zionist because of eschatology. My commitment to Israel isn't as dynamic or as apocalyptic as it is in the minds of some of my evangelical friends." In Haggard's belief-system, Christ's return is not contingent on Israel's occupying all of the land covenanted to Abraham. His advice to Sharon was consistent with that conviction.[24]

Different Theological Routes to the Same Conclusion

Ray Sanders, director of Christian Friends of Israel, one of the major evangelical philanthropic organizations in Jerusalem, takes a different theological route to arrive at the same position as Land, Robertson, and Haggard. He also accepts that Israel may make political compromises with covenanted land. But his reasoning is that the disengagement from Gaza is God's punishment of the Israelis for not keeping his commandments—for being secular rather than observant Jews.[25]

David Parsons and Malcolm Hedding of the International Christian Embassy in Jerusalem (ICEJ) reach a similar conclusion. Parsons, the ICEJ public relations officer, says that the fact that Israel owns the land by divine right doesn't mean that God wants the Jews to live on all of it now. The Lord, says Parsons, was never able to place all of the land in his Chosen People's hands because they were disobedient (Nehemiah 9:15). "Our reading of the Bible leads us to believe this will only be fully realized in the Messianic kingdom," says Parsons. The troubles that the Jewish state is facing are part of a process of affliction aimed at redemption (Hosea 5:14–6:3). "For Christians to insist that Israel should keep all the land that God has brought her back to without reference to her spiritual condition is an error and many are making it," Parsons concludes. "We must be patient with God and trust that He who brought her back thus far will not fail her now."[26]

In 2004 Hedding, the ICEJ executive director, asked fellow Christian Zionists, "So, what do we say about the [Gaza] Disengagement Plan?" His answer? "Nothing." Like Land, Haggard, Robertson, and Falwell, Hedding says that born-again Christians are not called to give Israel's leaders political advice. If the Israelis dismantle settlements on covenant land, said Hedding, evangelicals will acquiesce.[27] In the event, that is exactly what happened. During the disengagement from Gaza in 2005, Christian Zionist leaders were frustrated and baffled, but few spoke up to object. Rather, most watched in passive discomfort as Israeli forces removed thousands of Jewish settlers from their homes. The Israelis drew a red line in the sand," my senior source Faith told me. "We didn't know what to think or do."[28] The comparative silence among evangelicals at the time prompted the Web-based Christian Zionist *Jerusalem Newswire* to run the despairing headline "Where are the Christians?"[29]

Hedding acknowledges the power of eschatology on evangelicals' political views. "What you think of the end will always determine the present," he told me. Evangelical Christians have a hard time accepting that Israel, which they love so much and idealize too much, chose to go down the road of surrendering Gaza, he said. He added, however, "There has to be a call to reason here." Evangelicals are proud that Israel is a democracy, he said, though, to prevent disengagement, they wish it were a theocracy. But that will only come with Christ's return, Hedding declared, and "the King is not here yet!" Jesus Christ has not yet established his millennial kingdom.[30] Politics accords with faith, as ever. Hedding's acceptance of disengagement fits with his biblical perspective, as he made clear in a speech in October 2004: "Israel has lost her land and will probably lose more because God is dealing with her. We are Biblical Zionists; not political Zionists. Our position must be to call out to God, 'Save them and bring them to yourself.' . . . 'All Israel shall be saved' and THEN she will have all the land."[31] In 2006 Hedding and Jurgen Buhler made this point plainly: most Israelis are secular, unfaithful to God, they said. Therefore He shrinks their land to correct and save them, and it is naïve for Christians to expect otherwise. This does not legitimize the PLO, Hamas, and others who work for Israel's destruction, however. God promised two exiles and two returns and these have already taken place. Israel will never be exiled again.[32]

Becky Brimmer, international president of Bridges for Peace, told me that giving back covenant land goes against God's ultimate intentions. But "don't put God in a box," she cautioned. "How it will fit into God's plan, I don't know." Is ceding the land part of Satan's scheme to undo God's intentions for Israel? "Many Christians do believe that," she said. "I don't think that Disengagement fits in with the plan in the Tanach [the Hebrew Bible]. But God thinks differently than people do," she told me, and she offered some examples, with her characteristic good humor, of how she wouldn't have thought as God did. "I would build boats, not part the Red Sea," she said, citing Exodus. And "I wouldn't send people to Nineveh by way of a big fish," she remarked of the Jonah story. God moves on his own timetable, she observed, just as Robert Stearns and many others said. "There's an old joke," she told me. "God says, 'Yeah, I'll do it in just a minute'"—and the minute takes centuries.[33]

Jack Hayford, one of the most senior and prominent Christian Zionists in America, made the same point. "I am a friend of Israel's, sink or swim," he said, and he affirmed, "Yes! Israel will have all its land, but it will be in God's time, not man's." Hayford added a surprising twist, though, one that illustrates the striking diversity that marks evangelical thought: he declared that Sharon's "giveaway" of the Gaza Strip in 2005 was Christ-like. It did not invite God's wrath, as some evangelical leaders had declared, said Hayford. The Israeli prime minister wanted to make peace. Jesus said that God approves of that, Hayford reminded us (Matthew 5:9).[34]

Christians United for Israel

John Hagee, pastor of the 17,000-member Cornerstone Church in San Antonio, Texas, is one of the most dedicated and outspoken American Christian Zionists. He ardently supports Israel as a heroic outpost of Judeo-Christian values on the front lines of the fight against Islamic fascists. Yet he also expresses a surprising willingness to accept Israel's right to cede land for peace.

"In June of 1978, I went to Israel as a tourist and came home as a Zionist," Hagee recalled. "I have traveled the world but as I walked the cobblestone streets of the Holy City, I knew I was home! My roots were there! I felt a very special presence in that sacred city that changed my life forever!"[35] His public advocacy of Israel began in 1981, when Israeli jets bombed the Iraqi nuclear reactor at Osirak. He was shocked by the public hostility to this act in the West. Hagee, by contrast, felt that Israel had done the world a favor and he proposed to his congregation and to other pastors in San Antonio that they organize an event to celebrate the Jewish state. They've been mounting a gala Night to

Honor Israel every year since, and raising money for Israel. At the 2007 event alone, John Hagee Ministries gave Israel over $8 million dollars, as we have seen.[36]

In February 2006 Hagee announced the formation of a potentially important umbrella organization called the Christians United for Israel (CUFI), which he intends to be a Christian version of the influential Jewish lobby, AIPAC, only stronger. The new Christian Zionist lobby will be a "political earthquake," Hagee declared. It comprises a dozen regional directors and a network of evangelical political activists who can be reached within twenty-four hours to lobby senators and congressmen. Robert Stearns is regional director of New York and four other states in the Northeast, and the board of directors includes Benny Hinn and Jack Hayford, major supporters of Israel. Hagee intends CUFI to have teeth: he plans to establish a rapid-response center to flood Capitol Hill with e-mails, faxes, and phone calls on issues of immediate concern to the Jewish state.[37] CUFI also plans to organize nights to celebrate Israel in every major U.S. city, in Canada, and around the world, and will provide a canopy for Christians to speak with one voice in support of Israel. It claims a membership of 50,000.

In CUFI's first lobbying effort, in July 2006, over 3400 Christian Zionists from all fifty states answered Hagee's call to come to Washington, D.C. The event began with a banquet in the main ballroom of the Hilton Hotel. Charismatic Christians and Baptists danced in the aisles, waved American and Israeli flags, and sang the U.S. national anthem and *Hatikvah* as the sound of a shofar rang out. An evangelical group sang in Hebrew. From a stage adorned with an enormous Israeli flag, Jerusalem's ambassador to the United States, Danny Ayalon, set the tone for the evening by naming Iran as the center of Islamofascism. Hagee, in the keynote speech, cited Isaiah 62: "For Zion's sake I will not be silent. You are not alone," to which the audience replied, "Amen!" He read greetings from President Bush and from Prime Minister Olmert, who praised CUFI's acknowledgment of Israel's biblical birthright. Though the CUFI event had been planned months before, it happened to take place as Israel was conducting military operations in Gaza and Lebanon, following attacks by Hamas and Hezbollah. Hagee said of the recent terrorist acts, "The dots are there to be connected and it is not some big thing called terrorism." Rather, he declared, the problem is Islamic fascism, which is waging a war against Western civilization. He called the president of Iran a new Hitler, a comparison that religious and political conservatives made with increasing frequency in 2006, as we have seen. "The ghost of Hitler is walking across Europe and the Middle East," Hagee warned. Echoing Churchill's admonition about the Nazi threat seventy years earlier, Hagee declared, "What is America's and Israel's aim in fighting

Islamo-fascism? Victory at all costs." Israel, he declared, was doing God's work in a war of good versus evil, to which the crowd applauded wildly and said, "Amen."

Hagee then introduced his old ally from San Antonio, Rabbi Aryeh Scheinberg, who recited the *Motzee* (the Hebrew blessing over the bread).[38] Ken Mehlman, chairman of the Republican National Committee, declared, "Today, if you love freedom, whether you are Christian, Jewish, or Muslim, whether you are American, Japanese, or Indian, today we are all Israelis." Then-Senator Rick Santorum (R-Pennsylvania) warned that Iran's leaders intend to destroy Israel in order to bring on the twelfth Imam. Elliot Engel, a Democratic congressman from New York who is Jewish, used the language of prominent Christian Zionists: Israel's enemies do the work of Satan, he declared. Gary Bauer also spoke, assuring the assembled Christian Zionists of their potency in opposing Islamic extremism: "You are Hezbollah's greatest nightmare," he told them. Jerry Falwell bluntly put the Bush administration on notice that he would rebuke the State Department for ever telling Israel to stand down and show restraint. The packed audience applauded enthusiastically.[39]

The next day, the participants deployed on Capitol Hill to hold 280 meetings with their congressional representatives. David Brog, Senator Arlen Specter's former chief of staff and now executive director of CUFI, had spelled out the talking points for the Christians. One was that "Israel must not be pressured to withdraw its troops before the job has been completed." Another, given the continued terrorism against Israel after its withdrawal from southern Lebanon and Gaza, was that the United States "should never pressure Israel to give up land that it believes is necessary for its security."[40] CUFI leaders already had pressed these points at the White House in a series of off-the-record meet-and-greet sessions with Bush advisers. Hagee specifically had stressed to Elliott Abrams that, in the past, whenever the State Department had imposed a cease-fire on Israel, the Palestinians had used that time to rearm and retaliate. According to Hagee, Abrams essentially agreed. Leaving the White House, "we felt we were on the right track," Hagee said later. Congress, for its part, needed little persuasion. On the day of the CUFI banquet, the Senate passed a bipartisan, AIPAC-sponsored resolution supporting Israel's military campaign and blaming Hezbollah, Iran, and Syria for the conflict. The House then passed a strongly pro-Israel resolution by 410 to 8.[41]

CUFI's second mass lobbying effort in Washington, in 2007, drew over 4,000 delegates from around the country. The speakers renewed the denunciations of Islamic fascism that had informed the 2006 event, along with repudiations of Ahmadinejad as the new Hitler. One warned that Iran would try to destroy Israel first, then America, a variation on a theme that dispensationalists first applied to Russia, then to Islamic extremists.[42] Speakers also denounced appeasement, a major concern among Christian Zionists. Hagee, for example, warned that the State Department and the Europeans wanted to turn Israel into "crocodile food," a reference to Churchill's definition of appeasers as people who feed a crocodile hoping that they'll be eaten last. Newt Gingrich, the former Speaker of the House, charged that Bush's recent proposal of a regional Mideast peace conference was nothing more than appeasement of the Arabs. "We don't have a peace process. We have a surrender process," said Gingrich, who was thinking of seeking the Republican nomination for president at the time. And Gary Bauer showed the temperament of the CUFI participants when he declared that evangelicals were praying that Israel will never give up one centimeter of land, even under American pressure. The audience burst into applause and stood up waving Israeli flags.[43]

The speakers also reflected the debate then under way in Washington on whether to set a deadline for withdrawing U.S. troops from Iraq. They skewed their remarks to focus on Israel. Senator John McCain (R-Arizona), then beginning his campaign for the Republican presidential nomination, asserted that for America to prematurely draw down its forces would lead to catastrophe—and would threaten the Jewish state. McCain, who was trying to rebuild bridges he had burned with conservative evangelicals in 2000 when he called Robertson and Falwell "agents of intolerance," drew loud and repeated standing ovations. "Israel will survive!" he assured the audience. "There will always be an Israel." Hamas must be isolated, Hezbollah disarmed, and Iran chastened by economic sanctions, said McCain. Senator Joe Lieberman (Independent-Connecticut) also warned of catastrophe to America and Israel if the U.S. pulled out of Iraq hastily. Lieberman called Hagee an *Ish Elochim* (a "man of God" in Hebrew) and compared him to Moses: both led "a mighty multitude in pursuit and defense of Israel," said Lieberman. Rabbi Scheinberg added that Hagee "personifies God's living words" and Roy Blunt, the House Republican Whip, declared that CUFI is "part of God's plan."[44]

CUFI set out several issues for the amateur lobbyists to support when they met with their legislators, including increased foreign aid to Israel, steps to enable the international force in Lebanon to contain Hezbollah, and the Iran Counter-Proliferation Act, which would impose sanctions on Tehran for pursuing nuclear arms. The delegates also were told to urge legislators from their home states to keep all options on the table for dealing with Iran, including a preemptive military strike. On the third day of the conference, they met with fifty-seven senators and over 220 congressmen, many of whom responded warmly. There was some sharp debate, though, in the office of Congresswoman Betty McCollum (D-Minnesota). McCollum had declined to come to CUFI's Night to Honor Israel in Minnesota three months earlier, citing Hagee's "repugnant" statements, such as his charge that the Qur'an requires Muslims to kill Christians and Jews. Now Bill Harper, McCollum's chief of staff, called the CUFI leaders radicals. "They are dangerous to any prospects of ending the conflict between Israelis and Palestinians," he said. Senator Bob Corker (R-Tennessee), on the other hand, praised the group after meeting with eighty-five CUFI delegates on the Capitol steps. The clarity of their message has endeared them to many people, said Corker diplomatically. After this meeting, several CUFI members lingered. Forming a circle, they held hands and prayed. "We know we'll get blessed because we're blessing Israel," said one of them, the organization's co-director for Tennessee.[45]

"They Out-Likud the Likudniks"

CUFI's politics are the subject of anxious debate, not least among Jews. Michelle Goldberg, critic of the Christian right and author of *Kingdom Coming: The Rise of Christian Nationalism,* commented that Hagee's influence is dangerous because it makes Americans support Bush's "completely one-sided, hawkishly pro-Israel stance" in support of Israel's military action in Lebanon.[46] Journalist Max Blumenthal accused Hagee of praying for Armageddon and trying to get America and Israel to base their foreign policy on his Armageddon-based worldview. In a series of articles, the journalist Sarah Posner charged that Hagee exaggerated the Iranian threat and served Bush administration hawks by firing up grass-roots support for a preemptive strike on Iran.[47] In his book *Jerusalem Countdown,* however, Hagee dreads an Iranian attack on the West and seeks to prevent it. He believes the prophecies about the tribulations of the end-times are inevitable, and he thinks those times may be imminent. He does not cheer for the end to come, however.

Some critics worried that CUFI would work to undermine Olmert's plan to pull out of 90 percent of the West Bank by 2010. The organization's Web site expresses "support of Israel's right to the land by Biblical Mandate," citing the Lord's promise to give Abraham and his offspring all of the land within his range of sight, to the north, south, east, and west, forever (Genesis 13:14–17). "They out-Likud the Likudniks," said the NAE's Richard Cizik, referring to the right-wing Israeli political party. "I think they're more adamant about the land than Israel itself."[48] "If they oppose the government, it's an anti-Israeli lobby as far as I'm concerned," declared Rabbi Eric Yoffie, president of the Union for Reformed Judaism. "I would consider that dangerous to Israel." He has no doubt that Hagee's policies contradict those of the Bush administration and the state of Israel. Yoffie also considers it deeply disturbing that AIPAC conferred legitimacy on Hagee by inviting him to speak at its policy conference in 2007. A principal reason for this, he says, is to get evangelical dollars for Jewish federation coffers, and he warns that young Jewish adults will see this as selling their souls. In April 2008, as 1000 Christians were in Israel on a CUFI tour, Yoffee called on Reform Jews to reject alliances with Hagee and his group. These conservative Christians' rejection of land for peace and other extreme views do not represent those of most evangelicals, said Yoffee.[49]

One month later, John McCain rejected Hagee's endorsement for president. He had sought Hagee's support for a year and got it in February 2008. Shortly after that, though, Hagee was publicly criticized for alleged having associated the Catholic Church with the Great Whore of Revelation 17. He apologized, declaring that he had never made that connection and is not anti-Catholic. The notoriety intensified when bloggers publicized the fact that Hagee had interpreted Jeremiah 16:16 to mean that God had used Hitler as his instrument. In the verse, the Lord says that he will send fishers to catch the people of Israel and hunters to hunt them from every mountain and hill in order to bring them back to their own land. Hagee, in fact, was repeating an interpretation that Derek Prince had suggested in 1978: that the fishers were the early Zionists who sought to persuade the European Jews to return to Palestine and the hunters were the Nazis, who drove out those that they did not kill. Rather than reading this verse as referring to ancient times, Hagee applied the prophecy to the modern period, as Prince had. The idea that prophecy is being fulfilled today is, of course, at the heart of dispensationalism. The result in this instance was an explosion of outrage from some sources, but continued support from others.

Hagee retorted that he has dedicated his life to combating anti-Semitism and supporting Israel, and he insisted that this attack on him had mischaracterized his life's work. He knew that the idea that God had used the Holocaust to serve His ends was repulsive and he made it clear that this biblical interpretation was an attempt to understand evil, not to condone it. McCain nonetheless ended his association with Hagee, who told friends that the senator "threw me under the bus."[50] Colette Avital, a Labor Party Member of Knesset, called for an end to the "the sick marriage of convenience" between American Jewish leaders and "Hageeism," and David Saperstein, director of the Religious Action Center of Reform Judaism, called Hagee's words anti-Semitic. The audience at the annual AIPAC policy conference in Washington, D.C., disagreed, however. No doubt recalling Hagee's ringing support for Israel at the conference the year before, they rose for a standing ovation at the mention of his name.[51]

Paul Boyer, author of *When Time Shall Be No More*, believes that although Hagee talks publicly about the Jews' eternal possession of the land, he privately believes in bad news for the Jews too: that the Antichrist will persecute and slaughter the Jews. In keeping with this prophetic worldview, Boyer says, Hagee considers any compromise on Jewish ownership of the land, and especially of the Temple Mount, as contrary to God's will.[52] CUFI appears to pose little practical threat to Olmert's plan for convergence, though. At the time of this writing, the Second Lebanon War in 2006, the continuing rocket attacks on Israel from Gaza, and Olmert's political instability make it unlikely that the Israelis will conduct further unilateral withdrawals in the near future. But even if they do, Hagee, like so many other Christian Zionist leaders, says that he will accept them. Like Robertson and others, he shows unexpected flexibility about Israel's right to trade land for peace. True, he believes that God gave the sacred biblical land to the Jews. "It's yours," Hagee said. "Don't give it away." He will acquiesce, though, if Israel cedes territory. "If you choose to give land away, that's your business," says Hagee. "We're still friends, although we feel you make the wrong choice. I wouldn't stop supporting Israel because of your choice."[53]

Despite warning against feeding Israel to crocodiles, Hagee repeated this conciliatory position at the 2007 CUFI conference. "We are supportive of Israel even if they make decisions that are contrary to what we believe are their best interests," he said.[54] One CUFI member at the conference said the same, though with a little more political bite. Michelle Stephens said that her own position is not to give away an inch. She drew an analogy: "I live in southern California," she said. Is anyone going to tell her to give San Diego to Mexico? "That is not going to happen," just as Israel should not surrender any of the West Bank. But Stephens confirmed Hagee's point that CUFI is not interested in telling Israel what to do.[55]

Hagee notes that "Christians United for Israel is completely loyal to the positions of the Bible," meaning that it will oppose relinquishing covenant land. But his willingness to acquiesce if Israel should take such steps is also based on his reading of Scripture. "Our support for Israel is without condition," he says. "We have a Bible mandate by St. Paul, by the prophets Isaiah and Jeremiah, to be supportive of Israel and the city of Jerusalem, period. We are not swayed by political personalities or parties." This is consistent with his understanding of the end-times. The most crucial consideration on Doomsday, he believes, will be whether Christians supported Israel, as we saw in Chapter 2.

"A Shared Jerusalem? Never!"

In *Standing with Israel,* David Brog properly disputes the claim that all conservative Christians, for dark theological motives, insist that Israel must make no territorial compromise in exchange for peace. The lunatic fringe of the Christian right may take this position, he says, but it's wrong to project it onto all Christian Zionists. Brog attributes Jewish fears about this to a Pavlovian knee-jerk discomfort with robust Christianity.[56] That is debatable. There have been so many press reports highlighting doctrinaire evangelical opposition to giving land-for-peace that it is quite reasonable that many Jews believe it.

Jerusalem may be another matter, though, and possibly a fighting issue. Prominent and influential evangelical leaders forcefully oppose the idea of dividing the city. For them, retaining the entire capital in Jewish hands is the bottom line, both politically and theologically. Robertson has warned that Christian acquiescence in Israeli decisions would change completely if Israel tried to divide Jerusalem. Gaza is one thing, he said. But if Bush touches Jerusalem, "he'll lose virtually all Evangelical support, and they will go and form a third party." This isn't a question of politics, Robertson declared one month before the 2004 presidential election. "It's just a question of God's plan."[57] Richard Land told me that if Israel were to give back the Old City of Jerusalem and the Temple Mount, evangelicals would rise up in protest. Even the Israeli government would have trouble convincing them that should be done, he added, though ultimately born-again Christians would acquiesce.[58] But if the United States imposed this on Israel, there could be a severe evangelical response.

Hagee, too, takes a very strong position on Jerusalem. He says in his 1998 book, *Final Dawn over Jerusalem*, "A shared Jerusalem? Never! A 'shared Jerusalem' means control of the Holy City would be wrested away from the Jewish people and given, at least in part, to the Palestine Liberation Organization. I say 'never' not because I dislike Arab people or Palestinians, but because the Word of God says it is God's will for Jerusalem to be under the exclusive control of the Jewish people until the Messiah comes." Scripture mentions Jerusalem 811 times, Hagee notes in *Jerusalem Countdown*. It is the city where Solomon built his Temple, one of the Seven Wonders of the World. It is the city where Jeremiah and Isaiah shaped the standards of righteousness for the nations. Israel may give up land to the Palestinians, he concedes, though it should not do so until every terrorist organization lays down its weapons (a highly unlikely event in itself). But, he insists, "Jerusalem is not to be divided again, for any reason with anyone regardless of the requirements of the Roadmap for peace."[59]

In the dispensational view, it is critical that Israel retain control of Jerusalem. That will be the site to which Christ will return. The Temple Mount is especially precious, since the building of the Third Temple is a necessary step in this prophetically based understanding of the end-times. Hagee observes that Jesus speaks of abomination in "the holy place" before the Tribulation (Matthew 24:15–18). The "holy place," he explains, is the Temple in Jerusalem.

"The Jews are in control of the temple at this time right before the Tribulation. How could they control the temple without being in control of Jerusalem?"[60]

That is why Robertson, in his 2004 speech, warned that if President Bush touched Jerusalem, he'd lose all evangelical support.[61] In fact, Robertson has given voice to the profound anxiety felt by many evangelicals that God's wrath will be directed at the United States if it urges Israel to make concessions with the Holy City. On his Web site, Robertson says of dividing Jerusalem: "I am telling you, ladies and gentlemen, this is suicide. If the United States . . . takes a role in ripping half of Jerusalem away from Israel and giving it to Yasser Arafat and a group of terrorists, we are going to see the wrath of God fall on this nation that will make tornadoes look like a Sunday school picnic."[62]

Even evangelicals who are not deeply invested in end-times theology regard Jerusalem as the ultimate red line. Congressman Mike Pence (R-Indiana), who declares himself relatively incurious about eschatology, says that for him Israel was a childhood dream that became a reality. Its territorial integrity is a core belief, founded on his understanding of the Bible. In 2003, with great respect for Israel's right to determine its own policies, Pence told Prime Minister Sharon in his private office in Jerusalem that he was concerned that territorial withdrawal would lead only to a terrorist state. "Congressman," Sharon replied, "any time people wonder whether I will ever do anything that endangers the people of Israel and the survival of the state of Israel, I remind them that most of the men in my first unit in 1948 had numbers tattooed on their arms." Pence is a pragmatist. When Israel withdrew from Gaza in 2005, he bit his lip. But there is a limit to what evangelical supporters of Israel will accept, he said. They may well reach that limit if an Israeli government offers to divide Jerusalem. "There is a point when Americans who cherish Israel will push back," Pence told me. That point, he said, may be in the precincts of Jerusalem.[63]

Dispensationalism: Convert or Die?

Since dispensationalism posits invasion of Israel, the battle of Armageddon, and massive Jewish deaths or conversions to Christianity, critics have claimed that evangelicals support Israel precisely to bring those tribulations upon the Jews, as we have seen. In fact, Christian Zionists, like many other devout Christians, do await the culmination of history in Jesus Christ's return. This doesn't mean that they focus on the horrors that will be visited on the Jewish people, though. Nor does it necessarily mean that they look forward to the day in which the Jews will ultimately accept Christ or die.

Indeed, many evangelical leaders openly dispute key aspects of the standard dispensational account of the end-times. Robert Stearns told me that he had never heard of the Antichrist's slaughter of two-thirds of the Jews until he read stories about it in the press.[64] Paul Charles Merkley, in *Christian Attitudes towards the State of Israel,* calls it a canard to say that Christian Zionists believe the scenario of the slaughter of most Jews and the conversion of the rest. None of the major organizations holds such a view, says Merkley, despite false claims by anti-Zionists. The ICEJ, he notes, believes that a final war awaits all of mankind, not just the Jews, and will culminate in the annihilation not of Israel, but of her enemies.[65]

Indeed, the ICEJ's David Parsons rejects dispensationalism outright. He traces his convictions not to Darby and Scofield, but to the infancy of the Protestant Reformation and the Christians who were excommunicated and burned at the stake for saying that God still loves the Jews. Parsons considers the massive convert-or-die scenario to be especially repulsive.[66] One primary source for this notion is Zechariah 13:8–9, which includes the prophecy,

> In the whole land, says the Lord, two thirds shall be cut off and perish,
> and one third shall be left alive. And I will put this third into the fire,
> and refine them as one refines silver, and test them as gold is tested.
> They will call on my name, and I will answer them. I will say, "They
> are my people"; and they will say, "The Lord is my God."

These verses actually describe the times of the Jewish uprisings against Rome in the first and second centuries A.D., and don't apply today, says Parsons. Satan inflicted the Holocaust on the Jews and they will not face another one, he says. He refutes the idea that the Church and Israel will have different fates at the close of time. Rather, both will meet the Lord in the air.[67] Malcolm Hedding, the ICEJ's executive director, says that his organization, which represents millions of evangelicals worldwide, bases its support for Israel on God's promises to Abraham in Genesis, not on "shaky" prophetic schemes and end-times scenarios. Indeed, most evangelicals outside the United States reject a pre-Tribulationist, premillennial rapture theory, he told me.[68] Susan Michael, the ICEJ's U.S. director, says that most born-again Americans, too, have outgrown dispensational ideas about Israel. Some of the pioneers of modern evangelicalism in the 1960s and 1970s did see the Jews' return to Israel as the necessary prelude to the Rapture and the end of time, with its convert-or-die scenario, Michael acknowledges. But evangelicals have evolved since then. Prophecy is no longer really part of their thinking about Israel, she declares.[69]

The Jews will not need to convert to Christianity in the end of days, Becky Brimmer, the Bridges for Peace leader, told me. She agreed with Parsons that this idea takes the prophecy in Zechariah 13 out of context. The Jews will call out to God, not necessarily to Christ. Most evangelicals do expect a battle of Armageddon, Brimmer conceded, but how it will play out she didn't know. And as for the crucial question, whether the messiah has come before or not, she said, "I think there's probably going to be a lot of surprises here for all of us. Whether we're right or wrong, I'm going to follow him."[70]

John Hagee was once widely credited with espousing a "dual covenant" theology, according which the Jews would find salvation at the end of time without accepting Christ. In 2006 he denied ever holding that position.[71] He did assert, however, that in Romans 11:5, Paul declares that a portion of the Jewish people have the favor of God by the election of grace. As for the Second Coming, Hagee offers a variant of the story told by so many Jews. He tells his rabbi friends, "When we're standing in Jerusalem and the messiah is coming down the street, one of us is going to have a very major theological adjustment to make. But until that time, let's walk together in support of Israel and in defense of the Jewish people, because Israel needs our help."[72]

Gary Bauer, who served in the Reagan administration and ran for the Republican nomination for president in 2000, holds that the biblical Judea and Samaria are covenant land, deeded to Abraham and his descendants eternally. The solution to the Palestinian problem, he contends, is to transfer the Arab inhabitants of the West Bank to the kingdom of Jordan. "Jordan is that Palestinian state," Bauer told me. He believes that there will be an end of times in which good will clash with evil. But he said that he's very cautious about pretending to know what biblical verses mean, whether they're symbolic or actual descriptions. Though many critics in Europe zero in on the end-times as the explanation of evangelical support for Israel, it's not his motive, he said.[73]

Bauer made that perfectly clear at the fifth annual Israel Solidarity Event in the Israeli embassy in Washington, D.C., in June 2006. "Yesterday I completed my two hundredth interview on why Christians support Israel," Bauer told an appreciative audience of 200 people, mostly Christians with a sprinkling of Jews, including me. "They want us, they want me, they want you to cite some relatively obscure end-of-time Bible verse that the reason we support Israel is because we want to get all of the Jews there, where very bad things will happen to them so that the Messiah will come back." He can feel the disappointment in the room when he doesn't cite any of those verses, said Bauer. "I grew up in a Southern Baptist church, and as I go around speaking in churches, I never hear Christians cite such verses." Christians' true motive, he tells reporters, is Genesis 12:3, God's promise to bless those who bless Israel. "And, gosh," said Bauer facetiously, "being simple people, that's good enough for us!" (Laughter and applause from the crowd.) "When we look at the Middle East and we see Israel, we see ourselves, don't we?" ("YES!" said the audience.) "I remember after 9/11 how shocked I was to see people in Damascus, in Tehran, in Gaza celebrating, passing out candy before we buried our three thousand dead," he said. "I saw that Israel declared a day of mourning." These are the reasons Christians support Israel, he said, not some yearning for events in the *Left Behind* novels.[74]

Hagee says the same. He asserts that his backing of Israel has absolutely nothing to do with end-times prophecy. Rather, CUFI's support is based on the unprecedented danger that now confronts the Jewish state, says Hagee. "As a religious person, I find that hard to believe," comments Rabbi Eric Yoffie skeptically, adding that his own theology and reading of the Bible and other sacred texts inevitably has a major impact on how he sees politics and the world. The same must be true of evangelicals, Yoffie suggests.[75] But Ralph Reed, who emerged as an eloquent advocate for Israel during his years as executive director of the Christian Coalition (1989–97), has implied that theology isn't a factor at all in his support for the Jewish state! In 2002, he said that he is driven by a humanitarian impulse to preserve a safe homeland for the Jews, given their history of anti-Semitism and persecution. He is motivated, too, he said, by a sense of shared "democratic values, national security interests, and historic friendship with Israel, *not theology*" (emphasis mine). He also backs Israel in order to safeguard free access to the holy sites in Jerusalem. Most Christians have the same motives, said Reed, though he acknowledges that most evangelicals see the modern Jewish state as fulfilling God's promise to the Israel of old.[76] It is curious that so outspoken an evangelical supporter of Israel would minimize or even omit faith as his reason, and five years later Reed amended his position. In fact, he went to the opposite extreme. In 2007, when Arab diplomats asked American evangelical leaders to become more balanced toward the Palestinians, Reed replied flatly that their support for Israel comes from the Bible, and so is not subject to negotiation.[77]

Hastening the End-Times

A common rebuke to Christian Zionists is that they seek to hasten Armageddon. North Park College professor Donald Wagner charges, for example, that extreme right-wing evangelicals support Israel's Likud Party specifically to speed up the end of the world. George Monbiot, a columnist for *The Guardian,* put it succinctly: Christian fundamentalists are bonkers. They sponsor Jewish settlements in the occupied territories and seek to provoke a final battle with the Muslim world in order to bring on the Rapture and the last days, he said. Stephen Sizer, author of *Christian Zionism: Road-map to Armageddon?*, repeats the charge that Christian Zionists have one goal: "to facilitate God's hand to waft them up to heaven, free from all the trouble, from where they will watch Armageddon and the destruction of planet earth." Former president Jimmy Carter makes the same point: members of the Christian right, he says, "are convinced that they have a personal responsibility to hasten the coming of the 'rapture' in order to fulfill biblical prophecy."[78]

But David Brog argues in *Standing with Israel* that, to the contrary, conservative Christians support Israel to secure God's blessing, to express gratitude to Jews and Judaism, and to join an ally in combating radical political Islam. He asserts that evangelicals don't believe that they can hurry the return of Christ, that this has never been their goal. It is a sinister motive conjured up by the media, he contends, "not an argument but a caricature." Most conservative Christians do believe that the birth of the state of Israel will lead to the Second Coming, he concedes, but, he says, "It is a mistake to confuse this belief for a motive."

Brog attempts to prove his point with a remarkable argument: if evangelicals really wanted to speed Christ's return, he says, they would open up abortion clinics, brothels, and casinos to advance the social and moral decay that are preconditions for the Second Coming. They also would try to weaken Israel's defenses, to entice the prophesized invasion of the Jewish state.[79] The concept of born-again Christian abortion clinics and brothels is, of course, deliberately outrageous. As for casinos, for an evangelical to profit from one even indirectly would be scandalous. Ralph Reed discovered that when it became public that he took casino money from his close friend, lobbyist Jack Abramoff—to lobby against opening other casinos. Reed had had a brilliant career to that point. He had guided the Christian Coalition to political power and along the way had ameliorated strained relations between Robertson and the Anti-Defamation League's Abe Foxman. Reed had declared the separation between church and state complete and inviolable, assuaging Jewish anxieties about the intentions of the Christian right. And he had eloquently expressed such empathy and support for Israel and the Jews that he had won the trust of Foxman and other Jewish leaders. "I understand your fears, and I'm not dismissive of them," Reed said. He allied with Yechiel Eckstein to co-chair Stand for Israel, which organizes a day of prayer and solidarity with Israel for evangelicals and Jews. He also founded Century Strategies, a public relations firm that advises Fortune 500 companies, and he became a political strategist inside the Bush administration. But in 2006 he paid a political price for involvement in the Abramoff scandal: he lost the Republican primary election for lieutenant governor of Georgia. A significant factor in his defeat was that suburban Atlanta precincts with large evangelical megachurches turned against him. Reed "has shamed the evangelical community," wrote Marvin Olasky, a born-again Christian and a journalism professor at the University of Texas who helped conceive of the notion of compassionate conservatism.[80] Evangelicals will not abide unrepentant moral corruption. But the fact that they oppose casinos does not prove that they have no intention of hurrying the Last Days.

Not one of the prominent evangelical leaders I talked with gave hastening the end-times as his reason for championing Israel. Even Jerry Jenkins, co-author with Tim LaHaye of the *Left Behind* books, the phenomenally successful popular accounts of events following the Rapture, says that he isn't eager for the Rapture to occur. The Left Behind series fictionalizes the events that are predicted by premillennial dispensationalism. It begins with the mysterious disappearance of millions of believing Christians. They have been raptured, caught up to meet Jesus in the heavens. Ordinary people are left behind to live through the seven years of the Tribulations. The hero, airline pilot Rayford Steele, rallies forces to combat the Antichrist, who turns out to be the secretary general of the United Nations, a supporter of abortion, ecumenicalism, and one-world government. Ultimately, heaven opens and Christ appears on a white horse to defeat the forces of evil and usher in the millennial kingdom. The books have grossed more than $650 million, according to *Business Week*.[81] Despite the astonishing appeal of these stories, Jenkins himself doesn't look forward to the Rapture. Anyone who expects to be raptured looks forward to escaping perilous times on earth, he says. But gloating about it isn't in line with core Christian values. "Why hurry an event that will assure that untold millions will be left behind?" he asks. "'Good for us, too bad for you' seems an attitude wholly antithetical to the teachings of Christ." The writer George Eliot made the same point 150 years earlier: that anticipation of the Rapture represents the belief that "our party" will triumph while others suffer. That is nothing more than "the transportation of political passions on to a so-called religious platform," said Eliot.[82]

LaHaye isn't eager for the end-times to come, either. Asked in August 2006, as Hezbollah's rockets were falling on Israel, if the war was good news for believers who thought that Jesus' return might be near, he declared, "I'm praying that this whole thing will die down and that as many lives as possible will be saved."[83]

This doesn't mean that dispensationalism is dead. Nor does it suggest that every Christian reader dismisses the end-of-days scenarios in the *Left Behind* books as an action fantasy. It is unreasonable to expect such conformity of faith in so diverse and individualistic a religious culture. Motives can be complex and sometimes uncomfortable to express. People may not fully appreciate the forces that drive them. At the same time, the public representatives of Christian Zionists are comparatively erudite spokespeople, seasoned in dealing with the Jewish community and the press. Are they representative of the larger evangelical community? Or, as some critics suggest, have they simply learned how to speak to Jews without giving offense? Are they being deceptive about conservative Christians' true motives?

I put that question to Martin E. Marty, the eminent scholar of religion. In 2002 Marty had said that, yes, evangelicals were indeed deceiving Israel. They were Zionists before the Jews were, he acknowledged, but only because a strong Israel is necessary for Jesus to come again. Then all the Jews will be converted or killed. When Prime Minister Menachem Begin began to court conservative Christian leaders like Jerry Falwell in the late 1970s, Marty noted, "We all thought Jews were getting snookered."[84] I asked Marty, Are evangelical leaders sincere now when they cite their love of Israel and God's promises to bless those who bless the Jews as their principal motives? Or are they secretly hoping to hurry Armageddon? "You are being snookered if you think that it's only the love of Israel that motivates them," he told me. But Marty added, "I believe that they're all sincere motives."[85]

Marty offered Tim LaHaye's *Left Behind* novels as proof of this complication. He cautioned that one shouldn't measure any movement by its extremists. Marty observed, however, that tens of millions of the people have bought these books. For many of them, it's probably just another fantasy. But it's hard to get away from the hunch that a lot of them believe it, he told me. "There have got to be millions and millions in that camp," Marty said.[86] That applies to Hal Lindsey's *Late Great Planet Earth* as well.

Late Great Planet Earth-Thinking

In an important and strikingly candid admission at the Israel Solidarity Event at the Israeli embassy in June 2006, Ted Haggard conceded that end-time prophecy books have indeed affected evangelicals, including the movement's elites. And, he declared, the books are wrong! "Evangelicals, those that are my age or older," said the forty-nine-year-old Haggard, "are persuaded by what I call *Late Great Planet Earth*-thinking—which is somewhat bombastic and highly inaccurate." He recapitulated the predictions about the final days that never came true: "The Soviet Union never invaded Israel," said Pastor Ted. "The Temple wasn't being rebuilt in the 1970s. Red heifers weren't being prepared, as they said [see Chapter 9 below]. There was not the great falling away from the Church. Instead, we have had the greatest increase in the Church, since those books were written, that we have ever seen. And so," Haggard concluded, "actually we missed it."[87]

Haggard's views comport with his theology, of course. He rejects the dispensationalism that underlies the *Late Great Planet Earth* and the *Left Behind* novels. Dispensationalists believe that mankind is hurtling toward catastrophe, but Pastor Ted is, characteristically, far more positive. "There is no reason that we should be anything but optimists," he says. "The trends in the last 40 years should make us optimistic. More people are living under representative government than ever before in history. More people's civil liberties are protected than ever before in history. Women have greater opportunity than ever before in history. Fewer wars than ever before in history. We are doing a really good job of improving global economics and food distribution systems."[88]

And what about an impending showdown between the forces of good and evil at Armageddon? Pastor Ted dismisses it as fantasy.[89] He also suspects that many people think of the *Left Behind* novels as a good read but don't endorse their theological premises. "Everyone in my church has read the *Left Behind* series," he told me, "but none of them is preaching the Rapture." They love Jerry Jenkins, who lives near Haggard's New Life Church and who actually writes the books, based on Tim LaHaye's story ideas. But they don't believe the Rapture theology on which the books are based.[90] One prominent evangelical leader told me off the record, in fact, that he doesn't think that LaHaye and Jenkins believe in the Rapture either. "They kept the money!" he said of their book royalties. If they really thought that the end-times were imminent, "they'd be giving it to the poor and to missionary activity all over the world. Instead they have huge houses and big endowments for their kids and grandkids. Pay attention to what people do and not what they say."

This source noted that in the early 1970s, people did believe the Rapture theory. Paul Crouch, president of the Trinity Broadcasting Network, and his wife, for example, felt that there was no reason for young people to go to college and get married. "To this day they have preparations for the Rapture. But their kids don't," my source told me.

In fact, even firm belief in the Rapture doesn't necessarily stop premillennialists from planning for the future, since no man knows the hour of its coming. Zev Chafets points out that Jerry Falwell, for example, launched a long-term building program at his Liberty University and that Tim LaHaye donated millions for a hockey rink on the campus.[91] This does not in itself suggest a lapse of faith, however. LaHaye humorously describes his gift as "Evangelicalism with a hockey puck." He intends the rink to attract hockey players from Canada and North America to Liberty University, where they'll accept Christ. Some have already returned to Canada and started churches, says LaHaye. This is part of the evangelical goal of winning people to Christ before the coming end of time, he notes.[92]

A Huge Generation Gap in Support for Israel?

There were lots of things wrong with *Late Great Planet Earth*-thinking, Ted Haggard told me in June 2006, but it had a positive side too: "It created a generation that would unconditionally support Israel." Many of those ideas have not come to the younger generation, which doesn't have that eschatology, he observed. As a result, they don't back Israel in the same way that their parents did, Pastor Ted said. Isn't Genesis 12:3 sufficient reason for their support? I asked him, startled that the president of the NAE would suggest that it's not. Yes, it helps, Haggard replied, but it lacks the undergirding of a strong eschatology. He believes that the Genesis 12 promise of blessing refers in any case to Jews worldwide, as we have seen. It applies to Jews in Colorado Springs, or Manhattan, or Baton Rouge as much as to those in Jerusalem. If younger evangelicals are indifferent to dispensational ideas about Israel, as Haggard himself is, Genesis 12 will not in itself guarantee the kind of alliance with Israel that their parents have forged, he said. Haggard believes from anecdotal experience that there is already a huge chasm in support for Israel between evangelicals aged forty-five to fifty and those who are younger. "That should be of concern," he warned.

The *Late Great Planet Earth*-generation's eschatology made evangelical support for Israel unshakeable, Haggard told me, but for the next generation that sympathy may have to be earned. If in ten years American evangelicals soften on Israel, he cautioned, the Jewish state may have a hard time getting U.S. support. That's not a threat, he was quick to add; it's an analysis that worries him.[93]

Pastor Ted's argument is stunning. It turns on its head the critics' assertions that dispensational eschatology delegitimizes evangelical support for Israel. Skeptics insist that evangelicals' backing is inimical because their love is hypothetical rather than real and their true goal is to bring the end-times, including tribulations and death for the Jews. Haggard's point is the opposite: that dispensational beliefs about the end-times engendered evangelicals' love for Israel and the Jewish people rather than subverting it. Without that eschatology, he warns, Christian Zionism may wither. He also challenges the advocates' reassurance that Genesis 12:3 is the main basis of Christian Zionism. Despite the insistence of very many evangelicals, Pastor Ted says that Genesis 12 is not sufficient in itself to assure the continued alliance between conservative Christians and Jews.

To maintain that connection, Haggard told me, American Jews should be friendlier to evangelicals. He cited two recent points of conflict: Mel Gibson's *The Passion of the Christ* and a suit by Mikey Weinstein, a Jewish graduate of the Air Force Academy and a White House attorney for Ronald Reagan, to prevent evangelical chaplains from using Christ's name at events at the Academy. American Jews need to realize that evangelical enthusiasm for Gibson's film was not anti-Semitic, noted Haggard. And they should accept that prayer in the name of Christ in public places is a protected expression of religious freedom. Young evangelicals need to see that American Jews are friends and not enemies on issues like these, which are deeply significant to evangelicals, Pastor Ted said. Otherwise the strong alliance between them may fray. Maybe the Islamist threat will bring Christians and Jews together by forcing us into a global struggle for civil liberties, he said but added, "I don't want us to love each other because of a common enemy."[94]

Haggard expressed similar complaints and fears in an interview with Chafets, who conjectures that evangelical Christians may, in the future, stop loving Jews and Israel. Chafets, noting that the NAE did not express support for the Jewish state during the 2006 Lebanon war, wonders whether this might signal a weakening of Christian Zionism. Pastor Ted replied that the NAE's silence was pragmatic: "There are evangelical Christians in just about every totalitarian nation in the Middle East," he said, and 480 of them are martyred every year. Other evangelical leaders have disparaged Islam, provoking Muslims to violence. Haggard didn't want to say anything that would further endanger evangelicals in that region. "So there is a possible clash between our principled argument for Israel and the safety of Christians," he said. But the NAE's support is unequivocal, he declared.[95]

The NAE's backing of Israel is not unequivocal, however. The organization has never issued a policy statement about Israel because its constituents don't necessarily agree on the subject. Timothy Weber points out that any position that the NAE adopted would have to reflect some of its nondispensational members' conviction that Israel needs to do justice to the Palestinians and deal with the settlements.[96] Indeed, three members of the NAE board and a former NAE president signed a letter to Bush in 2007 asking him to be even-handed in his treatment of the Palestinians.[97]

Haggard's observations about a loss of support for Israel are anecdotal and are not necessarily right. John Green confirms that older doctrines, including dispensationalism, are being challenged, redefined, and even rejected by the younger generation. "The many predictions that failed to happen have had a sobering effect on many evangelicals, especially the better educated ones," he notes. But Green's polling data do not corroborate Pastor Ted's observation that this has lessened support for Israel among young evangelicals. "If anything," Green says, "the pattern is reversed, with older folks less supportive and less positive about prophecy." That is consistent with the older evangelicals' disappointment with *Late Great Planet Earth*-thinking that Pastor Ted described, a disillusion that Haggard shares. But Israel is the exception to this pattern of disenchantment, says Green. "Interestingly enough, the state of Israel is the best concrete example of prophecy coming true—so even disillusioned evangelicals tend to see that as a bright spot for prophecy," he notes. Was Pastor Ted right to question whether Genesis 12:3 alone, without the reinforcement of dispensational eschatology, can inspire love and blessing for Israel and the Jewish people? Green responds that his data continue to show that the promise to Abraham in Genesis 12 is very important to evangelical support for Israel, but so is prophecy. That's only logical: biblical literalism demands that all parts of Scripture be true elements of divine revelation. Bible-believers who read the text in that way can't disentangle the promise from the prophecies. Green adds that he isn't sure that younger evangelicals are less interested in eschatology than their parents are, in any case.[98]

Jerry Falwell declared, in fact, that evangelical support for Israel and the Jewish people has grown, not declined, over the generations. "We didn't talk much about Jews, or Israel, in the 1950s," he said. "It wasn't much of an issue. My kids' generation has a positive attitude toward Israel and Jews, far more than mine did." Falwell's three children are all in their forties, and their generation is not necessarily the one that Pastor Ted was worried about. But Falwell was confident that evangelical support for Israel will endure. "That's not going to change," he observed. "Places like Liberty University will see to it," he said of the evangelical university that he founded and owns in Lynchburg, Virginia.[99]

9

❦

Prophecy, Policy, and the
Unfolding of God's Plan

Christian Zionists' Motives: What the Surveys Say

The difference between what high-profile televangelists say and what people in the pews actually believe can be dramatic. That is especially true of Pat Robertson and the late Jerry Falwell, whose vibrant support and unconditional love for Israel are not shared by every born-again Christian. Evangelical elites in the seminaries and the heads of parachurch organizations and denominations also are significantly more devoted to the Jewish state than are evangelicals generally.[1] So what do born-again Christians themselves say about Israel? How many are premillennial dispensationalists, supporting Israel to bring on the Second Coming, with its convert-or-die scenario for the Jews? Polling data provide tantalizing but incomplete answers and most experts agree that no one can say for sure.

Most of the survey evidence is generally unsurprising. It indicates, for example, that white evangelicals support Israel far more than they do its Arab enemies. A Pew Research Center poll in 2003 found that 55 percent of white American evangelicals sympathized with the Jewish state while only 6 percent favored the Palestinians. Surprisingly, that left nearly four in ten, a substantial minority, who expressed no view—a pattern not often found on foreign policy questions.[2] But the evangelicals showed a significantly stronger level of support for Israel than Americans in general expressed at that time (41% of the overall sample of Americans sided more with Israel, and 13% with the Palestinians). White evangelicals also were almost twice as likely to see Israel as the fulfillment of biblical prophecies of the Second Coming of Christ: nearly two-thirds (63%) of them viewed modern Israel in that light, as compared to a little more than one-third of the overall U.S. population. That religious conviction was strongly connected to their political sympathies: a 2006 Pew survey found that Americans who hold that belief sympathize with Israel over the Palestinians by a lopsided 60 percent to 7 percent. That poll also showed that the vast majority of white evangelicals (69%) believe that God gave Israel to the Jews.[3]

This correlation between support for Israel and biblically based convictions about the Jewish state doesn't in itself establish evangelicals' motives, though. Believing that Israel will be the site of Christ's return doesn't necessarily impel one to try to hasten that event by aiding the Jewish state. There are can be several other factors at work.[4] A poll for Yechiel Eckstein's Stand for Israel organization, an offshoot of his International Fellowship of Christians and Jews (IFCJ), found in 2002 that many white evangelicals backed Israel for reasons other than religion: 24 percent because it is a democracy, and 19 percent because it is a strong ally in the war on terrorism. More than one in every three, though, based their support on their belief that Jerusalem is the prophesied place of the Second Coming.[5] None of these questions discovered how many Christians support Israel in order to help summon the end of time.

Narishkeit and the Number of American Dispensationalists

Eckstein himself says that it's pure narishkeit (Yiddish for "foolishness") and hogwash to say that evangelicals back Israel to get the Jews to go there so they will convert or die. "You're all on the wrong track" if you think that," he said at the 92nd Street Y in Manhattan one night in March 2006. "It's not this eschatology scenario that you're familiar with. It's been a myth. It's just not there." Eckstein noted that his IFCJ gets 3,000 pieces of mail a day from evangelicals who support Israel, and few of them mention the end of days. And though the mainstream press has never reported it, he said, evangelical children give up their Christmas presents to assist elderly Jews in the former Soviet Union through the IFCJ's Isaiah 58 program. So do thousands of senior born-again Christians from around North America, who donate 10 percent of each Social Security check. These suffering Jews are not going to emigrate to Israel, said Eckstein, yet Christians are tithing to help send them food and clothing. The end-times don't even come into play in evangelicals' backing for Israel, he said. If we press them for their motive, it's Genesis 12:3, Eckstein concluded.[6] The IFCJ's own survey refuted that, however, as we have seen: it indicated that more than a third of evangelicals specifically *do* link their support for Israel to the fact that it is the prophesied site of the Second Coming. Whether they hope to actually hasten that event is another question, though—one that's difficult to answer empirically.

Frank Newport, the Gallup organization's editor in chief, told me that he's been unable to measure whether hurrying Christ's return is a significant motive for evangelicals. A Gallup poll in spring 2003 showed that nearly 30 percent of Americans felt that Israel has a personal religious significance for them because the Bible predicts events that actually will occur there.[7] But Gallup couldn't ask people if they are premillennial dispensationalists, Newport said, because the terminology would only confuse many of them. Even those who fit the description would be surprised to learn that they are one of those, he told me. "I've always felt, without data to back it up," Newport said, "or perhaps your book will illuminate this, that perhaps some of the relationship between evangelical Christians and Israel is even simpler than [end-time beliefs]. Israel is just a country with which they identify as the seat of their religion, too. It may be extremely uncomplicated. . . . I believe experts make these things much more complex than the average Christian does."[8]

John Green told me pretty much the same thing. The 2003 Pew poll didn't address dispensationalism—belief in the Rapture, seven years of Tribulations, the Antichrist's desecration of the Temple, and other end-times events. He himself finds it impossible to frame a survey question that would yield unambiguous results about those beliefs, Green said. So there are no good data about the prevalence of dispensationalism. The Pew survey did find in 2006, however, that nearly half of all white evangelicals (48%) express a broadly pessimistic premillennial eschatology: they believe that the world situation will steadily worsen, and when it hits a low point, Christ will return.[9] This doesn't necessarily mean that they accept or even know the dispensationalist view of Israel's key role at the close of history, however. So it does not speak to their motives for backing the Jewish state. Green's guess, like Newport's, is that most evangelicals' beliefs about the end are not founded on an elaborate theology. Rather, they support Israel in order to be on God's side in the coming unfolding of history.[10]

Interestingly, Green is able to speculate about how many Americans are hard-core dispensationalists. Survey data show that biblical prophecy leads 33 million American adults to support Israel. It influences half of that number strongly. A much smaller subgroup of those, about five million, are dispensationalists, says Green. They comprise about 2.5 percent of the adult population of the United States.[11]

Avoiding Specific End-Times Stuff Like an Embarrassment

The Reverend Jim Denison's practical experience confirms the idea that dispensationalists are a minor stream of evangelicals. His city of Dallas is a center of dispensational thought because it's the home of the theologically conservative Dallas Theological Seminary, which was founded in 1924 to advance dispensational doctrine. But when Denison was on the faculty of the School of Theology of Southwestern Seminary in nearby Fort Worth years ago, only one of his seventy colleagues was a dispensationalist. That was indicative of how marginal dispensationalism was among Baptists at the time, he told me. "Dispensationalism is a pretty recent phenomenon in the larger evangelical world," said Denison, who has a Ph.D. in philosophy and is Distinguished Adjunct Professor at Dallas Baptist University. Until the 1960s, he said, the dominant perspective was amillennial, which holds that Christ will not reign on earth. In this view, the prophecy of Christ's thousand-year kingship is just a symbol in the Book of Revelation. Next came the belief that Christ will return and establish his kingdom, but that Israel isn't necessary for that to happen, Denison noted. In the last twenty years, however, premillennial dispensationalism has become far more influential than it was, thanks to the influence of Dallas Theological Seminary and other conservative religious institutions. Nearly all of the theology professors left Southwest Seminary, and the majority of their replacements were dispensationalists, he told me. The Southern Baptist Convention also has become much more theologically conservative, with the result that dispensationalism has become far more important in Baptist life.

Still, premillennial dispensationalism remains a minor influence among evangelical Christians overall, said Denison. Using Dallas as a point of reference, he noted that Mark Craig, pastor of Highland Park Methodist Church, whom President Bush calls his pastor and his friend, isn't a dispensationalist. The largest Presbyterian Church of America congregation in the United States, a strongly evangelical house of worship, is also in Dallas, and the pastor there isn't a dispensationalist either. In fact, "There isn't a church in Dallas, except for the large fundamentalist Baptist churches here, that I'd say is probably dispensationalist," Denison told me. Interestingly, the large majority of Baptists in Dallas do believe in the Rapture, even members of churches whose pastors don't preach about it, he remarked.[12] That's because the concept of the Rapture appears in the Bible (1 Thessalonians 4:16–17) and because Dallas Theological Seminary is in town, he said. But many people who accept this doctrine have no idea about any of the other tenets of dispensationalism, Denison noted. For example, the recent Billy Graham crusade in Dallas "attracted a broad cross-section of people," he recalled, and "within that group you'd find almost no dispensationalists."[13] That is consistent with John Green's estimate that only 2.5 percent of Americans fit into that category.

University of Notre Dame professor Chris Smith has conducted hundreds of in-depth, personal interviews with evangelicals, reaching striking conclusions about their convictions, and he agrees that probably a very small percentage of Americans have a theory of hastening the end-times. Though he hasn't researched this question, Smith's definite sense is that many evangelicals believe that the Jews are still God's chosen, covenant people and that their nation deserves protection. For many of them, this probably isn't very well thought out. As for dispensational theories, Smith believes that "the majority of evangelicals avoid such specific end-times stuff like an embarrassment." They avoid trying to manipulate God's timing of events even more, he said.[14]

Even if the polling data did address end-times beliefs, they would not necessarily get to the heart of evangelical motivations concerning Israel and the Jewish people. Smith warns that to think that surveys can tell us what we need to know about evangelicals is like believing that one can know Manhattan by flying over it in a Lear jet.[15] To appreciate the range of beliefs and spiritual life within individual evangelical churches, one needs to experience them. The Eagles' Wings events described in Chapter 1 represented one kind of Christian Zionist devotion. The service in Pastor Omar's little church in Queens, New York, was something different altogether.[16]

Pastor Omar

"Are you a Christian?" Pastor Omar asked me. "No, I'm Jewish," I told him. "Oh!" he replied enthusiastically, "Your Messiah is my Messiah!" I had phoned him to arrange to attend a service at his church and he was filling me in on his background. Pastor Omar was born in British Guyana, where he grew up as a devout Muslim, he said. When he was twenty-eight, he became a born-again Christian. A girl had deceived him, disturbing him deeply. "I was going mad as a Muslim," he told me. "Then a voice came to me and said, 'Why don't you try this Jesus?' Immediately I was healed." Within weeks of that experience, Omar discovered that he had the power to heal others, he said. An old Christian man he knew dropped his glasses and the lenses broke. "I told him, 'You don't need those glasses anymore!' and he was healed. So Jesus is real, my brother," Omar assured me. In 1989 he came to America and learned for the first time how Hitler had tried to destroy the Jews. "God gave me a love for the Jewish people," Pastor Omar said. "You know, the devil and the Muslims and most of the world hate the Jews. It's amazing that God put it into my heart to help them. To love them. To bless them."[17]

Pastor Omar is the minister of New Birth Ministries, one of thousands of evangelical churches worldwide that joined in the annual Day of Prayer and Solidarity with Israel that Yechiel Eckstein's Stand for Israel organized in January 2006. The Israeli diplomatic community, including the ambassador to the United States and people from the consulates and the Israeli Foreign Ministry, turn out for this event each year, a measure of Eckstein's clout. He was the pioneer of Jewish ties with evangelical Christians in the United States, an alliance that he's nurtured since 1977.[18] Prior to that, American Jews were only partially aware of evangelicals' desire to support them and had only occasional contact with their leadership. "No Jewish spokesman would receive us," my anonymous senior evangelical source Faith told me. "We waited. Yechiel was the one who did." Eckstein is a good Orthodox Jewish man who can talk to the Jewish people, and yet he understands us, Faith said. "He saw this vision when no one else did." He endured derision and exclusion by the Jewish leaders, Faith noted. "He was put on earth for what he's doing, and no one's paid a higher price."[19] Even now, some top American Jewish leaders hold him in suspicion and consider him a publicity hound. Eckstein needs public notice and financial transparency, though, in order for his Christian donors to know the good that their gifts are doing. Some Orthodox rabbis in Israel, including two former chief rabbis, call on Jews to refuse to accept his money. But he's been vindicated in the eyes of needy Israelis to whom he annually gives millions of dollars in aid donated by North American evangelicals.[20]

On Stand for Israel's 2006 day of prayer, Eckstein himself appeared at the huge New Life Church in Colorado Springs, where Ted Haggard was just beginning what would turn out to be his last year as pastor. Eckstein told the congregants that Jews and Christians need to reverse history and support one another. He also urged the evangelical audience not to expect Jews to convert and not to try to figure out whether recent events in the Middle East signify the coming of the final days.[21] Pastor Ted's megachurch is one of the most influential in the United States. The little church I went to for the Israel solidarity event, by contrast, was not the kind to attract the attention of the press. I'd already attended evangelical services that were diplomatic, decorous, and attuned to the sensibilities of Jewish guests. Pastor Omar's New Birth Ministries, was very different: it was charismatic, with emphasis on the Gifts of the Spirit: faith healing, speaking in tongues, prophecy. I wanted to see how this group viewed Israel and the Jews.

"It's Like Christmas!"

Pastor Omar's church is in a hall over a row of stores. The setting is modest. It sits above a beauty salon, next to a shop with a large yellow banner advertising kerosene sales. As I entered, people greeted me warmly, thinking that I might be the guest speaker, Amir Ofek, an Israeli consul from the city. "I'm with him," I explained, and people nodded and smiled warmly. There were about sixty in the congregation, mostly black, but several white people and a few others, all mixing easily. Most were in churchgoing suits and dresses, though a few of the younger people wore jeans. One congregant came up to say hello. "I was a Catholic," he told me, "now I'm a Christian." Some people resent the fact that evangelicals seem to have arrogated the term "Christian" to themselves alone, but this man explained that a Christian is someone who follows in the footsteps of Christ. Some Catholics do that, but not all, he said.[22] In this church, though, I would see the Holy Spirit moving through the entire congregation, he said. "Is this a charismatic church?" I asked. "And how!" he replied. The pastor truly works through the power of God, he assured me. He moved on to discuss Judaism, noting that the Old Testament is filled with prophecy that Jesus would be the Messiah. As for Israel, he said, God struck down Sharon. You can't divide that land. "That's what Pat Robertson said," I pointed out. He skipped a beat, then said, "Whoever gave him that revelation, it was right."

Then Pastor Omar entered, fifty-eight years old, short, dark-complexioned, in a suit and vest with no tie and the top shirt button buttoned. He went up to the podium as Amir, the Israeli consul, entered the hall and sat next to me. "The Jews are indestructible," Pastor Omar told his congregation. "They exist because of the love of God." "Amen," said the worshippers. "I've told you this for years, not just today. One of the best ways to be blessed is to bless the Jews," said Omar, and the crowd responded, "Amen." "We are grafted in by the Jewish Messiah," he went on. Then he turned to Amir and me. "Two of our brothers are here. Our brothers are here to commend us and thank us. You know that they are the richest people on the planet," and to that the congregants responded with a cheer and applause while my jaw dropped a little in surprise. "They own almost half the planet," he added, "all of those big apartment buildings." Startling as these comments were, they weren't said in envy or accusation, but in approval. They were confirmation that God has blessed his Chosen People, the apple of his eye. They illustrate an observation that David A. Rausch made in his 1991 book, *Communities in Conflict*: that evangelicals often see Jews as wealthy, talented, and blessed by God despite being limited by their failure to acknowledge Jesus' special gift to the world. Jerry Falwell, for example, has reported wisecracked that a Jew "can make more money accidentally than you can on purpose." Jews similarly tend to believe stereotypes of evangelicals, said Rausch.[23]

Pastor Omar went on. In 1967, he said, Arab nations came against Israel and tried to destroy it, but they couldn't do it "because God says, he who touches them touches me." You know I've been telling you this all the time, not just because our brothers are here." "Yes, yes," came the response. Then he turned to Amir and me again and expressed his joy at our presence. "It's like Christmas! It's a holiday for me, I'm telling you," he said, and the small congregation applauded us. "Do not pressure them with any doctrine, please," he told them, and repeated this admonition twice. "Don't forget, they being here, we're gong to be exceedingly blessed. Do you believe that?" he asked them. "AMEN!" they replied. "We have two of God's covenant people with us," he told them. "That means this ministry will never be the same. By biblical revelation, wherever they are, people are gonna be blessed. A lot of churches don't like the Jews, but I'm proud to have Jews with us. Watch how all of you, if your heart is with us, are gonna be blessed. Stay put. This ministry's gonna explode after today! God is gonna give me millions of dollars supernaturally. I cannot wait to go to Jerusalem. I want all of you to go and help God's people," he told them. "Because the Messiah is coming soon."

The service continued for four hours. Pastor Omar spoke of bringing the Jews of the former Soviet Union back home to Israel. It was a poor church, but he wanted to help. "We want to bring them back," he said. "We don't have the finances, but God has the finances." "Yes!" the congregants cried out. Music played as he said, "We're going to have millions of dollars—not for nice houses and cars, but to support Israel." Later I was surprised to hear the pastor's wife say that this small church, in which some people were struggling to get by, had somehow contributed enough money to bring over 100 Jews from the former Soviet Union to Israel last year.

Pastor Omar told Amir and me not to be frightened as people came forward to be healed. The Holy Spirit was working through him, he said, and as he put his hand on each person, he shot the word "FIRE!" into the microphone on his lapel.[24] As he touched people and healed them, they wobbled in place, their hands and arms jerking as if subjected to electric shock. Some managed to stay upright, but most fell backward, one after the other. Men stood behind them, calmly easing their fall as they went down to the floor as if slain. Each of them lay there supine for several minutes, their heads trembling as people called out, "Thank you, Jesus!" I'd heard of being slain in the spirit in this way but had never seen it. The whole experience was completely new to Amir and his eyes were open wide as he took it in. But he recovered quickly enough to deliver a very nice, brief talk about how it's important to give when one receives. The

Dead Sea receives water from the Jordan River, he said, but doesn't give any. That's why it's dead. Amir hadn't come to ask for money, but evangelical Christians are major donors to Israel. His small sermon affirmed that their generosity is natural and appropriate, a source of life to the giver as well as the receiver.

Pastor Omar returned to the podium. "Every day we pray for the Jewish people," he said. "They are our brethren. I say, 'My God, what a wonderful people. God is using us to bless Israel." Why did the Arabs and the Communist bloc try to destroy the Chosen People in 1967? he asked. Because Satan knows that the Messiah will come from the Jews. Why are the Jews so hated? Because Satan knew the Messiah would come from the Jews' bowels, through Abraham. Besides, the Russians want the immense mineral wealth in the Dead Sea, said Omar. This supposed enormous financial potential would come as news to the Israeli and Jordanian production facilities that use the Dead Sea to mine potash and produce cosmetics, but it is no surprise to readers of Hal Lindsey's *Late Great Planet Earth,* which was the source of Omar's statement. Applying contemporary conditions to understand Ezekiel 38:10, Lindsey says that prior to Armageddon, Russia will invade Israel to conquer the strategically important land bridge of the Middle East. He adds that the Russians "will be motivated by the great material wealth of the restored nation of Israel," which they will seize and carry off, as Ezekiel prophesies. He notes that the value of the mineral deposits in the Dead Sea alone has been estimated at $1,270,000,000,000. "This is more than the combined wealth of France, England, and the United States!" says Lindsey.[25] This fits with Pastor Omar's theme of the enormous prosperity of the Jews, if not with the point of Amir's sermon.

Omar continued. "I'm proud of my brothers," he declared, "but I'm also proud that I've got their Messiah!" "Yes!" came the response. "They're gonna receive their Messiah in good time," he said. "So don't try to push them." Pastor Omar wanted to respect us, to not press doctrine on us, but it was too integral to his faith for him not to declare that we would find the Messiah. "God is restoring Israel now," he said. "God is still allowing Israel to suffer a little bit more, but Jews are leaving America and going to Israel. You can imagine how close the Messiah is!" That recalled something that Pat Robertson had said in his book *The New Millennium* sixteen years earlier. Robertson doubted that American Jews would conduct a mass exodus to Israel, and he hoped that no catastrophic event would ever occur to drive them out. But if the Jews ever do emigrate, he declared, "we will certainly know that the last days are upon us."[26]

Amir had to leave and Pastor Omar announced that Brother Stephen was staying. I don't often think that my mere presence is a blessing to others, but Omar made it clear that they all felt that way. Then seven people stood

successively and gave testimony. One man confessed that he'd originally been
a doubter but had come to believe in Pastor Omar's power. "Do you think
that I'd be here now if I didn't know that God works through this man?"
he asked. Seven more people came forward together and touched a manila
envelope containing written prayers for healing, for jobs. Pastor Omar, holding the envelope, looked straight over at me as if posing a spiritual challenge
and declared, "The signs that the Bible says the Jews require are happening
right here![27] Watch the miracle happen! FIRE!" he said directly into his lapel
mike, his voice exploding for an instant, and the seven staggered backward as
if stricken. One laughed, some breathed hard as if recovering from the blow.
Pastor Omar stood calmly, speaking softly, the spiritual lightning rod chan-
neling divine power and grace into his parishioners. Others come forward and
were healed, then toppled backward to the carpet, trembling. Their heads
continued to shake as people covered them in white sheets.

A pretty girl, perhaps Italian, maybe twenty years old, wearing jeans, stood
before Omar. "This girl doesn't just think about boys," the pastor said approvingly in his gentle voice. "She thinks about God." Then, suddenly, he shot the
word "FIRE!" into the microphone and she very slowly dropped backward to
a seated position on the floor and wept. "My brother, are you seeing the signs
performed by Jesus?" Pastor Omar asked me from the podium, looking me
straight in the eye. As one very large man fell backward, I realized that there
was no one to catch him, so I hurried to the front of the hall and slowed his
backward fall. "Beautiful," said Omar, seeing this. The man was heavy and
would have gone down really hard if I hadn't held his weight. He may have
been healed, I thought, but my old neck problem had flared up, a pulled muscle
down into my right shoulder. Then, surprisingly and atypically (I won't say
miraculously), the pain went away. Pastor Omar called me up to get a blessing.
"No way," I answered, and somebody behind me laughed. "Then I'll come to
you," he said and walked over to me. "Keep it ecumenical," I cautioned him
softly. "Don't worry," he replied reassuringly and placed three fingers gently on
my forehead. He blessed me in the name of Jesus Christ. It wasn't exactly the
ecumenism I had hoped for, but I understood that, from his faith perspective,
he did it in a spirit of generous inclusion.

We moved on to a reading of Scripture, appropriately a story in Genesis
about Abraham. One of the congregants hurried over to lend me a Bible, which,
I saw, he had underlined throughout and annotated in the margins. Pastor
Omar looked over again and said directly to me, "The Bible is right there, my
brother! Are you reading it? SO GET YOUR MESSIAH QUICKLY!" He concluded the service with a prophecy straight out of John Darby and Hal Lindsey.
The whole world is going to go against Israel—except me and my church, he

said, and people laughed. "No, other churches too," he conceded in good humored clarification. "God gave Israel the land and the world hates Israel. And when Jews are leaving America, you know we don't have much time on earth. I'm gonna be raptured totally healthy and totally wealthy. Do you believe?" he asked his congregation. Yes, of course they did.

A Benefit beyond Measure

Pastor Omar had clearly linked the ingathering of the Jews to Israel with the imminent arrival of the Rapture. His congregation's support for the Jewish return to the Holy Land thus would yield a double benefit: God would bless those who blessed the Jews, and Christ would return more quickly. The issues that the evangelical elites finesse or treat delicately had not only surfaced, they had become the whole point. Martin Marty was right: all of the motives for evangelical support of Israel were valid, at least in this little charismatic church. They were acting through love. At the same time, a congregation in need of healing, and jobs, and reconciliation with their children translated the key verse, Genesis 12:3, to match their yearnings. The very presence of two Jews promised to make that come true. They would receive a benefit beyond measure. Their prayers would be answered, the ministry would profit immensely, and the very real financial sacrifices they had made to help Jews emigrate to Israel would have a prompt reward: they would soon be raptured, to enjoy health and wealth in the company of Christ.

In the standard dispensational view, that is very bad news for the Jewish people, most of whom will suffer a very different fate. Pastor Omar offered hope on that point, though. Many Jews would be saved without accepting Christ, as Abraham had been, he said. Still it would be far better if Jews found their Messiah, Jesus, and Omar had explicitly extended an invitation to me to do that quickly. I admit that I was a little embarrassed. It reminded me of something that Susan Michael, the director of the Washington, D.C., office of the International Christian Embassy Jerusalem (ICEJ) had told me a few weeks earlier. She put all such conversionary statements in perspective. "The segment of Christians that are the staunchest supporters of Israel are actually the weakest and least experienced at interfaith dialogue and relations," she said. "We get letters every day from people praying for Israel and the Jews, but a lot of them have never spoken to a Jewish person. Could they carry out a conversation with a Jew without offending one? No. But you learn from your mistakes. We encourage Jews to forgive us when we make mistakes. Because that's really the way you learn."[28]

The truth is, I felt the warmth and generosity of spirit in that room, as I had in the very different setting of the Eagles' Wings Rend the Heavens conference in New Jersey. The love for Israel and the Jewish people was as intense. There were fewer restraints here, though, as befits a ministry in the charismatic stream of belief.

Fishers in the North Country

Many evangelicals, Christian Zionists among them, disavow any intention of hastening scriptural prophecy, as we have seen. David Brog argues that evangelical Christians have no interest in speeding the end of days. Their Zionism is driven, he says, by the promises in Genesis, not by prophecy. As evidence, he notes that their fund-raising literature never mentions the Second Coming.[29] That is not entirely true, however. Syndicated columnist Cal Thomas reports that Pat Robertson did send precisely such a letter. Thomas, a former vice president of the Moral Majority, says that Robertson's fund-raising message asserted that God wanted him to bring on the Second Coming. Robertson therefore asked for money to support his Middle East radio station, which beamed evangelizing messages to Israel. Bringing the Jews to belief in Christ, Robertson said, would usher in the Messiah's return.[30] Robertson does not speak for all evangelicals, however, as we have seen.

Brog, like Eckstein, points out that Christians make charitable donations to poor elderly Jews in the former Soviet Union not because of prophecy but out of a sincere desire to bless the Jews. That raises a crucial question, however: If Christians can express their love for the Jewish people by supporting them in the countries where they now live, why do evangelical organizations urge all Jews to emigrate to Israel? Why do Christian Zionist groups maintain a hundreds of "fishers" in remote areas of the FSU to teach secular Jews about their religious heritage and to encourage them to move to Israel? Why do they pay the cost of the Jews' emigration? It may be out of concern for their safety in some cases. The Proclamation of the Third International Christian Zionist Congress, which the ICEJ organized in Jerusalem in 1996, said that explicitly: "We remain concerned for the fate of imperiled Jewish People in diverse places, and seek to encourage and assist in the continuing process of the Return of the Exiles to Eretz Yisrael [the land of Israel]."[31] Fair enough. But why, then, do evangelicals rejoice when North American Jews make aliyah, exposing themselves to greater risk in Israel than in their former homes? Pastor Omar was very definite on that point: he sees it as a sign that Christ is coming soon.

Clearly, these devout Christians are participating in God's plan. Bridges for Peace makes this explicit in calling its workers "fishers." This is a reference to a prophecy in Jeremiah:

> Therefore. behold, the days are coming, says the Lord, when it shall no longer be said, "As the Lord lives who brought up the people out of the land of Egypt," but "As the Lord lives who brought up the people of Israel out of the north country and out of all the countries where he had driven them." For I will bring them back to their own land which I gave to their fathers. *Behold, I am sending for many fishers,* says the Lord, and they shall catch them; and afterwards I will send for many hunters, and they shall hunt them from every mountain . . . (Jeremiah 16:14–16, emphasis mine)

This is the text that John Hagee got in hot water for in 2008 because he interpreted the fishers as early Zionists and the hunters as Nazis, as we saw in Chapter 8. Many other Christian Zionist preachers and writers also apply this passage to modern events, though with a different result: they see themselves as the fishers and they understand the "north country" to be the former Soviet Union, which is north of Israel.[32] The born-again fishers, then, are working to fulfill Jeremiah's prophecy. Other evangelical volunteers in the former Soviet Union also help to bring the prophecy to pass, filling out emigration forms for Jews, busing them to airports, and even providing ships to bring them to Israel. Christians for Israel has actively assisted the aliyah, sponsoring the Exobus program in partnership with the Jewish Agency to find Jews in Ukraine and transport them to Israel.[33] The international Christian Embassy Jerusalem has invested large sums in bringing *olim* ("immigrants") from Russia.[34] John Hagee Ministries reported having donated more than $8.5 million to help Jews make aliyah by August 2007.[35] Yechiel Eckstein's International Fellowship of Christians and Jews has also transported tens of thousands of Jews to Israel from the former Soviet Union, Ethiopia, and, most recently, India, through its On Wings of Eagles program, which is principally supported by evangelicals.

Conservative Christians' motives go beyond the promises of Genesis. Certainly they bless the Jews to express their gratitude and love and to win God's blessing, as in Genesis 12:3. They also are fulfilling Paul's prescription that Christians should share their material blessings with the Jews (Romans 15:27). But these scriptural considerations do not require them to encourage the Jewish people to emigrate to Israel. Nor do they oblige Christians to pay for the aliyah. Isaiah does prophesy that the nations will help carry the sons and daughters of the Hebrew people to Zion (49:22), and Christian Zionist activists are making that happen.[36] There is no biblical injunction to do it, however. So why do they?

For enormous numbers of born-again Christians, supporting the Jewish return to the Holy Land allows them to join in the unfolding of divine history. That is why evangelicals who work hard to make ends meet—from the scores of them in Pastor Omar's church in Queens to the hundreds of thousands who contribute to Yechiel Eckstein's charities—give their money to help Jews make aliyah. It is also a principal reason that hundreds of Christian volunteers seek out Jews in the former Soviet Union: to instill in them their own religious heritage and a desire to move to Israel.

Virtually every critic of Christian Zionism and every news source seeking a balanced report charges that these acts are overt attempts to hurry the Second Coming of Christ. For Israelis, immigration is a humanitarian cause, says Gershom Gorenberg. For conservative Christians, by contrast, part of the attraction is "to speed fulfillment of Endtime prophecy by helping with the ingathering of the exiles." Bill Moyers makes a similar claim: "Christians intoxicated with the delusional doctrine of [dispensationalism] not only await the rapture but believe they have an obligation to get involved politically to hasten the divine scenario for the Apocalypse," says Moyers.[37]

Ted Haggard, by contrast, asserts that the fishers are *cooperating* with biblical prophecy, not trying to speed it. "I don't know of any evangelicals, not even the John Hagees among them, who believe that they can hasten prophecy," he told me. In fact, American Christians are divided on this point: nearly one in four (23%) do believe that human actions can influence the timing of Christ's return, while half say that they cannot.[38] Haggard is one of the doubters on that score, but he does think that people can help *fulfill* prophecy, if God wills it. "Nineteen forty-eight was fulfillment of prophecy by the sovereign hand of God through a confluence of events," he said. Evangelicals believe that the realization of prophecy will continue as they assist people who want to go back to Israel, he noted. Haggard himself was one of the fishers earlier in his life. He understands the impulse to reach out to secular Jews in the former Soviet Union and educate them in Judaism. Even in America, he says, evangelicals love to see Jews recover their heritage and practice their traditional faith.[39]

So, do evangelicals intend to hasten the apocalypse or don't they? The answer is, both. Call it paradox, or mystery if you prefer. Most born-again Christians do not believe that they can determine God's timetable, since that is the Lord's business and no one knows the day or the hour of God's coming.[40] But millions of them are convinced that the divine clock is ticking and has been since the founding of the Israeli state. Nearly two-thirds of white American evangelicals believe that Israel, simply by virtue of its existence, helps fulfill the prophecies of Christ's Second Coming, as we have seen.[41] As these prophecies come true for the first time ever, many Bible-believers are certain that the final days are near. The fishers in the North and the donors in the West are acting accordingly. So are the evangelizers in Israel, the United States, and elsewhere: they are all doing their part to facilitate the unfolding of divine history. They are humbly aware that man's plans and man's time are not God's. They know that reversals, delays, and catastrophes can occur and that people cannot always shape or even know the outcome of their actions. But at the same time, by cooperating with prophecy, they are working to achieve its fulfillment. They are forwarding God's plan in the hope, if not the firm expectation, of speeding its end. "We are indeed told to pray that the Lord would hasten His return and that the times of the end would be hastened," says the International Christian Embassy's David Parsons. "Perhaps our actions do speed things up in that regard."[42]

Pat Robertson's fund-raising letter, asking for support for his evangelizing radio broadcasts in the Middle East, made that explicit: converting the Jews would fulfill prophecy and hasten Christ's return.[43]

The Billion Souls Initiative

The "Billion Souls Initiative" provides a parallel. The Global Pastors Network has set the goal of planting five million new churches worldwide in ten years. James Davis, president of the campaign, notes that Christ commissioned his disciples to tell everyone on earth how to achieve eternal life. "As we advance around the world," he says, "we'll be shortening the time needed to fulfill that Great Commission. Then, the Bible says, the end will come." The current generation may actually live long enough to see this," Davis adds. This pastors' group, which was established in 2001 by Bill Bright, founder of Campus Crusade for Christ, represents tens of thousands of congregations. Twenty thousand church leaders have attended its events, including prominent evangelicals who also happen to be Christian Zionists: Jerry Falwell, executives of Pat Robertson's 700 Club, Ted Haggard, and Bobby Welch, former president of the Southern Baptist Convention. (In January 2006, former New York City mayor Rudy Giuliani, seeking conservative Christian support in a run for president, addressed this pastors' group in Orlando, Florida.)[44] It seems logical that many of the pastors who so openly seek to hasten the end in this respect may well have the same hopes for Israel.

The Third Temple

Another way to hasten the end-times is to build the Third Temple in Jerusalem. In this, the yearnings of the Christian and Jewish religious right converge, sometimes issuing in a common enterprise. For dispensationalists, two of the three major events that serve as prelude to the Rapture have already occurred: the Jews have returned to their ancestral home and they have taken control of Jerusalem and much of the biblical Land of Israel. Premillennialists expect the next decisive step in prophetic history to be the rebuilding of the Temple, which the Antichrist will desecrate.[45] For many Jewish religious nationalists, too, salvation and the arrival of the Messiah depend on the existence of the Temple. Only there can Jewish priests carry out the ritual sacrifices and other rites prescribed by the Torah. From this perspective, the restored Temple is crucial to the redemption of the Jewish people and, through them, of all mankind.[46]

Gershon Salomon, the Israeli leader of a group dedicated to rebuilding the Temple, sounds almost like a dispensationalist himself when he talks about that. According to Salomon, "God brought us back to the Temple Mount to say to all the world, 'Not only do I continue my relationship with Israel, and Jews continue to be my Chosen People, but I now open up the fulfillment of my End Time plans.'" Salomon was on the Mount on June 7, 1967, the day that Israeli paratroopers rushed through the Lion's Gate, captured the Old City of Jerusalem, and raised the flag of Israel over the Dome of the Rock. But Moshe Dayan, acting on his own initiative as defense minister, yielded the day-to-day authority over the site to the Muslim religious authorities. Salomon considers that a sin and a terrible mistake. In response, he founded the Temple Mount and Land of Israel Faithful Movement, dedicated to removing the mosques and rebuilding the Temple.

In 1990, Salomon led a contingent of followers toward the Temple Mount in an attempt to lay a cornerstone for the Third Temple. Perhaps 5,000 Arabs defended the site, and when Israeli border guards arrived, at least seventeen Muslims were killed and hundreds injured.[47] Several times a year after that, Salomon returned to the ramp that leads from the Western Wall plaza to the Mount, demanding that he be allowed to go up and lay the cornerstone for the Temple. He typically was accompanied by a small group of the Temple Mount Faithful, often older ultranationalists and youngsters from the national-religious fringe of Zionism. In 2001, Arafat declared a Day of Rage in response. Arabs on the Mount threw down stones on Jewish worshippers at the Wall below and Israeli riot police stormed into the Muslim sacred site, firing tear gas and stun grenades. Twenty Palestinians and a dozen police were injured.[48]

Salomon has developed a close relationship with American evangelicals. Gorenberg observes that although Salomon is a messianic nationalist of the secular far right, he has learned to speak the language of Christian Zionism. His Internet mailings contain assertions like, "These are the godly, prophetic end-times and God is redeeming the people of Israel."[49] In 1991, appearing on Pat Robertson's 700 *Club*, Salomon asserted that he was engaged not only in a struggle for the Temple Mount but also for the redemption of the world. Robertson, for his part, declared, "We will never have peace until the Mount of the House of the Lord is restored."[50] Another example: in 1999, in a Jerusalem hotel, Salomon addressed a group of born-again tourists led by Reverend Irvin Baxter. He assured them that the Dome of the Rock will be moved to Mecca and the Third Temple will be built in their lifetimes. Evangelicals respond by sending him gifts, including gold and jewelry. Salomon describes the building of the Temple as the last act of the divine drama. Baxter, by contrast, considers it the penultimate act: still to come will be the Antichrist's desecration of the sanctuary, Armageddon, and Christ's return. They know each other's position, Gorenberg concludes, and each believes that he is exploiting the other.[51]

Another Israeli who urges the rebuilding of the Temple is Shlomo Goren. The chief rabbi of the army in 1967, he also was present when the Israeli forces captured the Temple Mount. According to one widely cited story, Goren, carrying a Torah scroll and a shofar, excitedly urged the head of the IDF Central Command to blow up the Dome of the Rock, an act that he believed would usher in the Messianic era. The officer, Major General Uzi Narkiss, threatened to imprison him.[52] In language that rivaled any dispensationalist's, Goren declared that the conquest of Jerusalem heralded redemption and was the most exalted moment in the history of the Jewish people.[53] Two months later, Goren and fifty followers returned to the Mount, where they fought off Arab and Israeli security and held a prayer service. Muslims saw that as a spiritual contamination and a political provocation. Soon afterward, the Chief Rabbinate formally forbade Jews to set foot there.[54] Despite this controversy, Goren was appointed the Ashkenazi chief rabbi of Israel in 1973 and served until 1983.

For centuries, Jews believed that only the Messiah could build the Temple. The great twelfth-century Rabbi Moses Maimonides wrote in the *Mishneh Torah,* his code of Jewish law, that building the Mikdash (Temple) on its site and gathering in the dispersed remnant of Israel were, in fact, two of the defining qualities of the Moshiach (Messiah).[55] Many ultra-Orthodox Jews still hold to that and to the conviction that only the Messiah can establish a legitimate Jewish state. For mankind to "force the End" by taking those things on himself is the work of Satan, they say. Rabbi Zvi Yehuda Kook, the head of the Merkaz Harav Yeshiva in Jerusalem, taught, by contrast, that the redemption had already begun. His followers could advance God's plan by settling in the whole of Israel permanently, said Kook. Still, like his father, former chief rabbi Abraham Yitzhak Kook, he declared that it was not yet time to build the Temple.[56] In the years following the Six-Day War, however, "redemptive Zionists" spoke openly of doing just that, undaunted by the catastrophic war that could follow. According to one estimate, by 1998 perhaps 1,000 ultra-nationalists were active in radical Temple Mount movements.[57]

There have been occasional isolated attacks on the Mount, including one in 1969 by an Australian Christian tourist whom Israeli judges found insane. The best organized and most extensively planned scheme to destroy the Dome of the Rock was developed by the Gush Emunim underground. In 1984, Israeli police learned of the plot when they thwarted an attempt by West Bank Gush activists to bomb five Arab buses. During the investigation, it came out that members of the same group had planted bombs on the cars of five West Bank Arab mayors and attacked Hebron's Islamic College. Several of them also had plotted from 1978 to 1982 to destroy the Dome of the Rock. They considered the Dome, the oldest major Islamic building and one of the most beautiful, to be an "abomination" and a contamination of the site of the Temple. The Gush terrorists aborted the plan in 1982, in part because they couldn't get rabbinic approval for it.[58]

The Red Heifer

A major obstacle to any such plot is the absence of a red heifer. According to Numbers 19, anyone who comes into contact with a human corpse or bone, or even a grave, is unclean until he is cleansed with water containing the ashes of a perfectly unblemished red heifer. Only that can remove the impurity that comes with even indirect contact with the dead. Without it, the contaminated person who enters the tabernacle of the Lord defiles it and must be "cut off from the midst of the assembly" (19:20). The ashes of the last red heifer are said to have run out after the destruction of the Temple in the year 70, however, leaving all Jews presumably impure, and so, unfit to tread on the site of the Holy of Holies. As a result, there was no way for Orthodox Jews to try to build the Third Temple. Maimonides said that there have been only nine red heifers in history. The tenth, he predicted, would arrive at the time of the Messiah.

In the 1990s, one born-again Christian tried to supply that cow: Clyde Lott, a cattle breeder and Pentecostal preacher from Mississippi. Lott knew the significance of the heifer from his Bible study. And from the prophecy preaching that he had heard, Lott understood that to actually produce such a creature promised to be one of the most significant events in nearly two thousand years. His plan was to use modern breeding techniques with champion Red Angus stock, and he allied with the Temple Institute in Jerusalem, an organization that is dedicated to building the Temple. Over time, Lott's thinking evolved. Rather than shipping a few hundred Red Angus cattle to Israel, he decided to bring 50,000, to build the Israeli livestock industry until the end-times arrived. He began to breed the cows in Nebraska and formed a nonprofit company in 1998, with pastors from Pennsylvania to California as officers and board members. He sent out a fund-raising letter that citied Genesis 12:3. In the end, though, the project faltered over financial disagreements and an allegation that Lott had spoken in Florida about spreading the Gospel in Israel.[59]

Timothy Weber quite reasonably calls this episode "one of the most blatant attempts by dispensationalists to help prophecy happen."[60] Interestingly, Lott doesn't agree, and his reasoning provides another example of paradox in evangelical thinking about the end-times. Lott says that he actually opposes efforts to hasten the End! He considers it very sad that Christians want the Temple to be rebuilt solely to bring on the Rapture and the Antichrist. The people who advocate that are selfish and anti-Semitic, Lott declares. He denies any connection with extremists who want to destroy the Dome of the Rock and the Al-Aqsa mosque and says that he doesn't know how or when the Temple will be built. "In God's timing, we know that all Bible prophecy will be fulfilled," he observes. His own intention, Lott says, was to simply bring the red cows to Israel, to create the circumstances in which God might or might not choose to act. Lott sees his role in the context of God's promise in Isaiah 30:23, which speaks of a day when "your cattle will graze in large pastures." "If God chooses to use the Numbers 19 red heifer from that standpoint, that's up to God," he concludes.[61]

In 1996, while these events were still unfolding, a red heifer named Melody was born on a farm near Haifa. The mainstream press in Israel and the West covered the story, which ignited "Jewish longing for the Temple, Christian hopes for the rapture, and Muslim paranoia about the destruction of the mosques," as the author Lawrence Wright observed later.[62] Yisrael Ariel, the founder of the Temple Institute, visited Melody, along with fifteen or twenty others from the Temple movement. So did a group of 100 clergymen from Texas. Reverend Irvin Baxter featured Melody on the cover of his *Endtime* magazine, and televangelist Jack Van Impe wondered if her ashes would be available by the millennial year 2000.[63] The media treated this story as a curiosity or an amusement. One Israeli journalist realized how dangerous it was, though. David Landau, writing in *Haaretz,* called Melody "a four-legged bomb" and suggested putting a bullet in her head. At the age of eighteen months, however, Melody sprouted a cluster of white hair and became just another cow. In 2002 another red heifer was born in Israel and things worked out the same way for her.[64]

That did not end evangelical interest in finding a red heifer and allowing Israeli extremists to take matters from there. By the end of 1999, Israeli authorities were afraid that premillennialist Christians would try to blow up the mosques, and their fear, says Yaakov Ariel, bordered on hysteria.[65] That moment passed, but the danger hasn't gone away, says Gorenberg. "The Temple Mount is potentially a detonator of a full-scale war, and a few people trying to rush the end could set it off."[66] Carmi Gillon, former chief of Israel's Shin Bet internal security agency, is well aware of the threat. "Every day in Jerusalem that ends peacefully is a miracle" and protecting the Dome of the Rock is Mission Impossible, he says. The catastrophe that Gillon dreads is the redemption that Gershon Salomon eagerly anticipates. "God is waiting for us to move the mosques and rebuild," says Salomon. "The Jews may not be ready, but the Christians are."[67] Some people suspect that George W. Bush is one of those Christians.

Is George W. Bush a Christian Zionist?

Several commentators have speculated that Bush sympathizes with Israel because in Scripture the entire Holy Land belongs to the Jews, the apple of God's eye.[68] In *Standing with Israel,* David Brog appears to assume that because Bush is an evangelical, he is a Christian Zionist, and that this shaped his Middle East policy. "To a certain extent," says Brog, "evangelical Christians are preaching to the converted when they speak to George Bush about Israel." Brog acknowledges that Bush had domestic and geopolitical reasons for supporting the Jewish state. Still, he argues, George W.'s faith affected his foreign and domestic policy. "Look at the major differences between the way this President Bush treats Israel and the way his father did," he says. "Have the geopolitics really changed so much since Bush 41 left the White House? No. Has the religious orientation of the president changed? You bet."[69] This implies that faith was the principal difference between the policies of Bush father and son. It fails to take into account the impact of 9/11 and other intervening events, as well as experience, character, and political philosophy. And it attributes religious convictions to George W. without offering proof.

John Green observes that George W. does not embrace the Christian Zionist agenda down the line as he would if he were one of them. The reason, says Green, is simple: "He isn't one of them." Bush reads the Bible faithfully. And, says Green, he no doubt sees Israel as positive and admirable. Green would be very surprised, though, if his policies were motivated by a particular reading of Scripture.[70] Richard Land confirms that. Bush is "a plain vanilla evangelical," he told me. "His personal faith is based on his relationship with Jesus. He believes that God is still working in history."[71] Bush probably isn't engaged by many theological details far beyond that, though. Land calls him a "mere Christian" in C. S. Lewis's sense: Bush believes in the lordship of Jesus, the Crucifixion, the Resurrection, and other elements of the faith that have been "common to nearly all Christians at all times."[72] Bush describes himself in that way.[73] Doug Wead, who worked closely with George W. on his father's 1988 presidential run, says the same. Bush "has absolutely zero interest in anything theological—nothing," says Wead.[74] That does not impugn the depth and fervor of Bush's faith, though. As Ted Haggard said before his fall from grace, Bush's religious convictions run deep.[75]

People who worked with Bush agree that his faith did not influence his Mideast policy. "I absolutely do not believe that his religion dictates his policies, absolutely," says Wead. His faith in God is about if there is a God and [if] there is eternity. It relates to those issues."[76] David Frum agrees. Bush's religion is a great source of personal psychic strength, he says, but his faith didn't prejudge his policy conclusions. Asked about some evangelicals' claims that God punished Sharon for dividing the land, Frum responded succinctly, "That's not the way the president would think."[77] Former presidential counselor Dan Bartlett also says that Bush divorced policy making from personal faith. "I have never heard him describe the broader context of our times in biblical terms—not even the Middle East," he says. Ari Fleischer, former White House spokesman, says the same. Fleischer observes that he never saw any evidence, publicly or privately, that the president's faith had anything to do with his pro-Israel position. "I would have been very uncomfortable with that," says Fleischer, who, incidentally, is Jewish.[78]

Is Bush a Dispensationalist?

Some journalists and other observers have gone even further, however, suggesting that Bush secretly subscribes to dispensational views of the end-times and that he designed American policy around Christian eschatology. Deanne Stillman, writing in the *Nation* in 2002, said that "Bush may (reluctantly and with great difficulty) regard himself as an usher of the Second Coming." Analysts who tried to understand Bush's policies according to political events missed the point, she argued. "To many evangelical Christians, what's playing out in the Middle East is all part of God's plan. The only thing a born-again President can do is stand at the helm and occasionally turn the rudder, making sure that Israel survives."[79] The late Edward Said wrote in *Al-Ahram* in 2002 that "strange fundamentalist Christian sects" are "a menace to the world and furnish the Bush government with its rationale for punishing evil."[80]

Some critics charge that Bush was particularly influenced by Tim LaHaye's *Left Behind* novels, the best-selling action series depicting fictional events that will follow the Rapture.[81] LaHaye himself said that he has no idea whether his prophecy teaching has had an impact on George W. Jerry Falwell, by contrast, offered a startling speculation on how Bush's beliefs about the end-times compare with LaHaye's: "My guess is that his views would differ very little, but that's conjecture," he said.[82]

Esther Kaplan argued in her 2004 book, *With God on Their Side,* that Bush's Middle East policy accorded perfectly with LaHaye's theology. "From his unflinching support of Israel's far right government to his invasion of Iraq," Kaplan concluded, "Bush's Middle East policy perfectly aligns with the worldview of LaHaye and his millions of readers."[83] Especially early in its first term, however, the Bush administration's support of Israel was far from unflinching. It hardly reflected an unwavering pro-Israel religious commitment, as we shall see in Chapter 10. And Bush's endorsement of a Palestinian state on the West Bank and of Israel's withdrawal from Gaza, both on the record by 2004, starkly conflicted with the convictions of LaHaye and other Christian Zionists. Indeed, in taking these positions, Bush baffled and antagonized many of his evangelical backers. "Gaza broke the evangelicals' heart," my senior source Faith told me in February 2006. One pro-Israel evangelical activist and educator in Texas confided, "Every Christian Zionist is in total shock over what Bush is doing. Arab oil is more important than Jewish lives."[84] In 2007, Pat Robertson denounced the Bush administration's recently revived interest in a two-state solution. Citing God Himself as his source, Robertson declared that the president's policies were pushing Israel toward national suicide. Then he went so far as to question Bush's character as well as his beliefs: the president and his advisers were only feigning friendship with Israel, Robertson declared. He was charging the president with hypocrisy about an issue that Robertson and many others regard as central to their faith. Hal Lindsey seconded Robertson's skepticism. Bush must be aware of the "avalanche of hard evidence" that the Palestinians' goal is to destroy Israel, Lindsey declared. So Israel's destruction must be okay with the president and other world leaders, he concluded.[85]

Craig Unger wrote in *Vanity Fair* in 2005, however, that political views derived from the dispensational apocalyptic vision "have shaped the political discourse all the way to Jerusalem and the White House."[86] In the same year, former president Jimmy Carter asserted that Bush had injected the belief system of the *Left Behind* books into American policy in the Middle East. This theology, said Carter, calls for war against Islam (Iraq?) and the expulsion of all non-Jews from the Holy Land. "I think that's a completely stupid and ridiculous premise on which to base foreign policy and on which to base support for Israel," Carter added in 2006.[87] He offered no proof that a fundamentalist eschatology inspired the war in Iraq, however. As for transferring Arabs out of Israel and the occupied territories, it is an extreme position, not widely advocated by Christian Zionist leaders.

Surprisingly, Karen Armstrong, the distinguished author of *The Battle for God,* made similar unsubstantiated assertions about Bush's faith. Writing during Israel's war with Hezbollah in July 2006, she claimed that fundamentalist notions of the Rapture, Armageddon, and the Millennium are all familiar and congenial to Bush. These end-times beliefs, Armstrong opined, "can perhaps throw light on the behaviour of a president who, *it is said,* believes that God chose him to lead the world to Rapture" (emphasis mine). These claims, based on unnamed sources, were wholly unsupported by evidence. So was Armstrong's statement that Bush's embrace of fundamentalist belief "explains his unconditional and uncritical support for Israel, his willingness to use 'Jewish End-time warriors' to fulfill a vision of his own."[88] Curiously, Armstrong subverted her own argument. She listed the conviction that the Jews must control all of the Holy Land in order for Christ to return as one the fundamentalist beliefs that Bush finds congenial. If so, his policy was in direct conflict with his faith.

White House officials dismissed the idea that John Darby's premillennial beliefs had any role in policy making. After leaving the Bush administration, Michael Gerson wrote that he couldn't imagine that the president or the secretary of state shares dispensational views. "But I wouldn't know for sure," said Gerson, "because I never heard such views advocated or mentioned in five years of policy discussions I participated in at the White House."[89] Based on extensive interviews with administration officials, D. Michael Lindsay confirms that the apocalyptic eschatology of conservative biblical prophecy is completely foreign to Bush and his approach toward Israel. Not even Bush's critics could cite a single instance of such views being part of a policy discussion in the administration.[90]

Don Poage, Bush's longtime friend who studied Bible with him in the Community Bible Study program in Midland, Texas, in the mid-1980s, put this in perspective. Poage doubts that God's promise in Genesis 12:3 to bless those who bless Israel is significant to Bush as a specific verse. He does believe, though, that the Holy Spirit has woven the concept within the verse into the fiber of the former president's being. But when I asked him the inevitable question, could Bush privately be a dispensationalist, he replied with good-natured derision: "Is a guy who gets his words mixed up as much as this guy secretly planning to battle Satan?" The former president would have to be as smooth as butter to keep something like that from coming out, Poage told me, and George W. Bush definitely is not.[91] Mark Leaverton, who taught the Community Bible Study course when Bush was a member, also believes that the president is familiar with the special relationship between the Jews and the land. Bush must be impressed by the Abrahamic covenant deeding the land to the Jews eternally, he said. "I wouldn't be surprised if he took it as an irrevocable promise that God made to the Jews," Leaverton noted. "The president knows that God doesn't break his promises," but the covenant is something that we have to leave to God, he said. "Our job is to make peace."[92] David Aikens, in A Man of Faith, his spiritual biography of Bush, also suggests that the president privately holds a biblically favorable view of Israel's existence.[93] That is not the same thing as a dogmatic view of the end-times and Armageddon, however.

Richard Land confirms that the president is deeply committed to Israel's survival, but not for religious reasons. "The president doesn't do the backstroke in that particular stream of evangelicalism," he told me. Bush's position on abortion offers an instructive contrast. Land has said that the president's pro-life position is grounded in faith and conviction. I asked him if the same is true of Bush's allegiance to Israel. No, Land replied: the president's commitment to the Jewish state may be as deep, but it's not based on religion.[94] Bush's support is founded on humanitarian and geopolitical grounds. He sees Israel as a nation conceived after horrific experiences in the Holocaust, a democracy in a sea of dictatorships, and a firm ally in the war on terror.

Bush has explicitly acknowledged the religious significance of the modern State of Israel, however. In his speech before the Knesset in May 2008 marking the sixtieth anniversary of Israel's birth, Bush affirmed that the Jewish state represents "the redemption of an ancient promise given to Abraham and Moses and David—a homeland for the chosen people." He based this conviction purely on Scripture, with no theological elaboration. Bush added that the friendship between the United States and Israel derives from a number of considerations. Americans admire Israel's many accomplishments and its modern society based on the love of justice, liberty, and human dignity, he said. The United States stands with Israel in defending those values against people who claim the mantle of Islam, but who in reality are irreligious. The enemy pursues "a narrow vision of cruelty and control by committing murder, inciting fear, and spreading lies," Bush said. It is an ancient battle between good and evil, he concluded.[95]

"He's Damned if He Does and Damned if He Doesn't"

Bush himself flatly denied that he based his policy on end-times theology, though he said this a little uncomfortably, in an awkward moment in March 2006. After the president gave a speech in Cleveland, a questioner referred to Kevin Phillips's best-selling *American Theology*. Phillips says that members of the administration have reached out to prophetic Christians who see the war in Iraq and the rise of terrorism as signs of the apocalypse, the questioner noted. "Do you believe this? And if not, why not?" she asked. "Hmmm," the president replied and laughed along with the audience. "The answer is, I haven't really thought of it that way. (LAUGHTER) Here's how I think of it. First I've heard of that, by the way," he said, adding, "I guess I'm more of a practical fellow." It was the attack on 9/11 that shaped his attitude, fortifying his resolve to protect America, he explained.[96] CNN commentator Lou Dobbs, in an interview with Phillips that evening, observed that a simple yes or no answer would have sufficed. Bush couldn't give such a response, Phillips replied. About 55 percent of Republican voters believe in Armageddon and the Antichrist, and the president couldn't alienate them by denying those articles of faith, he said. On the other hand, he couldn't publicly endorse these views either. "He's damned if he does and damned if he doesn't," said Phillips.[97]

"The President Views This as One of His Challenges as President"

After the 2000 election, Karl Rove concluded that four million conservative religious voters hadn't voted and he determined to court them for 2004. As a result, the Bush presidency accorded evangelicals frequent access to the White House. They have been regularly briefed and consulted in telephone conferences and meetings, and they are entirely capable of reminding the administration of their clout and their convictions on specific issues, including Israel. Devout Christians have made the biblical grounds for supporting Israel very clear to the president. My senior evangelical source Faith told me that Bush invited the late Christian Zionist Ed McAteer and twenty prominent evangelicals and religious Jews to speak to him at the White House, to make sure that he understood their scriptural views on this matter.[98] In July 2003, Yechiel Eckstein, the orthodox rabbi who has allied with evangelicals since 1977, brought a delegation of Christian Zionists to the White House for a "quiet meeting" with Condoleezza Rice, then the national security adviser, and Elliott Abrams, then the National Security Council director of Near East and North African Affairs. The evangelicals fervently opposed the Road Map to Peace. Rice expressed the administration's sympathy for their concerns and stressed her own born-again convictions. She declared that it was Bush's faith that prompted him to take the positions he did.[99] Pat Robertson has said straightforwardly that Bush, Cheney, Rumsfeld, and Wolfowitz all grasp the "spiritual significance" of what's going on in Israel.[100] In 2002, more than one influential evangelical made public and private declarations that Israel's security had become their number one concern, as we shall see.

Bush listened to these views but there is reason to question whether he took them seriously. In fact, Bush regarded end-times believers as a problem, according to his White House spokesman. At a July 2006 press conference, Tony Snow perhaps inadvertently revealed Bush's discomfort with those important members of his electoral base. At the time, LaHaye, Falwell, Hal Lindsey, and other Christian Zionist leaders were interpreting Israel's conflict with Hezbollah as a precursor of Armageddon. One journalist asked Snow what Bush thought about these beliefs among some of his strongest supporters. With disarming candor, Snow replied, "The President views this as one of his challenges as President." Bush does not look through a theological lens, said Snow, but rather through the perspective of national interest and the expansion of democracy.[101] Implicit in this response was the fact that the president was walking a political tightrope. He needed to retain the allegiance of prominent conservative Christians without necessarily acting on their convictions about Israel. On that subject, Bush embraced their support but evidently not their theology.

10

✦

Christion Zionists, Bush, and
the Al-Aqsa Intifada

Analyses of George W. Bush's Middle East policy often speak of his unprecedented tilt toward Israel. Thomas Pickering, former U.S. ambassador to Israel, Russia, and the United Nations, for example, says that "Bush was more overtly, publicly, and ideologically attached to Sharon and Israel than any previous American leader has been attached to an Israeli leader or a party."[1] Matt Brooks, executive director of the Republican Jewish Coalition, goes even further. Bush, he says, was "not only the most pro-Israel president, [he] redefined what it means to be pro-Israel."[2]

The Bush administration was not always skewed in favor of Israel, though. To the contrary, from late summer 2001 until the spring of 2002, U.S. policy hardly gave Jerusalem the unwavering support for which it later became known. This period saw the height of the Al-Aqsa Intifada and Israel's massive military response, Operation Defensive Shield. Christian Zionist leaders, alarmed by the Palestinian violence and acutely sensitive to the threat to the Israeli Jews, rose to Israel's support. In rallies and e-mail and telephone campaigns, they pressed Bush to stop equivocating: they exhorted him to put aside other considerations and side definitively with Jerusalem's efforts to root out terrorism. That was Washington's own policy toward Muslim radicals, they declared, so it would be hypocritical to ask Israel to do otherwise. Bush, they insisted, should allow Prime Minister Ariel Sharon to do that as he saw fit. Gary Bauer and other evangelicals later claimed that their pressure tactics worked: they induced Bush to change his position, giving Sharon free rein in dealing with the Palestinians. Media reports largely accepted that narrative.[3]

The Al-Aqsa Intifada

The Al-Aqsa Intifada ("uprising," literally "shaking off") was ignited when Sharon made a tour of the Temple Mount in September 2000. Following that visit, Palestinians rioted on the site, throwing stones at Jews and tourists praying at the Western Wall below, and held demonstrations on the West Bank. Within days, the Israeli army and police killed scores of Palestinians and wounded very many more. Israelis charged that Yasser Arafat and the Palestinian Authority had planned the revolt, while the PLO asserted that it was a spontaneous reaction to excessive Israeli use of force. A cycle of violence and severe response followed. One attack that particularly disturbed Israelis was a Hamas suicide bombing that killed twenty-one, mostly teenagers, at the Dolphinarium dance club in Tel Aviv. That impeded American attempts to establish a cease-fire.

Sharon, who had been elected prime minister in February 2001 on the promise of restoring security to Israel, attempted to suppress the Intifada by force. Saudi Arabia's Crown Prince Abdullah and other pro-Western Arab leaders then pressed Bush to restrain him. Televised scenes of Israeli police and army attacks on rioting Palestinians had enraged Arabs and other Muslims, along with many others around the world. As a result, friendly Arab rulers warned Washington that their ties to the United States could destabilize their regimes. During a visit to the White House in the spring of 2001, Abdullah said that he could not afford even to be photographed with Bush. Polls showed that over 95 percent of Saudis considered the Palestinian issue to be the most important *domestic* political problem in Saudi Arabia. That galvanized the White House and the State Department.[4] Secretary of State Colin Powell's staff worked throughout August 2001 on a speech that would establish a timetable for declaring a Palestinian state within three years. When a suicide bomber killed fifteen people at a Sbarro's pizza restaurant in the heart of Jerusalem that month, the State Department was undeterred. In fact, one of their spokesmen condemned Israel for retaliating. At the same time, the United States and Britain were developing a plan for an international peacekeeping force that could conceivably protect Arafat when other terrorists hit Israel.[5]

In late August, after watching television footage of an Israeli soldier brutally mistreating an elderly Palestinian woman, Abdullah dispatched Prince Bandar bin Sultan, the Saudi ambassador to the United States, to deliver a decisive message to Bush. It now appeared that the marriage between their nations must end in divorce, Bandar told him. According to a Saudi account of the story, Bandar said that the president had allowed Sharon "to determine everything in the Middle East," permitting Israel to act "as if a drop of Jewish blood is equal to thousands of Palestinians' lives." As a result, the crown prince would now cease all communication with Bush. Two days later, on August 29, the president sent Abdullah a letter supporting the Palestinian people's right to a state of their own. That was a very significant step. Even Bill Clinton had never specifically endorsed a discrete Palestinian state. Bush planned to announce his position publicly during the week of September 10, 2001, but events the next day prevented that from happening.[6]

Israel Will Not Be "Sacrificed to the Arabs"

The attacks of 9/11 are often cited as a turning point in American foreign policy, but there was no instant course correction regarding Israel. To the contrary, the United States sought to court Arab leaders as allies in the war on terrorism. When Arafat denounced Osama bin Laden, seeking to dissociate himself from America's enemies, Bush began to look for ways to reward the Palestinian leader.[7] In late September, the president urged Sharon to show restraint in the West Bank, then pressed him to allow Shimon Peres, Israel's foreign minister at the time, to meet with Arafat. In early October, Bush publicly announced his support for a Palestinian state. Though Bush and Sharon had agreed not to take each other by surprise, the Israeli leader was caught off guard and felt betrayed. Sharon lashed out at the president, warning him not to adopt a policy of appeasement, as British Prime Minister Neville Chamberlain had done with Czechoslovakia in 1938. Israel will not be "sacrificed to the Arabs" for a momentary gain, Sharon vowed. "From now on, we will only count on ourselves." Bush was reportedly furious and Sharon apologized. The bond that the two had established during then-Governor Bush's visit to Israel in 1998 was wearing thin.

Powell called Sharon almost every day to press him to renew talks with the Palestinians and to contain violent clashes in the territories. Israeli leaders, for their part, were bitter toward the Bush administration. Sharon was reportedly upset that Israel was supplying the United States with intelligence for the upcoming invasion of Afghanistan and getting in return only pressure to bargain with Arafat.[8] Then, on October 17, 2001, came a turning point that hardened Israel's resolve to ignore American pressure to moderate its responses to terrorist attacks. Instead, Sharon determined to root out the militants' infrastructure in the West Bank. The critical event was the assassination of an Israeli called Gandhi.

The Assassination of Gandhi

Gandhi's real name was Rehavam Ze'evi. He had been nicknamed Gandhi in his youth because he was extremely thin and shaved his head. The name turned out to be exquisitely ironic. Ze'evi was the polar opposite of India's Mohandas K. Gandhi, who dedicated himself to achieving tolerant coexistence with Muslims. The Israeli Gandhi advocated the reverse. He was on the extreme right of Israeli politics, seeking the "transfer" of the Palestinians from the West Bank and Gaza Strip to Arab nations.[9] As a result, he was a highly controversial figure, hated and feared by many Palestinians. Many Israelis respected his war record and his love of the land, while others considered him a racist and a fascist.

Whatever people thought of him, Ze'evi was one of the founding generation of the State of Israel. Born in Jerusalem in 1926, he had served in the Palmach, the elite force of the Jewish underground in British mandatory Palestine, and fought in the 1948, 1956, and 1967 wars. In 1967 he led a ruthless hunt for Palestine Liberation Organization guerillas who were infiltrating into the West Bank from Jordan, and he became a major-general in the IDF. In 1972, when Prime Minister Golda Meir was looking for the toughest general she could find to hunt down the Black September terrorists who had slaughtered Israeli athletes at the Munich Olympics, she chose Ze'evi. He then served as his friend Prime Minister Yitzhak Rabin's adviser on terrorism from 1974 to 1977. Gandhi was part of the flesh and blood of the Israeli establishment and so was accepted in positions of power despite the extremity of his political views.

In 1988 Ze'evi was elected to the Knesset as the leader of Moledet ("Motherland"), a fringe political party he had founded. He soon earned notoriety when one member of the Knesset deplored the loss of Palestinian lives in the first intifada, which was then under way. Gandhi's shocking response was, "For every Jew, a thousand Arabs."[10] He advocated a "negative magnet policy" through which Israel would deny Palestinians work or an education so they would leave of their own accord.[11] Ze'evi was appointed minister of tourism in March 2001, a relatively unimportant cabinet post at that time but one for which he was highly qualified because of his extensive knowledge of biblical archaeology. He sparked further controversy when he compared Palestinians living and working illegally in Israel to lice and a cancer.

Ze'evi resigned from the Knesset in October 2001 to protest the government's acquiescence to American demands that Israel withdraw its forces from the area of Hebron in the West Bank. He also rejected American plans for a Palestinian state. Israel should wipe out terrorists, he said, not partner with Arafat, whom he called a viper, a scorpion, a vampire, and a Hitler. It wasn't murder to kill terrorists, he added, and he called on the IDF to destroy Arafat's house. Ze'evi loathed the peace process, which he believed would lead to the second genocide of the Jews within a century. The biggest challenge facing Israel, he declared, was how to thwart Colin Powell's initiative to create two states.

Two days after Ze'evi's resignation, assassins from the Popular Front for the Liberation of Palestine (PFLP), a radical Marxist wing of the PLO, entered the Jerusalem Hyatt Regency Hotel and put three bullets in his head and neck in the hallway outside of his room. The PFLP later declared that the killing was revenge for Israel's slaying of its leader three weeks earlier. They had targeted Ze'evi, they said, because he was a symbol of racism and extremism. The PFLP had a history of opposing all Middle East peace efforts, including the Oslo Accords, a point, ironically, on which it agreed with Ze'evi.

Ze'evi, who was still officially a member of the cabinet at the time of his death, is the only Israeli government minister ever to have been killed by Arab terrorists. Sharon eulogized him as the greatest lover of *Eretz Yisrael* ("the Land of Israel"), who knew its shards, its crevices, its citadels. "May God avenge his blood," said the prime minister. Arafat sent his condolences, but Jerusalem held the Palestinian Authority responsible for the killing. Sharon demanded that Arafat turn over the captured assassins. Fearful that a harsh response by Israel could upset the attempt to bring Arab and Muslim states into a global war on terrorism, Washington did not support Sharon in this.[12]

There were two immediate consequences of the assassination. First, the already strong ties between evangelical Christians and Israel deepened. This happened on a symbolic level even as Ze'evi lay dying. In a nearby room, the Reverend David Hocking, an American evangelical pastor, heard a thud as Gandhi's body hit the hallway floor. Hearing Mrs. Ze'evi's screams, he rushed out to see the bloody scene. Hocking, who had led Christian tourists to Israel for thirty years, was shaken by this experience, but he continues to bring believers to the Holy Land. His father and his wife were Jewish and he considered himself to be Jewish as well, having supported Israel his whole life. His goal is to educate the American public about the justice of Israel's cause. Dr. Hocking is now the pastor of the Hope for Today ministry in Tustin, California, which maintains a strong interest in the Jewish state. His ministry's Web site in 2008 advertised a tour of Israel and carried an image of the Israeli flag with the caption "Pray for the peace of Israel." The site also had an archive of news stories about Israel, one of which praised the pope and the Italian prime minister for shunning Iranian president Ahmadinejad during his recent visit to Italy. Earlier articles on the site included a report that Senator Barack Obama is secretly anti-Israel, a warning by former IDF chief of staff Moshe Yaalon against the current Mideast peace initiative, and a denunciation of "God's Warriors," a CNN series in which Christiane Amanpour presented an allegedly biased depiction of West Bank settlers.[13]

The more long-term measure of the new strengthening of the conservative Christian bond to Israel was that Ze'evi's successor as tourism minister was Rabbi Benny Elon. Although Hocking said that many Christians loved Ze'evi, Gandhi was not invested in tourism.[14] Elon, by contrast, used his position to quickly become one of the most influential Israelis in the American evangelical world.

Benny Elon and the "Road Map to Hell"

A ninth-generation Jerusalemite, Elon is the son of a deputy chief justice of Israel's Supreme Court. Like Ze'evi, he seemed destined to be part of the Israeli establishment until he emerged as a leader of the political far right. He first came to prominence as the founder of an East Jerusalem yeshiva, built on land taken from Jordan in 1967. Upon succeeding Ze'evi as minister of tourism, he courted American evangelicals, both to attract them as tourists and to strengthen Israel's political alliance with them. "Benny Elon was the first guy to do the things we're involved with now," Ronn Torossian told me later. Torossian runs his own public relations firm in New York and, amazingly, has represented both the Christian Coalition and the Government of Israel. His current client list includes John Hagee, Christians United for Israel, and Benny Hinn Ministries, on the one hand, and the American Jewish Congress and the Zionist Organization of America on the other.[15] It was Elon who helped make such a connection possible, Torossian observed. "The Jewish establishment doesn't help us. They're afraid of their own shadow," he said. Rather it was the Israelis who built the ties to evangelicals in the United States, he noted. Former prime minister Netanyahu developed a political alliance with Jerry Falwell and Pat Robertson, Torossian observed, but Netanyahu doesn't know their right-hand people. He wouldn't know how to get things done. Benny Elon does. Elon "believed in creating an infrastructure with the Christian Right [to] influence policy within the White House." Elon is the best-known Jewish figure to evangelicals, bar none, and is very well respected among the Christian right, Torossian told me. Since 2001, it was Elon who had put the most effort into getting their attention, he added. In that year Elon met Roberta Combs, head of the Christian Coalition, and started lobbying in the halls of the Senate and Congress, trying to influence U.S. policy to favor Israel.[16]

In 2003, Elon led the first major campaign to attract tourists since the start of the intifada, and he focused on evangelicals. Revenue from tourism to the Holy Land had dropped drastically, from $4 billion prior to the conflict to $1 billion in 2002, and Elon credited Christian tourists with keeping it from collapsing altogether. When American Jews called off their trips to Israel, evangelicals didn't. "They were not afraid," he said. "They saved the industry." So in this campaign Elon aimed to attract born-again Christians in particular. Tourism Ministry officials visited U.S. churches and placed ads on Christian radio stations with the theme "Don't put your soul on hold."[17]

At the same time that Elon attempted to revive Israel economically through tourism, he also tried to revive it spiritually, according to his biblical understanding of the world. He argued that the Jewish state should keep its God-given inheritance of Judea and Samaria, which he called the nation's heartland, and he offered a solution to the problem of the Palestinians who lived there. Ze'evi had advocated "voluntary transfer" of Palestinians to other Arab countries. Elon went further: he proposed forcibly removing them as punishment for the intifada. He added that the quiet majority of his countrymen supported transfer. In fact, 35 percent of Israelis favored that approach as the violence raged in 2002, far from a majority but a surprisingly strong endorsement of a policy that many liberal Israelis considered racist. Elon later modified that plan, proposing incentives of up to $200,000 per family to encourage Palestinian refugees to leave the West Bank for other countries.[18]

In frequent radio and newspaper interviews, Elon fervently opposed the Road Map to Peace that the United States, the European Union, Russia, and the UN had proposed. In May 2003, he took his case to Washington, D.C. According to Salon.com, Elon told 800 Christian supporters at the Israeli embassy's Solidarity and Prayer Breakfast that Israel would never give up the West Bank. Then he met with Dick Armey, the former House majority leader, who also had publicly supported the "transfer" of Palestinians to Arab states. From there Elon met with Senator Lindsey Graham (R-South Carolina), who greeted him like an old friend and accepted Elon's invitation to tour the Temple Mount. Elon professed not to care that President Bush would not meet with him, since evangelicals with access to the president would convey his ideas. "I prefer to have the message come to him through my Christian contacts here in the United States," he said.[19]

Elon warned Gary Bauer that month that Bush was about to pressure Sharon to accept the Road Map, and American evangelicals rose up in protest. At a Washington, D.C., conference, speakers denounced it as a "Road Map to hell." Bauer then organized a letter to Bush declaring that it would be reprehensible to be evenhanded in dealing with the Israelis and the Palestinian terrorists.[20]

"This is not a road map, it is a road trap," Elon told Pat Robertson from Jerusalem in an appearance on the *700 Club* later that month. The State Department had put great pressure on Sharon to accept the Road Map, Elon replied. Yet this plan was a trap because Arafat would never, never accept a real peace, he said. Robertson agreed. If the Road Map is implemented, Robertson said, "it will be the beginning of the end of the state of Israel as we know it. I think that the President of the United States is imperiling the nation of Israel. Not only is he going against the clear mandate of the Bible, which is very important, but he's also setting up a situation where Israel will no longer have secure borders."[21]

To counter the Road Map, Elon floated his own "peace plan." It called for Israel to immediately dissolve the Palestinian Authority, uproot the terrorist infrastructure in Samaria and Judea, and recognize Jordan as the Palestinian national state. Israel would then declare its sovereignty over Judea and Samaria, "the historical 'spinal cord' of the land of Israel," as well as Gaza. The Jewish state would complete "the exchange of populations that began in 1948," transferring Palestinian refugees from the territories to Arab countries. In the meantime, he asked his Christian Zionist allies to "go from mosque to mosque and bring Muslims into the light," converting to Christianity those who preach murder. Michael Melchior, a member of the Knesset who has supported interfaith dialogue, called Elon's comments crazy. "There is no greater insult for Muslims than this," he said.[22]

In June 2004, Prime Minister Sharon fired Elon from his cabinet to improve the chances of winning approval for his plan to disengage from the Gaza Strip. Elon later criticized the disengagement as "a plan to whet the appetite of our enemies" and denounced Sharon in the Knesset as "evil, evil, evil."[23] Though no longer the tourism minister, Elon maintains his close contacts with American evangelicals. According to *Haaretz* in 2005, he "invests more time and effort than perhaps any other Israeli in nurturing the relationship with Evangelical Christians in the U.S."[24]

Pull Back Immediately

Another consequence of the assassination of Rechavam Ze'evi in October 2001 was the most intense Israeli military response to terrorism since the formation of the Palestinian Authority in 1994. Sharon had not achieved his promise to bring peace and security. Now his countrymen were outraged by this assassination and he had to act forcefully. Most Israelis opposed Ze'evi's politics, but they demanded that Arafat arrest and surrender his killers. When he refused, the IDF moved into six West Bank cities, occupying or choking off most of the Palestinian population centers. The action was intended to arrest or kill terrorists and to pressure Arafat to dismantle terrorist organizations and surrender Ze'evi's assassins.

The Bush administration, far from being one-sidedly pro-Israel, denounced the Israeli incursion. A State Department spokesman, using unusually tough language, deplored it. President Bush called on Israel to pull back immediately. He was worried that renewed violence could undermine Arab and Muslim support for the war on terror and was reportedly alarmed by news of Palestinian casualties. Many Israelis, for their part, felt that Washington was more concerned with building support for the invasion of Afghanistan than with their security. They complained that the Bush administration practiced a double standard, striking at terrorists in Afghanistan while insisting that Israel not do the same in the West Bank. Jerusalem initially defied the American calls for restraint, then began a slow phased withdrawal.

Arafat, who had received warm welcomes in European capitals shortly before, denounced the assassination and outlawed the militant wing of the PFLP. Washington, in direct contradiction to Israel's position, then declared that Arafat could not be held directly responsible for Ze'evi's death.[25] Bush's desire to reward Arafat for having denounced bin Laden was frustrated, though, when the Sharon government labeled the Palestinian leader a sponsor of terrorism. Still, according to a source close to the prime minister, Sharon believed that the Bush team thought the Palestinians had crossed a red line when they assassinated Ze'evi.[26]

The Passover Massacre ~~2002~~

Tensions between Washington and Jerusalem heightened again in the spring of 2002. In late March of that year, on the first night of Passover, a young Palestinian named Abdel-Basset Odeh entered the luxury Park Hotel in the northern Israeli seaside city of Netanya. Somehow he slipped past an armed security guard and walked into the banquet hall, where 250 people were just sitting down for a seder. Many of them were elderly. Some had come from abroad to spend Passover with their families. Odeh concealed on his body a forty-pound bag of explosives studded with shrapnel, by far the largest bomb that the Palestinians had employed in the eighteen months that the Al-Aqsa Intifada had been raging. A few of the guests noticed that he seemed peculiar, coming to the seder alone rather than with a family, and, more strangely, wearing a woman's wig. "What are you doing here?" a desk clerk shouted at him. At that, Odeh set off his bomb, launching a hail of nails through the banquet hall. The blast killed thirty people and wounded 140. It hurled mangled chairs and tables out the windows, blew a deep crater in the banquet room floor, shredded the hotel lobby ceiling, and crumpled cars in the street outside. "This is not just terror," Israel's minister of public security, Uzi Landau, said later. "This is a massacre." A Hamas spokesman took credit for the attack, noting that it was timed as a warning to the Arab summit meeting in Beirut, where Saudi Crown Prince Abdullah had just presented a peace plan for Israel. Hamas wanted to send the message to Arab leaders that it had chosen the path of "resistance," not peace. The attack also undermined American emissary General Anthony Zinni's mission, then under way, to broker a cease-fire between the Israelis and the Palestinians. Although Arafat denounced the bombing, Israeli officials again held him responsible. They had asked the Palestinian Authority several times to arrest Odeh, but Arafat had done nothing to apprehend him and other militants, or to rein in Hamas, they said.[27]

"Enough Is Enough"

March 2002

Sharon responded immediately, calling up 20,000 reserve soldiers and mounting Operation Defensive Shield, the largest Israeli ground offensive since the invasion of Lebanon twenty years earlier. Israeli tanks ripped through every Palestinian city, seeking to wipe out terrorist networks. They even moved into refugee camps, which were such strongholds of resistance that the IDF generally had avoided full-scale assaults on them. The Israelis advanced in particularly heavy fighting in the camp at Jenin, which they considered the heart of Palestinian militancy, the site from which twenty-three suicide bombers had attacked Israel. The army expected to clean up the camp in two days, but the insurgents resisted fiercely for ten. Palestinians accused the IDF of a massacre. That charge was vastly exaggerated, but Terje Roed-Larsen, the UN special envoy to the region, later spoke of horrifying scenes of human suffering in the camp. International organizations and human rights groups demanded to know why Israel had kept the Red Cross and the Red Crescent out for thirteen days. Palestinians accused Israel of using people as human shields, paralyzing civilian life, and seizing control of security that had devolved to them under the Olso agreement.

The Israeli dragnet in the West Bank was highly effective, however. It resulted in the arrest of 1,500 militants, over 800 of whom had direct involvement in terrorist attacks, according to the IDF. Israeli forces also discovered sixty labs that made TATP, the crude explosive used in suicide-bomb belts.

Meanwhile, in Bethlehem, 190 Palestinians, thirty to fifty of them armed, took refuge in the Church of the Nativity, which marks the traditional birthplace of Jesus. In Ramallah, Arafat gave sanctuary to the five men Israel accused of killing Rehavam Ze'evi and Israeli tanks and troops then laid siege to his offices. In the north, Hezbollah fired missiles from Lebanon into Israel. The United Nations Security Council voted, with American support, to demand that Israel withdraw from the West Bank "without delay."

Bush initially said that he understood Sharon's decision to mount this incursion, but early in April he reversed himself. The president now declared that he expected Israel to withdraw its forces. "Enough is enough," he said in a Rose Garden speech. He also called on the Palestinians to renounce terror and asked the Arab states to acknowledge that Israel and a Palestinian state have the equal right to exist. The president had particularly harsh words for Arafat, saying bluntly that he did not regard him as a trustworthy negotiating partner. Arafat had crossed the line for good three months earlier by being involved in an attempt to import arms on a ship called the *Karine-A,* then lying about it.

"No Israeli Prime Minister Can Openly Defy the President of the United States, at Least for Long"

All sides ignored the president's admonitions. As the IDF continued its mission, reporters asked Bush at his Texas ranch whether Sharon was publicly defying him. Obviously annoyed, the president raised his voice and called on Israel to pull out of the West Bank "without delay." That echoed the language of the UN resolution. British Prime Minister Tony Blair, standing beside Bush, declared that the time had come for Israel to "heed the words of President Bush." Then Bush had a "frank and direct" telephone conversation with Sharon, their first talk in two months. The Israeli told the president that he would accelerate efforts to root out terrorist infrastructures in the West Bank but gave him no assurance when that would be finished. The Israeli public, feeling more beleaguered than they had in decades, overwhelmingly supported the military operation. A year and a half of attacks against Jewish civilians, reaching a crescendo with the massacre at the Passover seder in March, left people feeling that they were in a fight for survival. To pull back would only lead to renewed suicide bombings and a right-wing backlash, Israeli sources said. The IDF predicted that they would need two months to clean up the Palestinian areas. But Colin Powell was about to embark on a mission to Morocco, Madrid, and the Middle East, and Israeli officials cautioned that if Sharon didn't give him a firm commitment to end the hostilities, Israel would face the wrath of the Bush administration.[28]

Extended Israeli defiance would call into question American prestige and influence, and possibly damage U.S. relations with moderate Arab states. Sharon, however, cast the operation in the West Bank as an existential struggle against the Palestinian "kingdom of terror." The result was a standoff. It was a contest of wills between the American and the Israeli leaders, one that Sharon could not sustain indefinitely. "No Israeli prime minister can openly defy the president of the United States, at least for long," Stephen P. Cohen, a Middle East expert at the Israel Policy Forum, commented at the time.[29]

George W. Bush as Everyman

Evangelicals rallied to Israel's side, and they weren't alone. A Gallup poll showed that in April 2002, 67 percent of Republicans supported Israel, as against only 8 percent who favored the Palestinians. As David Frum points out, born-again Christians had a lot to do with that, but they didn't constitute 67 percent of the GOP. Rather, he says, Republicans supported Israel because they intuitively sensed that the people who hated the Jewish state also hated America.[30] The general American public was somewhat less supportive. They sympathized far more with Israel than with the Palestinians, but the vast majority (71%) thought that the United States should not take sides. Precisely the same percentage said that Bush had done the right thing in demanding that Israel withdraw from the Palestinian territories.[31]

Conservative stalwarts, by contrast, insisted that the president should put no pressure on Sharon. William Kristol, William J. Bennett, and the *National Review* rebuked the Bush administration's effort to promote peace talks with Arafat as an "amateur hour" exemplifying "moral confusion" and "Clintonite wishful thinking."[32] The *Wall Street Journal* ran an editorial saying, "Suddenly the President who soared by standing on principle seems to have been replaced by an imposter who's lost his foreign-policy bearings."[33] Senator Sam Brownback (R-Kansas), a Methodist convert to Catholicism who is a staunch Christian Zionist, said, "I don't think there is anybody who puts much stock in talks right now. Many people are saying, 'How can we tell Israel to pull back when, if terrorists were hitting us that way, we would be going back at them hammer and tong?'" Kristol and Bennett made the same point, arguing that it was hypocritical for the United States to tell Israel not to respond to terrorism.[34] Tom DeLay (R-Texas), then the House majority whip, declared that "Israel is resisting a campaign of death." Noting that Arafat had proven his total contempt for human life, he concluded, "This hellish strategy of destruction menaces far more than the state of Israel. It is a threat to the entire civilized world." (DeLay, once considered cool toward Israel, had become one of its most ardent supporters.) In April, Powell met privately with Senate and House conservatives and asked them to withdraw resolutions expressing solidarity with Israel in Operation Defensive Shield. These endorsements of the Israeli military action would complicate attempts to set up peace talks in the region, Powell argued. Both resolutions were approved overwhelmingly with bipartisan support, though, despite opposition from Bush, who felt they would tie his hands.[35]

Many Christian Zionists were alarmed by the bloodshed and suffering in Israel. "The Israelis are very depressed," said Susan Michael, director of the ICEJ's office in Washington, at the time. "We want them to know that they have friends who understand the battle they're in."[36] Mike Evans now established the Jerusalem Prayer Team, saying that the Jewish people are "experiencing the same type of terror that was experienced in America on September 11"—a sentiment that the Israeli public also expressed. Evans called for a bridge of love, with each American Christian praying for the peace and protection of one Jew in Israel. "You can't love Jesus without loving the Jewish people," he said. Pat Boone, Pat Robertson, and Tim LaHaye joined a hundred other Christian leaders in supporting this prayer campaign.[37]

Many Christian Zionists considered Bush to be a friend of Israel who had to be reminded of his better instincts—and of his supporters' profound commitment to the Jewish state. Some of them were infuriated by Bush's Rose Garden speech, which appeared to equate Palestinian terrorism with the Israeli response to it.[38] Some evangelical leaders feared that the president would come under the influence of the State Department, which, in their view, had always been pro-Arab. Several spoke derisively of the Arabists and bureaucrats at State who are interested only in Middle East oil. The president is a good man, they said, but too influenced by Colin Powell.

Bush, in their minds, was virtually an Everyman figure in a medieval morality play, with Powell whispering seductive bad advice into one ear while evangelicals uttered words of moral clarity into the other.[39] The danger they saw in the secretary of state was exemplified by a comment that Powell made during a stopover in Madrid on his way to the Middle East that month: "I think we are all in agreement, and the world is in agreement, that the solution will not be produced by terror or a response to terror." That statement denied the value and the virtue of Israel's striking back after terrorist attacks. It "sent waves of confusion into the already chaotic state in the Middle East," said Jerry Falwell. "With that one sentence," Gary Bauer commented, "Powell abandoned moral clarity and embraced the moral relativists who see no difference between terrorism and fighting terrorism."[40] Powell's position was inconsistent with the approach that the United States itself was pursuing, said John Hagee, who expressed concern that "there's a duplicitous interpretation of the Bush doctrine—one for America and one for Israel." "A good administration had succumbed to a double standard," said Bauer. Pat Robertson told CNN that evangelical support for the president was wavering.[41]

Netanyahu came to the United States to drive home the same points. In a speech to the Senate on April 10, he declared that the war on terror can be won with moral and strategic clarity. But for the first time, he said, he was concerned that America might succumb to confusion and vacillation. "The free world is muddling its principles, losing its nerve," Netanyahu said. By demanding that Israel stop fighting terror and return to the negotiating table with a regime committed to its destruction, the United States was permitting the main engine of Palestinian terror to remain intact. If the Bush administration selectively abandoned its principles in that way, holding a different standard for Israel than for itself, Netanyahu suggested, it would lose its moral clarity and jeopardize the entire war on terror.[42] That agreed perfectly with the views that Christian Zionists were expressing.

"The Bible Belt Is Israel's Safety Belt"

Reports now circulated in the press that evangelicals were in constant communication with the White House—and with Karl Rove in particular. There was, in fact, a weekly telephone conference with the White House, and Falwell said in June 2002, "Let's just say that the Middle East comes up during most of these calls."[43] Richard Land, who participated in these teleconferences, said in May of that year that the Mideast crisis was the primary concern among evangelical Christians. In his travels to Baptist churches across America, Land noted, people constantly asked him to tell the president not to abandon Israel. "The Bible Belt is Israel's safety belt," said Land, repeating a familiar phrase among evangelicals.[44] Israel had become the hottest political button for American evangelicals, *Time* magazine reported. Ralph Reed said of the attacks on Israel, "You hear about it in the churches, on talk radio. In the past 30 days I have seen this move to the top of public policy concern." Reed saw the alliance between evangelicals and Jews as the remedy. Bauer said that April, "I do e-mail every day to 100,000 people, and I'm just inundated with very emotional responses saying, 'Keep standing up, we've got to stand shoulder to shoulder with Israel.'"[45] Janet Parshall, whose nationally syndicated radio show, *Janet Parshall's America,* reaches 3.5 million listeners a day, couched the same point in stark political terms: "For me and my voting power, the number one issue is,

Where do you stand on Israel? You get that one right and we can start talking about where you stand on other issues . . . Fifty million evangelicals in America will not be silent about this."[46]

The Washington, D.C., Rally for Israel, April 2002

In April 2002, Christian Zionists leaders took a firm stand to stop Bush from restraining Israel. On April 10, the same day as Netanyahu's speech at the Senate, Trent Lott, the Senate minority leader, informed the president that the religious right was placing increasing pressure on Republicans to back Sharon.[47] The next day, Bauer, Falwell, John Hagee, Ed McAteer, and two other Christian Zionist leaders sent Bush a letter urging him to "end the pressure on Israeli Prime Minister Ariel Sharon so that he has the time necessary to complete the mission he has undertaken—the elimination of terrorist cells and infrastructure from the West Bank territories." The letter added that Powell's peacemaking trip was sending the dangerous message that Israel must negotiate with Arafat "in spite of his complicity in promoting terror."[48]

On April 15, Christian Zionists joined with American Jews, Israelis, and other supporters of the Jewish state at a huge pro-Israel rally on the Washington, D.C., mall that over 100,000 people reportedly attended.[49] A persistent theme among the speakers was the call for moral clarity. Bill Bennett, who has been chairman of the National Endowment for the Humanities, secretary of education, and drug czar, was one of the first to speak. Bennett recalled that Israel rallied for the United States on 9/11 while Palestinians honked their horns for joy at America's losses. September 11 was a moment of moral clarity, he said, and moral clarity means understanding the distinction between a democracy like Israel that is fighting for survival and a dictatorship that is fighting to push it into the sea. Arab states are deeply anti-Semitic, Bennett told the crowd. "A Saudi newspaper recently published a story about Jews using Arab blood for the Purim celebration," he noted. "We are reading reports from the Arab press that speak of 'Hitler of blessed memory.'"

Netanyahu spoke next. "No greater friend of Israel has ever been in the White House," he said of George W. Bush, "and no president has ever championed a cause that was more just." An enemy that sends children to die and to kill other children cannot be placated, Netanyahu added, to the applause of the crowd. "An enemy that openly preaches the destruction of our state is not a partner for peace. (*Applause.*) The only way to defeat it is to destroy it." (*Applause.*) Arafat is the quintessential terrorist, "Osama bin Laden with good PR."

(*Applause.*) Terror will be given no quarter until it is wiped out from our world, Netanyahu said, again to applause.[50]

Natan Sharansky then saluted President Bush's determination in waging a global battle against Islamic terrorism. Israel today is in the very same battle, he told the audience. A former prisoner of conscience in the Soviet Union and, at the time of the rally, deputy prime minister of Israel, Sharansky warned, "Every compromise with Palestinian terror will encourage potential terrorists everywhere to try and achieve political goals through terror." Personalizing the threat, he noted that terror in Israel means that when couples say goodbye in the morning, they say, "Know that I love you, just in case I don't come home in the evening." "Make no mistake about it," Sharansky pointed out, "Arafat is at the root of terror." (*Applause*). There are documents signed by Arafat to prove this, he noted. "But what about Jenin?" he asked, referring to Palestinian claims that the IDF had perpetrated a massacre in the refugee camp there. "Dear friends, let me tell you the true story about Jenin," said Sharansky. Dozens of terrorists went from there to kill hundreds and thousands of civilians, he told them. "And when we came to the camp, where for 10 years no soldier dared to enter, we found out that every house is a fortress." Rather than use artillery, tanks, or airplanes, Israel chose to take the camp by going house to house. This risked the lives of Israeli soldiers, Sharansky noted, but saved the lives of hundreds of Palestinian civilians.

Paul Wolfowitz, who was then deputy secretary of defense, represented the Bush administration at the rally. Wolfowitz hadn't wanted to go, but Karl Rove had played a key role in dispatching him.[51] "President Bush wants you to know that he stands in solidarity with you," Wolfowitz began, to applause and cheers. Then, astonishingly, he expressed sympathy for Palestinian suffering. He called for a hopeful future for Palestinian as well as Israeli children. "In the words of Malachi," Wolfowitz said, "'Have we not all one Father? Did not one God create us?'" Perhaps Woflowitz didn't fully appreciate the mood of his audience. Or maybe he was making that rarest of gestures, a show of empathy for both sides in a conflict. Social commentator Christopher Hitchens says that the thing that would surprise most people is that Wolfowitz is a bleeding heart, with sympathy for those who suffer. In any event, Wolfowitz wasn't prepared for the boos and catcalls that he received from the crowd.[52] They were in no mood to sympathize with the enemy whom the other speakers had denounced with such moral clarity. "No more Arafat!" the audience chanted. Bill Bennett had said the week before on CNN that Bush's Mideast policy was angering "his entire political base" and some observers conjectured that sending Wolfowitz to the rally was the administration's attempt to quell that anger. If so, it failed. He was the right person, said Gary Bauer, but he gave the wrong speech.[53]

The most enthusiastic applause of the day went to Janet Parshall, She pointed out that the Hebrew word for "waver" means "to limp, to vacillate." "I am here to tell you today," Parshall assured the audience, "we Christians and Jews together will never limp, we will never wimp, we will never vacillate in our support of Israel." (*Applause. Cheers.*) Some people have the strange idea that "land for peace" means giving away one piece of land at a time, Parshall told them. She utterly rejected that: "We will never give up the Golan! (*Applause. Cheers.*) We will never divide Jerusalem! And we will call Yasser Arafat what Yasser Arafat is: a terrorist!" (*Applause. Cheers.*) "Stand firm," she exhorted her "Jewish bothers and sisters" in closing. "Be courageous." No Jewish speaker that day made such hawkish statements, and none was as well received.[54]

House Majority Leader Dick Armey (R-Texas), a staunch Christian Zionist, offered another endorsement of moral clarity. "Ladies and gentlemen, I'm from Texas," he said, "and in Texas, we've got a reputation for straight talk. We don't believe in ambiguity and we believe in clarity." Armey said that it is perfectly clear that a deliberate attack on innocent civilians is terrorism, whether it happens in New York City, at the Pentagon, in the skies over Pennsylvania, or in the heart of Jerusalem. Israel and the United States, in other words, were fighting a war against a common enemy.

A Flood of E-Mails and Telephone Calls in Support of Israel

To further influence the Bush administration, Gary Bauer, Pat Robertson, and Jerry Falwell each independently engineered a massive e-mail and letter-writing campaign exhorting Bush not to restrain the Israelis.[55] In a clear warning to the president, Falwell announced that Israel and abortion are the two issues that "surpass all human alliances and friendships." He urged his followers to flood the White House with e-mails and phone calls backing Israel. The next day, senior Bush aides called Falwell to assure him of the president's continued support for Sharon.[56] Bauer, for his part, asked the 100,000 readers on his e-mail address list to forward a message to the White House conveying both loyalty and an explicit threat. "Mr. President," it said, "we pray for you every day. I believe God wanted you to be president. If you abandon Israel, you will never get my vote again."

Bauer is convinced that this large-scale electronic lobbying helped persuade the president to stop calling on Israel to withdraw from the West Bank. "I do believe that in this White House, with Karl Rove, who is a very bright and political man, it had an impact," Bauer said at the time. The president's instincts were good, Bauer added, but the State Department and Bush's father had led him astray. The e-mail campaign, and the revelation that Arafat had made payments to support terrorism, helped Bush's best impulses reassert themselves, Bauer noted. "No White House wants to look like it bent to political pressure," he told me later, "but it was clear to us that there was a change in tone."[57]

"A Man of Peace" versus a Homicide Bomber

That change in tone actually began before Bauer's e-mail campaign, though. It started to emerge unmistakably soon after Powell left on his diplomatic mission, when Ari Fleischer, the White House press secretary, said that President Bush believed Sharon was "a man of peace." By sharp contrast, Fleischer called Arafat a homicide bomber, a phrase that Israelis often used to describe him. That undermined the secretary of state's denunciation of both Palestinian terrorism and the Israeli response to it. Fleischer also distanced the White House from Powell's decision to meet with Arafat. That, he said, was the secretary's idea, not Bush's.[58] Meanwhile the Israelis were encouraged by the fact that the administration's chief hawks, Vice President Cheney and Defense Secretary Donald Rumsfeld, were silent about their action in the West Bank. Martin Indyk, who had been Clinton's ambassador to Israel, said at the time that Israeli officials had picked up on Bush's reluctance to stop them. They believed that the president was fighting his own instincts, which he had expressed initially, to understand the need to strike back against terrorism, said Indyk. Some Christian Zionist leaders agreed, as we have seen. Indyk added that Bush wasn't interested in doing anything more at that time "because of the backlash he has confronted."[59]

On April 18, Secretary Powell came back from his ten-day mission empty-handed. The president praised his initiative but compromised his diplomatic efforts. One day earlier, before leaving Jerusalem, Powell had placed the onus on Sharon, saying that negotiations could not proceed until Israel ended its military operation. That represented a shift in the American stance that Arafat would have to act first by cracking down on terrorist groups. Bush, by contrast, repeatedly spoke of Sharon as a man of peace, the phrase that Fleischer had employed, while castigating Arafat. The president praised the Israeli leader for taking the first steps toward winding down the three-week-old incursion by beginning to withdraw from Nablus and Jenin. History will show that Israel responded, Bush declared.

"President Bush is as wrong as wrong can be," Saeb Erekat, a top Palestinian negotiator, said in response. With Israeli tanks and troops still forming a cordon around the major Palestinian cities, Bush's comments were provocative to Arab opinion. The timing was particularly delicate, since in one week Saudi Arabia's Crown Prince Abdullah was scheduled to visit him at his Texas ranch. The president also angered Palestinians when he essentially endorsed the Israeli siege of Arafat's offices: he said that he could understand why Sharon wanted to bring the "Ze'evi Five killers" to justice. Gandhi's alleged assassins were being sheltered in Arafat's compound in Ramallah and Palestinian spokesmen said that they had no obligation to turn them over to Israel as long as the Palestinians arrested and tried the five themselves. They had done neither, however.[60] Meanwhile, King Abdullah II of Jordan called Bush to say that the Israeli-Palestinian conflict had so infuriated the Arab public that moderate Arab regimes, including his own, were at risk. Prince Saud al-Faisal, the Saudi foreign minister, warned that events in the region were headed for an abyss. He accused Israel of war crimes.[61]

The Administration's Mideast Policy Was "Dead in the Water"

Throughout the month of April 2002, Powell tried to persuade the president to halt the Israeli operation. When Bush refused, the secretary concluded that Karl Rove was shaping policy in response to crass political concerns.[62] State Department officials described themselves as despondent that the administration's Mideast policy was "dead in the water." They believed that this resulted from a battle between Defense and State. Rumsfeld and his advisers Wolfowitz and Douglas J. Feith sympathized with Israel's need to defend itself, as did Cheney. "Israel has a very small margin for error," Rumsfeld observed. Such a small country can't make many mistakes and survive. Powell, on the other hand, favored an energetic diplomatic campaign to address both Israeli and Palestinian concerns. Condoleezza Rice, then the national security adviser, was supposed to broker such differences, but her position on Israel was unclear. Critics said that the National Security Council (NSC) was weaker than it had been at any time since the end of the Reagan administration. The NSC senior director for the Middle East, Zalmay Khalilzad, was relatively new to the issue and was focused on Afghanistan. When officials from the Pentagon and Cheney's office presented their views to Bush, there was nobody in the White House to contradict them, said one official who was critical of Rice.[63] Flynt Leverett, her top aide on Middle East issues at the time, recalled later that she had wanted to be bolder in helping the Palestinians but had folded when Cheney and Rumsfeld opposed her.[64] All of this contributed to Bush's inaction.

Born-Again Christians: "The Most Influential
Pro-Israel Lobby"

Gary Bauer and others, however, attributed the president's softening on Israel largely to evangelical pressure. *Time* adopted this view, saying in early May, "When the G.O.P.'s right wing unleashed a tide of e-mails and telephone calls in support of Israel, Bush appeared to revert to his instinctive support of the country. And that is pretty much where things stand—back where they started a month ago." The most influential pro-Israel lobbying, the article added, was being done not by Jews but by born-again Christians, whom Bush was courting for the 2004 election.[65] Deborah Caldwell, the senior religious producer for *Beliefnet,* claimed in October 2002 that the president had backed down specifically in response to Christian eschatological views. It was very probable that Bush didn't curb Israel's crackdown on the Palestinians, she contended, because of evangelical leaders' belief that Rapture and the end-times won't happen unless Israel continues to exist in the Holy Land.[66] Though Caldwell and others offered no evidence to support these assertions about Bush, both friends and opponents of Christian Zionism have often cited them to illustrate the power that evangelicals are thought to have over him. There were claims that 100,000 e-mails and phone calls descended on the White House that spring. *Newsweek* reported that there were *several* hundred thousand, and accepted the narrative that this, along with heavy lobbying by Christian Zionists, caused the Bush administration to stop pressuring Sharon. Bob Simon repeated that interpretation of events on *60 Minutes*, as David Brog does in *Standing with Israel.*[67] In fact, Bauer has no idea how many e-mails were sent, since he was not copied on them.[68] And the question of this campaign's impact on the president is open to debate, as we shall see.

America's Last Chance

Far from being thoroughly chastened by evangelical opposition, Bush continued to vacillate about Israel through the spring of 2002. In late April, Saudi Arabia's Crown Prince Abdullah came to the president's Crawford, Texas, ranch and told him bluntly that their nations' strategic relationship would be in danger if Bush did not moderate his support for Jerusalem. The Saudis regarded this as America's last chance for constructive relations with the Arab world. "The perception in the Middle East, from the far left to the far right, is that America is totally sponsoring Sharon—not Israel's policies but Sharon's policies—and anyone who tells you less is insulting your intelligence," said a source familiar with Abdullah's thinking. "If Sharon is left to his own devices, he will drag the region over a cliff," said an adviser to the crown prince.[69]

Although Israel had largely withdrawn from the West Bank, the IDF was employing rapid attacks and helicopter strikes to seize militants and at times sending in heavy armored vehicles and infantry. Israel also retained tanks and troops outside of Arafat's quarters in Ramallah, keeping him penned in. The Saudis wanted the United States to make Sharon release Arafat from confinement, but, according to one eyewitness account, Bush's response was a blank stare. A list of Saudi requests had been diverted to Cheney's office and Bush, not having seen it, had no idea what the Saudis would ask for.[70] One day after his five-hour meeting with Abdullah, though, Bush told the Israelis, "It's time to end this." There had been some progress, the president said, but now it was time to quit it altogether. Bush then pressured Sharon to accept a deal on Ze'evi's assassins that would result in Israel's lifting its siege on Arafat's compound. Israel acquiesced and withdrew its tanks and soldiers from Ramallah. "It would have been stupid and impolite to say no," said an Israeli cabinet minister.[71]

In May 2002, observers were saying that the Bush administration had no Middle East strategy. Rather, it was answering to disparate voices and trying to keep up with events. Colin Powell proposed an international conference, but the next day it was downgraded to a "meeting." American officials vilified Arafat, as Sharon did, but accepted Saudi, Egyptian, and Jordanian advice that he had to be included in any meaningful talks. "There is no policy. It's tactical," said Judith Kipper, the director of the Middle East Forum at the Council on Foreign Relations. Edward S. Walker, former assistant secretary of state for Near Eastern affairs, concurred: "There is a superficial nature to the policy. It isn't deeply rooted at all."[72] Bush's positions on Israel seemed improvised.

The Christian Coalition's Rally for Israel

Christian Zionists kept up the pressure. In October, the Christian Coalition held its 2002 Road to Victory conference in Washington, D.C., organized around the theme of supporting Israel. Pat Robertson, Tom DeLay, and Benny Elon were among the speakers. The *Washington Post* dismissed this event as a desperate effort by a once-powerful organization to return to the national political stage. With the departure of Ralph Reed in 1997, its loss of tax-exempt status in 1999, Pat Robertson's resignation, and a decline in membership, the Christian Coalition was a shadow of itself.[73] But the point of the rally, said one of the organizers, was not so much to pressure Bush as to allow him to respond to the *appearance* of pressure. That would give the president the political opportunity to do what he wanted to do anyway. Ronn Torossian, the public relations executive whose client lists includes Christian Zionist, Israeli, and American Jewish organizations and officials, asserts that an evangelical rally had much greater impact with the Bush administration than do Jewish events. "I know on a firsthand basis that [the Christian Coalition] Pro-Israel rally this past weekend at which 10,000 people attended had more influence on the White House and world leaders than the Jewish community's pro-Israel rally did a few months ago," he wrote in October 2002. "One Christian rally does more than 100 Jewish rallies."[74] Asked about that provocative statement, Torossian replied that two extremely important people in American politics had discussed that with him both before and after the rally. One was a senior member of the Bush administration and the other a very senior elected official. They wanted the pro-Israel events to have an impact, and the Christian Coalition rally was far more significant than the ecumenical one in April.[75] If this account is accurate, important figures in and outside of the Bush administration were complicit in creating the circumstances that would justify supporting Israel.

In the spring of 2002, Bush's decisions about Israel seemed deracinated, reactions to the tumultuous events and passions of the time rather than expressions of a consistent policy. The president was aware of the evangelicals' pressure and may even have used it as the occasion to say what he already believed.[76] Whether or not Christian Zionists' exhortations and threats that April influenced the president tactically, the radically new strategic policy that he introduced two months later was directly contrary to their convictions, as we shall see in the next chapter.

11

⚜

Evangelicals and the Dynamics
of George W. Bush's Middle
East Policy

By April 2002, evangelical leaders had become so assertive in supporting Israel that many observers understandably concluded that it was
they who had caused George W. Bush's softening of tone regarding
Ariel Sharon. Prominent Christian Zionists encouraged the view that they had
extraordinary clout with the White House. Ralph Reed said at the time, for
example, that born-again Christians in alliance with Jews "could be the most
important constituency to influence foreign policy since the end of the Cold
War."[1] But the change in Bush's Middle East policy that June has to be seen in
the larger context of his character, his political calculus, and his evolving position on the Israeli-Palestinian question.

People who know and admire Bush consider it ludicrous to suppose that
evangelical pressure forced him to recast his policy about Israeli military action on the West Bank. It is true that there were limits to Bush's latitude in
dealing with Israel, of course. To compromise the Jewish state's security or to
force the division of Jerusalem would certainly alienate much of his base. "I've
been at the White House where they've said that God will strike him dead"
(if he ever undermined Israel), said the NAE's Rich Cizik.[2] Richard Land, who
has known the president for eighteen years and meets with him several times
a year, says that Bush is singularly unsusceptible to coercion, however. In fact,
coercive pressure is often counter-productive with him. "I strongly believe that
this president is going to do what he believes is right regardless of political
consequence," Land told me.[3]

David Frum, the former Bush speechwriter, concedes that it's not impossible that the evangelical e-mail, letter-writing, and telephone campaign in

behalf of Israel influenced the president at that crucial moment in April 2002. Frum acknowledges that the views of Bush's Christian Zionist supporters are "absolutely a factor in his thinking. And I'm sure that they say things that touch his conscience." He dismisses the idea that it was evangelical pressure that compelled Bush to change his position on Israel, however. "That would be ridiculous," he told me. "I shouldn't say ridiculous. It is not realistic to think that in 2002, if there had been a trial of political strength between Robertson and Bauer on the one side and the president on the other for the support of the Republican base, that Bauer and Robertson could have hoped to win." That isn't the way pressure exerts itself anyway, Frum observed. One reason that presidents respond to their base is that they react to the same things that their supporters do. In that sense, he said, they are their base, said Frum. "So if the government does something that the base hates, it's quite possible that the president, if he had known about it in advance, would have hated it too."

In any case, Bush was far more attentive to his core constituency than he was to ultraconservative Christian Zionists, said Frum. "He could certainly have afforded to kiss off those Republicans who believe that, if the U.S. does not support the outermost conceivable demands of the state of Israel, then God will curse it," Frum told me. David Kuo, the former number two man in the White House Office of Faith-Based and Community Initiatives, substantiates that conclusion. In *Tempting Faith: An Inside Story of Political Seduction*, Kuo reports that most of the Bush White House barely tolerated the leaders of the religious right. "National Christian leaders received hugs and smiles in person and then were dismissed behind their backs," says Kuo, who is born-again himself. White House strategists considered evangelicals politically invaluable but personally boorish, tiresome, annoying, ridiculous, goofy, and out of control, he says. Top officials in Rove's political affairs shop referred to conservative Christian elites as "the nuts."[4]

The administration allowed conservative Christians a significant voice in federal judicial appointments and was responsive on a limited number of other issues, notably opposition to "partial birth" abortion. On the question of Israel, though, Bush could afford to dismiss his fringe supporters on the Christian right if he had to, said Frum. In fact, it did not come to that. Bush endorsed the creation of a Palestinian state and supported Sharon's disengagement from Gaza, and Christian Zionists were distressed but quiescent. What the president could not dismiss, said Frum, were the people who saw Sharon's forceful response to terrorism and thought, "If I were an Israeli, I'd be doing exactly what the Israelis are doing now." Bush needed to be responsive to the many Americans who thought that if the president pressed the Israelis to go soft, he would go soft himself in the defense of the United States. That, said

Frum, was the subtext of the president's policy. Bush understood that his base would know instinctively that a president who was tough on Hamas would also be tough on Al Qaeda. The president didn't need to do polling on that, Frum said. He could look inside himself and see the connection between President Clinton's mollifying Arafat and his inaction when Al Qaeda hit American targets, Frum added. Bush firmly wanted to distinguish himself from that approach.

The Mongol Emperor of China

Frum's perspective on the events leading up to April 2002 is totally different from Gary Bauer's narrative about the impact of the e-mail blitz of the White House. Bush initially had no plan for Israel, Frum told me. Quite the contrary, "he had learned, maybe over-learned, the lesson of his father . . . that too much attention to foreign policy will lose you reelection." The president intended to devote his first two or three years in office to educational policy and faith-based initiatives, issues on which he had some expertise from his time as governor of Texas. "That's where he thought he would make his mark," said Frum.[5] Bob Woodward confirms that in *State of Denial,* adding that for Karl Rove, the top policy objective in the first months of the Bush presidency was also a domestic issue: tax cuts.[6]

Bush left Israel to the State Department and, through the summer of 2001, Secretary of State Colin Powell worked on rededicating the United States to a Clinton-style peace process. "The State Department is the Department of Negotiations," Frum observed. But people in the Defense Department and the National Security Council staff, and above all the vice president, said that the timing was wrong: the moment to negotiate a settlement would not come until the Israelis, the Palestinians, or both, had had enough of fighting. "August of 2001 was not that moment," Frum said. But "after September 11th, the whole world looked different. There are two administrations we're talking about: the one that leaves office on September 10th, 2001, and the one that takes office on September 12th."[7]

The Middle East was now far more urgent to Bush, as Secretary of State Condoleezza Rice confirmed later. "The dream of some, that we could avoid this conflict, that we did not have to take sides in this battle in the Middle East, that dream was demolished on September the 11th," said Rice. The United States learned on that day, she explained, that the security of America is inextricably linked to the success of freedom, moderation, and democracy in the Middle East.[8]

Still, it took Bush time to arrive at a policy for Israel, Frum noted. "Bush, between September 11th and the summer of 2002, just did not allot that much of his thinking time to the Israeli-Palestinian problem," Frum said. He was thinking instead about Afghanistan, Iraq, and domestic security. Frum offered an analogy: any new president feels a bit like the Mongol emperor of China. "You and your 5,000 warriors have ridden into China and conquered it. Now you're emperor and they are the nobles. Your 5,000 Mongols rule the three hundred million people of China, but you don't speak the language and you don't know what's going on." This tiny occupying force sits atop a vast alien civilization. "A lot of the time you're as surprised as anybody about what's going on," said Frum. Similarly, it takes a new chief executive time to learn what the government is doing. Even when he does, he can't change a policy until he comes up with a new one. Bush was obviously uncomfortable with the Clinton policy on Israel and the Palestinians, Frum observed, but until he devised an alternative, he had to stick with it.

The result was that it was very easy for people who worked on the problem full time—i.e., those in the State Department—to get the conventional American policy answer onto his desk. "So when Bush said, 'The Israelis must stop' " in April 2002, Frum observed, "he's really saying exactly what American presidents have said consistently since the late 1960s, and probably since the early 1950s." Those were not Bush's own views, however. When he read these things out loud, Frum noted, "you can see often even in his body language, in that April statement, you see how as he's saying it, he realizes, 'I hate this. I don't believe in this. Who gave me this?' That's why he lost it so quickly." When Bush abruptly stopped issuing demands that Israel withdraw from the West Bank, said Frum, it looked as though he was being inconsistent. In reality, he was breaking away from a four-to-five-decades-old American policy.[9]

"We're Going to Tilt Back toward Israel"

In fact, Bush firmly aligned himself with Jerusalem long before 9/11. Almost immediately after taking office he made this clear, setting out a policy of American inaction that would allow Israel wide latitude in dealing with the Palestinians. At Bush's first National Security Council principals meeting, on January 30, 2001, he said that the United States should withdraw from the Israeli-Palestinian conflict, which was hopelessly mired in distrust and minutia. Bill Clinton had overreached, accommodating Arafat too much. Bush was going to change direction. "We're going to tilt back toward Israel," he declared. Colin Powell objected, warning that this decision would reverse thirty years of U.S.

policy and unleash Sharon. "Sometimes a show of force by one side can really clarify things," replied the president, for whom clarity is a valued goal. His focus would be on Iraq, Bush announced.[10]

Two months later, Bush stated his pro-Israel policy plainly to Sharon. At their first meeting in Washington, in March 2001, he assured the prime minister that he would use force to protect the Jewish state, startling everyone else in the room.[11] This bias in favor of Jerusalem dictated a hands-off stance, allowing his foreign policy to concentrate on Afghanistan and Iraq that spring. By mid-2002, though, the bloodshed in Israel and the territories demanded the president's attention. He then developed, however fitfully, the articulated policy that he announced in early June of that year.

"The Landscape Was Turning Fast in a Bad Direction"

A State Department official who was actively involved in Israeli-Palestinian diplomacy in April 2002 linked Bush's shift of tone about Sharon to changes in the way Powell and his entourage saw the situation as they moved through the Middle East that month. He acknowledged that evangelical pressure may have influenced Bush's stance to some extent but said that he'd be surprised if it had anything like the impact that Bauer and the others claim. Instead, events themselves dictated the softening of the American position on Israel's incursion into the West Bank, he observed. "In Middle East policy, the landscape was turning fast in a bad direction," he noted. The area was in the throes of terrible violence. As Powell and his team traveled through the region, they saw that "the choices were pretty unappealing. It was just a very, very hard slog to bring about any diminution of the violence." A hard line would have had little impact, and that influenced the president's decision to tone down his rhetoric. In addition, "there was sympathy for the needs of the Israeli government to respond, and respond strongly." Still Bush's reference to Sharon as a man of peace made Powell's job more difficult, this official conceded. The secretary of state "felt that the weakening of support from Washington was yet another complication, making it that much harder" to do diplomacy.

Bush's Rose Garden Speech of June 24, 2002

By the early summer of 2002, Bush had charted an entirely new course. In his groundbreaking speech on June 24, he set out preconditions for American recognition of a Palestinian state, including the demand that the Palestinians remove leaders tainted by violence and adopt a democratic system based on tolerance. This emphasis on democracy, Frum observed, was a paradigm shift. U.S. policy now would concentrate more on the nature of the Palestinian government than on the traditional questions of the borders of a Palestinian state, refugees, and Jerusalem.[12] Bush had instituted a new focus: on whether the Palestinian leaders would fight terrorism, govern justly, and create opportunity for their people.[13] That approach was confirmed and developed by Natan Sharansky, the Israeli former Soviet refusenik, whose ideas in his book *The Case for Democracy* Bush later described as "part of my presidential DNA."[14]

Efraim Halevy, who was head of the Mossad at the time, broadly corroborates Frum's account but adds a startling twist: he claims that it was the Mossad that conceived of Bush's new policy. Halevy confirms that in 2001 the Bush administration was not working on ideas of its own regarding the Israeli-Palestinian conflict. So, according to Halevy, Bush invited the Israelis to develop new proposals for joint action with the United States—with the proviso that they should gave due weight to America's position in the Arab world; i.e., any plans should not lean too obviously in Israel's favor. In the meantime, Bush sent CIA director George Tenet to the region to craft a solution. Israel accepted the Tenet plan, says Halevy, and Arafat ultimately did as well, but the violence did not diminish. Bush dispatched General Anthony Zinni to implement the Tenet plan, but he failed and withdrew. In March 2002, Palestinian terrorists blew up the Passover seder in Netanya, and the IDF entered the West Bank in force to clean up the terrorist infrastructure. Knowing that they would have to withdraw before completing the job, though, the Israelis stepped into the policy-making vacuum. So the Mossad devised the new strategy, says Halevy. Convinced that Arafat had no real interest in accommodation, they created a plan for the Palestinian parliament to create a new position, a prime minister empowered to control security and finances. In essence, that would effect a regime change without removing Arafat entirely. Sharon quickly approved the plan and passed it on to Washington, says Halevy. Two months later, Bush made it the centerpiece of his June 24th Rose Garden speech.[15]

The president may have reached this paradigm shift gradually, and it may have been inspired philosophically by Sharansky, but, if Halevy's account is right, it was energized and given specific form by the Mossad and Ariel Sharon. Indeed, the respected Israeli commentator Nahum Barnea said at the time that Sharon was the inspiration for Bush's speech. The president not only called on the Palestinians to discard Arafat, he also declined to set a firm timetable, said Barnea. This fit precisely with the views of Sharon, who "added Bush as a temporary member of the Likud Party."[16] Halevy also says that "Bush's statement of June 2002 was without doubt a spectacular achievement of Prime

Minister Ariel Sharon." Sharon felt that there was too much hatred and distrust between the Israelis and Palestinians for them to enter final status negotiations at that time. As a new Palestinian leadership asserted itself, establishing law and order and putting a stop to terrorism, the two sides could move ahead to negotiations on a final agreement.[17] Bush also hoped that a democratically elected Palestinian leadership would concentrate on providing services to their people and be less hung up on questions of borders and Jerusalem. Flynt Leverett, Rice's former aide, who became a critic of Bush, called that "one of the most profoundly ignorant statements anyone has ever uttered on the Israeli-Palestinian conflict."[18] Bush had other considerations at the time, however. He and Rice had realized that the Arab states and the Europeans would not support the upcoming American invasion of Iraq until the administration had made progress toward resolving the Palestinian question. Bush's speech that June addressed that issue, and he gave it over the objections of Defense Secretary Donald Rumsfeld, who eventually relented, and of Vice President Cheney, who did not.[19]

The June 24th speech was reportedly crafted to take into account the views of pro-Israel domestic supporters, including evangelicals. According to *Newsweek,* Rove, Cheney, Rumsfeld, then-National Security Adviser Rice, and her deputy, Stephen Hadley, all reviewed the speech and "walked back" any language that favored the Palestinians. Hadley said that the speech had to be politically viable. Through a spokeswoman, he later denied that politics was a factor.[20]

Bush's Relationship with Sharon

Some observers say that Bush aligned firmly with Israel because of his personal relationship with Sharon. These two leaders shared policy objectives and personal inclinations: both inclined toward unilateralism and military preemption in dealing with terrorists, and both developed transformational visions regarding the Middle East. They first met in December 1998, when the Republican Jewish Coalition sponsored a trip by then-Governor Bush and three other governors to Israel. Sharon gave him a helicopter tour and Bush was impressed by how vulnerable Israel is. Sharon believed that, in its pre-1967 borders, the coastal plain of Israel, with its population centers, industry, power stations, and airport, is so narrow as to be indefensible. Israel is only nine miles wide at its narrowest point, he told Bush. "In Texas, some of our driveways are longer than that," Bush joked later.[21] George W. expressed strong admiration for all that

Israel had been able to accomplish, telling Sharon, "If you believe in the Bible, as I believe in the Bible, you know that extraordinary things happen." During that flight and over dinner, Bush and Sharon seemed to bond. When he left, George W. shook the Israeli's hand and said, "You know Arik, it's possible that I might be president of the United States, and you might be prime minister of Israel." Sharon laughed. He had been forced to resign as defense minister in the early 1980s after an Israeli court found him indirectly responsible for a Lebanese Christian militia's massacre of Palestinian civilians in the Sabra and Shatila refugee camps of Beirut. It seemed improbable at that moment that he ever would be rehabilitated politically. When Sharon was elected prime minister in February 2001, Bush, who had been inaugurated as president only a few weeks earlier, was one of the first foreign leaders to congratulate him. Journalist Uri Dan reported that when the two met as leaders for the first time, it was clear that no American president and Israeli prime minister had ever shared such mutual trust.[22] Bush said later that the trip to Israel was one of the most moving experiences of his life. On that helicopter trip, he made an enduring commitment to Israel's security.[23]

Both Bush and Sharon felt disdain for Arafat but kept open the possibility of dialogue with him until events convinced them otherwise. For Sharon the turning point came in the spring of 2001, when a Palestinian suicide bomber blew up the Dolphinarium nightclub in Tel Aviv, killing twenty-one Israelis, most of them teenagers. Until then, suicide bombings had been infrequent. Sharon had been using his son Omri as a back-channel to Arafat, but now he ended that connection. For Bush the tipping point came in January 2002 when Israel intercepted the *Karine A.*, a merchant ship carrying arms intended to reach Palestinian terrorists in Gaza. Arafat denied any connection to it, and Israel provided documents proving that he was lying. "Bush does not lie to you," says David Frum. "You had better not lie to him. The *Karine A.* incident finished off Arafat in Bush's eyes."[24]

Brent Scowcroft, who was national security adviser to both Gerald Ford and George H. W. Bush, believes that Sharon had a mesmerizing effect on Bush. "Sharon just has him wrapped around his little finger," Scowcroft told the *Financial Times* in 2004 (a comment that was meant to be off the record). After 9/11, said Scowcroft, Sharon persuaded Bush that Israel is the front line in the war on terrorism. Sharon, he added, "has been nothing but trouble."[25] Former ambassador Chas. W. Freeman, a critic of both Bush and Sharon, agrees. "From the point of view of Sharon and the Israeli right-wing expansionists," Freeman says, "Bush is the most manipulable thing that ever came along."[26] That directly contradicts the views of supporters who are familiar with him, as we have seen.

If Sharon had the president mesmerized, the spell was intermittent. Lawrence Wilkerson, Colin Powell's chief of staff during his term as secretary of state, says that after 9/11, Bush and Sharon "had an intellectual mind-meld. Bush thought, 'You have a worse problem than I do and now I feel for you, because now I understand it.' He made a conscious decision that he would help Sharon in any way that he could." Wilkerson, who has been far more outspoken than Powell in criticizing Bush's Mideast policy, nonetheless sees nuance in the president's relationship with Sharon. Bush always felt free to change direction, says Wilkerson. When he went too far in support of Israel or when Sharon carried his policies too far, Bush would back up with a tactical move. George W. gave the appearance of being buddy-buddy with Sharon, Wilkerson adds, and would say that he'd do whatever the Israeli asked him to. He always allowed himself the freedom to distance himself from Sharon, though.[27]

Indeed, Sharon's anxiety that Bush would pressure him politically was a factor in the Israeli leader's decision to withdraw from the Gaza Strip, according to Aluf Benn, diplomatic editor of the Israeli daily *Haaretz*. In September 2003, Sharon feared that the U.S. president was about to impose a settlement in the Middle East. Mahmoud Abbas, who was then the Palestinian prime minister, had resigned and the Road Map appeared to have collapsed. Rice sent Jerusalem the message that the United States would not let the peace process freeze, however. Sharon was afraid that Bush would demand that Israel withdraw from the occupied territories, which he compared to being corralled, like cattle sent to be slaughtered. It was then that the Israeli prime minister first seriously considered evacuating all Israeli settlements from Gaza, says Benn. Such a move would preempt American diplomatic pressure on Israel and preserve the outlines of the Road Map. At the end of 2003, Sharon unveiled this disengagement plan to the public.[28]

By 2005, American Jewish leaders associated with the Republican Party believed that Sharon's alliance with Bush was thinner than their public declarations had made it seem; Sharon himself reportedly agreed. Tom Pickering, the highly respected former U.S. ambassador to Jerusalem, Moscow, and the UN, believes that Rice's forceful intervention in the minute details of the Gaza border crossings following the disengagement showed that if Bush ever was wrapped around Sharon's finger, the wrapping wasn't so tight anymore. Still, Bush's relationship with Sharon was more significant than many people tend to believe, Malcolm Hoenlein, executive vice chairman of the Presidents Conference, told me.[29] Nor should one underestimate the president's identification with Israeli suffering after 9/11. From that point on, said Ari Fleischer, former White House spokesman, Bush knew what little Israel was going through. It was a democracy trying to protect its people against terrorists, just as he was trying to do. In an interview in December 2001, Bush spoke of how sympathetic he was to Sharon, who stood in his office "obviously agonizing over the loss of innocent life." Laura Bush, the president's wife, said in the same interview that she and her husband talked at night about how the Israeli people are terrorized, and they identified with Israel's having to endure "the same sort of situation we're facing in our country now."[30]

Bill Clinton's Failure

Another perspective is that the Bush administration maintained a hands-off policy in the Middle East because of Bill Clinton's failure, despite great effort, to achieve a diplomatic breakthrough. The Bush team, in this view, avoided getting deeply involved in the peace process out of a desire not to get bogged down in an effort that was sure to fail. Dennis Ross, a top Middle East negotiator for both President Bush 41 and Clinton, warned the Palestinians in December 2000, toward the close of Clinton's presidency, that this would happen. If Yasser Arafat didn't agree to the deal that Israeli Prime Minister Ehud Barak had accepted, said Ross, the incoming Bush administration would keep a distance from him.[31] Arafat turned down the offer and Bush never met with him.

Ross says that the Bush administration operated on other assumptions as well: that Clinton had wanted peace more than the parties themselves, had gotten too involved, and had overindulged Arafat. Bush and his advisers believed that little could be accomplished with the newly elected hard-line Sharon anyway. As a result, they didn't have much interest in pursuing peace negotiations and even avoided the phrase "peace process" in their first months in office. Ross adds that the Bush administration's reluctance was reinforced by the belief that Arafat hadn't seriously acted to stop terrorism and that he was essentially dishonest, as demonstrated by the *Karine-A* incident. Bush and his advisers thought that they would be more likely to transform the Middle East by dealing with Iraq, as opposed to the intractable Israeli-Palestinian conflict.[32]

Frum offers a corollary. Many of Bush's advisers believed that Bill Clinton had committed too much of the prestige of the country and the presidency to an uncertain outcome on the one issue of Israel, he notes. "Clinton was pretty persuasive and hardworking, and it still didn't work. People complained that [Bush] did not assert himself. But what were we going to accomplish in March 2001 that Clinton could not accomplish in December of 2000?" Bush's advisers felt that the war between Israel and the Palestinians eventually would exhaust itself, opening an opportunity for the United States to play a role. Till then, it was neither possible nor wise for the United States to intervene.[33]

President Bush felt that the parties themselves have to make peace, that you can't impose it, the Conference of Presidents' Malcolm Hoenlein notes. Hoenlein, who has regular access to the White House and State Department, says that "the efforts by [Ehud] Barak and Clinton in the last days before the [U.S. 2000] election were, by most estimates, frenetic, unproductive, and in fact counter-productive." Bush's advisers, by contrast, came in trying to be realistic. "They didn't want to put Bush out there until there was some basis on which to do it."[34]

As a result, according to Ross, the Bush 43 administration didn't act on the Israeli-Palestinian dispute soon enough. Bush waited four and a half years to become seriously involved, says Ross. If the president didn't move with a sense of urgency, Ross warned in 2005, Palestinian president Mahmoud Abbas's government was likely to collapse.[35] In the Palestinian elections in January 2006, Abbas's Fatah Party did lose to Hamas, though there were other reasons than American inaction, as we have seen. Chas. W. Freeman calls the Bush administration's long failure to act on the problem "an incredible error of judgment." It was, he says, a misunderstanding of America's historical role in the region that allowed the violence to escalate until 4,000 Palestinians and 1,000 Israelis had died and 40,000 Palestinians and 7,000 to 8,000 Israelis had been grievously injured. It was a default policy that has never been fully rectified, Freeman observed in 2005.[36]

The Question of Iraq

Another issue was whether to act first on Iraq or on the Israeli-Palestinian question. James Mann, in *The Rise of the Vulcans,* says that the hawks in the new Bush administration believed that removing Saddam Hussein from power in Iraq would isolate Arafat, making him more conciliatory. That was the position of Cheney, Rumsfeld, and Paul Wolfowitz, who was then the third-highest ranking civilian in the Pentagon.[37] Colin Powell and his deputy Richard Armitage believed, to the contrary, that there would have to be progress toward peace between Israel and the Palestinians before Arab governments would support a U.S. war against Iraq. Their short-term goal in 2002, therefore, was to induce Jerusalem to relax its crackdown in the occupied territories.[38] As we have seen, Bush went along with that for a time. It was the policy of the hawks that won out, however. Frum says that the president believed that even if the Palestinian problem were solved, it wouldn't make much difference to the larger war on terror.[39]

The Jewish Lobby

Tom Pickering argues that Bush's strategy toward Israel was shaped by domestic considerations. In Pickering's view, because of conservative political pressures at home, it was much easier for Bush to support Israel when Sharon was intransigent. When the Israeli prime minister began to consider disengagement from Gaza, says Pickering, he was out on his own for a while. The United States stood on the sidelines and the neocons watched with their mouths agape. It was left to Rice to step in and assert U.S. support of the withdrawal.[40]

Freeman also argues that domestic considerations determined foreign policy in the Bush administration. He believes that Bush wanted to wean the American Jewish community from their traditional loyalty to the Democrats.[41] Jews represent about 2 percent of the American population. They are, however, concentrated in a few big states that control almost half of the Electoral College, including Florida and Ohio, key swing states in recent presidential elections. Jews are also enthusiastic volunteers for Democratic candidates ("All you have in Democratic campaigns are Catholics and Jews," says James Carville, the campaign consultant. "I don't know why, but it's a standing joke.") Even more significantly, Jews donate up to half of the total funds given to the Democratic National Committee, which coordinates and supports individual electoral races. In addition, Jewish donors provide about half of the funding for Democratic presidential candidates—more than that for a friend of Israel like Bill Clinton, less for Jimmy Carter. Jews give to Republican candidates too, but, as of 1996, they had never provided more than 20 percent of the total amount.[42] Some Republican strategists hoped that Bush's strongly pro-Israel policy could divert enough Jewish funds from the Democrats to cripple them in 2004. That did not happen, but as the 2006 elections approached, Republicans received the highest percentage of Jewish political donations ever: 42 percent of the money from Jewish political action committees went to the GOP.[43]

Many observers focus more on Jewish than Christian influence on U.S. policy toward Israel. They believe that the combination of the powerful pro-Israel lobby in Washington, the presence of Jewish voters in swing states, and disproportionately large Jewish contributions in election campaigns has made it very difficult for any administration to stand up to Israel. This, they argue, accounted for Bush's one-sided support of the Jewish state. Former Democratic congressman Lee Hamilton, for example, noted that "the American Jewish community has developed a lobbying campaign that is unmatched in Washington." The cultural and psychological symbiosis between Americans and Israelis, combined with the lobbyists' outreach to labor unions on the left and evangelicals on the right, and the massive Jewish contributions to candidates of both parties, said Hamilton, had produced a fascinating result: "Politically, Israel is absolutely untouchable." Former president Jimmy Carter added that the historical American role as a strong and objective mediator in the Middle East "is constrained by powerful lobbying forces."[44] The lobbyists he had in mind were, of course, Jewish.

The United States gives Israel a remarkable level of material and diplomatic support. John Mearsheimer of the University of Chicago and Stephen Walt of Harvard have argued that America doesn't do this because of shared strategic interests or compelling moral imperatives but rather because of the "Israel Lobby." As Mearsheimer and Walt define it, that lobby includes not only the American-Israel Public Affairs Committee (AIPAC) and the Conference of Presidents but also evangelical Christians. Among the latter are Gary Bauer, Ralph Reed, Pat Robertson, and two former Republican leaders of the House of Representatives, Dick Armey and Tom DeLay, all of whom believe that Israel represents the fulfillment of biblical prophecy. Mearsheimer and Walt list the late Jerry Falwell as well. They point out that neoconservative gentiles also are involved, notably former U.S. ambassador to the United Nations John Bolton, former secretary of education William Bennett, and columnist George Will; they also implicate the late former UN ambassador Jeanne Kirkpatrick. No other lobby has managed to divert the United States as far from its own national interests, the authors say. No other such group has been able to convince Americans that their interests and those of another country are essentially identical. Especially after 9/11, Mearsheimer and Walt argue, the assertion has been made that Israel's enemies and America's are the same. "In fact, Israel is a liability in the war on terror," they claim. "The U.S. has a terrorism problem in good part because it is so closely allied with Israel, not the other way around." Many leaders of Al Qaeda are motivated, they declare, by Israel's presence in Jerusalem and the plight of the Palestinians. Meanwhile, "the Palestinians barely have an effective police force, let alone an army that could pose a threat to Israel," they assert. The Bush team is persuaded otherwise, they say, by domestic politics.[45]

The response to this study was immediate and outraged. Michael Oren, author of the acclaimed *Six Days of War,* accused Mearsheimer and Walt of slipshod work that drew on neither declassified records, presidential memoirs, nor State Department documents. Those sources, Oren said, would "unimpeachably show that Arab oil (and not Israel) was America's persistent focus in the Middle East—and that presidents have supported Israel for strategic and moral reasons, not political ones."[46] Benny Morris, a prominent Israeli "new historian" who has offered critical views of Zionism, also was dismissive of the study.

Mearsheimer and Walt often cite his books, said Morris, "yet their work is a travesty of the history that I have studied and written for the past two decades. Their work is riddled with shoddiness and defiled by mendacity."[47]

Dennis Ross concluded that Mearsheimer and Walt are ignorant and their study is "incredibly simple-minded."[48] Fouad Ajami, director of the Middle East Studies Program at Johns Hopkins (whom the study accused of persuading Dick Cheney to attack Iraq) characterized it as "nonsense scholarship" that purveys "lurid fantasies endemic to the Arab world."[49] Harvard professor Alan Dershowitz, author of *The Case for Israel,* noted that Mearsheimer and Walt, by their own admission, employed no original documentation or interviews. Rather, they used anti-Israeli charges that "can be found on the Web sites of extremists of the hard right, like David Duke, and the hard left, like Alexander Cockburn. They appear daily in the Arab and Muslim press." The authors' claims, said Dershowitz, are variations on old anti-Semitic themes of the kind found in the notorious czarist forgery *The Protocols of the Elders of Zion* and in Nazi literature.[50]

David Gergen, who advised Presidents Nixon, Ford, Reagan, and Clinton and who, like Walt, is a professor at the Kennedy School of Government at Harvard, also rebutted the study. "Over the course of four tours in the White House," he wrote, "I never once saw a decision in the Oval Office to tilt U.S. foreign policy in favor of Israel at the expense of America's interest." Aside from Nixon, Gergen added, he couldn't remember any president even talking about an Israeli lobby—though there were plenty of conversations about the power of the gun lobby, environmentalist, evangelicals, small-business owners, and teachers' unions.[51] David Frum commented, "Is Fouad Ajami Jewish? Trent Lott? Tom DeLay? Seems to me that Walt & Mearsheimer are conflating the actual Jewish lobby with the broad and deep support Americans feel for the state of Israel. It's a little like proponents of a higher gasoline tax complaining that they were defeated by the 'driver lobby'—all 240 million of them working together in a shadowy covert conspiracy."[52] David Remnick, the editor of *The New Yorker,* observed that Walt and Mearsheimer's "account is not so much a diagnosis of our polarized era as a symptom of it."[53] Former secretary of state George P. Shultz characterized the thinking behind their argument as "conspiracy theory, pure and simple." Schultz argued that the United States supports Israel because that position is politically sound and morally just, not because of political pressure or influence. "We are not babes in the woods. We act in our own interests," he concluded.[54]

Michael Gerson, the former Bush speechwriter and adviser, said in 2007 that Walt and Mearsheimer are naïve to think that the United States has a terrorism problem because it is so closely allied with Israel. That's like saying that Britain had a Nazi problem in the 1930s because it was so closely allied with Czechoslovakia, said Gerson. Far from shaping Bush's Middle East policy, as the two authors claim, Israel was consistently skeptical of Bush's agenda to plant democracy in the region. Nor did Christian Zionism ever come up in any policy discussion, said Gerson. Mearsheimer and Walt are thinking conspiratorially, he said, and their charge against the Israel lobby "is not only rubbish, it is dangerous rubbish."[55]

One attack on Mearsheimer and Walt's contentions came from a wholly unexpected source: Columbia professor Joseph Massad, whose radical criticism of Israel and U.S. foreign policy has been highly controversial. Writing in the Egyptian *Al-Ahram Weekly,* Massad claimed that the Mearsheimer-Walt study makes a crucial error in that it shifts the blame for United States policies to Israel and its supporters. The real problem, he said, is that America is the implacable enemy of all Third World liberation groups; U.S. policy toward the Palestinians merely falls into that pattern.[56]

Given the eminence of its authors, the Mearsheimer-Walt study is remarkably reductivist and tendentious. The authors seem to hear only one voice in the complex narrative of Middle East history and politics. The fact remains, however, that the pro-Israeli lobby is profoundly influential in Washington, and Jewish votes and electoral participation are political considerations that candidates for office ignore at their peril.

George Bush senior's experience proved the point. He played tough with Israeli Prime Minister Yitzhak Shamir, threatening to withhold loan guarantees unless Shamir froze construction of settlements in the West Bank. American Jewish voters came to Washington to lobby Congress on behalf of Israel, the president appeared to criticize them, and he lost Jewish support. In fact, he got only 11 percent of the Jewish vote in 1992, a dramatic decline from this group's turnout for Nixon and Reagan as well as for Bush himself in 1988.[57] Bush's defeat still hangs like a cloud over Washington, Pickering notes.[58] More than one American diplomat told me that the president and Karl Rove learned a lesson from that experience, and that George W. Bush had no intention of making a similar mistake.

After the Second Lebanon War

By the autumn of 2006, Israelis began to worry that the Bush administration would be far less supportive than it had been in recent years. The White House was disappointed by Israel's failure to deliver a decisive blow to Hezbollah in the war that July and August. Some Israeli officials worried that Washington was reassessing the Jewish state's effectiveness and even its value as an ally in the war on terror. Iran, by contrast, was emboldened by its proxy's performance in Lebanon, and moderate Arab states were anxious about Teheran's new influence in the region.

By 2007, the administration was on the defensive. The Democrats were in control of both houses of Congress, discussing a timetable for withdrawing American troops. There were widespread complaints that Iraq had become a quagmire, and the president's approval ratings had hit new lows. Israeli and Christian Zionist leaders became concerned that Bush would need to build a coalition among Arab states to oppose Iran and ease the exit from Iraq. That could mean U.S. pressure on Israel to make concessions to the Palestinians. Bridges for Peace, reporting on Hamas's insistence that it would never recognize Israel's right to exist, continued to warn of the Palestinians' plan to use a state as a base to obliterate Israel.[59] The Christian Zionist Stan Goodenough complained that George W. Bush was oblivious to the theological dimension of the conflict. The president believed that a two-state solution will bring peace, Goodenough lamented. "What Bush apparently does not see at all, is that this is a conflict involving God and His Word on the one side against Satan and his determined effort to thwart that Word and its Author on the other."[60]

The Annapolis Summit, 2007

In the summer of 2007, after Hamas had forcibly seized control of the Gaza Strip, the Bush administration sought to prop up the Fatah-led government in the West Bank and to sponsor Israeli-Palestinian peace negotiations. Abbas had dissolved the national unity government and separated politically from Hamas, and the United States and Israel were ready to support him. In July, Bush offered $190 million in aid to the Palestinian Authority (PA) and $80 million in security assistance. He also called for a regional peace conference, to be held in Annapolis, Maryland, that would lead to a Palestinian state.

Christian Zionists denounced the new peace initiative. Gary Bauer was deeply disappointed that Bush was trying to resuscitate the moribund 2003 Road Map. "I don't know how many times we can say this: This dispute is not about a Palestinian state," Bauer told his readers. Al Qaeda, Hezbollah, Hamas, and even some elements of Fatah, the people who are killing Americans and Israelis, don't want a Palestinian state, he said. "They want it all, 'from the river to the sea.'" It is delusional, added Bauer, to imagine that there can be peace when one side promotes a culture of death and anti-Semitism.[61] The International Christian Embassy's David Parsons warned that it was too risky to agree to a Palestinian state that would likely be overrun by Hamas. Previous IDF withdrawals had only brought terrorists' rockets closer to Israel, he noted.[62] Bridges for Peace exhorted its readers to "pray that Israel will not be deceived into a position of peace while its neighbors prepare for war."[63] The Unity Coalition for Israel warned its evangelical and Jewish readers that Bush, Rice, and Abbas were leading the weak and unpopular Olmert to accept a suicide pact. It involved "unthinkable concessions": giving away half of the Land of Israel, including the Temple Mount; accepting the Palestinian refugees' "right of return" to Israel; and releasing Palestinian criminals. The UCI asked its members to sign a petition calling on two small Israeli parties to bring down Olmert's government by resigning from it.[64] Joseph Farah, an evangelical American journalist and radio talk show host of Arab descent, denounced the peace process as "never-ending appeasement of the Islamists by Israel." In yielding to Palestinian demands, especially in ceding control of the Temple Mount, the Israeli elite were selling out their birthright, he declared. They were lying down before their enemies.[65] The heads of the three major Christian Zionist organizations in Israel made public statements warning against dividing Jerusalem. They stressed its historical importance to Jews and the fear that if Muslim Palestinians controlled the Old City, Christians there would be forced to live as inferiors, in dhimmihood.[66]

All of these arguments were grounded in history and secular politics, though, of course, they comported perfectly with faith. Christian Friends of Israel's Carolyn Jacobson, by contrast, spoke directly from religious conviction: she reminded her readers in an e-mail Prayer Letter that only the King of Kings—not the Annapolis summit—would bring peace. The process preparing Jews to accept the Antichrist as their Messiah is accelerating, she warned. The dispensational time of Tribulation is approaching.[67]

Meanwhile, American evangelical and Jewish leaders met with national security adviser Stephen J. Hadley and Elliott Abrams to express the depth of their concern about dividing Jerusalem. Hadley assured them that Washington was not pressuring Olmert to make concessions.[68]

A number of Middle East experts opposed investing political or financial capital in Fatah. Armed Fatah gangs ruled the streets of the West Bank and elected Hamas officials languished in Israeli prisons, but most Palestinians were not loyal to the timid and feckless Abbas. He had utterly failed to enact his promise to impose "one law, one authority, one gun" in the territories. And under his leadership, Fatah had not reformed itself after its humiliating defeat in the elections of January 2006.[69] Fatah officials remained corrupt and its security services were still divided. Fouad Ajami warned that "Nablus in the West Bank is no more amenable to reason than is Gaza." Both are ruled by pitiless preachers and masked gunmen, he noted. And there is no way to create a normal state in the West Bank while Gaza goes under, said Ajami.[70] The Shin Bet (the General Security Service), the Mossad, and Israeli military intelligence expressed the joint opinion that even if agreements were reached in Annapolis, Abbas would be incapable of implementing them. "There is a total disconnection between the leadership and the Palestinian people," read their report.[71] Abbas was a powerless leader. He would need the support of the key Arab states to even consider reaching an accord with Israel.

The Americans hoped to have a peace agreement in place while Bush was still in office. So did Olmert. He knew that Israel would "never have a more comfortable administration," as one of his aides put it.[72] But Bush himself was said to be skeptical that the Arab side would make the compromises necessary for peace, and he was deeply resistant to repeating what he considered to have been Bill Clinton's mistake: getting too involved because he wanted peace more than the parties did. Bush's critics warned that after seven years of a mostly hands-off policy, the president would have to follow through.[73]

Whether or not the summit led to much, the speech in which Bush had called for it was important in its own right. It confirmed the policy in his landmark Rose Garden speech of five years before, calling on the Palestinian Authority to end terrorism and corruption as steps toward achieving a state. It reiterated a statement Bush had made in a letter to Ariel Sharon on April 14, 2004, that a final agreement would take into account the "new realities on the ground": Israel could retain its major settlements rather than returning to the 1949 armistice borders. The speech also declared that the United States would never abandon its commitment to Israel's security as a "Jewish state and homeland for the Jewish people." That obliquely confirmed another statement that Bush made in the 2004 letter: that Palestinian refugees should settle in their own state (not in Israel).[74] That in essence denied the Arab demand that millions of Palestinian refugees be allowed to return to Israel, a right expressed in UN General Assembly Resolution 194. Moreover, the president's speech called on the Arab states to recognize Israel, ending the fiction that it does not exist, and to stop inciting hatred against it. All of that would have to happen to before there would be a Palestinian state.[75]

The Annapolis summit took place in November 2007. The Israelis and Palestinians left with the goal of reaching an accord by the end of 2008 and Bush told them, "We will use our power to help you."[76] Three-quarters of Israeli Jews and most Palestinians (59%) considered the conference a failure.[77] And though most Israeli Jews thought that the Palestinians genuinely wanted peace and were justified in demanding a state, more than six in ten believed that even if there were a two-state solution, there would be no peace: without

Hamas's agreement, terrorism against Israel would continue. The vast majority of Israeli Arabs, for their part, said that Abbas had no mandate to make concessions.[78] But Rice believed that a moment of opportunity had finally arrived: the Israeli and Palestinian leadership and a majority of their peoples wanted a two-state solution, and the rise of violent extremism in the region had compelled neighboring Arab states to support the peace conference.[79]

All parties were driven by an unspoken goal, the fear of Iran and the militant radicalism that it sponsored. Hezbollah's success in the Second Lebanon War and Hamas's takeover of Gaza had shaken moderate Arab rulers, who feared for the stability of their own regimes. From their perspective, to solve the Israeli-Palestinian conflict, which had festered for so long and occasioned so much hatred, would frustrate their Islamist opponents and help calm domestic unrest. Many Israelis, too, felt that their circumstances required action. Olmert warned that if a two-state solution failed, leaving Israel with a growing Palestinian population demanding equality in a South Africa-style confrontation, even the American Jews would turn against Israel: they would refuse to support a state that denies equal rights to its residents.[80]

Following the conference, a group of over eighty politically moderate and liberal evangelicals declared that they would work diligently for peace and a flourishing economy for both Israel and the Palestinians. Focusing on hopelessness, not religious or cultural conflict, as the source of militancy, they warned that "Palestinians—especially the youth who have no economic opportunity— are increasingly sympathetic to radical solutions and terrorism."[81] Rice, who met with five of these evangelicals at the White House prior to the conference, expressed similar views. "Deprivation and humiliation can radicalize even normal people," she said. She empathized with both sides. And she noted that Olmert, too, had spoken of his concern for the indignity and hardship that Palestinians feel.[82]

Christian Zionists saw an entirely different reality. Olive Tree Ministries, in Minnesota, responded to the summit with disdain and alarm. The conference had resembled the tea party with the Mad Hatter, an absurd descent into a land of make-believe, said an Olive Tree e-mail. If the Annapolis accords were put into place, it warned, Israel could be erased from the map—yet the left-leaning evangelicals had put their blessing on it.[83]

The Jerusalem Prayer Team's Mike Evans also denounced the conference. He warned that the Arab vultures were gathering again, sensing that the City of David would be laid on the altar as a sacrifice. How could Bush cavalierly shake hands with Abbas, "the man responsible for the Munich [Olympics] massacre?" Evans asked. He was appalled to have to admit that Bush actually believed that the Palestinian issue was the root of Islamic hatred for America, he added.[84] Bush's plan to establish a PLO state by the end of 2008 was a bat-tle between light and darkness, politics and prophecy, Evans declared, and he revealed that God had spoken to him. The Lord had inspired him to launch the Save Jerusalem Campaign, and to that end he asked his Jerusalem Prayer Team readers to sign a petition against dividing Jerusalem. By late January 2008, 128,000 of them had. "Satan knows his command and control center for spiritual warfa re is Jerusalem," Evans cautioned. "God will oppose any nation that attempts to touch Jerusalem."[85]

Bridges for Peace carried a report that, on the day after the summit, Pal-estinian Authority–controlled television showed a map in which Israel was painted in the colors of the Palestinian flag. The message was clear: the Jewish state remained under existential threat. "Pray that no negotiator will be de-ceived," urged Bridges. It asked its readers to pray that God's Road Map—not Bush's—would be implemented.[86]

"The whole affair is so childishly transparent that even the Bush adminis-tration ought to be able to grasp it," declared Hal Lindsey dismissively. The Annapolis conference was little more than an attempt to appease an enemy on a scale not seen since Neville Chamberlain betrayed Czechoslovakia at Munich, he said. Chamberlain returned home with the tragically empty promise of "Peace in our time." Similarly, Olmert was leading his people to disaster, Lindsey warned. He concluded, as always, by embedding current events in the matrix of prophecy: "Thank God that the 'times of the Gentiles' are almost complete," Lindsey said, quoting Luke 21:24. "Then, as God has sworn, He will liberate His people Israel and bring a remnant to true faith in His Messiah."[87]

Notes

PREFACE

1. Eric Uslaner and Mark Lichbach, "Why the GOP Can't Convert the Jewish Vote," *The Forward*, February 24, 2006, and "The Two Front War: Jews, Identity, Liberalism, and Voting (undated, http://www.bsos.umd.edu/gvpt/uslaner/uslanerlichbachjewishvotingbehavioriii.pdf).

2. Figures presented by John Green at the "Uneasy Allies" conference, Jewish Theological Seminary, New York, November 30, 2005; John C. Green, "Evangelical Protestants and Jews: A View from the Polls, in Alan Mittleman, Byron Johnson, and Nancy Isserman, eds., *Uneasy Allies? Evangelical and Jewish Relations* (Lanham, Md: Lexington Books, 2007), 26.

3. Green, "Evangelical Protestants and Jews: A View from the Polls," 37.

4. "American Jewish Committee's 2006 Annual Survey of American Jewish Opinion" (http://www.ajc.org/site/apps/nl/content2.asp?c=ijITI2PHKoG&b=2174431&ct=3152891). In 1976, Rabbi Alexander M. Schindler, the leader of the Reform Jewish movement, warned that fundamentalism was the source of anti-Semitism, and the National Jewish Community Relations Advisory Council and the Anti-Defamation League urged rabbis to seek the help of liberal Protestant clergy in countering evangelicals' "negative influence." As early as 1979, however, scholar David Rausch called that perception of fundamentalists' bias "totally inaccurate," asserting that they were firmly committed to Israel and the Jewish people (David A. Rausch, *Zionism within Early American Fundamentalism, 1878–1918: A Convergence of Two Traditions* [New York: Edwin Mellen Press, 1979], 1–2, 4). In 1988, 58 percent of American Jews saw fundamentalist Protestants as anti-Semitic (Kenneth D. Wald and Lee Sigelman, "Romancing the Jews: The Christian Right in Search of Strange Bedfellows," in Corwin E. Smidt and James M. Penning, eds., *Sojourners in the Wilderness: The Christian Right in Comparative Perspective* [Lanham: Rowman & Littlefield, 1997], 155).

5. Council on Foreign Relations Meeting Subject: Peace versus Democracy in Palestine, with Former U.S. President Jimmy Carter, Federal News Service, March 2, 2006.

CHAPTER I

1. Interview with Robert Stearns, May 16, 2005. In 2007, the scholar of Islam Bernard Lewis expressed a similar view about Europe. He quoted a Syrian philosopher who said that the

only question about the future of Europe is, "Will it be an Islamized Europe or a Europeanized Islam?" Lewis added that Muslims "seem to be about to take over Europe" and noted that "the outlook for the Jewish communities of Europe is dim (Tovah Lazaroff and David Horovitz, "The Iranians Do Not Expect to Be Attacked," *Jerusalem Post,* January 31, 2007).

2. Sokolow referred to William Hechler, who assisted Theodor Herzl's efforts to create a Jewish state, as a "Christian 'Lover of Zion'" and a "Christian Zionist" (Nahum Sokolow, *History of Zionism 1600–1918* [1919; reprint New York: Ktav, 1969], I. 270, 468). See Donald Wagner, "A Christian Zionist Primer (Part II) Defining Christian Zionism," *Cornerstone,* 31 (Winter 2003) (http://sabeel.org/documents/CornerStone31.pdf); Walter Riggans, *Israel and Zionism* (London: Handsel Press, 1988), 18–19.

3. David A. Rausch, *Communities in Conflict: Evangelicals and Jews* (Philadelphia: Trinity Press International, 1991), 151. Young founded a Jerusalem-based organization to educate Christians in Hebraic understandings of the Bible and to break down walls between Christians and Jews. In 1977, it split into a school and the pro-Zionist Bridges for Peace, which now has a staff of eighty. Among its philanthropic functions is running the largest Christian food bank in Israel, distributing seventy tons of food a month to poor Israelis (interview with Rebecca Brimmer, August 8, 2005).

4. David K. Shipler, "1,000 Christian 'Zionists' Rally in Jerusalem," *New York Times,* September 25, 1980 (which includes an account of Dr. Larry Samuels's influence on Prime Minister Menachem Begin); David Firestone, "DeLay Is to Carry Dissenting Message on a Mideast Tour," *New York Times,* July 25, 2003.

5. Riggans, *Israel and Zionism,* 19.

6. Guilt has been a factor in many Christians' support for returning the Jews to Israel. Walter Russell Mead observes that in the nineteenth century, it contributed to a "progressive Zionism" that was grounded less in prophecy than in the liberal belief that God was actively making a better world. In this view, one way He was doing that was by restoring the oppressed and degraded Jews to the Holy Land to shield them from further persecution and to uplift their character. Gentiles who held this conviction joined with Christian Zionists in signing William Blackstone's petition to Benjamin Harrison in 1891, which I note later in this chapter (Walter Russell Mead, "The New Israel and the Old: Why Gentile Americans Back the Jewish State," *Foreign Affairs,* July/August 2008).

7. Wagner, "A Christian Zionist Primer (Part II)."

8. Interview with Richard Booker, August 17, 2005. Booker says that the term "Christian" has been used so generically that it has lost its true meaning. He defines a biblical Christian as someone who has "a personal relationship with the God of Abraham, Isaac, and Jacob through Jesus (Richard Booker, "Christian Zionists, Jews and Israel" [2004, booklet], 2).

9. Interview with Booker, August 17, 2005; interview with Ted Haggard, June 26, 2006.

10. Joel Baker defined Christian Zionism as "affirming the Word of God regarding His eternal covenant with the Jewish people and their return to Zion." He asserted that Christianity is Zionist by its biblical nature, but to focus on Israel and the Jewish people as ultimate goals in themselves would be idolatry. Rather, Christian Zionism should be one aspect of acting in accordance with the Word of Jesus ("Christian Zionism" in Matt Johnson and Nicola Goodenough, eds., *Christians and Israel: Essays on Biblical Zionism and on Islamic Fundamentalism* [Jerusalem: International Christian Embassy Jerusalem, 1996], 1–3, cited by Maria Leppakari, "The End Is a Beginning: Contemporary Apocalyptic Representations of Jerusalem" [Abo, Finland: Abo Akademi University Press, 2002], 140–43).

11. Interviews with Joel James, March 22, 2005, and Robert Stearns, May 16, 2005.

12. Eagles' Wings also educates American volunteers in the history of the Jews and anti-Semitism, then sends them to Jerusalem. When they return, these devout Christians serve as unofficial ambassadors for Israel called Watchmen on the Wall and they counter the anti-Zionism that they find in the news. This is inspired by Isaiah 62:6–7: "Upon your walls, O Jerusalem,

I have set watchmen; all the day and all the night they shall never be silent. You who put the Lord in remembrance, take no rest, and give him no rest until he establishes Jerusalem and makes it a praise in the earth." Eagles' Wings also sends Christian college students on three-week trips to Israel. They then act as ambassadors for the Israeli view of events on college campuses (Interviews with Joel James, March 22, 2005, and January 19, 2006).

13. Isaiah 62: 6–7.

14. Interview with Miriam Rodlyn Park, March 23, 2005.

15. Eagles' Wings reported that Christians in 200,000 congregations in 167 nations participated in the 2007 Day of Prayer for the Peace of Jerusalem. Evangelicals from a dozen countries, including China and Uganda, prayed with Robert Stearns in Jerusalem. Among the participants were Rabbi Benny Elon and Daniel Ayalon, Israel's former ambassador to the United States. David Davis, senior pastor of the Messianic Jewish Kehilat HaCarmel congregation in Haifa, also spoke. There was also a nonstop twenty-four-hour global prayer teleconference. Evangelicals from around the world also have joined Eagles' Wings in a daily prayer call since October 2006 (Eagles' Wings: Jerusalem Project [http://ew.us.churchinsight.com/Group/Group. aspx?id=1000002764]; Jerusalem's Watchman Prayer Update, October 12, 2007; "Prayers for Peace in Jerusalem Have Global Impact," retrieved October 16, 2007 [http://www.earnedmedia. org/alrc1015.htm]; EWM Report, December 27, 2007).

16. Jeremiah 31: 15.

17. Ezekiel 36:26.

18. Ephesians 2:15–16.

19. The respected Christian Zionist writer Derek Prince, a fervent supporter of Israel, declared in 1978 that God is giving the Jews hearts of flesh in fulfillment of Ezekiel's prophecy. He added that Christians were preparing the Jews to accept their messiah, by whom he certainly meant Jesus Christ (*Promised Land: God's Word and the Nation of Israel* [1978; reprint, Charlotte, N.C.: Derek Prince Ministries, 2003], 86 and 131).

20. Paul Boyer, *When Time Shall Be No More: Prophecy Belief in Modern American Culture* (Cambridge, Mass.: Belknap Press of Harvard University Press, 1992), 88–89; Increase Mather, *The Mystery of Israel's Salvation Explained and Applied,* cited by Boyer, 183.

21. Timothy P. Weber, *On the Road to Armageddon: How Evangelicals Became Israel's Best Friend* (Grand Rapids, Mich.: Baker Academic, 2004), 23–26; Yaakov Ariel, *On Behalf of Israel: American Fundamentalist Attitudes toward Jews, Judaism, and Zionism, 1865–1945* (Brooklyn, N.Y.: Carlson, 1991), 15. Dispensationalists also find support for the Rapture in 1 Corinthians 15:53 (Gershom Gorenberg, *The End of Days: Fundamentalism and the Struggle for the Temple Mount* [2000; paperback, New York: Oxford University Press, 2000], 33).

22. There are no hard polling data on this, but the estimate of 10 percent is by John Green, a premier authority on the subject. See Chapter 9 below.

23. Weber, *On the Road to Armageddon,* 13.

24. Donald Wagner, "Christians and Zion: British Stirrings," Information Clearing House, October 9, 2003 (http://www.informationclearinghouse.info/article4959.htm); Robert W. Hanning, *The Vision of History in Early Britain* (New York: Columbia University Press, 1966), 55.

25. Ariel, *On Behalf of Israel,* 1–10; Michael B. Oren, *Power, Faith, and Fantasy: America in the Middle East, 1776 to the Present* (New York: Norton, 2007), 89.

26. Barbara W. Tuchman, *Bible and Sword: England and Palestine from the Bronze Age to Balfour* (1956; reprint, New York: Ballantine Books, 1984), 121–22, 131.

27. Gershom Scholem, *Sabbatai Sevi: The Mystical Messiah* (Princeton, N.J.: Princeton University Press, 1973), 549, n207; Ariel, *On Behalf of Israel,* 3. Millenarian expectations were also a factor in Oliver Cromwell's allowing the Jews to return to England in the mid-1650s after having been expelled in 1290.

28. S. Snobelen, "'The Mystery of This Restitution of All Things': Isaac Newton on the Return of the Jews," in J. E. Force and R. H. Popkin (eds.), *Millenarianism and Messianism in Early*

Modern European Culture: The Millenarian Turn (Dordrecht, The Netherlands: Kluwer Academic, 2001), 95–118. Newton's dating of the apocalypse is based on Daniel. It appears in a manuscript collection that was exhibited for the first time in 2007 at the Jewish National and University Library's Givat Ram campus in Jerusalem (Yaakov Lappin, "The First Christian Zionist?" *Ynet*, June 22, 2007; Matti Friedman, "Now on Display in Jerusalem: Newton's Temple Drawings," *Jerusalem Post Christian Edition*, July 2007).

29. *The Complete Poetical Works of John Milton*, ed. Douglas Bush (Boston, Mass.: Houghton Mifflin, 1965), 496; *The Poems of Alexander Pope*, ed. John Butt (New Haven, Conn.: Yale University Press, 1963), 189–94; Clifford R. Ames, "False Advertising: The Influence of Virgil and Isaiah on Pope's Messiah," *Studies in English Literature, 1500–1900*, 28 (Summer 1988), 401–26; Gerhard Falk, *The Restoration of Israel: Christian Zionism in Religion, Literature, and Politics* (New York: Peter Lang, 2006), 9–14.

30. Tuchman, *Bible and Sword*, 175–76, 190; Benny Morris, *Righteous Victims: A History of the Zionist-Arab Conflict, 1881–2001* (New York: Vintage Books, 1999), 42.

31. Paul Charles Merkley, *The Politics of Christian Zionism, 1891–1948* (London: Frank Cass, 1998), 11 and 16; Amos Elon, *Herzl* (New York: Holt, Rinehart and Winston, 1975), 187.

32. Howard M. Sachar, *A History of Israel from the Rise of Zionism to Our Time* (1976; reprint, New York: Alfred A. Knopf, 1996), 6–16.

33. Elon, 126–31, 187–94, passim; Merkley, *The Politics of Christian Zionism*, 16–34.

34. Yaakov Ariel, "An Unexpected Alliance: Christian Zionism and Its Historical Significance," *Modern Judaism*, 26.1 (2006), 78; Michael J. Pragai, *Faith and Fulfilment: Christians and the Return to the Promised Land* (London: Vallentine Mitchell, 1985), 61.

35. See Tom Segev, *One Palestine Complete: Jews and Arabs under the British Mandate*, translated by Haim Watzman (New York: Holt, 1999), 37–38.

36. Tuchman, *Bible and Sword*, 311–47. Tuchman accepted the traditional view that Lloyd George also wanted to reward chemist and Zionist leader Chaim Weizmann for his contribution to the Allied war effort.

37. Oren, *Power, Faith, and Fantasy*, 90, 141–42.

38. Ariel, *On Behalf of Israel*, 10.

39. Yaakov Ariel, "An Unexpected Alliance," 78–79; Merkley, *Politics of Christian Zionism*, 88–89.

40. Ariel, *On Behalf of Israel*, 25, 70–91, and "An Unexpected Alliance," 76–77.

41. Ariel, "An Unexpected Alliance," 78–79.

42. In the dispensational view, the promises to Abraham are literal, though John F. Walvoord, then-president of the Dallas Theological Seminary, said in 1962 that the references to Abraham's seed apply in three different ways: (1) They can refer to his actual physical descendants, through Isaac and Jacob. (2) They can denote those among his physical descendants who kept God's law. They are the "spiritual Israel" of Romans 9:6–8. (3) They are the Gentiles who are not Abraham's physical descendants but who "are of faith" and so are blessed with Abraham (Galatians 3:3–9). These people receive the promises given to the Gentiles, not those given to Abraham's physical seed. Walvoord warns that it is wrong to conclude from Galatians that all distinctions between the natural and spiritual seed of Abraham are erased (*Israel in Prophecy* [Grand Rapids, Mich.: Zondervan, 1962], 36–37).

43. Clarence H. Wagner, Jr., "The Error of Replacement Theology," *Bridges for Peace*, May 9, 2002, http://www.ldolphin.org/replacement. For an account of a prominent evangelical's internal debate about supersessionist belief, see Richard J. Mouw, "The Chosen People Puzzle," *Christianity Today*, March 5, 2001. In 2007, John Hagee refuted replacement theologians' claim that God broke his covenant with Israel because the Jews rejected Jesus. It was never God's plan for Jesus to be Israel's Messiah, said Hagee. That would have required Jesus to live, and God had always intended him to die. "If Jesus refused by his words or actions to claim to be the Messiah to the Jews," Hagee argues, "then *how can the Jews be blamed for rejecting*

what was never offered?" (John Hagee, *In Defense of Israel* [Lake Mary, Fla.: Strang, 2007]), 132, 135–36).

CHAPTER 2

1. Jerry Falwell, *Listen, America!* (Toronto, New York: Bantam Books, 1980), 98.

2. Interview with Richard Land, September 27, 2005. The Southern Baptists are the largest Protestant denomination in America, representing 43,000 churches.

3. John Eidsmore, *God and Caesar: BiblicalFaith and Political Action* (Westchester, Ill: Crossway Books, 1984), 226–27, cited by Michael Lienesch, *Redeeming America* (Chapel Hill: University of North Carolina Press, 1993), 231.

4. "Pastor John Hagee AIPAC Policy Conference, March 11, 2007 (www.aipac.org/Publictions/SpeechesByPolicymakers/Hagee/PC-2007.pdf); Stan Goodenough, "Hagee: Giant of Christian Zionism Has Awakened," *Jerusalem Newswire*, March 15, 2007.

5. Jan Markell, "Are There Consequences When Harming Israel?" *Understanding the Times*, Olive Tree Ministries, February 8, 2007.

6. Yaakov Lappin, "Christians Offer 'Repentance," *Ynet*, March 28, 2007.

7. David Parsons, "The Blessing of Abraham," *Jerusalem Post Christian Edition*, October 2006. For studies of the ICEJ, see Timothy P. Weber, *On the Road to Armageddon: How Evangelicals Became Israel's Best Friend* (Grand Rapids: Baker Academic, 2004), 215–18, 230–31; Yaakov Ariel, "An Unexpected Alliance: Christian Zionism and Its Historical Significance," *Modern Judaism*, 26.1 (2006), 83–87.

8. Franklin Graham, with Bruce Nygren, *The Name* (Nashville: Nelson Books, 2002), 186–88.

9. Hal Lindsey, *The Everlasting Hatred: The Roots of Jihad* (Murrieta, Calif.: Oracle, 2002), 55–57. Jerry Falwell similarly said that the "deep-seeded roots" of the Israeli-Palestinian crisis began with Ishmael and Isaac: "The enmity that began between these two boys continues today," he noted in the July 21, 2006, issue of Falwell Confidential. Richard Booker too speaks of the Arab-Israeli conflict as "a centuries-old family feud that is spiritual in nature" ("The Battle for Truth: Middle East Myths and the Arab-Israeli Conflict," page 3).

10. Jerry Falwell, "The Twenty-First Century and the End of the World," *Fundamentalist Journal*, May 1988, p. 10, cited by Boyer, p. 189; Craig Unger, "American 'Rapture,'" *Vanity Fair*, December 2005.

11. David Parsons, "Witness to Prophecy: An Interview with Dr. Jack Hayford," *Jerusalem Post Christian Edition*, October 2006.

12. Luke 21: 24. Dwight Wilson notes that the end of the "times of the Gentiles" has been placed in 1895, 1917, and 1948, as well as 1967 (*Armageddon Now! The Premillenarian Response to Russia and Israel since 1917* [1977; reprint, Tyler, Tex.: Institute for Christian Economics, 1991], 216).

13. Debbie White, "CBN: Israel's Friend to the End," CBNNews.com, June 1, 2007 (http://www.cbn.com/CBNnews/169124.aspx?option=print).

14. Falwell, "The Twenty-First Century and the End of the World."

15. Weber, *On the Road to Armageddon*, 184–86; John F. Walvoord, "The Amazing Rise of Israel," *Moody Monthly* 68 (October 1967), 22; and L. Nelson Bell, "Unfolding Destiny," *Christianity Today* (July 21, 1967), 1044–45, cited by Weber, *On the Road to Armageddon*, 184.

16. Harold Sevener, "Israel: The World's Timetable," *Christian Life* 35 (August 1973), 28, cited by Weber, *On the Road to Armageddon* , 291 n78. Sevener also cited Obadiah 17–20.

17. Walid Shoebat, "Why I Left Jihad," *Jerusalem Post Christian Edition*, October 2006..

18. "The Saga of Jerusalem and the Temple Mount," Christian Friends of Israel, *On Watch in Jerusalem*, September 3, 2007.

19. Derek Prince, *Promised Land: God's Word and the Nation of Israel* (1978; reprint, Charlotte, N.C.: Derek Prince Ministries, 2003), 135–36.

20. David Horovitz, "Most Evangelicals Are Seeing the Error of 'Replacement Theology,'" *Jerusalem Post,* March 20, 2006.

21. Art Toalston, "Lack of NAE Stance on Israel-Hezbollah Clash Is 'Grave Disappointment,' Baptist Says," *BP News,* August 17, 2006 (www.bpnews.net/printerfriendly. asp?ID=23808); Steve Gushee, "Why Are the Southern Baptists Trying to Bring Jews to Jesus?" *Palm Beach Post,* June 28, 1996; Andrea Stone, "A Mission to Bring Jews to Jesus," *USA Today,* August 19, 1996.

22. Interview with Esther Levens, August 25, 2005. Levens, a Jewish woman from Kansas, founded Voices United for Israel, which became the Unity Coalition for Israel in 1991. Its Web site says that it represents more than 200 pro-Israel groups, mostly Christian, the others Jewish, with a combined membership of 40 million people (http://www.israelunitycoalition).

23. "The Apple of His Eye," John Hagee Ministries (www.jhm.org/support-israel.asp).

24. Interview with Malcolm Hedding, July 20, 2005.

25. Interview with Ray Sanders, July 25, 2005.

26. Interview with Rodlyn Park, March 23, 2005.

27. Interview with Glenn Plummer, October 17, 2005; Glenn Plummer at Stand for Israel conference, Washington, D.C., September 28, 2005.

28. "The Apple of His Eye."

29. Brad A. Greenberg, "Evangelical Prayer Banquet Promotes Love for Israel," *Jewish Journal of Greater Los Angeles,* May 25, 2007; "The Apple of His Eye;" Saul Elbein, "Evangelicals Raise $8.5 m. for Jewish State," *Jerusalem Post,* October 17, 2007.

30. Abe Levy, "5,000 Pack Church in Israel's Honor," *San Antonio Express-News,* October 23, 2006; Elbein, "Evangelicals Raise $8.5 m. for Jewish State."

31. Prince, *Promised Land,* 116–17.

32. Yaakov Lappin, "Christians Offer 'Repentance."

33. Don Finto, *Your People Shall Be My People: How Israel, the Jews, and the Christian Church Will Come Together in the Last Days* (1973; reprint, Ventura, California: Regal Books, 2001), 70–74.

34. "Report Reveals Anti-Semitic Acts Increased in 2006," Bridges for Peace, *Israel Current News Update and Prayer Focus,* April 20, 2007; "Watchmen on the Wall: A Practical Guide to Prayer for Jerusalem and Her People," Robert Stearns, general editor, written and compiled by Miriam Rodlyn Park.

35. David Parsons, "Witness to Prophecy: An Interview with Dr. Jack Hayford."

36. Greenberg, "Evangelical Prayer Banquet Promotes Love for Israel."

37. Ibid

38. Jack Hayford, "Why Stand with Israel Today?" Jack Hayford Ministries (www.jackhayford.org/israel/pdf/stand_with_israel.pdf).

39. Victoria Clark hypothesizes that Christian Zionists in the United States are motivated by boredom and fear. She suggests that their attempt to escape from boredom into "a disaster-movie scenario with a happy Rapture ending for the born-again good guys" accounts for the spread of their ideology in America, as does their fear that America's days as a superpower are numbered. Clark argues that modern American Christian Zionism is a simplistic and irrational ideology with a repellent eschatology, and is harmful to both Palestinians and Israelis (Victoria Clark, *Allies for Armageddon: The Rise of Christian Zionism* [New Haven: Yale University Press, 2007], 230, 242, 258, 286–87).

CHAPTER 3

1. Randall VanderMey, cited in Wendy Murray Zoba, *The Beliefnet Guide to Evangelical Christianity* (New York: Doubleday, 2005), xiv.

2. Mark A. Noll, *The Rise of Evangelicalism: The Age of Edwards, Whitefield and the Wesleys* (Downers Grove, Ill.: InterVarsity Press, 2003), 16–17. The Franciscan friar Roger Bacon (1214–94) antedated Luther in insisting on the final authority of Scripture. Bacon also championed the literal interpretation of the Bible rather than the allegorical or other levels of meaning.

3. Donald G. Bloesch, *Essentials of Evangelical Theology* (San Francisco: Harper and Row, 1978), 1: 7.

4. The Second Great Awakening revived the commitment to Christianity in America, resulting in expansion of churches and enhanced religious influence in the culture. Noll argues that historians mistakenly trace its origins to local Congregational revivals in New England in the 1790s or large-scale revivalism in upstate New York thirty years later. Instead, says Noll, it began in the mid-1780s in the South and rural New England (Noll, *Rise of Evangelicalism,* 212).

5. George M. Marsden, *Fundamentalism and American Culture* (Oxford: Oxford University Press, 2006), 221–25.

6. Walter Russell Mead, "God's Country?" *Foreign Affairs* (September/October 2006); "What Would Wilberforce Do?" *Christianity Today* editorial, February 19, 2007.

7. Marsden, *Fundamentalism and American Culture,* 225–26.

8. Ibid., 226.

9. Interview with Martin Marty, January 11, 2006; Martin E. Marty, *When Faiths Collide* (Malden, Mass.: Blackwell, 2005), 16.

10. Malise Ruthven, *Fundamentalism: The Search for Meaning* (Oxford: Oxford University Press, 2004), 10–14.

11. Marsden, *Fundamentalism and American Culture,* 322, n6.

12. Garry Wills, *Under God: Religion and American Politics* (New York: Simon and Schuster, 1990), 97–114.

13. See George M. Marsden, *Understanding Fundamentalism and Evangelicalism* (Grand Rapids: W.B. Eerdmans, 1991), 1–6; Mark Noll in "Understanding American Evangelicals," Ethics and Public Policy Center, Washington, D.C., June 2, 2004; and Harvey Cox, "Old-time Religion," *Boston Globe,* July 9, 2006. Jeff Sharlet argues that, in addition to the populist fundamentalists, an elite branch emerged after the Scopes trial. They created a new civil religion that conflated the nation with the faith, enabling Cold Warriors and the projection of American influence around the globe, he says (*The Family: The Secret Fundamentalism at the Heart of American Power* [New York: HarperCollins, 2008], 277).

14. Christian Smith, *Christian America? What Evangelicals Really Want* (Berkeley: University of California Press, 2000), 13.

15. Christian Smith, *American Evangelicalism: Embattled and Thriving* (Chicago: University of Chicago Press, 1998), 1–12; Mark Silk, *Spiritual Politics: Religion and America since WW II* (New York: Simon and Schuster, 1988), 55–57; "History of the NAE," www.nae.net.

16. Marsden, *Fundamentalism and American Culture,* 233–36.

17. Martin E. Marty, "What Is Fundamentalism? Theological Perspectives," in Hans Kung and Jurgen Moltmann, eds., *Fundamentalism as an Ecumenical Challenge,* Concilium 1992/93 (London: SCM Press, 1992), 3–13.

18. Marsden, *Fundamentalism and American Culture,* 233–38; Peter Applebome, "Jerry Falwell, Moral Majority Founder, Dies at 73," *New York Times,* May 16, 2007. For analysis of fundamentalists' optimistically advocating political action despite an essentially tragic and pessimistic view of history, see Stephen D. O'Leary, *Arguing the Apocalypse: A Theory of Millennial Rhetoric* (New York: Oxford University Press, 1994).

19. Randall Balmer, *Thy Kingdom Come: How the Religious Right Distorts the Faith and Threatens America* (New York: Basic Books, 2006), 13–17.

20. "The American Religious Landscape and Politics, 2004," Pew Forum on Religion and Public Life, Washington, D.C.

21. "Evangelical Reflections on the U.S. Role in the World," Carnegie Council on Ethics and International Affairs, New York, September 15, 2005; "Understanding American Evangelicals: A Conversation with Mark Noll and Jay Tolson," Ethics and Public Policy Center, Washington, D.C., June 2, 2004; Richard Cizik, "New Moral Awakening, or How I Changed My Mind," *Reflections*, Yale Divinity School (Spring 2007), 58–60. In 2008 *Time* Magazine listed Cizik as one of the one hundred most influential people in the world.

22. Paul Nussbaum, "An Evangelical Voice Strikes Different Notes," *Philadelphia Inquirer*, June 19, 2005.

23. Jim Wallis, *God's Politics: Why the Right Gets It Wrong and the Left Doesn't Get It* (San Francisco: Harper San Francisco, 2005), 3, passim.

24. Ann Rodgers, "Centrist Evangelicals Lift Their Political Voice," *Pittsburgh Post-Gazette*, March 9, 2008.

25. "The American Religious Landscape and Politics, 2004"; Michael Luo, "Evangelicals Debate the Meaning of 'Evangelical,'" *New York Times*, April 16, 2006; Ruth Marcus, "The New Temptation of Democrats," *Washington Post*, May 23, 2006; "Evangelical Reflections on the U.S. Role in the World"; "Many Americans Uneasy with Mix of Religion and Politics." The Pew Forum on Religion & Public Life, Washington, D.C., August 24, 2006.

26. In 2003–4, 64 percent of traditionalist evangelicals favored Israel over the Palestinians, as compared to 52 percent of white evangelicals overall (Pew Forum on Religion & Public Life, cited in Ori Nir, "Evangelicals Eye Middle Ground on Middle East," *The Forward*, July 1, 2005; "American Piety in the 21st Century," The Baylor Religion Survey, Waco, Texas, September 2006, Baylor Institute for Studies of Religion).

27. Mark Lilla, "Getting Religion," *New York Times*, September 18, 2005.

28. Joseph B. Tamney, *The Resilience of Conservative Religion: The Case of Popular, Conservative, Protestant Congregations* (New York: Cambridge University Press, 2002), 84 and 87, and Alan Wolfe, *The Transformation of American Religion: How We Actually Live Our Faith* (New York: Free Press, 2003), 191–92; "Survey Shows How Christians Share Their Faith," *Barna Update*, January 31, 2005 (http://www.barna.org/FlexPage.aspx?Page=BarnaUpdate&BarnaUpdateID=181).

29. Interview with Robert Stearns, May 16, 2005.

30. D. W. Bebbington, *Evangelicalism in Modern Britain: A History from the 1730's to the 1980's* (London: Unwin Hyman, 1989), 1–17, and "Not so Exceptional after All," *Christianity Today*, May/June 2007; Yancy, "A Quirky and Vibrant Mosaic," *Christianity Today*, June 3, 2005.

31. Zoba, *The Beliefnet Guide*, 18.

32. Carl F. H. Henry, *The Uneasy Conscience of Modern Fundamentalism* (Grand Rapids: Eerdmans, 1947), 16.

33. Noll, *Rise of Evangelicalism*, 18–20.

34. Randall Balmer, *Mine Eyes Have Seen the Glory: A Journey into the Evangelical Subculture in America* (New York: Oxford University Press, 1989), 8–9, 24.

35. Wolfe, *The Transformation of American Religion*, 70–74; Kimon Howland Sargent, *Seeker Churches: Promoting Traditional Religion in Non-Traditional Ways* (New Brunswick, N.J.: Rutgers University Press, 2000), 31, 101.

36. Interview with James Denison, February 13, 2006.

37. Mark Simon, "Ex-Provost Lends a Hand to Bush, GOP," *San Francisco Chronicle*, July 1, 1999.

38. Sarah Vowell, "A Pat on the Back," *New York Times*, July 6, 2005; Daniel Burke, "Rift Opens among Evangelicals on AIDS Funding," *Christianity Today*, June 2, 2006.

39. "Robertson: U.S. Shouldn't Interfere with China's Forced Abortion Policy," CNN, April 16, 2001 (http://archives.cnn.com/2001/US/04/16/robertson.abortion); Joel Miller, "Pat Robertson's Brain Abortion," *WorldNetDaily*, April 18, 2001.

40. Jean Gordon, "Falwell Speaks Mind," *Jackson, Mississippi, Clarion-Ledger*, July 28, 2006.

41. Interview with Haggard, June 26, 2006. See Chapter 8 below for a discussion of Haggard's reasoning on this point.

42. Laurie Goodstein and Neela Banerjee, "Minister Admits Buying Drug but Denies Tryst," *New York Times*, November 4, 2006.

43. Edsall, "Possible Frist '08 Bid Splits Religious Right," *Washington Post*, August 16, 2005; Eric Gorski, "Push to Nix Gay Nuptials Begins," *Denver Post*, December 12, 2005; Eric Gorski, "Man of Cloth and Clout," *Denver Post*, October 30, 2005; Erin Emery, "Colorado Springs' Evangelical Image Out of Focus, Officials Believe," *Denver Post*, August 2, 2002 (http://www.rickross.com/reference/fundamentalists/fund168.html); Stan Guthrie, "Evangelicals in a Secular Society," *Christianity Today*, November 4, 2005; Goodstein and Banerjee, "Minister Admits Buying Drug but Denies Tryst."

44. Hector Gutierrez, "At war with himself," *Rocky Mountain News.com*, November 23, 2006 (http://www.rockymountainnews.com/drmn/local/article/0,1299,DRMN_15_5165412,00.html).

45. Susannah Meadows, "Evangelicals and the Vitter Effect," *Newsweek*, July 19, 2007 (http://www.msnbc.msn.com/id/19852389/site/newsweek/). Cromartie was commenting on another scandal among the devout: the revelation that Senator David Vitter (Republican-Louisiana), a staunch Catholic who had crusaded to impeach Bill Clinton during the Lewinsky affair, had patronized an escort service.

46. Henry Abelove, *The Evangelist of Desire: John Wesley and the Methodists* (Stanford: Stanford University Press, 1990), 3.

47. Steven Waldman, "The Pearly Gates Are Wide Open," *Beliefnet*, August 21, 2005; "In Search of the Spiritual," *Newsweek*, September 5, 2005; e-mail interview with John Green, March 6, 2006. In 2008 the Pew Forum on Religion & Public Life found similar results: 57% of members of American evangelical churches agreed that many religions can lead to eternal life ("U.S. Religious Landscape Survey: Religious Beliefs and Practices: Diverse and Politically Relevant," June 2008).

48. "Poll: America's Evangelicals More and More Mainstream, but Insecure," *Religion and Ethics Newsweekly*, April 16, 2004 and PSRA/Newsweek Poll, May 2004, cited by Green at the Uneasy Allies conference, Jewish Theological Center, New York, November 30, 2005; John C. Green, "Evangelical Protestants and Jews: A View from the Polls, *Uneasy Allies? Evangelical and Jewish Relations*, eds. Alan Mittleman, Byron Johnson, and Nancy Isserman (Lanham, Maryland: Lexington Books, 2007, 28.

49. Jon Meacham, "Pilgrim's Progress," *Newsweek*, August 14, 2006.

50. Interview with James Denison, February 13, 2006.

CHAPTER 4

1. Noll, *The Scandal of the Evangelical Mind* (Grand Rapids, Mich.: Eerdmans, 1994), 132.

2. "2007 Annual Survey of Jewish Opinion," American Jewish Committee (http://www.ajc.org/site/c.ijITI2PHKoG/b.3642857/); "Peace Index: December 2006," JCPA Middle East Briefing, Washington, D.C., January 10, 2007. The Peace Index survey for December 2006 was carried out on 1–2 January 2007.

3. Kinsella's report depended on Benjamin Netanyahu's 1993 account of this plan ("Phase Plan for Israel's Destruction Alive and Well," *Omega Letter*, January 10, 2006).

4. Bridges for Peace was founded in 1977 in Jerusalem as an educational organization by G. Douglas Young. It now has a staff of eighty, mostly volunteers, supported mainly by churches, family, friends, and worldwide gifts. In 2004 it received $7.1 million in charitable donations from around the world (interview with Rebecca Brimmer, August 8, 2005). Bridges sponsors fourteen different aid projects in Israel, running the largest food bank in the country, providing

social assistance inside Israel, and helping poor immigrate to Israel. It runs educational programs abroad for Christians to learn about the Jewish roots of Christianity, operates Bible study tours of Israel, and produces several publications, including the *Israel Current News and Update*, which I cite frequently in this book. In late 2007, it set the goal of doubling its food distribution to the poor in Israel, to one hundred tons a month (http://www.bridgesforpeace.com/h2n.php?fn=whoarewe.html; "30% Price Hike! Social Effects Far Reaching—Israel Report." Bridges for Peace, *Israel Current News and Update*, December 20, 2007).

5. Lindsey, *The Everlasting Hatred: The Roots of Jihad* (Murrieta, Calif.: Oracle, 2002), 221–22; Uri Dan, "Yasser Feels Ariel's Angry Boot Again," *New York Post,* August 12, 2001.

6. "Why Evangelical Christians Support Israel," December 17, 2003 (http://www.patrobertson.com/Speeches/IsraelLauder.asp). By "the man who yearned to finish the work of Adolf Hitler," Robertson meant Haj Amin Muhammed al-Husseini, the Mufti of Jerusalem, a Palestinian nationalist leader who courted and allied with Germany in World War II. In 1941 the Mufti met with Hitler, who pledged to destroy Jewry in Palestine. In 2002 Arafat reportedly referred to the Mufti as "our hero." Jan Willem van der Hoeven says that Arafat was the Mufti's blood relative (*Babylon or Jerusalem?* [Shippensburg, PA: Destiny Image Publishers, 1993], 136), but such claims have been disputed.

7. Psalm 2:1–4; "Abbas: A Moderate or a Calculator?" Bridges for Peace, *Israel Current News Update and Prayer Focus,* October 6, 2006.

8. "Abbas Sends Warmest Greetings to Iran's Ahmadinejad," Bridges for Peace *Israel Current News Update and Prayer Focus* February 16, 2007.

9. "International Aid: Is It Financing More Disaster?" Bridges for Peace, *Israel Current News Update and Prayer Focus,* June 22, 2007.

10. Carolyn Jacobson, "Evacuees," *On Watch in Jerusalem,* Christian Friends of Israel, July 31, 2007. Three days later, Bridges for Peace issued the same appeal explicitly, urging its readers to "pray that Israel will not be like Esau and despise their inheritance" ("US Signs On to Arab Peace Plan," Bridges for Peace, *Israel Current News Update and Prayer Focus,* August 3, 2007).

11. Gary Bauer, "Fund Fatah?" *American Values,* July 20, 2007.

12. "The Results Are In!" International Fellowship of Christians and Jews newsletter, July 27, 2007.

13. Jan Willem van der Hoeven, "A Clever People, yet So Self-destructive!" International Christian Zionist Center, January 30, 2007, reprinted in Unity Coalition for Israel, *Today's News Summaries* (http://www.israelunitycoalition.org/news/article.php?id=816).

14. Gary Bauer, "Amazing Hubris," *American Values,* July 24, 2006. A World Public Opinion Survey released in 2007 reported that large majorities in Morocco, Egypt, and Pakistan, and 53 percent in Indonesia, support strict application of Shari'a ("Muslim Public Opinion on US Policy, Attacks on Civilians and al Qaeda," World Public Opinion.org, University of Maryland, April 24, 2007).

15. Roger Cohen, "Jews and Evangelicals Find Common Political Ground," *International Herald Tribune,* February 10, 2007.

16. Christian Friends of Israel, *On Watch in Jerusalem,* October 3, 2006.

17. Hal Lindsey, "Israel's Political Earthquake," *Oracle Commentaries,* hallindseyoracle.com, January 27, 2006.

18. Gary Bauer, "Listen to What They Say," *American Values,* January 31, 2006; "Evil," Stand for Israel Web site, March 15, 2006. Palestine Media Watch reported that this video, from 2004, was newly posted on the Hamas Web site in February 2006 (Orly Halpern, "Hamas Working on New 'Charter' . . . Which Will Still Call for End to Israel," *Jerusalem Post,* February 17, 2006).

19. Stan Goodenough, "Always Darkest before Dawn," stangoodenough.com, March 2, 2006, carried on Jerusalem Newswire.

20. The Covenant of the Islamic Resistance Movement (http://www.yale.edu/lawweb/avalon/mideast/hamas.htm).

21. Mohammed Daraghmeh, "Hamas Seeks Grass-roots Support in Islamic World to Wrest Additional Arab Aid?" AP, April 11, 2005; "The Iran Phenomenon in the Middle East—An Israeli Perspective," Saban Center; reprinted in *Jewish Council for Public Affairs Briefing*, November 1, 2006.

22. Fouad Ajami, "Brothers to the Bitter End," *New York Times,* June 19, 2007.

23. Shahar Smooha, "All the Dreams We Had Are Now Gone,'" *Haaretz,* July 21, 2007.

24. Gershom Gorenberg, "Minor Change Marks Major Shift in Vote," *The Forward,* February 24, 2006; Jarrett Blanc, "Just How Weak Is Hamas after Months of Pressure?" *Daily Star* (Lebanon), October 31, 2006; Khaled Abu Toameh, "What to Do Now about the Palestinian Authority," Jerusalem Center for Public Affairs, 7, July 12, 2007.

25. In one poll, three times as many Palestinians said that they would vote for a Fatah presidential candidate as those who would vote for one from Hamas if new elections were scheduled ("Results of Palestinian Public Opinion Poll No. 30," 13–15 September 2007, Al-Najah National University, Center for Opinion Polls and Survey Studies). Polls in 2008 continued to show a preference for Fatah, though some indicated that Hamas's Ismail Haniyeh was more popular than Abbas.

26. "PSR Poll No, 25," Palestinian Center for Policy and Survey Research, poll taken September 6–8, 2007 (http://www.pcpsr.org/survey/polls/2007/p25e2.html). Forty-eight percent opposed a permanent settlement with a Palestinian state within pre-1967 borders except for some settlements on 5 percent of the land, which would be exchanged for Israeli land elsewhere; 46 percent supported such a plan.

27. David Frum, *The Right Man: An Inside Account of the Bush White House* (New York: Random House, 2003), 259.

28. Tim LaHaye, *The Coming Peace in the Middle East* (Grand Rapids: Zondervan, 1984), 167.

29. Timothy P. Weber, *On the Road to Armageddon: How Evangelicals Became Israel's Best Friend* (Grand Rapids: Baker Academic, 2004), 207–10.

30. Laurie Goodstein, "Seeing Islam as 'Evil' Faith, Evangelicals Seek Converts," *New York Times,* May 27, 2003.

31. Bill Sherman, "Robertson: Iraq invasion a mistake," *Tulsa World,* August 20, 2007; Gorski, "Evangelicals' Issue: Radical Islam"; Naomi Schaefer Riley, "Evangelicals and Evil Empires," *Wall Street Journal*, November 16, 2007; David D. Kirkpatrick and Michael Cooper, "In a Surprise, Pat Robertson Backs Giuliani," *New York Times*, November 7, 2007; Erik Gorski, "Evangelicals' Issue: Radical Islam," AP, November 9, 2007.

32. A May 1, 1991, editorial in the *Jerusalem Post* cited this phrase in graffiti scrawled by Hamas intifada activists in Bethlehem. An editorial in the same newspaper on October 4, 1992, said that Palestinian Arabs have desecrated Christian religious sites and cemeteries with this slogan since 1967. A 1995 article in the *New York Times Magazine,* possibly referring to the 1991 *Jerusalem Post* report, said that that this graffito had been written near Bethlehem several years earlier (Andre Aciman, "In the Muslim City of Bethlehem," *New York Times,* December 24, 1995).

33. Jack Kinsella, "The West's Achilles' Heel" and "So Where ARE the Moderates?" *Omega Letter*, November 12 and April 22, 2006.

34. Robert Spencer, "The War Is Over; the Jihad Isn't," *Front Page,* August 18, 2004, retrieved from Focus on the Family Web site on September 4, 2006. The spirit of the Qur'an is pluralistic, but Shari'a law never accepted the equality of nonbelievers, says Abdullaziz A. Sachedina, professor of religious studies at the University of Virginia. Muslim jurists instituted the dhimmi system to protect the well-being of the Muslim public order (Abdulaziz A. Sachedina,

"A Crisis of Interpretation," On Faith, *Washington Post.com,* July 27, 1997 [http://newsweek. washingtonpost.com/onfaith/abdulaziz_a_sachedina/2007/07/a_crisis_of_interpretation.html]). In Ottoman Arab lands, the concept of the *ahl al-dhimma* ("the people of the contract") guaranteed non-Muslims' rights to property, livelihood, and freedom of worship. In return, they paid the *jizya,* which, though irksome, was typically light and based on one's ability to pay (Bruce Masters, *Christians and Jews in the Ottoman Arab World: The Roots of Sectarianism* [Cambridge: Cambridge University Press, 2001], 17–19).

35. Reza F. Safa, *Inside Islam: Exposing and Reaching the World of Islam* (Lake Mary, Fla: Charisma House, 1996), 34.

36. Carolyn Jacobson, "The Fall of Islam," *On Watch in Jerusalem,* Christian Friends of Israel, March 20, 2006.

37. Carolyn Jacobson, "An Islamic Caliphate," *On Watch in Jerusalem,* Christian Friends of Israel, August 28 and "The Forked Tongue," October 30, 2006; Nedra Pickler, "Bush Welcomes Muslims to Dinner," *Charleston Gazette,* October 17, 2006.

38. Barry Harrin, "The Islamic Conquest of Europe 2020," *Today's News Summaries,* Unity Coalition for Israel, May 30, 2006.

39. Brigitte Gabriel, "Have the Presbyterians Lost Their Conscience?" June 17, 2006, reprinted in *Today's News Summaries,* Unity Coalition for Israel, June 21, 2006, and "When a Big Lie Meets a Little Truth," *Jerusalem Post Christian Edition,* September 2006. Ms. Gabriel, former anchor of *World News* for Middle East Television, has been described as "a survivor of Islam's Jihad against Lebanese Christians" (Jamie Glazov, "Islam's Torture of Lebanon," FrontPage.com, August 11, 2005).

40. "Hamas: Islam Will Conquer USA and Britain" and "Speaker of PA Legislature: Kill Every Last Jew and American," Bridges for Peace, *Israel Current News Update and Prayer Focus,* June 23, 2006, and May 4, 2007.

41. David Parsons, "Killing Off the Messenger," *Jerusalem Post Christian Edition,* August 2007. On the program an Israeli official killed Farfur. Hamas television then introduced a bee puppet named Nahool, who vowed to take Jerusalem back from the "criminal Jews." (Dan Murphy, "Hamas' Approach to Jihad: Start 'Em Young," *Christian Science Monitor,* August 20, 2007).

42. "Puppet Child on Hamas TV 'Kills' US President," AP, in *Ynet,* April 1, 2008; "Hamas Puppet Show Kills President Bush," Bridges for Peace, Israel Current News Update & Prayer Focus, April 4, 2008. Gary Bauer cited this show as evidence that Muslim extremists are poisoning the minds of potential future jihadists, and that the West deceives itself by believing that Israeli concessions will end the conflict (Gary Bauer, "Turning Children into Killers," American Values, April 1, 2008).

43. Steven Erlanger, "Israel Seeks Hint of Victory," *New York Times,* August 13, 2006.

44. Brian Whitaker, "Bin Laden's Deputy Calls for Global War on 'Crusaders,'" *The Guardian,* July 28, 2006; Gary Bauer, "We Will Attack Everywhere," *American Values,* July 27, 2006.

45. Gary Bauer, "Evil," in Stand for Israel newsletter, March 18, 2006.

46. Gary Bauer, "London One Year Later," *American Values,* July 7, 2006.

47. Bauer referred to North Korea because it had supplied missiles to Iran. (Gary Bauer, "It's Bush's Fault," *American Values,* July 13, 2006, and "Moral Confusion," *American Values,* September 12, 2006); Rowan Scarborough and Jerry Seper, "Unanswered Questions of September 11," *Washington Times,* September 10, 2006.

48. Bernard Lewis, *Islam and the West* (New York: Oxford University Press, 1993), 9.

49. Benny Morris, "Hamas: Alms and Arms by Benny Morris," *New Republic,* July 11, 2006.

50. Scott Shane, "Fighting Locally, Fighting Globally," *New York Times,* July 16, 2006.

51. Thomas H. Kean and Lee H. Hamilton with Benjamin Rhodes, *Without Precedent: The Inside Story of the 9/11 Commission* (New York: Knopf, 2006), 245–46.

52. Shane, "Fighting Locally, Fighting Globally"; John Ward Anderson, "Hezbollah, Hamas United by Tactics," *Washington Post,* July 16, 2006.

53. Interview with John Esposito, May 3, 2007. Goldstein, a disciple of Meir Kahane, believed in "redemptive Zionism." He acted to avenge the slaughter of Jews in Hebron in 1929. Gershom Gorenberg notes that Goldstein's family and friends insisted that he'd acted out of ideology, not insanity, as evidenced by the fact that he attacked on Purim, which commemorates the Jews' revenge against their enemies (Gershom Gorenberg, *The End of Days: Fundamentalism and the Struggle for the Temple Mount* [2000; paperback, Oxford: Oxford University Press, 2000], 203–8).

54. John L. Esposito, *Unholy War: Terror in the Name of Islam* (Oxford: Oxford University Press, 2002), 65.

55. Martin E. Marty, *When Faiths Collide* (Malden, Mass.: Blackwell, 2005), 78–79.

56. Interview with John Esposito, May 3, 2007.

57. "Muslim Public Opinion on US Policy, Attacks on Civilians and al Qaeda." Forty-nine percent of Indonesians also desire a caliphate.

58. *Meet the Press,* transcript for July 16, 2006 (www.msnbc.com/id13839698/print/1/displaymode/1098/); David Postman, "Let's Face It, It's WWIII, Gingrich says," *Seattle Times,* July 16, 2006.

59. *Larry King Live,* July 16, 200 (transcripts.cnn.com/TRANSCRIPTS/0607/16/lk1.01.html). Bauer excerpted Gingrich's argument the next day in his e-mail to his readers ("World War III," *American Values,* July 17, 2006); William J. Bennett, "Why Israel Fights," National Review Online, August 11, 2006; Margy Pezdirtz, "A Matter of Clarity," *Christian Friends of Israeli Communities,* July 25, 2006; "Ahmadinejad: 'Death to Israel,'" Bridges for Peace, *Israel Current News Update and Prayer Focus,* August 11, 2006.

60. Betsy Hiel, "Pat Robertson Shows Support in War Zone," *Pittsburgh Tribune-Review,* August 9, 2006; Mike Allen, "Take about Five People with You and Vote. It Would Be a Sin Not to," *Time,* October 22, 2006.

61. Michael Melchior, then Israel's deputy foreign minister, quoted this passage in 2002 at a meeting in the Israeli consulate in New York with Robert Stearns and other evangelicals. That inspired Eagles' Wings to sponsor its annual Day of Prayer for the Peace of Jerusalem (interview with Stearns, May 16, 2005). Laura Bush, campaigning for her husband in 2004, spoke of a woman in Ohio who told her, "President Bush was born for such a time as this" ("Mrs. Bush's Remarks at Bush-Cheney '04 Rally in Charleston, West Virginia," September 17, 2007, www.whitehouse.gov/news/releases/2004/09/print/20040917–1.html).

62. Falwell also spoke of the Iran-Syria-Hezbollah and Hamas alliance as the start of World War III (*Falwell Confidential,* "Bible History, Prophecy and 'World War III,'" July 21, 2006).

63. Ezekiel 38, Isaiah 17: 1,4 (Hal Lindsey, "Uncovered" Russian-Syrian-Iranian Axis," www.hallindseyoracle.com/article_print.asp?ArticleID=13165, July 22, 2006).

64. Alexandra Alter, "For Some Evangelicals, Mideast War Stirs Hope," *Miami Herald,* August 8, 2006; Steven G. Vegh, "Pat Robertson Reports from Israel-Lebanon Border," *Hampton Roads Virginian-Pilot,* August 9, 2006; Etgar Lefkovits, "Robertson, Olmert Pray for Victory," *Jerusalem Post,* August 9, 2006. Two prophecy devotees who maintain the Rapture Ready Web site use forty-five categories, including false messiahs, inflation, famine, and floods. They rate each variable from 1 to 6 to determine "how fast we're heading toward the tribulation" (Nancy Haught, "On the Fast Track to 'The Rapture,'" *Beliefnet,* 2005).

65. Sheera Claire Frenkel and Gil Hoffman, "Is This the Start of World War III?" *Jerusalem Post,* July 17, 2006.

66. Interview with Thomas Pickering, September 5, 2006. Pickering's point about bin Laden's goal is supported by "The Management of Savagery," an Al Qaeda training manual. It prescribes the strategy of forcing America to abandon its war on Islam "by proxy" and provoking it to attack a Muslim state (Jessica Stern, "Keep American Muslims on Our Side," *New York Times,* September 10, 2006).

67. Richard Wolffe and Holly Bailey, "The 'Islamofascists,'" *Newsweek*, September 11, 2006; "Five Years after 9/11: The Clash of Civilizations Revisited," *Pew Forum on Religion & Public Life*, August 18, 2006.

68. Fareed Zakaria, "True or False: We Are Losing the War against Radical Islam," *Newsweek*, July 2, 2007. Bernard Lewis argues that the only way to deal with Islamism is to "mobilize Muslims themselves on our side. . . . We must free them or they will destroy us" (Amanda Gordon, "Leadership and Ideas at Washington Institute Gala," *New York Sun*, October 19, 2007). For discussion of successful strategies against terrorist groups, see Louise Richardson, *What Terrorists Want: Understanding the Enemy, Containing the Threat* (New York: Random House, 2006).

69. Ian Shapiro, *Containment: Rebuilding a Strategy against Global Terror* (Princeton: Princeton University Press, 2007), 7, 34.

70. Count de Marenches and David A. Andelman, *The Fourth World War: Diplomacy and Espionage in the Age of Terrorism* (New York: William Morrow, 1992), 30–31.

71. Eliot A. Cohen, "World War IV: Let's Call This Conflict What It Is," *Wall Street Journal*, November 20, 2001; R. James Woolsey, "World War IV," *Front Page*, November 22, 2002. See also Charles Feldman and Stan Wilson, "Ex-CIA Director: U.S. Faces 'World War IV,'" CNN.com, April 3, 2003, and Norman Podhoretz, "World War IV: How It Started, What It Means, and Why We Have to Win," *Commentary*, September 2004.

72. John Hagee, *Jerusalem Countdown; a Warning to the World* (Lake Mary, Fla: Frontline, 2006), 1–20, 29. For criticism of Hagee, see, for example, Kathleen Parker, "The Christians Are Coming, the Christians Are Coming," Townhall.com, August 4, 2006, and Max Blumenthal, "Birth Pangs of a New Christian Zionism," *The Nation*, August 8, 2006.

73. Hagee, *Jerusalem Countdown*, 3–16, 26–29.

74. Zev Chafets, *A Match Made in Heaven: American Jews, Christian Zionists, and One Man's Exploration of the Weird and Wonderful Judeo-Evangelical Alliance* (New York: HarperCollins, 2007), 151–53.

75. "Iran Bought Long-range Missiles from N. Korea—Report," *Al Jazeera*, December 16, 2005; "Iran Test-fires Long-range Missiles," AP, in *Jerusalem Post*, May 23, 2006; Toby Harnden, "Iran Admits It Gave Hezbollah Missiles to Strike All Israel," *Daily Telegraph*, August 6, 2006; "Highlights of U.S. Broadcast News Coverage of the Middle East from June 16–18, 2006," Federal News Service, August 19, 2006.

76. Ronny Sofer, "Israel Cannot Be Destroyed, Says Former Mossad Chief," *Ynet*, October 18, 2007; Gidi Weitz and Na'ama Lanski, "Livni Behind Closed Doors: Iran Nukes Pose Little Threat to Israel," *Haaretz*, October 25, 2007.

77. Dennis Ross, "The Can't-Win Kids," *New Republic*, December 11, 2007.

78. Mark Mazzetti, "U.S. Finds Iran Halted Its Nuclear Arms Effort in 2003," *New York Times*, December 3, 2007; Aluf Benn, Shmuel Rosner, and Yossi Melman, "Olmert: Nuke Report on Iran Shows Need for Tighter Sanctions," *Haaretz*, December 4, 2007; Marc Perelman, "Intel Bombshell Sends Community Scrambling to Hold Line on Iran Threat," *The Forward*, December 5, 2007.

79. Yossi Klein Halevi, "An Insult to Intelligence," *New Republic*, December 6, 2007.

80. Chafets, *A Match Made in Heaven*, 193.

81. Azar Nafisi, "America's Best Weapon Is the Iranian People," *New Republic*, April 23, 2007. Nafisi praises the moderating influence of Western nongovernmental organizations and human rights groups.

82. See, for example, Trita Parsi, "The Case for Talking to Iran," *The Forward*, December 19, 2007.

83. Seymour M. Hersh, "The Iran Plans," *New Yorker*, April 17, 2006.

84. Robert Baer, "Commentary: Was Bush behind the Iran Report?" *Time*, December 4, 2007. Israeli security analysts pointed out that Syria had a nuclear project for seven years before they found out about it (Halevi, "An Insult to Intelligence").

85. Bernard Lewis, "Allah Will Know His Own," *Wall Street Journal* (Europe), August 8, 2006. *Newsweek*'s Fareed Zakaria said that Lewis's perspective on Iran "would be funny if weren't so dangerous." He added, "The American discussion about Iran has lost all connection to reality" (Fareed Zakaria, "Stalin, Mao and . . . Ahmadinejad?" *Newsweek*, October 29, 2007).

86. Aaron Klein, "'Hizbullah Youths' Train in Terrorism," *World Net Daily*, reprinted in *Ynet*, September 15, 2006.

87. Lonnie C. Mings, "A Relentless Enemy," Christian Friends of Israel, *Watchman's Prayer Letter*, November 23, 2006.

88. Gary Bauer, "London One Year Later"; Bauer, "A Striking Contrast," *American Values*, August 23, 2006; Dan Gilgoff, *The Jesus Machine: How James Dobson, Focus on the Family, and Evangelical America Are Winning the Culture War* (New York: St. Martin's Press, 2007), 10. Rumsfeld referred to feeding a crocodile at an American Legion convention in August 2006 (Donald Rumsfeld, "Address at the 88th Annual American Legion National Convention," U.S. Department of Defense, August 29, 2006 (http://www.defenselink.mil/Utility/Print Item.aspx?print=http://www.defenselink.mil/Speeches/Speech.aspx?SpeechID=1033). John Hagee reiterated Bauer's warning at the Christians United for Israel summit in July 2006.

89. Lynne Olson, "Why Winston Wouldn't Stand for W," *Washington Post*, July 1, 2007.

90. Pastor John Hagee, AIPAC Policy Conference, March 11, 2007 (http://www.aipac. org/about_AIPAC/Learn_About_AIPAC/2841_2859.asp). See Chapter 6 in the present book; also Hagee, *Jerusalem Countdown*, vii. Mike Evans speaks of Ahmadinejad as a "little Hitler on Steroids" (*Jerusalem Prayer Team Action Alert*, September 18, 2006).

91. Ryan Jones, "Bibi: Lebanon War Proves Retreat Is Bankrupt Policy," *Jerusalem Newswire*, August 15, 2006; Yaakov Lappin, "Bibi: Iran President More Dangerous than Hitler," *Ynet*, September 12, 2006; Aluf Benn and Mazal Mualem, "Netanyahu, Mossad Chief's Comments on Iran Are Warning, Not All-clear Signal," *Haaretz*, December 19, 2006. Shimon Peres also equated Ahmadinejad with Hitler (Yossi Melman, "Peres: Israel Should Regard Ahmadinejad as It Would Hitler," *Haaretz*, October 21, 2006).

92. "General Moshe Yaalon Addresses 650 in NYC," *Americans for a Safe Israel*, August 16, 2006. This speech was carried in the online news summary of the Unity Coalition for Israel, which coordinates Christian Zionist groups around the United States, August 18, 2006 (www.israelunitycoaliton.org/news/article.php?id=226); Gil Hoffman, "Ya'alon: Israeli Leaders Should Quit," *Jerusalem Post*, September 1, 2006.

93. William Kristol, "It's Our War," *Weekly Standard*, July 24, 2006.

94. Rick Santorum, "The Great Test of This Generation," July 20, 2006, an NRO Primary Document (http://article.nationalreview.com/?q=ODk3NWI3ZmFiMWU3ZjMzNDI2 MWE1NzkooGFhMjZiNTI=).

95. Tom Raum, "Fascism Is New Buzz Word among Republicans," AP, August 30, 2006.

96. "President Discusses War on Terror at National Endowment for Democracy," October 6, 2005 (www.whitehouse.gov/news/releaes/2005/10/print/20051006–3.html); David E. Sanger, "Does Calling It Jihad Make It So?" *New York Times*, August 13, 2006; "Senate Ready to Up War Aid," CBS News, October 7, 2005 (www.cbsnews.com/stories/20005/10/06/iraq/main91740.html).

97. "President George W. Bush, War on Terror and Operation Iraqi Freedom," March 20, 2006 (http://www.state.gov/p/nea/rls/rm/2006/63493.htm). In 2002, then-White House spokesman Ari Fleischer declined to use this term in describing the hunt for Bin Laden "Bush Likens 'War on Terror' to WWIII," ABC Online, May 6, 2006 (www.abc.net.au/cgi-bin/common/printfriendly.pl?http://www.anc.net.au/news/newsi).

98. "President Bush Addresses American Legion National Convention Center, Salt Lake City, Utah," August 31, 2006 (http://www.whitehouse.gov/news/releases/2006/08/print/20060831–1.html).

99. "President Discusses Global War on Terror, Capital Hill Hotel, Washington, D.C." September 5, 2006 (http://www.whitehouse.gov/news/releases/2006/09/20060905-4.html).

100. According to Stephen J. Hadley, the national security adviser, the officials told Bush that this would take some time to evaluate. The new National Intelligence Estimate appeared in December (Peter Baker and Robin Wright, "A Blow to Bush's Tehran Policy," *Washington Post*, December 4, 2007).

101. Vali Nasr, "After Lebanon, There's Iran," *Christian Science Monitor*, August 9, 2006; Seymour Hersh, "Watching Lebanon: Washington's Interests in Israel's War," *The New Yorker*, August 21, 2006.

102. Shapiro, *Containment*, 46.

103. Khalid al-Dakhil, "Muslims Speak Out." On Faith, Washingtonpost.com, July 26, 2007.

104. Joshua Mitnick, "Iran Threat Steals Show at Herzliya," *Jewish Week*, January 26, 2007; Chemi Shalev, "Could This War Produce a Sunni-Israeli Alliance?" *Haaretz*, August 28, 2006.

105. "'Bush Will Be Tried Just like Saddam,'" AP, in *Jerusalem Post*, September 14, 2007.

106. Badih Chayban, "Nasrallah Alleges 'Christian Zionist' Plot," *Daily Star* (Lebanon), October 23, 2002.

107. Yoginder Sikand, "The Faith of George W. Bush; Christian Supremacy, American Imperialism and Global Disaster," *The American Muslim*, May 10, 2006, and "Christian Zionism: Terror in Jesus' Name," July 8, 2006 (www.mukto-mona.com/Articles/yogi_s/christian_zionism011205.htm).

108. Ghassan Rubeiz, "U.S. and Israel Have Their Jihadists Too," *Arab American News*, March 24, 2007.

109. Interview with Thomas Pickering, September 5, 2005.

CHAPTER 5

1. "Robertson Labeled Islam a 'Bloody, Brutal Type of Religion,'" *Media Matters for America*, May 1, 2006 (http://mediamatters.org/items/printable/200605010007).

2. Marvin Olasky, "The Panda in Winter," *World* Magazine, February 18, 2006; "Evangelical Broadcaster Pat Robertson Calls Radical Muslims 'Satanic,'" AP, March 14, 2006.

3. From the April 28, 2006, edition of the *700 Club*, cited in "Robertson Labeled Islam a "Bloody, Brutal Type of Religion"; "Robertson: 'Islam Is Not a Religion. It Is a Worldwide Political Movement Meant on Domination [*sic*],'" *Media Matters for America*, June 12, 2007 (http://mediamatters.org/items/200706120009?f=h_topic).

4. "Why Evangelical Christians Support Israel," December 17, 2003 (http://www.patrobertson.com/Speeches/IsraelLauder.asp).

5. Interview with Ted Haggard, June 26, 2006.

6. Reza F. Safa, *Inside Islam: Exposing and Reaching the World of Islam* (Lake Mary, Fla.: Charisma House, 1996), 17–23. Pastor Reza based his observation on E. M. Wherry's *Comprehensive Commentary on the Quran* (Osnaburck, Germany: Otto Zeller Verlag, 1973), 36; Richard Cimino, "New Boundaries—Evangelicals and Islam after 9/11" (www.religionnews.com/press02/PR121405.html, 1.

7. Walid, Shoebat, *Why I Left Jihad: The Root of Terrorism and the Rise of Islam* (Newtown, Penn.: Top Executive Media, 2005), 272: Jack Kinsella, "Under the Ramadan Moon . . . 2005," *Omega Letter*, October 19, 2005. Walid Shoebat is an assumed name. In 2006, the messianic Jewish writer Yoel Natan argued that "the 'Allah' demon masqueraded as both the God of the Bible and as a war and moon god." Islam, he concluded, is a modified pagan moon god religion (*Moon-O-Theism* [Edition 1.0, 2006], 32 passim).

8. Miriam Rodlyn Park, "Watchmen on the Wall: A Practical Guide to Prayer for Jerusalem and Her People," Robert Stearns, gen. ed. (Training manual), 97–99. Chuck Missler and Don Stewart say that Muslim holy sites are pagan. Missler, a prominent Bible teacher associated with Pastor Chuck Smith's Calvary Chapel in Costa Mesa, California, is the former chairman of Western Digital Corporation; Stewart is an award-winning author of Christian books. In their *The Coming Temple,* they assert that the Dome of the Rock and the Al-Aqsa mosque, which sit the Temple Mount in Jerusalem, are "'pagan' holy places." These buildings profane the area where the sacred Temple once stood, they say (Chuck Missler and Don Stewart, *The Coming Temple: Center Stage for the Final Countdown* [Orange, Calif.: Dart Press, 1991], 100, 104).

9. C. Peter Wagner, "Allah 'A' and Allah 'B,'" *Global Prayer News,* April–June 2002 (http://lyris.strategicprayer.net/cgi-bin/lyris.pl?sub=67908&id=203515133), cited by Richard Cimino, "New Boundaries—Evangelicals and Islam after 9/11" (www.religionnews.com/press02/PR121405.html), 12.

10. William M. Arkin, "The Pentagon Unleashes a Holy Warrior," *Los Angeles Times,* October 16, 2003; Douglas Jehl, "The Struggle for Iraq," *New York Times,* October 18, 2003; Richard W. Stevenson, "For Muslims, a Mixture of White House Signals," *New York Times,* April 28, 2003. In August 2004, an inspector general's report recommended that Boykin be subjected to corrective action but specified no details (Douglas Jehl, "Report Urged Action against General for Speeches," *New York Times,* March 4, 2005). In 2002, the conservative evangelical *World* magazine gave Franklin Graham its Daniel of the Year award for speaking "hard truths about Islam," even though his words brought death sentences from radical Muslim clerics upon him ("Daniel of the Year 2002," *World,* December 7, 2002). Martin Durham notes that Boykin claimed to have been misrepresented: he had attacked the Somali's worship of money and power, not Allah, he said, and asserted that God had helped put Bill Clinton as well as Bush in office ("Evangelical Protestantism and Foreign Policy in the United States after September 11," *Patterns of Prejudice,* 38 [2004]).

11. Jan Willem van der Hoeven, "Allah Is Not God," March 30, 2004 (www.isrealmybeloved.com/history_prophecy/islam_arabs/God_allah.htm).

12. Laurie Goodstein, "Seeing Islam as 'Evil' Faith, Evangelicals Seek Converts," *New York Times,* May 27, 2003; "In U.S., Fear and Ignorance Feed Christian-Muslim Divide," *The Peninsula* (Qatar), February 20, 2007.

13. Interview with Ted Haggard, June 26, 2006.

14. Steven Waldman, "Commandment the First: Do Muslims and Christians Worship the Same God?" *Slate,* December 17, 2003; William Wallis, "Evangelicals See Opportunity in Promised Land," *Financial Times,* July 16, 2005; Jeff Sharlett, "Soldiers of Christ: Inside America's Most Powerful Megachurch with Pastor Ted Haggard," *Harper's,* May 2005.

15. Safa, *Inside Islam,* 10, 16–18, 36–49.

16. Jon Meacham, "Pilgrim's Progress," *Newsweek,* August 14, 2006; "Billy Graham: Aging with Faith," *Washington Post,* April 14, 2007. Franklin Graham states more than once in his 2002 book, *The Name,* that the God of Islam is not the God of Christianity, 69–76.

17. Hal Lindsey, "The Religion of Peace," *Oracle Commentary,* http://www.hallindseyoracle.com/articles.asp?ArticleID=13400, September 18, 2006.

18. David Nirenberg, "What Benedict Really Said: Paleologus and Us," *The New Republic,* September 28, 2006. Shortly after the pope's speech, Pat Robertson endorsed the idea that Muslims are violent and irrational. "It's amazing how the Muslims deal with history and the truth with violence," he said on the *700 Club.* "They don't understand what reasoned dialogue is" ("Robertson: "Muslims Deal with History and the Truth with Violence," *Media Matters for America,* September 25, 2006 [http://mediamatters.org/items/printable/200609250007]).

19. Dorothee Metlitzki, *The Matter of Araby in Medieval England* (New Haven, Conn.: Yale University Press, 1977), 6, 11.

20. Dan Murphy, "Pope's Comments on Islam Hit 'Civilization Clash' Fault Line," *Christian Science Monitor,* September 19, 2006; Daniel Pipes, "The Pope and the Byzantine Emperor," *Jerusalem Post,* September 20, 2006; Alessandra Rizzo, "Pope Says He Was Misunderstood," AP, in *Deseret News,* September 21, 2006.

21. Lindsey, "The Religion of Peace."

22. Ron Ross, "Gaza Christians Threatened: Choose Islam or Death," in Bridges for Peace, *Israel Current News Update and Prayer Focus,* September 22, 2006.

23. Aaron Klein, "Sheikh: All Must Convert to Islam," *World Net Daily,* reprinted in *Ynet,* September 28, 2006; "Al Qaida No. 2 Urges Pope, Christians to Convert to Islam," AP, in *Haaretz,* September 30, 2006.

24. In 2007, 57 percent of white evangelicals had a negative view of Muslims and 56 percent said that Islam encourages violence ("Benedict XVI Viewed Favorably but Faulted on Religious Outreach," Pew Research Center for the People & the Press, September 25, 2007).

25. "Most Evangelical Leaders Favor 'Evangelizing Muslims Abroad,'" Ethics and Public Policy Center press release, April 7, 2003; "Evangelical Views of Islam," EPPC-*Beliefnet,* April 7, 2003. By way of contrast, in 2005 only 36 percent of the general American population had an unfavorable view of Islam versus 40 percent who had a favorable view from 2002 to 2005; 60 percent said that terrorist attacks represent a conflict with a small group of radicals ("Poll: Fewer People Link Islam, Violence," AP, July 26, 2005). By March of 2006, however, a *Washington Post*-ABC News poll found that 46 percent of Americans held negative views of Islam (Jim Lobe, "Evangelical Christians Most Distrustful of Muslims," Inter Press Service, March 22, 2006).

26. Interview with Richard Land, June 6, 2006; Deborah Caldwell, "How Islam-Bashing Got Cool," *Beliefnet,* August 8, 2002.

27. Paul S. Boyer, *When Time Shall Be No More: Prophecy Belief in Modern American* Culture (Cambridge, Mass.: Belknap Press of Harvard University Press, 1992), 202; *Falwell Confidential,* "Bible History, Prophecy and 'World War III,'" July 21, 2006.

28. Interview with Robert Stearns, May 16, 2005; Gary Bauer, "We Will Attack Everywhere," *American Values,* July 27, 2006; Gary Bauer, "A Ray of Hope," *American Values,* April 30, 2007, and "A Glimmer of Hope," Human Events.com, May 4, 2007 (http://www.humanevents.com/article.php?id=20544).

29. Gary Bauer, "When Will We Wake Up?" *American Values,* December 27, 2007.

30. Psalm 21:8–9 (Bridges for Peace, *Israel Current News Update and Prayer Focus,* July 21, 2006).

31. Ken Silverstein and Michael Scherer, "Born-again Zionists," *Mother Jones,* 27: September/October 2002, 56–62.

32. Caldwell, "How Islam-Bashing Got Cool."

33. Broadcast on the *700 Club,* April 24, 2006: see "Robertson: The West Is Ignoring Threats from 'Islam in General,' Just as It Ignored 'What Adolf Hitler Said in *Mein Kampf,*'" *Media Matters for America,* April 24, 2006 (http.//mediamatters.org/items/printable/200604240007).

34. Broadcast on August 29, 2006: see "Robertson: Osama bin Laden May Be One of the True Disciples of the Teaching of the Quran . . . ," *Media Matters for America,* August 31, 2006 (http.//mediamatters.org/items/printable/200608310004).

35. Carolyn Jacobson, "Whose God Is God?" Christian Friends of Israel, *Watchman's Prayer Letter,* September 21, 2006, and "The Palestinian Authority Coalition Government," Christian Friends of Israel, *Watchman's Prayer Letter,* April 2, 2007.

36. Hal Lindsey, "The Myth of 'Measured Response,'" July 17, 2006 (www.halllindseyoracle.com/article_print.asp?ArticleID=13138).

37. James C. Dobson, "Is Political Islam a Threat?" Focus on the Family, November 10, 2003, updated August 1, 2006 (http://www.focusonthefamily.com/docstudy/newsletters/A000000639.cfm#); Peter Wallsten, "Evangelical Leaders Urging Followers to Back GOP in Nov.," *Baltimore Sun,* September 23, 2006.

38. John Hagee, *Jerusalem Countdown; a Warning to the World* (Lake Mary, Fla.: Frontline, 2006), 32–34, 42; Samuel P. Huntington, *The Clash of Civilizations and the Remaking of World Order* (New York: Simon and Schuster, 1996), 209. Evangelicals are not alone in asserting that violence is inherent in Islam. Syrian-born American psychologist Wafa Sultan, for example, says that "Islam is not only a religion. Islam is also a political ideology that preaches violence, and applies its agenda by force. . . . I don't believe there are moderate Muslims" (Yaakov Lappin, "Syrian-American: Islam Needs Transformation," *Ynet,* October 6, 2006).

39. Huntington, *Clash of Civilizations,* 209–18.

40. "Islam and the West: A Conversation with Bernard Lewis," Pew Forum on Religion and Public Life, April 27, 2006.

41. Bernard Lewis, *Islam and the West* (New York: Oxford University Press, 1993), 13.

42. Goodstein, "Seeing Islam as 'Evil' Faith, Evangelicals Seek Converts."

43. Boyer, *When Time Shall Be No More,* 51, 78, 200–203. Boyer (p. 327) observes that a prophecy writer's claim in 1989 that "the Muslims have declared war on the West, the United States, and especially the Christians" would have been familiar to Joachim of Fiore, Martin Luther, or Cotton Mather.

44. "Evangelicalism, Islam, and Humanitarian Aid: A Conversation with Lamin Sanneh," Ethics and Public Policy Center, eppc.org, December 15, 2003.

45. Derek Prince, *Promised Land: God's Word and the Nation of Israel* (1978; reprint, Charlotte, N.C.: Derek Prince Ministries, 2003), 70–71.

46. Cimino, "New Boundaries," 7; Todd Hertz, "Riots, Condemnation, Fatwa, and Apology Follow Falwell's CBS Comments," *Christianity Today,* October 2002.

47. Michelle Boorstein, "Rising Star in Falwell Orbit." *Washington Post,* May 8, 2005; Cimino, "New Boundaries," 8.

48. Ergun Mehmet Caner and Emir Fethi Caner, *Unveiling Islam* (Grand Rapids, Mich.: Kregel, 2002), 105–9, 117, 203–22.

49. David Parsons, "The Ways of Abraham," *Jerusalem Post Christian Edition,* September 2006.

50. Shoebat, "Why I Left Jihad." This passage is from the sunnah of Sahih Bukhari, Volume 4, Book 52, #176; see also #177 (http://www.usc.edu/dept/MSA/fundamentals/hadith sunnah/bukhari/052.sbt.html#004.052.176); "The Covenant of the Islamic Resistance Movement" (http://www.yale.edu/lawweb/avalon/mideast/hamas.htm).

51. James Gray, "Editorial," *Moody Bible Institute Monthly* 31 (1931), 346 (cited by Ariel, *Philosemites or Antisemites? Evangelical Christian Attitudes toward Jews, Judaism, and the State of Israel* [Jerusalem: Hebrew University, Vidal Sassoon International Center for the Study of Antisemitism, Analysis of Current Trends in Antisemitism, 20 (2002)], 7).

52. Prince, *Promised Land,* chapter 4 and pages 101, 142–43.

53. John Hagee, *Beginning of the End: The Assassination of Yitzhak Rabin and the Coming Antichrist* (Nashville: Thomas Nelson, 1996), 24, 27. In 2002, Pastor C. Peter Wagner wrote to his followers that the war in Afghanistan was not the Taliban versus the Americans but Allah versus God the Father (C. Peter Wagner, "Allah 'A' and Allah 'B,'" cited by Cimino, "New Boundaries," 12).

54. "Peace in the Middle East Speech by U.S. Sen. James M. Inhofe" (R-Okla)," March 4, 2002 (http://inhofe.senate.gov/public/index.cfm?FuseAction=PressRoom.Speeches&Content Record_id=73a47d47-802a-23ad-4d61-336bcd0c370f&Region_id=&Issue_id=&CFID=587 2324&CFTOKEN=81269357).

55. Pat Robertson, "Why Evangelical Christians Support Israel"; "Peace in the Middle East," Senate Floor.

56. Hal Lindsey, "The Enemy Within," February 16, 2006; reprinted in *Worldnet,* November 3, 2006 (http://www.worldnetdaily.com/news/article.asp?ARTICLE_ID=52752).

57. David Chanoff, "The Israeli Landscape I Saw through Ariel Sharon's Eyes," *The Forward,* March 17, 2006.

58. Haviv Rettig, "Melchior: Alert Abbas to PA textbooks," *Jerusalem Post,* March 20, 2007; Hal Lindsey, "Desperate Search for 'Peace-loving' Palestinians," *World Net Daily,* March 23, 3007; reprinted in Unity Coalition for Israel *Daily News* (http://www.israelunitycoalition.org/news/article.php?id=1051); "Zohar: Koran forbids recognizing Israel," *Jerusalem Post,* April 20, 2007.

59. Benny Morris, "From Dove to Hawk," *Newsweek,* May 8, 2008.

60. Timothy P. Weber, *On the Road to Armageddon: How Evangelicals Became Israel's Best Friend* (Grand Rapids, Mich.: Baker Academic, 2004), 207.

61. Merrill Simon, *Jerry Falwell and the Jews* (Middle Village, N.Y.: Jonathan David, 1984), 25–26, 53. John Hagee, *Day of Deception* (Nashville: Thomas Nelson, 1997), 99. Jan Willem van der Hoeven adds Haman to the list, saying that Satan tried to use him to murder all of the Jews in Persia until Queen Esther saved them (*Babylon or Jerusalem?* [Shippensburg, Penn.: Destiny Image Publishers, 1993], 131).

62. Don Finto, Your People Shall Be My People: How Israel, the Jews, and the Christian Church Will Come Together in the Last Days (1973; reprint, Ventura, Calif.: Regal Books, 2001), 70–74.

63. Hal Lindsey, *The Everlasting Hatred: The Roots of Jihad* (Murrieta, Calif.: Oracle, 2002) 17–21.

64. Malcolm Hedding, "The Root of Anti-Semitism," *Jerusalem Post Christian Edition,* May 2007.

65. In 1962, Walvoord blamed Satan for the trials (of Israel since the time of Abraham but did not focus on the Arabs as demonic agents (*Israel in Prophecy* [Grand Rapids, Mich.: Zondervan, 1962], 101ff). The 1976 proclamation of the Bicentennial Congress of Prophecy in Philadelphia declared that "the perpetrators of the holocaust were in essence the enemies of God, working against God" and "any nation who bitterly assails Israel . . . can be seen [as] . . . the enemies of God" (cited by Rausch, *Zionism within Early American Fundamentalism* [New York: Edwin Mellen Press, 1979], 2–3).

66. Shoebat, "Why I Left Jihad."

67. Prince, *Promised Land,* 105.

68. Stan Goodenough, "Why the Temple Mount?" Jerusalem Newswire; reprinted in *The Jerusalem Connection,* December 2007.

69. Caldwell, "How Islam-Bashing Got Cool."

70. Jack Hayford, "Why Stand with Israel Today?" Jack Hayford Ministries (www.jackhayford.org/israel/pdf/stand_with_israel.pdf).

71. Mike Evans, "Has America Lost Her Courage to Confront Evil?" *Jerusalem Prayer Team Action Alert,* May 4, 2007.

72. Malcolm Hedding, "The Saga of the Vulture," *Jerusalem Post Christian Edition,* May 2006.

73. Hal Lindsey, "Shock Waves from North Korea," *Hal Lindsey Oracle Commentaries,* October 14, 2006 (http://www.hallindseyoracle.com/articles.asp?ArticleID=13428).

74. EWM Report, September 1, 2006.

75. EWM Report, September 8, 2006; Eli Lake, "Big Protest Rally Taking Shape to Greet Ahmadinejad at U.N.," *New York Sun,* September 8, 2006; Gary Bauer, "Solidarity with Israel," *American Values,* September 14, 2006; Jacob Berkman, "Supporters of Israel Rally Near U.N., but Inside, Israel, U.S. on Defensive," *JTA (Jewish Telegraphic Agency),* September 20, 2006; Annie Karni, "Thousands of Israel Supporters Rally for Release of Kidnapped Soldiers," *New York Sun,* September 21, 2006; "Report on September 20 Rally at the U.N.," *Jerusalem's Watchmen Prayer Update,* September 29, 2006. The Jewish Community Relations Council co-sponsored the protest at the UN, in cooperation with the United Jewish Communities, UJA-Federation of New York, and the Jewish Council for Public Affairs.

76. *Jerusalem Watchmen Prayer Update*, September 18, 2007; *EWM* Report, September 18, 2007.

77. Yechiel Eckstein, "This Week with Rabbi Eckstein," September 21, 2007 (http://www.ifcj.org/site/PageServer?pagename=rabbistudy_thisweekwithrabbi&autologin=true&JServSessionIdr007=asodph8b41.app7b); Mike Evans, *Jerusalem Prayer Team Action Alert*, September 20, 2007. The rally was organized by the Conference of Presidents, the Jewish Community Relations Council of New York, the United Jewish Communities, the UJA-Federation of New York, and the Jewish Council for Public Affairs (Ben Harris, "Ahmadinejad Met with Protests," *JTA*, September 24, 2007. John Hagee's lobby, Christians United for Israel, co-sponsored the event.

78. Prince, *Promised Land*, 54–55.

79. The cleric, Mohsen Mojtahed Shabestari, was a representative of Iran's Supreme Leader, Ali Khamenei, but there was some doubt that the fatwa would have any weight outside Iran (Todd Hertz, "Riots, Condemnation, Fatwa, and Apology Follow Falwell's CBS Comments." *Christianity Today*, October 2002).

80. Boyer, *When Time Shall Be No More*, 327.

81. Dudi Cohen, "Iranian President: Israel Will Soon disappear," *Ynet*, October 20, 2006.

82. "Ahmadinejad's letter to Bush," May 9, 2006 (http://cnn.worldnews.printthis.clickability.com/pt/cpt?action=cpt&title=CNN.com+-+Ahm).

83. "The World toward Illumination" (http://english.irib.ir/IRAN/Leader/Illumination.htm).

84. Vali Nasr, *The Shia Revival: How Conflicts within Islam Will Shape the Future* (New York: W.W. Norton, 2006) , 67–68; Marshall Hodgson, *The Venture of Islam* (Chicago: University of Chicago Press, 1974), I, 373–74; Scott Peterson, "True Believers Dial Messiah Hotline in Iran," *Christian Science Monitor*, January 4, 2006; Jay Tolson, "Aiming for Apocalypse," *U.S. News & World Report*, May 22, 2006; "God's Country? Evangelicals and U.S. Foreign Policy," The Pew Forum on Religion and Public Life, Washington, D.C., September 26, 2006.

85. Scott Peterson, "Waiting for the Rapture in Iran," *Christian Science Monitor*, December 21, 2005, and "True Believers Dial Messiah Hotline in Iran"; Irshad Manji, "Armageddon? Great, Bring It On," *Times Online*, May 1, 2006.

86. A. Savyon and Y. Mansharof cite criticism of Ahmadinejad's theology by the senior Shia cleric Ayatollah Hossein Ali Montazeri and others in "The Doctrine of Mahdism: In the Ideological and Political Philosophy of Mahmoud Ahmadinejad and Ayatollah Mesbah-e Yazdi," MEMRI, May 31, 2007.

87. "Iranian opposition group criticized by top leadership," Xinua General Overseas News Service, August 5, 1983; "Iran's revolution starts to settle for domesticity," *The Economist*, August 25, 1984; "Iran's presidential race gets underway," *Mideast Mirror*, October 22, 1996; "Iran: Deputy says conservative right-wing group exacerbating sectarian conflict," BBC Worldwide Monitoring, September 3, 2002; "Head of Iranian president's office comments on oil minister debate, other issues," BBC Worldwide Monitoring, November 23, 2005; Alan Isenberg et al., "Periscope," *Newsweek*, December 5, 2005; Arnaud de Borchgrave, "Later than we think," UPI, February 2, 2006; Nasr, *Shia Revival*, 133-34; Tolson, "Aiming for Apocalypse"; Amir Taheri, "Rafsanjani revelations," *Jerusalem Post*, October 6, 2006; "God's Country? Evangelicals and U.S. Foreign Policy"; David Horovitz, "Iran the vulnerable?" *Jerusalem Post*, December 8, 2006; Nazila Fathi, "Iranian Clerics Tell the President to Leave the Theology to Them," *New York Times*, May 20, 2008.

88. Tovah Lazaroff and David Horovitz, "The Iranians Do Not Expect to Be Attacked," *Jerusalem Post*, January 31, 2007.

89. Peterson, "Waiting for the Rapture in Iran"; Manji, "Armageddon? Great, Bring it On."

90. Joseph Farah, "Iran's Leader's Messianic End-times Mission," *WorldNetDaily*, January 6, 2006.

91. Gary Bauer, "Nuclear Nightmare," *American Values*, August 28, 2006; Bauer, "Who's Afraid of the Truth?" *American Values*, September 21, 2006.

92. Hal Lindsey, "Iran's Expanding Threat," *Hal Lindsey Oracle Commentaries*, October 28, 2006 (http://www.hallindseyoracle.com/articles.asp?ArticleID=13434). The book Lindsey cites is Muhammad Ibn 'Izzat and Muhammad 'Arif's *Al Mahdi and the End of Time*. See Joel Richardson's *Antichrist: Islam's Awaited Messiah* (Enumclaw, Wash.: Pleasant Word, 2006), which received generous praise from Robert Spencer, director of Jihadwatch.com, and Ergun Caner, dean of Jerry Falwell's Liberty Theological Seminary.

93. Jan Markell, "Come, Lord Jeus, but Not Too Soon," Olive Tree Ministries, *Understanding the Times Weekly Update*, February 24, 2007; "Jan Markel" (www.olivetreeviews.org/about.shtml).

94. Jerusalem Prayer Team, *Action Alert*, May 1 and 5, September 12 and 13, and October 2, 2006.

95. Carolyn Jacobson, "Islam—Satan's 'I Will,'"Christian Friends of Israel, *Watchman's Prayer Letter*, May 30, 2006. The article cites Isaiah 14:13: "You said in your heart, 'I will ascend to heaven; above the stars of God I will set my throne on high," a central verse in understanding Satan's rebellion against God. It also cites Revelation 12:12.

96. Jacobson, "Whose God Is God?"

97. "Ahmadinejad: Zionists Different from Jews," Bridges for Peace, *Israel Current News Update and Prayer Focus*, September 22, 2006, and "Iran Says 2007 Could Bring Islamic Messiah, Possibly This Spring," Bridges for Peace, *Israel Current News Update and Prayer Focus*, January 5, 2007; Pat Robertson, "Praying for a 'Decisive' Victory," Pat Robertson.com (http://www.patrobertson.com/PressReleases/JPCE0906.asp).

98. Vali Nasr, "The New Hegemon," *The New Republic Online*, December 12, 2006.

99. Interview with Said Arjomand, December 7, 2006.

100. The show was intended to show that Iran is sympathetic to Jews while opposing Israel (Farnaz Fassihi, "Iran's Unlikely TV Hit," *Wall Street Journal*, September 7, 2007).

101. Trita Parsi, "A Sober Analysis of Iran," *Ynet*, October 14, 2007.

102. Michael Slackman, "U.S. Focus on Ahmadinejad Puzzles Iranians," *New York Times*, September 24, 2007.

103. Michael Slackman, "Deep Roots of Denial for Iran's True Believer," *New York Times*, December 13, 2006; Arash Norouzi, "The Rumor of the Century," *Al Jazeera*, January 19, 2007; confirmed by Said Arjomand, e-mail interview, January 21, 2007.

104. Rabbi Eric H. Yoffie, "Remarks as Prepared to the Islamic Society of North America 44th Annual Convention, Chicago, Illinois, Friday, August 31, 2007" (http://urj.org/yoffie/isna/index.cfm?&printable=1).

105. Marc Perelman, "Top Reform Rabbi Gives Watershed Address to Largest U.S. Muslim Group," *The Forward*, September 5, 2007; Stewart Ain, "Reform Draws Fire for Muslim Outreach," *Jewish Week*, September 6, 2007. During the trial, the prosecution released previously classified documents showing that the Muslim Brotherhood, the parent of Hamas, planned to destroy Western civilization and establish Shari'a within the U.S. That appeared to confirm one of the most grievous charges about Islamists. Some scholars and Muslim leaders said that these documents, from 1991, were outdated and represented an extremist fringe, however. In 2008, the jurors cleared one defendant and deadlocked on charges against the others (Jason Trahan, "Muslim Brotherhood's papers detail plan to seize U.S.," *Dallas Morning News*, September 17, 2007; "U.S. Court declares mistrial on charges Muslim charity had Hamas ties," AP, in *Haaretz*, October 22, 2007; Carrie Johnson and Walter Pincus, "Few Clear Wins in U.S. Anti-Terror Cases," *Washington Post*, April 21, 2008).

106. John Esposito, e-mails, May 4, 2007.

107. See John Kelsey, *Arguing the Just War in Islam* (Cambridge, Mass.: Harvard University Press, 2007), 129ff.

108. Ali Gomaa, "The Meaning of Jihad in Islam," On Faith: Muslims Speak Out Blog, *Washington Post.com,* July 21, 2007 (http://newsweek.washingtonpost.com/onfaith/muslims_speak_out/2007/07/sheikh_ali_gomah.html).

109. G. Willow Wilson, "The Show-Me Sheikh," *Atlantic Monthly,* 29 (July/August, 2005), 29–31; Neil MacFarquhar, "Hezbollah's Prominence Has Many Arabs Worried," *New York Times,* August 4, 2006.

110. Abduallah al-Askar, On Faith: Muslims Speak Out Blog, *Washington Post.com,* July 21, 2007.

111. John Kelsay, Arguing the Just War in Islam (Cambridge, Mass.: Harvard University Press, 2007), 139–41.

112. John L. Esposito, *Unholy War: Terror in the Name of Islam* (Oxford: Oxford University Press, 2002), 100.

113. The poll surveyed attitudes of Muslims in Britain, Spain, Germany, and France as well as opinion in Pakistan, Egypt, Jordan, Indonesia, Turkey, Nigeria, and India. Only in Nigeria did a majority of Muslims say that many or most Muslims supported extremists like Al Qaeda ("The Great Divide: How Westerners and Muslims View Each Other," The Pew Global Attitudes Project, June 22, 2006). Pew released data in 2007 showing that large majorities of Muslims in the United States, Europe, Pakistan, and Indonesia are concerned about the rise of Islamic extremism around the world, as are smaller majorities in Jordan, Egypt, and Nigeria. In Turkey, only 39 percent of Muslims registered such concern. Five percent of American Muslims expressed favorable views of Al Qaeda ("Muslim Americans: Middle Class and Mostly Mainstream," Pew Research Center, May 22, 2007).

114. Populus survey for *The Times* and ITV, reported in Aexandra Frean and Rajeev Syal, "Muslim Britain Split over 'Martyrs' of 7/7," *Times Online,* July 4, 2006 9http://www.timesonline.co.uk/article/0,,22989-2254764,00.html).

115. Thirty percent of Pakistanis said that Islam opposes violence against civilians while 35 percent said that it doesn't ("Muslim Public Opinion on US Policy, Attacks on Civilians and al Qaeda").

116. Interview with John Esposito, May 3, 2007.

117. Malise Ruthven, *Islam in the World* (London: Penguin, 1994), 92–96; H.A.R. Gibb, *Mohammedanism: An Historical Survey* (1949; reprint, London: Oxford University Press, 1970), 26–31; W. Montgomery Watt, *Muhammad: Prophet and Statesman* (London: Oxford University Press, 1961), 25–26.

118. Karen Armstrong, *Islam: A Short History* (New York: Modern Library Chronicles, 2000), 3–10.

119. Evangelicals, Orthodox Jews, and Muslims in Israel agree on at least one point: disapproval of homosexuality. In the summer of 2006, the three main Christian Zionist organizations in Israel (Bridges for Peace, Christian Friends of Israel, and the International Christian Embassy Jerusalem), rabbis, and Muslim Arab civic and religious officials all condemned the World Pride gay parade planned for Jerusalem that August.

120. Philip Yancey, "The Lure of Theocracy," *Christianity Today,* July 10, 2006.

121. Joel C. Rosenberg, "A Different Sort of Radical Muslim," *National Review Online,* May 9, 2006; Daniel Ben Simon, "All the King's Mosques," *Haaretz,* October 5, 2006.

122. "Evangelical Reflections on the U.S. Role in the World," Carnegie Council on Ethics and International Affairs, New York, September 15, 2005; Neela Banerjee, "Jordan's Leader Calls for Unity among Religions," *New York Times,* February 3, 2006; Patricia Zapor, "Jordan's King Talks Islamic Moderation to Evangelical Christian G-roup," Catholic News Services, February 3, 2006. The *Mideast Mirror* found it ironic that one day before King Abdullah made his appeal for religious tolerance, the Jordanian parliament entertained proposals to make it illegal for any Jew to ever buy land in Jordan. The article concluded that "Abdullah's words are as empty as the vast deserts which dominate most of his homeland" (February 22, 2006).

123. D. Michael Lindsay, "Is the National Prayer Breakfast Surrounded by a 'Christian Mafia'? Religious Publicity and Secrecy within the Corridor of Power," *Journal of the American Academy of Religion*, 74 (2), June 2006, 390–419; David Van Biema, "The 25 Most Influential Evangelicals in America," *Time*, February 7, 2005.

124. Jeff Sharlet, *The Family: The Secret Fundamentalism at the Heart of American Power* (New York: HarperCollins, 2008), 281.

125. E-mail from D. Michael Lindsay, September 21, 2006.

126. Sharlet, *The Family*, 27.

127. Laurie Goodstein, "Coalition of Evangelicals Voices Support for Palestinian State," *New York Times*, July 29, 2007.

128. Steven G. Vegh, "Gordon Robertson Succeeds his Father, Pat, as CBN's Chief," *Hampton Roads Pilot*, December 4, 2007. This was not the first such contact between Arab leaders and born-again Americans. Jordan's King Abdullah said that he attended the National Prayer Breakfast in 2005 to conduct diplomacy with American evangelicals (Sharlet, *The Family*, 270).

129. Jonathan Falwell, "Christians and Muslims in Historic Meeting," *WorldNetDaily*, July 7, 2007; "Benny Hinn and Christian Leaders Meet with Arab Ambassadors," Benny Hinn Ministries (http://www.bennyhinn.org/articles/ambassadorsmeeting.cfm); Julia Duin, "Evangelicals, Muslims Meet," *Washington Times*, July 11, 2007; Bay Fang, "Evangelicals, Muslims Start a Rare Dialogue," *Chicago Tribune*, July 23, 2007; "Evangelicals and Muslims Meet," *NAE Insight*, July/August 2007 (www.nae.net/images/July-Aug%2007%20Personal$20edition%20final.pdf). The other evangelical of Arab ancestry was Joshua Youssef of Leading the Way Ministries. Jonathan Falwell's article in *World Net* was immediately followed by a link to a far more hostile assessment of Muslims: an ad for Jim Murk's book *Islam Rising*, which declares that "just like Nazism and Communism, Islam's goal for the last 1300 years has been to control the world." The ad includes an endorsement by a retired pastor from Tennessee saying that "Radical Islam may be Satan's final effort to take over the whole world."

130. Michael Melchior, moderator, Jewish Council for Public Affairs telephone conference, August 31, 2006.

131. See http://campus.northpark.edu/centers/middle/midest.letter_to_bush.htm. Signatories to the letter included Gary Burge, Richard Mouw, Tony Campolo (who mentored Bill Clinton spiritually during the Monica Lewinsky scandal), Ronald J. Sider, president of Evangelicals for Social Action, Richard Stearns, president of World Vision U.S., and author Philip Yancey.

132. "Letter to President Bush from Evangelical Leaders," *New York Times*, July 29, 2007.

133. "What It Means to Love Israel," *Christianity Today*, September 5, 2007 (http://www.christianitytoday.com/ct/2007/september/16.24.html).

134. "Letter to President Bush from Evangelical Leaders"; Laurie Goodstein, "Coalition of Evangelicals Voices Support for Palestinian State"; Abe Levy, "Some Evangelicals Counter Hagee View," *My San Antonio*, August 11, 2007. Another signer, Chris Seiple, president of the Institute for Global Engagement, affirmed that the traditional Christian Zionist believes that Jewish people have a special relationship with God and that Israel is America's greatest ally in the Middle East and will play a pivotal role in the end-times. He signed the letter, he said, for reasons of policy and principle, and because stereotypes of evangelicals as one-sidedly pro-Israel prevent Muslims and others from experiencing the love of Christ (Chris Seiple, "From the President: Why I Signed the Open Letter," Institute for Global Engagement, October 4, 2007).

135. Hutchens is a defender of Messianic Judaism who converted to Judaism while retaining his belief in Jesus as Messiah. His doctoral dissertation at Fuller Theological Seminary was "A Case for Messianic Judaism" (Yaakov Ariel, *Evangelizing the Chosen People: Missions to the Jews in America, 1880 to 2000* (Chapel Hill: University of North Carolina Press, 2000), 238). Hutchens is the editor and publisher of *The Jerusalem Connection*, a magazine that promotes a pro-Israel viewpoint and warns of the danger of Islamic radicalism.

136. Among the signatories were Gary Bauer, David Brog, Rod Parsley, Robert Stearns, and Hutchens (http://www.ouramericanvalues.org/images/CUFI%20Letter%20to%20President %20Bush.pdf).

137. Goodstein, "Coalition of Evangelicals Voices Support for Palestinian State"; Donna Russell, "Robertson: Evangelical Letter Applauding Two-States in Holy Land Unbiblical and Naïve," CBN News, July 31, 2007; Larry Cohler-Esses, "Evangelical Split over Israel Batters Bush," *Jewish Week,* August 3, 2007.

138. "The World toward Illumination," (http://english.irib.ir/IRAN/Leader/Illumination. htm). The World Public Opinion survey released in April 2007 showed that only 2 percent of Pakistanis believe that Al Qaeda perpetrated the 9/11 attacks; 27 percent think the U.S. government was behind them, and 7 percent blame Israel. Only minorities in Morocco (35%), Egypt (28%), and Indonesia (26%) put the blame on Al Qaeda ("Muslim Public Opinion on US Policy, Attacks on Civilians and al Qaeda"). A Pew Center survey showed that only 40 percent of Muslims in the United States believe that Arab groups were responsible for 9/11, while 7 percent blame the United States and 1 percent hold Israel and the Jews responsible. The Pew data confirm that only minorities of Muslims and Europe, the Middle East, Turkey, Indonesia, and Pakistan attribute the 9/11 attacks to Arabs ("Muslim Americans: Middle Class and Mostly Mainstream," Pew Research Center for the People and the Press, Washington, D.C., May 22, 2007).

139. Joel C. Rosenberg, "Iran Sobered Us Up on New Year's," *National Review Online,* January 3, 2007.

140. Stan Goodenough, "Christian Zionists Are Our Enemy," *Jerusalem Newswire,* May 9, 2006.

141. Ryan Jones, "Muslim Leader: Messiah Not Coming to Israel," *Jerusalem Newswire,* October 23, 2005.

142. See Gorenberg's fascinating analysis of Muslim writers' use of anti-Semitic and Christian millennialist materials to supplement classical Islamic material on the end-times (Gershom Gorenberg, *The End of Days: Fundamentalism and the Struggle for the Temple Mount,* [Oxford: Oxford University Press, 2000], 186–91).

CHAPTER 6

1. Marsden, *Understanding Fundamentalism and Evangelicalism* (Grand Rapids, Mich.: W.B. Eerdmans, 1991), 77.

2. Gershom Gorenberg, "Unorthodox Alliance," *Washington Post,* October 11, 2002.

3. "Understanding American Evangelicals: A Conversation with Mark Noll and Jay Tolson," Ethics and Public Policy Center, Washington, D.C., June 2, 2004.

4. Paul S. Boyer, *When Time Shall Be No More: Prophecy Belief in Modern American Culture* (Cambridge, Mass.: Belknap Press of Harvard University Press, 1992) 217.

5. Grace Halsell, *Prophecy and Politics: Militant Evangelists on the Road to Nuclear War* (1986; reprint, Bullsbrook, Western Australia: Veritas Publishing, 1987), 39.

6. Craig Unger, "American 'Rapture,'" *Vanity Fair,* December 2005.

7. Karen Armstrong, *The Battle for God* (New York: Ballantine Books, 2000), 218.

8. Abe Levy, "Some Evangelicals Counter Hagee View," *My San Antonio,* August 11, 2007.

9. "Evangelicals and Israel: A Conversation with Gerald R. McDermott," Ethics and Public Policy Center, Washington, D.C., November 20, 2003.

10. Timothy P. Weber, *On the Road to Armageddon: How Evangelicals Became Israel's Best Friend* (Grand Rapids: Baker Academic, 2004), 233.

11. David A. Rausch, *Communities in Conflict: Evangelicals and Jews* (Philadelphia: Trinity Press International, 1991), 114–21. See Moshe Aumann, *Conflict and Connection: The Jewish-Christian-Israel Triangle* (Jerusalem, N.Y.: Gefen, 2003), 77–78.

12. J. J. Goldberg, *Jewish Power: Inside the American Jewish Establishment* (Reading, Mass.: Addison-Wesley, 1996), 5–7.

13. Elliott Abrams, *Faith or Fear: How Jews Can Survive in a Christian America* (New York: Free Press, 1997), 37–39, 61–70. The 2006 American Jewish Committee Annual Survey of American Jewish Opinion found that 24 percent of American Jews consider many or most evangelical Protestants to be anti-Semitic. That is slightly less than the year before but higher than the anti-Semitic views that Jews attributed to other groups, except for Muslims (http://www.ajc.org/atf/cf/{42D75369-D582-4380-8395-D25925B85EAF}/2006_FINAL_QUESTIONNAIRE_SURVEY_FULL.PDF).

14. Bradley Burston, "Why 'Jews for Jesus' Is Evil," *Jerusalem Post,* May 20, 2006.

15. Billy Graham, "Billy Graham on Key '73," *Christianity Today,* March 16, 1973 (cited by Yaakov Ariel, *Evangelizing the Chosen People: Missions to the Jews in America, 1880 to 2000* (Chapel Hill: University of North Carolina Press, 2000), 214–15); Evangelical Council for Financial Accountability (http://www.ecfa.org/MemberProfile.aspx?ID=6322); Jews for Jesus Web site (www.jewsforjesus.org/about/finances); Michelle Boorstein, "Messianic Group's Touchy Mission," *Washington Post,* June 30, 2007. See Lawrence Grossman, "The Organized Jewish Community and Evangelical America: A Brief History," in Alan Mittleman, Byron Johnson, and Nancy Isserman, eds. *Uneasy Allies? Evangelical and Jewish Relations* (Lanham, Md.: Lexington Books, 2007), 49–72. Moishe Rosen made his own appeal to Billy Graham, who afterward did not speak against evangelizing Jews. Karen Sackville of the Jewish Community Relations Council says that the Southern Baptist Convention contributes $16 million annually to Jews for Jesus (interview with Sackville, July 28, 2005).

16. Donald E. Miller, *Reinventing American Protestantism: Christianity in the New Millennium* (Berkeley: University of California Press, 1997), 19.

17. Ibid., 120 and 242 n14.

18. Gershom Gorenberg, *The End of Days: Fundamentalism and the Struggle for the Temple Mount* (2000; paperback, Oxford: Oxford University Press, 2000), 118–19, 124–25.

19. "Calvary Chapel Jerusalem" (www.calverychapel.com/jeusalem/abut-us.html); "Bradley Antolovich" (http://calvarychapelcostamesa.org/high/chrchinfo/missionaries_display.php?id=20; "The Final Curtain by Chuck Smith" (http://www.calvarychapel.com/assets/pdf/ebooks/thefinalcurtain.pdf); Tom Sawicki, "Mission to the Soviet Jews," *Jerusalem Report,* December 19, 1991.

20. The 1978 Israeli law prohibiting giving money or economic benefits for conversion was a dead letter from the time it was passed. The attorney general had no intention of enforcing it. The former Soviet Union offers a rich opportunity to missions and Messianic Jewish organizations, which have sent dozens of evangelists and built Messianic congregations to attract Jewish converts (Ariel, *Evangelizing the Chosen People,* 277–79, 282, and "An Unexpected Alliance: Christian Zionism and Its Historical Significance," *Modern Judaism,* 26.1 [2006], 89).

21. Ron Kronish, "Is Christian Missionizing a Real Problem?" *Sh'ma,* May 2007. Kronish cites Daniel Rossing, director of the Jerusalem Center for Jewish-Christian Relations, to the effect that none of the indigenous Christian churches in Israel proselytizes. The small minority of individuals who do, says Rossing, often come from outside the country.

22. Kai Kjaer-Hansen and Bodil F. Skjott, "Facts and Myths about the Messianic Congregations in Israel, 1998–1999," *Mishkan,* Caspari Center, Jerusalem, 1999, 30–31; "Caspari Views from Jerusalem," November 2001 (www.caspari.com/newsletter/news01-11.html); Semy Kahan, "Easy Pray," *Jerusalem Post,* February 5, 1997; Jenny Hazan, "Jamming for Jesus," *Jerusalem Post,* July 30, 2004. In the United States, traditional evangelicals have been far more successful at converting Jews than Messianic Jews have been, and most of the people who attend Messianic congregations are Gentiles (Weber, *On the Road to Armageddon,* 242).

23. Ariel, *Evangelizing the Chosen People,* 273–75; Yad L'Achim (http://www.yadlachimusa.org/counter-missionary.asp).

24. This view did not originate with Rosen. By the 1890s, a congregation of immigrant Jews who had accepted Christ yet retained Jewish rites existed on the Lower East Side of Manhattan. By World War I, most Jewish missions had ceased to support separate congregations for Jewish converts. The Presbyterian Church promoted a few such fellowships between the wars and Jewish-Christian congregations proliferated in the 1970s, largely because of Jews for Jesus (Ariel, *Evangelizing the Chosen People*, 2, 9; Weber, *On the Road to Armageddon*, 238).

25. Ariel, *Evangelizing the Chosen People*, 273.

26. Kai Kjaer-Hansen and Bodil F. Skjott, "Facts and Myths about the Messianic Congregations in Israel, 1998–1999" (*Mishkan*, Caspari Center for Biblical and Jewish Studies, Jerusalem, 1999), 23, 27, 41, 48–52.

27. Marc H. Tanenbaum, "No, They Have Forsaken the Faith," *Christianity Today*, April 24, 1981 (cited by Rausch, *Communities in Conflict*, 129–30); Elie Wiesel, "The Missionary Menace," in *Smashing the Idols: A Jewish Inquiry into the Cult Phenomenon*, Gary D. Eisenberg, ed. (Northvale, N.J.: Jason Aronson, 1988), 162 (cited by Ariel, *Evangelizing the Chosen People*, 254; see also 270–75).

28. Michael McAteer, "Furor over Messianic Jews Accepting Christ Provokes Anger and Accusations," *Toronto Star*, March 27, 1993.

29. Interview with David Rosen, December 29, 2005.

30. Gorenberg, *End of Days*, 162.

31. Interview with Robert Stearns, May 16, 2005.

32. David Neff, "From an Evangelical Perch," *Sh'ma*. May 2007.

33. Weber, *On the Road to Armageddon*, 230–31.

34. Pat Robertson, *The New Millennium* (Dallas: Word Publishing, 1990), 289, 292.

35. Judy Lash Balint, "At Christian Rally for Israel, Robertson Pitches 'Messiah,'" *The Forward*, October 8, 2004.

36. Pat Robertson, "Praying for a 'Decisive' Victory," Pat Robertson.com (http://www.patrobertson.com/PressReleases/JPCE0906.asp).

37. Jerry Falwell, *Listen, America!*, (Toronto: Bantam Books, 1980), 98.

38. Julia Duin, "'Jews for Jesus Criticizes Evangelicals," *Washington Times*, January 6, 2004.

39. Jerry Falwell, "Bible History, Prophecy and 'World War III,'" *Falwell Confidential*, July 21, 2006.

40. Hana Levi Julian, "Shas Proposes Expanded Bill to Outlaw Missionary Activity," Israel National News, March 14, 2007 (http://www.wwrn.org/article.php?idd=24504&sec=36&cont=all); interview with Josh Reinstein, August 3, 2005; Jim Brown, "Prominent Evangelical Backs Out of Pro-Israel Event over Proselytizing Disclaimer," *Journal Chretien*, March 28, 2007; "Prominent Evangelical Leader Opposes 'Blind Support' for Israel," *Christian Post*, March 31, 2007; Hillel Fendel, "Chief Rabbinate Nixes Christian-Jewish Conference," *Arutz Sheva*, May 7, 2007. Yuri Shtern, founder of the Christian Allies Caucus, said that he was inspired by working with Israel's predominantly Christian allies in the South Lebanese Army (Etgar Lefkovits, "Growing Pains?" *Jerusalem Post*, January 16, 2006).

41. J.B. Soloveitchik "Confrontation," *Tradition*, 6 (Spring/Summer 1964), 5–28. In accordance with Soloveitchik's argument, the Conference of the Rabbinic Council of America concluded that Jewish-Christian cooperation should be restricted to "universal problems" that are "economic, social, scientific, and ethical." They held that there should be no discussion of faith, religious law, doctrine, or ritual. Although Rav Soloveitchik's position was not presented as a halakhic prohibition, it remains the policy of the Modern Orthodox community (Eugene Korn, "The Man of Faith and Religious Dialogue: Revisiting 'Confrontation,'" *Modern Judaism* [25], 2005, 290–315). Soloveitchik reportedly said that he intended to ensure only that sufficiently well educated rabbis participate in theological dialogue with Christians. Soloveitchik himself engaged in such conversations (David Rosen, "Orthodox Judaism and Jewish-Christian Dialogue" (http://www.bc.edu/research/cjl/meta-elements/texts/center/conferences/soloveitchik/sol_rosen.

htm). Perhaps ironically, he ordained Yechiel Eckstein, who later became the founder of the International Fellowship of Christians and Jews (interview with Eckstein, April 15, 2005).

42. Hillel Fendel, "Chief Rabbinate Nixes Christian-Jewish Conference," *Arutz Sheva*, May 7, 2007 (http://www.israelnationalnews.com/News/News.aspx/122358).

43. Ephesians 2:14–15; Colossians 3:11. David Davis, senior pastor of the Kehilat HaCarmel Messianic congregation in Haifa, noted at the 2007 Foursquare Church convention in Jerusalem that God desires Jews and Gentiles to become one olive tree, as in Romans 11:17–24 ("Foursquare Convention 2007 Continues in Jerusalem," July 23, 2007 (http://www.foursquare church.org/articles/427,1.html).

44. One of the people of Jewish descent who have risen to influence in the American evangelical movement after finding Christ is Jay Sekulow, who became the general legal counsel for Jews for Jesus, then chief counsel for Pat Robertson's American Center for Law and Justice. He is one of a small group of conservatives who have vetted Supreme Court candidates for the Bush administration. Another is Marvin Olasky, the editor in chief of *World* magazine, who helped then-governor George W. Bush develop his ideas of faith-based initiatives. Bush called him "compassionate conservatism's leading thinker" (Michelle Goldberg, *Kingdom Coming: The Rise of Christian Nationalism* [New York: W. W. Norton, 2006], 110). David Brody, another Jew who found Yeshua, covers politics for the Christian Broadcasting Network. His Brody File has become required reading for political insiders, receiving 100,000 hits a month (Michael Luo, "A Blogger's Blend of Prayer and Politics Gains Influence," *New York Times,* July 10, 2007). The best-selling author and communications strategist Joel C. Rosenberg was born to a Jewish father and Methodist mother, both of whom became evangelical. Joel committed to follow Jesus a few years later. He has worked for Steve Forbes, Benjamin Netanyahu, and Natan Sharansky (Joel C. Rosenthal, *Epicenter: Why the Current Rumblings in the Middle East Will Change Your Future* [Carol Stream, Ill.: Tyndale House, 2006], 21 passim).

45. Fifty-eight percent said that the purpose of interreligious dialogue about faith is evangelism and understanding. Another 6 percent said that its goal is evangelism alone, while 31 percent said that its intention is solely understanding (*Christianity Today* poll, retrieved October 15, 2007).

46. Ellen M. Horowitz, "Beware Theological Red Lines," *Jerusalem Post,* June 20, 2007; e-mail interview with Ellen M. Horowitz, August 9, 2007. Horowitz herself argued later that the "cultish metaphor of a grafted Judeo-Christian olive tree" represents a prohibited union and that Jews who advocate it are "dabbling with *avoda zara*"—"strange worship," by which she suggested idolatry ("A Jewish Mother's Guide to End Times," *Jerusalem Post,* August 27, 2007).

47. E-mail messages sent by the author to Rebecca Brimmer on June 20 and June 26, 2007; telephone message on December 17, 2007.

48. Amy Teibel, "Israeli Rabbis to Shun Christian Event," AP, in *The Guardian,* September 24, 2007.

49. Edgar Lefkovits, "Rabbinate Bans Jews from Succot March," *Jerusalem Post,* September 19, 2007; "Chief Rabbinate Forbids Jews to Attend Succot March," ICEJ Web site, September 19, 2007 (http://www.icej.org/article.php?operation=print&id=4395). Among the scheduled speakers at the 2007 Feast were Jack Hayford, Jane Hansen, Robert Stearns, and Malcolm Hedding.

50. "Over 6,000 Christian Pilgrims from 90 Countries Arrive for Succot," *Die Judische,* September 23, 2007.

51. "Rabbis Call on Jews to Refrain from Attending Christian Pilgrimage Events," *Israel Insider,* September 25, 2007.

52. Neta Sela, "55,000 Turn Out for Jerusalem March," *Ynet,* October 2, 2007; Shelly Paz, "Jerusalem March Draws 80,000," *Jerusalem Post,* October 2, 2007; Maria Hjort and Megan Jacobs, "Record Number of Jerusalem Marchers Despite Rabbinic Ban," *Jerusalem Post Christian Edition,* November 2007.

53. Ariel, *Evangelizing the Chosen People*, 276; Gorenberg, *End of Days*, 162–63; Weber, *On the Road to Armageddon*, 230. In 1990, *Mishkan*, a magazine associated with missionizing groups in Israel, devoted a special issue to criticizing the Christian Embassy for not evangelizing (Yaakov Ariel, *Philosemites or Antisemites? Evangelical Christian Attitudes toward Jews, Judaism, and the State of Israel* [Jerusalem: Hebrew University, Vidal Sassoon International Center for the Study of Antisemitism, Analysis of Current Trends in Antisemitism, 20 (2002)], 26).

54. Zev Nagel, "With Friends Like These," *Jerusalem Report*, September 6, 2004.

55. Brad A. Greenberg, "Evangelical prayer banquet promotes love for Israel," *Jewish Journal of Greater Los Angeles*, May 25, 2007 (http://www.jewishjournal.com/home/preview.php?id=17698). Hayford declares that when you receive the Lord, you become a Jew spiritually. He cites Romans 2:28-29 and Galatians 3:26-29 (Jack Hayford, "Why Stand with Israel Today?" Jack Hayford Ministries [www.jackhayford.org/israel/pdf/stand_with_israel.pdf]).

56. Shlomo Riskin, "In Praise of Christian-Jewish Interfaith Dialogue," *Jerusalem Post*, July 24, 2007.

57. "Foursquare Convention 2007," July 22–25, 2007 (http://www.foursquarechurch.org/convention/2007/). Linda Olmert, the prime minister's wife, spoke at this event and received a standing ovation. One Israeli critic charged that most of the featured speakers at the 2007 Feast of Tabernacles had called for Jews to embrace Jesus and, in some cases, were Messianic Jews themselves (Ellen W. Horowitz, "The Unkosher Feast," *Israel Insider*, September 21, 2007). A list of speakers and worship leaders at the 2007 Feast included several Messianic Jews, among them the publisher Stephen Strang, whom *Time* magazine listed as one of the top twenty-five evangelicals in America.

58. David Parson, "What Better Place Than in Israel?" *Jerusalem Post Christian Edition*, September 2007. Hayford and his wife are listed as endorsing a charity operated by a Messianic Jewish group, MaozIsrael Ministries (Ellen W. Horowitz, "WEA Launches Huge Campaign to 'Persuade' Jews to Accept Jesus [ADL Condemns Move]," March 31, 2008 [http://www.israelnews.com/web/view_printer.asp?ID=1610]).

59. Gorenberg, *End of Days*, 163.

60. Nagel, "With Friends Like These."

61. Horowitz, "Beware Theological Red Lines." The National Religious Party's Mina Fenton accused the ICEJ of being involved in the conversion of "the 50,000 Jews in Israel who have already converted" (Hjort and Jacobs, "Record Number of Jerusalem Marchers"). As we have seen, the number of Christian Jews in Israel is probably much smaller than that.

62. Interview with Malcolm Hedding, December 17, 2007.

63. Malcolm Hedding, "The 'Tension' of Jesus," *Jerusalem Post Christian Edition*, June 2008.

64. E-mail interview with David Parsons, August 13, 2007.

65. Ariel, *Evangelizing the Chosen People*, 278.

66. Interview with Ray Sanders, July 25, 2005.

67. Christian Friends of Israel, Mission Statement (www.cfijerusalem.org/aboutus.asp?id=2&cat=1).

68. Carloyn Jacobson, "Whose God Is God?".

69. Carolyn Jacobson, "Immigration and Emigration," Christian Friends of Israel, Watchman's Prayer Letter, April 28, 2006. The new heart in the passage from Ezekiel is a heart of flesh, replacing the heart of stone in Jews. When evoked by a writer anticipating the Jews' coming acceptance of Christ, the implication is that until that event, they are hard-hearted in their denial.

70. "Shanah Tovah!—Happy New Year," Christian Friends of Israel, *On Watch in Jerusalem*, September 12, 2007. Many evangelicals hope to reach the peoples in the "10/40 window," which comprises the fifty-five least evangelized nations of the eastern hemisphere, from North Africa to China, between 10° and 40° north of the equator. That includes hundreds of millions of Muslims, as well as Israel.

71. Don Finto, *Your People Shall Be My People: How Israel, the Jews, and the Christian Church Will Come Together in the Last Days* (1973; reprint, Ventura, Calif.: Regal Books, 2001), 73.

72. Christian-Zionism.org, e-mail of January 17, 2007.

73. Gary M. Burge, "Christian Zionism, Evangelicals and Israel," christianzionism.org, reprinted in *Al Jazeera,* July 31, 2006.

74. Wagner, *Anxious for Armageddon,* (Scottdale, Penn.: Herald Press, 1995), 62–84, 114–21. It was actually Ahab's wife, Jezebel, not Ahab, who conspired to take Naboth's vineyard. Elijah's consequent prophecy, that the dogs would lick Ahab's blood, seems particularly gruesome when used as an analogy for modern Israel. God relented when Ahab repented, deferring the evil that He would bring on Ahab's house.

75. Donald E. Wagner, *Dying in the Land of Promise: Palestine and Palestinian Christianity from Pentecost to 2000* (London: Melisende, 2001), 246–47.

76. Richard Mouw, "How to Bless Israel," *Beliefnet,* May 31, 2002. See also Mouw's "The Chosen People Puzzle," *Christianity Today,* March 5, 2001.

77. "Letter to President Bush," July 23, 2002 (http://campus.northpark.edu/centers/mid dle/midest.letter_to_bush.htm).

78. Gershom Gorenberg shows in *The Accidental Empire: Israel and the Birth of the Settlements, 1967–1977* (New York: Times Books, 2006) that the factors behind the initial growth of Israeli settlements were complex and, in important respects, not a matter of government planning. See also Idith Zertal and Akiva Eldar, *Lords of the Land: The War over Israel's Settlements in the Occupied Territories, 1967–2007* (New York: Nation Books, 2007).

79. Jim Wallis, *God's Politics: Why the Right Gets It Wrong and the Left Doesn't Get It* (San Francisco: Harper San Francisco, 2005), 144, 172–75.

80. "Peace versus Democracy in Palestine: A Conversation with Jimmy Carter," *Council on Foreign Relations,* March 2, 2006. Richard Nixon claimed in Billy Graham's magazine, *Decision,* that he had accepted Christ as his personal Lord and savior during a crusade service (Charles Marsh, *Wayward Christian Soldiers: Freeing the Gospel from Captivity* (Oxford: Oxford University Press, 2007), 61.

81. Jimmy Carter, *Palestine: Peace not Apartheid* (New York: Simon and Schuster, 2006), 174–76, 189–96.

82. Jimmy Carter, *Our Endangered Values: America's Moral Crisis* (New York: Simon and Schuster, 2005), 114–15. George P. Shultz, secretary of state from 1982 to 1989, characterized Carter's claim as a repulsive analogy. It ignores the fact that Israel built the fence to protect its people from terrorist attacks driven by an ideology bent on eradicating Israel, said Shultz (George P. Shultz, "The 'Israel Lobby' Myth," *US News and World Report,* September 9, 2007).

83. Carter, *Palestine: Peace not Apartheid,* 31–32.

84. John F. Walvoord, *Israel in* Prophecy (Grand Rapids, Mich.: Zondervan, 1962), 40–43 72–74.

85. W.E.B. (William E. Blackstone), *Jesus Is Coming* (London: Fleming H. Revell, 1898), 169. Blackstone cites Amos 9:15, Ezekiel 34:28 and 36:11–12, Isaiah 60:15–16 and 49:18, 22, 23; Micah 4:1–2, Zechariah 8:20–23 and 14:16.

86. Rabbi Yechiel Eckstein, "Five Myths about Israel's Security Fence," an IFCJ White paper, Stand for Israel, August 8, 2005. (http://www.ifcj.org/site/News2?abbr=rabbi_&page= NewsArticle&id=11061&security=1201&news_iv_ctrl=1341); "Mainline resolutions insult Jews," Stand for Israel, August 10, 2005. Sharon's government resurrected the idea of a security fence in 2002, when there were sixty suicide bombings in Israel. In 2006, there were five. A cause-and-effect correlation is not clear, however, since stepped-up army operations in the West Bank and the decision by most Palestinian factions to cease such attacks contributed to the decline in bombings (Scott Wilson, "Touring Israel's Barrier with Its Main Designer," *Washington Post,* August 7, 2007). Palestinian terrorists agree that the fence is an effective deterrent, though. Ramadan Shalah, the secretary-general of Palestinian Islamic Jihad, said in 2006 that "there is a

separation fence, which is an obstacle to resistance, and if it were not there the situation would be entirely different" ("Islamic Jihad Leader: Security Fence 'Obstacle to the Resistance," Israel Ministry of Foreign Affairs, November 20, 2006).

87. Interview with Yehiel Poupko, November 18, 2005.

88. Yehiel Poupko, "Protestants Talking about Israel," unpublished paper, May 5, 2005.

89. "What We've Learned from Each Other: A Report on a Jewish-Protestant Conversation about the Israel-Palestine Conflict," May 5, 2005.

90. Editorial, *Moody Bible Institute Monthly*, 31 (1931), 346–47. See Ariel, "An Unexpected Alliance," 78–79.

91. Wagner, *Anxious for Armageddon*, 77, 80–83.

92. David Parsons, "Preaching to the President," *Jerusalem Post Christian Edition*, October 2007.

93. The Old Testament scholar Walter Brueggemann argues that the single central symbol for the promise of the gospel is land, and that "the image is never robbed of its original, historical referent." He adds, "While the Arabs surely have rights and legitimate grievances, the Jewish people are peculiarly the pained voice of the land in the history of humanity, grieved Rachel weeping (Jer. 31:15)" (*The Land* [Philadelphia: Fortress Press, 1977], 170, 179, 190).

94. David Parsons, e-mail correspondence, August 9, 2007.

95. Naim Ateek, "Christian Zionism: The Dark Side of the Bible," *Cornerstone*, Issue 30, Winter 2003. *Cornerstone* is Sabeel's quarterly newsletter, published in English.

96. Naim Ateek, "A Biblical Reflection on Genesis 12:3," *Cornerstone*, Issue 31, Winter 2003.

97. Wallis, *God's Politics*, 182.

98. Dexter Van Zile, "Sabeel's Teachings of Contempt," *Judeo-Christian Alliance*, June 30, 2005; James D. Besser, "Palestinian Nationalists Seen behind Divestment," *Jewish Week*, July 22, 2005. Yehiel Poupko, noting that Ateek likens the Palestinian experience to Jesus' crucifixion, responds that it is the Jews through history who have lived the Passion narrative ("Letter to Presbyterian Friends," unpublished letter sent to the Presbytery of Chicago).

99. Naim Ateek, "The Massacre of the Innocents—A Christmas Reflection," *Cornerstone* 20, Christmas 2000, and "An Easter Message from Sabeel," April 6, 2001 (http://www.sabeel. org/pdfs/2001%20Easter%20Message.htm); Naim Stifan Ateek, *Justice and Only Justice: A Palestinian Theology of Liberation* (Maryknoll, N.Y.: Orbis Books, 1989), 164, 166.

100. Martin Bailey, "Palestinian Christian Offers Vision at UCC Synod," *Worldwide Faith News*, July 13, 2003. Ateek was active in the United Church of Christ's reviving its threat to divest from Israel, and Jewish leaders assert that Sabeel has been influential in each denomination's debates about divestment (Besser, "Palestinian Nationalists Seen behind Divestment").

101. Daniel Boyarin defines Midrash as "radical intertextual reading of the canon, in which potentially every part refers to and is interpretable by every other part." Midrash builds its discourse out of fragments of the Bible (*Intertextuality and the Reading of Midrash* [Bloomington: Indiana University Press, 1990], 16 and 39).

102. Elaine Pagels, in *The Origin of Satan* (New York: Random House, 1995), 47–50, notes that the story of the Fall of Lucifer joins Isaiah 14:12–15 with the apocryphal *Book of the Watchers* and *The First Book of Enoch*. Cf. Ezekiel 28:15–18, 2 Corinthians 11:14, Revelations 12.

103. Wagner, *Anxious for Armageddon*, 73. Barbara Rossing, a prominent critic of Christian Zionism theology, concurs. "Neither temple rebuilding nor the restoration of the nation of Israel is mandated in the New Testament," she says. In John 2:20–21, the temple that will be rebuilt is the temple of Christ's resurrected body, she notes (*The Rapture Exposed: The Message of Hope in the Book of Revelation* [Boulder, Colo.: Westview Press, 2004]. 58). Citing II Peter 1:19–20, Parsons charges that Wagner errs in dismissing the role of prophecy today (e-mail interview, August 9, 2007).

104. Jonathan Kuttab, "The Challenge of Christian Zionism," *Cornerstone*, 32 (Spring 2004). Rossing makes the same point about Christian Zionists' reading of prophecy (xi).

105. Charles Caldwell Ryrie, *Dispensationalism Today* (Chicago: Moody Press, 1965), 86–92.

106. Mouw argues that the "ethnocentric redemptive economy of the old covenant was never viewed . . . as the final arrangement. . . . There was never a time when the Israel of God had the right to think the covenant blessings were her exclusive property" ("The chosen people puzzle").

107. Kuttab, "The Challenge of Christian Zionism."

108. Ateek, "The Zionist Ideology of Dominion versus the Reign of God," sermon delivered on February 22, 2001 (http://www.sabeel.org/old/conf2001/ateek.htm).

109. Ateek, *Justice and Only Justice*, 7–13; "The Jerusalem Sabeel Document: Principle for a Just Peace in Palestine-Israel," (www.fosna.org/index.php?display=jerusalemsabeel). Sabeel's peace plan says that Israel must admit its injustices to the Palestinian people, pay reparations, return all lands conquered in 1967, allow all displaced Palestinians to return to their homeland, divide Jerusalem to allow it to be the capital of the Palestinian state, and discard its nuclear weapons.

110. Ateek, "The Zionist Ideology of Dominion versus the Reign of God."

111. Adam Gregerman, "Old Wine in New Bottles: Liberation Theology and the Israeli-Palestinian Conflict," *Journal of Ecumenical Studies*, 41 (Summer/Fall 2004), 313–40.

112. Rosemary Radford Ruether and Herman J. Ruether, *The Wrath of Jonah: The Crisis of Religious Nationalism in the Israeli-Palestinian Conflict* (Minneapolis: Fortress Press, 2002), 231.

113. Rosemary Radford Ruether, "Christian Zionism and Main Line Western Christian Churches," in *Challenging Christian Zionism: Theology, Politics and the Israel-Palestine Conflict* (London: Melisende, 2005), eds. Naim Ateek, Cedar Duaybis, and Maurine Tobin, 154–55.

114. "Sabeel holds 'Challenging Christian Zionism' Conference," *Worldwide Faith News*, April 28, 2004; Rosemary Radford Ruether, "Challenging Christian Zionism," *Catholic New Times*, May 9, 2004. Also at the conference were Gary Burge, Gershom Gorenberg, Donald Wagner, Jeff Halper, founder of the Israeli Committee against House Demolition, and Marc Ellis, a Jewish liberation theologian. Rossing says that Christian Zionism is based on "ridiculous interpretations of the Bible—Revelation and the book of Daniel, in particular." Its believers, she says, "look toward escape from this world rather than life in a 'peaceable kingdom' together with God on earth." She condemns this view as distorted, dangerous, and a hazard to peace (49).

115. "The 5th International Sabeel Conference Statement: 'Challenging Christian Zionism,'" *Cornerstone*, 33 (Summer 2004).

116. Kuttab, "The Challenge of Christian Zionism." Ateek similarly says that classical Judaism has limited the injunction to love your neighbor to "loving one's own fellow Jew" (Ateek, "The Zionist Ideology of Dominion versus the Reign of God"). Poupko calls that a falsehood out of the *adversus Judaeos* tradition ("A Letter to Presbyterian Friends").

117. Wallis, *God's Politics*, 176.

118. Naim Ateek, "Suicide Bombers: What Is Theologically and Morally Wrong with Suicide Bombings? A Palestinian Christian Perspective," *Cornerstone*, 25 (Summer 2002).

119. Interview with Martin Hoffman, November 14, 2006.

120. Mario Mukilincer, Phillip R. Shaver, et al., "Attachment, Caregiving, and Altruism: Boosting Attachment Security Increases Compassion and Helping," *Journal of Personality ad Social Psychology* 89 (November 2005), 817–39.

121. Edward W. Said, *Peace and Its Discontents: Essays on Palestine in the Middle East Peace Process* (New York: Vintage Books, 1996), 20.

122. Pagels, *The Origin of Satan*, xviii–xix and 36.

123. Halsell, *Prophecy and Politics*, 55.

124. Rossing, *The Rapture Exposed*, 62.

125. Weber, *On the Road to Armageddon*, 247–48.

126. Ariel notes that the Southern Baptists, the Christian and Missionary Alliance, the Assemblies of God, and the Plymouth Brethren have given relief and educational assistance to Palestinians (*Philosemites or Antisemites?* 16).

127. Tim LaHaye, *The Coming Peace in the Middle East* (Grand Rapids, Mich.: Zondervan, 1984), 170.

128. Pat Robertson, *The New Millennium,* 280–87. The Anti-Defamation League's Abe Foxman charges that Robertson's 1991 book *The New World Order* "traffics in . . . traditional anti-Semitic fare" (*Never Again? The Threat of the New Anti-Semitism* [New York: HarperCollins, 2003]. 142).

129. Franklin Graham with Bruce Nygren, *The Name.* (Nashville, Tenn.: Nelson Books, 2002), 195; Leviticus 25:23.

130. Rebecca Brimmer, Ray Sanders, and Malcolm Hedding, "The Jerusalem Declaration of Christian Zionism," reprinted in *The Jerusalem Connection,* December 2007.

131. Richard Booker, "Christian Zionists, Jews and Israel (2004 booklet)," 9.

132. Miriam Rodlyn Park, "Watchmen on the Wall: A Practical Guide to Prayer or Jerusalem and Her People," Robert Stearns, gen. ed. (Training manual.).60–69.

133. Maria Leppakari, "The End Is a Beginning: Contemporary Apocalyptic Representations of Jerusalem" (Abo, Finland: Abo Akademi University Press, 2002), 153.

134. Margaret Dudkevitch, "Pregnant Palestinian Woman and Niece Planned to Blow Up in Israel," Infolive.tv, June 13, 2007; reprinted in Bridges for Peace, *Israel Current News Update and Prayer Focus,* June 15, 2007; Christian Friends of Israel, *On Watch in Jerusalem,* June 14, 2007.

CHAPTER 7

1. Craig Unger, "American 'Rapture,'" *Vanity Fair,* December 2005.

2. Gershom Gorenberg, *The Accidental Empire: Israel and the Birth of the Settlements, 1967–1977* (New York: Times Books, 2006), 4.

3. Grace Halsell, *Prophecy and Politics: Militant Evangelists on the Road to Nuclear War* (1986; reprint, Bullsbrook, Western Australia: Veritas Publishing, 1987), 94, 106–7. Gush Emunim was formed in 1974, mainly by followers of Rabbi Tzvi Yehudah Kook, son of the former chief rabbi Abraham Yitzhak Kook. The younger Kook was head of the Merkaz Harav yeshiva in Jerusalem, where, like his father, he taught that secular Zionists had initiated the Messianic age. Rabbis, hawkish secularists, and religious Zionist IDF veterans also were founders of the movement. As a result, the Gush included a minority of secular ultranationalists. Members of the Gush followed the Kooks' teaching that the redemption was already under way and that hopes for the spiritual restoration of the Jews and peace in the world resided in the Jewish people's settling the whole Land of Israel (Ian Lustick, *For the Land and the Lord: Jewish Fundamentalism in Israel* [New York: Council on Foreign Relations, 1988], 29–35).

4. Roy Reed, "Carter Woos Jewish Vote; Some Gain in North Cited," *New York Times,* June 6, 1976; Yosef Bodansky, *Bin Laden: The Man Who Declared War on America* (New York: Forum, 1999), 338–43.

5. See Luis Lugo in "Evangelical Reflections on the U.S. Role in the World," Carnegie Council on Ethics and International Affairs, September 15, 2005; Jose Casanova, *Public Religions in the Modern World* (Chicago: University of Chicago Press, 1994), 3; Ralph Reed in "The Moral Majority of the Story, Jerry Falwell remembered," *National Review Online,* May 16, 2007.

6. David K. Shipler, "1,000 Christian 'Zionists' Rally in Jerusalem," *New York Times,* September 25, 1980; "When Larry Samuels and His Fellow Evangelical Christians Look . . . ," *Boston Globe,* September 30, 1980.

7. Naomi Shepherd, *Teddy Kollek: Mayor of Jerusalem* (New York: Harper and Row, 1988), 35–36. Kollek also allied with the Dutch group Christians for Israel, which invited him to Holland to meet its born-again donor-base in small fishing villages. During the first Gulf War, members of this group brought thousands of tulips to Israel and planted them (Interview with

Alan Freeman, October 31, 2007). Christians for Israel recruits Jews in the former Soviet Union to make aliyah, providing buses and other logistical support in the Exobus program, in partnership with the Jewish Agency and a British bus company (Timothy P. Weber, *On the Road to Armageddon: How Evangelicals Became Israel's Best Friend.* [Grand Rapids, Mich.: Baker Academic, 2004], 223).

8. See Yaakov Ariel, *Philosemites or Antisemites? Evangelical Christian Attitudes toward Jews, Judaism, and the State of Israel* (Jerusalem: Hebrew University, Vidal Sassoon International Center for the Study of Antisemitism, Analysis of Current Trends in Antisemitism, 20 [2002]).19–24.

9. Will King, "Begin and the Evangelicals," *Jerusalem Post Christian Edition,* December 2007. Zev Chafets notes that Hurwitz replaced Shmuel Katz, who had had some dealings with evangelicals in the United States (e-mail, December 14, 2007).

10. Deborah Caldwell, "The Rapture Factor," *Beliefnet,* May 30, 2002. In 1982, Criswell arranged through local Jewish leaders for Menachem Begin to speak at his First Baptist Church in Dallas, but Begin cancelled because of the death of his wife. In 1988, Begin honored Criswell for his backing of the Jewish state. In 1992, at the age of eighty-three, Criswell attended the "Washington for Israel Summit" in Washington, D.C., organized by the International Christian Embassy. Billy Graham considered Criswell his pastor for fifty years (Ariel, *Philosemites or Antisemites?,* 24, 30; "First Baptist Pastor Criswell Dead at 92," *The Alabama Baptist,* January 17, 2002; Charles Richards, "Former Baptist Leader Criswell Dies," AP in *Beliefnet,* January 10, 2002 (http://www.beliefnet.com/story/97/story_9744_1.html).

11. David E. Harrell, *Oral Roberts: An American Life* (Bloomington: Indiana University Press, 1985), 137 (cited by Ariel, *Philosemites or Antisemites,* 29.

12. Yona Malachy, *American Fundamentalism and Israel: The Relation of Fundamentalist Churches to Zionism and the State of Israel* (Jerusalem: Graph Press, Institute of Contemporary Jewry, Hebrew University, 1977), 106–11.

13. Yaakov Ariel, "An Unexpected Alliance: Christian Zionism and Its Historical Significance," *Modern Judaism,* 26.1 (2006), 87 and n 44. Rabbi Gerald Meister, whom we met in Chapter 1, serves in the Israel Foreign Ministry and is immensely learned on these questions.

14. R. J. Zwi Werblowsky in Malachy, *American Fundamentalism,* vii–x.

15. Dwight Wilson, *Armageddon Now! The Premillenarian Response to Russia and Israel since 1917* (1977 ; reprint, Tyler, Tex.: Institute for Christian Economics, 1991), 194–95; Weber, *On the Road to Armageddon,* 185.

16. Werblowsky in Malachy, *American Fundamentalism,* vii–x.

17. Weber, *On the Road to Armageddon,* 213–15; Zev Chafets, *A Match Made in Heaven: American Jews, Christian Zionists, and One Man's Exploration of the Weird and Wonderful Judeo-Evangelical Alliance* (New York: HarperCollins, 2007), 38. Chafets suggests that Ben-Gurion may have had private contacts with Lindsey (e-mail, December 14, 2007).

18. Weber, *On the Road to Armageddon,* 213–15. In 1967, Israel gave a free tour to Louis Goldberg, a Messianic Jew from the Moody Bible Institute. Goldberg returned every year, ministering to Messianic congregations. He also addressed prophecy conferences in the United States, becoming a spokesman for supporting Israel (David A. Rausch, *Zionism within Early American Fundamentalism, 1878–1918: A Convergence of Two Traditions* [New York: Edwin Mellen Press, 1979], 336–37).

19. Paul S. Boyer, *When Time Shall Be No More: Prophecy Belief in Modern American Culture* (Cambridge, Mass.: Belknap Press of Harvard University Press, 1992), 204–6.

20. Jerusalem Courier and Prophecy Digest, 1st Quarter, 1981 (cited by Ruth W. Mouly, *The Religious Right and Israel: The Politics of Armageddon* [Somerville, Mass.: Political Research Associates, 1985]).

21. Unger, "American 'Rapture.'"

22. Chafets, *A Match Made in Heaven,* 10–11.

23. Merill Simon, *Jerry Falwell and the Jews* (Middle Village, N.Y.: Jonathan David, 1984), 5–6, 60; Chafets, *A Match Made in Heaven*, 64–65.

24. Chafets, *A Match Made in Heaven*, 65–66; Colin Schindler, "Likud and the Christian Dispensationalists: A Symbiotic Relationship," *Israel Studies*, 5 (2000), 167.

25. Robert Wagmen, "Begin and Falwell," *Pittsburgh Press*, August 9, 1981 (cited by Mouly).

26. Voices United for Israel was founded by Esther Levens, the widow of an AIPAC activist in Kansas, to coordinate the pro-Israel activities of Christian groups. It is now known as the Unity Coalition for Israel and claims to include 200 organizations, churches, synagogues, prayer networks, think tanks, and individuals, mostly evangelical, the rest Jewish, representing 40 million people. Yechiel Eckstein helped it expand beyond its local roots and Douglas Feith has been its honorary policy chairman (interview with Levens, August 25, 2005). The Anti-Defamation League, the National Jewish Coalition, and Eckstein's IFCJ all withdrew from the board of the Unity Coalition for Israel, noting that it included groups that proselytize Jews and align with the Republican Party (Schindler, "Likud and the Christian Dispensationalists," 171).

27. Interview with Esther Levens, August 25, 2005; Laurie Goodstein, "Falwell Offers to Mobilize Churches to Oppose Israeli Pullback," *New York Times*, January 28, 1998; Unger, "American 'Rapture.'"

28. Chafets, *A Match Made in Heaven*, 67; Unger, "American 'Rapture.'" Voices United for Israel is now the Unity Coalition for Israel.

29. Chafets, *A Match Made in Heaven*, 66–67, 194.

30. "The Jerusalem Declaration on Christian Zionism," August 29, 2006 (http://www.hcef.org/index.cfm/mod/news/id/16/subMod/NewsView/NewsID/1595.cfm); Etgar Lefkovits, "Christian Zionists, Arab Clerics Spar over 'False Teaching,'" *Jerusalem Post Christian Edition*, October 2006; Brimmer, Sanders, and Hedding, "The Jerusalem Declaration of Christian Zionism," Reprinted in *The Jerusalem Connection*, December 2007.

31. "Evangelist Pat Robertson leads pilgrims to Israel," AP, October 4, 2004.

32. John Hagee, *Jerusalem Countdown; a Warning to the World* (Lake Mary, Fla.: Frontline, 2006), 24–25.

33. Stan Goodenough, "You Have Been Warned," *Jerusalem Newswire*, May 4, 2006.

34. Perry Stone, "Forming Two States—It Has Been Planned for Years," *Voice of Evangelism*, Perry Stone Ministries, December 14, 2007.

35. Sonja Baristic, "Robertson Links Sharon's Stroke to God's 'Enmity,'" AP, January 5, 2006; Mazal Mualem and Amiram Barkat, "White House Criticizes U.S. Evangelist Remark about Sharon," *Haaretz*, January 6, 2006; Larry B. Stammer, "Evangelical Leaders Criticize Pat Robertson," *Los Angeles Times*, January 7, 2006; Nathan Guttman, "Evangelist Pat Robertson Blasted for Saying God Punished Sharon," *Jerusalem Post*, January 8, 2006.

36. Jeffrey H. Birnbaum and Laurence I. Barrett, "The Gospel According to Ralph," *Time*, May 15, 1995; "Taking Over the Republican Party," June 18, 2004 (www.theocracywatch.com). The journalist Jo Freeman claimed that Robertson founded the Christian Coalition in 1989 with a $64,000 grant from the National Republican Senatorial Committee ("Christian Coalition Boosts Israel," *CounterPunch*, October 24, 2002). Senator Don Nickles, who was chairman of the Republican Senatorial Committee in 1989, says that this is false: there was no such grant (e-mail with Senator Rudy Boschwitz, June 21, 22, and 23, 2006).

37. Marvin Olasky, The Panda in Winter," *World* Magazine, February 18, 2006. Nielsen Media Research reports that the *700 Club's* average daily audience is 863,000 (Stephen Clark, "Ex-Stripper Spreads Gospel to Those in Sex Industry," *Los Angeles Times*, March 25, 2006).

38. Chafets, *A Match Made in Heaven*, 72.

39. Richardlandlive.com, January 7, 2006; Larry B. Stammer, "Evangelical Leaders Criticize Pat Robertson," *Los Angeles Times*, January 7, 2006. The politically conservative *eminence*

grise William F. Buckley wrote that there was no need for President Bush to put another spear in Robertson because "he's already dead" (William F. Buckley, Jr., "Robertson's Death Wishes," nationalreview.com, August 26, 2005.

40. Chafets, *A Match Made in Heaven,* 72; Jim Wallis, "Pat Robertson: An Embarrassment to the Church," *Sojourners,* August 25, 2005.

41. Álex Johnson, "In Evangelical World, a Liberal View Steps Up," MSNBC, June 9, 2005.

42. Charles Colson, with Anne Morse, "A More Excellent Way." *Christianity Today.com,* January 23, 2006; Paul Nussbaum, "The Surprising Spectrum of Evangelicals," *Philadelphia Inquirer,* June 19, 2006. Warren's *Purpose-Driven Church* is used as a training manual in 160 countries (David W. Bebbington, "Not so Exceptional After All," *Christianity Today,* May/June 2007).

43. Gary Stern, "Evangelical Analyst Calls for Religious Right Moderation," *The Journal News,* March 13, 2007. A 2007 study found that that the American media refer to conservative religious leaders nearly three times as often as they do to liberal and moderate religious spokes-people—even when not counting references to Jerry Falwell, Pat Robertson, and James Dobson! (Robert Marus, "Study Says American News Media Overplays Religious Conservatives," *Associated Baptist Press,* May 31, 2007 [www. abpnews.com/2266.article.print]).

44. Chafets, *A Match Made in Heaven,* 74–75.

45. Ibid, 73.

46. Michael Lind, "Bush Whistles Dixie," *Newsweek,* December 23, 2003; Craig Horowitz, "Israel's Christian Soldiers," newyorkmetro.com, September 29, 2003.

47. Interview on condition of anonymity, December 29, 2005.

48. "Pat's Out, but the Galilee Project Seems On," *Christianity Today,* January 13, 2006.

49. "Pastors Reveal Major Influencers on Churches," *Barna Update,* January 14, 2005.

50. "Israel Shuns Pat Robertson," AP, January 11, 2006; Sam Ser, "The Body Count," *Jerusalem Post,* March 6, 2006.

51. Chafets, *A Match Made in Heaven,* 204.

52. "Pat Robertson Prays for Israeli Victory," AP, in *Washington Post,* August 9, 2006; Michael Lando, "Come Home!" *Jerusalem Post Christian Edition,* November 2006; Steven G. Vegh, "Plans on Track for 'Galilee Christian Heritage Center' in Israel," *Virginian Pilot,* January 26, 2007; Chafets, *A Match Made in Heaven,* 75.

53. In the same statement, Robertson predicted massive deaths from a terrorist attack on the United States in 2007 ("Robertson Predicts Mass Killing," AP, January 2, 2007.)

54. "Zion's Christian Soldiers," *60 Minutes,* October 6, 2002 (http://www.cbsnews.com/stories/2002/10/03/60minutes/main524268.shtml). In a related line of thinking, Senator James Inhofe declared in a Senate speech that God opened the spiritual door for the 9/11 attacks because the United States had asked Israel not to retaliate against terrorist strikes ("Peace in the Middle East Speech by U.S. Sen. James M. Inhofe R-Okla," "Peace in the Middle East." March 4, 2002 [http://inhofe.senate.gov/public/index.cfm?FuseAction=PressRoom.Speeches&ContentRecord_id=73a47d47-802a-23ad-4d61-336bcd0c370f&Region_id=&Issue_id=&CFID=5872324&CFTOKEN=81269357]).

55. Hal Lindsey, "The Myth of 'Measured Response,'" Oracle Commentaries, July 17, 2006.

56. Stan Goodenough, "Katrina—The Fist of God?" *Jerusalem Newswire,* August 29, 2005.

57. Lonnie C. Mings, "Israel Hurries to Complete Fence," *Israel News Digest,* August 31, 2005.

58. Hansen cited a sermon by Rabbi Jonathan Cohen of New Jersey (Jane Hansen, "Rendezvous with Destiny," *Jerusalem Post Christian Edition,* November 2006).

59. Ryan Jones, "'Disengagement' HQ Hit with Bird Flu," *Jerusalem Newswire,* March 19, 2006. The biblical precedents are in 2 Chronicles 21: 12–14, 2 Samuel 24: 15, and Micah 6:13.

60. William Koenig, *Eye to Eye: Facing the Consequences of Dividing Israel* (Alexandria, Va.: About Him Publishing, 2004).

61. Ron Ross, "Annapolis: Religious Leaders Issue a Stern Warning," BFP Israel *Mosaic News*, Bridges for Peace, *Israel Current News Update and Prayer Focus*, November 9, 2007.

62. Interview with William Koenig, July 25, 2006.

63. Zvi Alush, "Rabbi Warns Leaders: No More Pullouts," *Ynet*, March 2, 2006; Efrat Weiss, "Rabbi: It's Forbidden to Vote for Kadima," *Ynet*, March 25, 2006. Zion Zohar argues that the pulsa denura ritual is actually a very recent innovation in which an outmoded ceremony of excommunication was given an ancient, mystical-sounding name ("Pulsa De-Nura: The Innovation of Modern Magic and Ritual," *Modern Judaism* (27 [2007], 72–99).

64. Ilan Marciano, "Rabbi: Vote Shas or Go to Hell," *Ynet*, March 19, 2006; Nadav Shragai, "Pullout Leaders Are Cursed, Argues the Religious Right," *Haaretz*, March 12, 2007.

65. Roee Nahmias, "Salah: Caliph Will Sit in Jerusalem," *Ynet*, September 15, 2006; Khald Amayreh, "Palestinian Leader Ends Israeli Jail Term," *Al Jazeera*, July 17, 2005.

CHAPTER 8

1. Maureen Dowd, "Rapture and Rupture," *New York Times*, October 6, 2002.

2. Timothy P. Weber, On the Road to Armageddon: How Evangelicals Became Israel's Best Friend (Grand Rapids: Baker Academic, 2004), 232.

3. Amos Oz, *How to Cure a Fanatic* (Princeton, N.J.: Princeton University Press, 2006), 68–69. Dr. David Flusser, professor of comparative religion at Hebrew University, and Teddy Kollek, the former mayor of Jerusalem, are among those to whom this story was first attributed.

4. Rabbi Yechiel Eckstein, Stand for Israel Washington Briefing, Washington, D.C., September 28, 2005.

5. Interview with Malcolm Hoenlein, February 27, 2006.

6. *The Religious Right: The Assault on Tolerance and Pluralism in America* (New York: Anti-Defamation League, 1994), page 21. Foxman continues to attack Pat Robertson's 1991 best seller, *The New World Order*, which uses what he calls "the waffling language of the conspiracy theorist who lacks factual evidence for the views he so desperately wants to purvey" (Abraham H. Foxman, *Never Again?*, 142–43).

7. Interview with Abraham Foxman, February 27, 2006. Elliott Abrams makes a corollary point in *Faith or Fear*: "The support of most Jews for Israel is based, even if indirectly, on their religious affiliation," he says, and asks why Christians shouldn't be allowed the same motivation (68).

8. Abe Foxman, *Never Again? The Threat of the New Anti-Semitism* (New York: HarperCollins, 2003), 150.

9. Elliott Abrams, Faith or Fear: How Jews Can Survive in a Christian America (New York, London: Free Press, 1997), 68.

10. Ted Haggard, *Primary Purpose: Making It Hard for People to Go to Hell from Your City* (Lake Mary, Fla: Charisma House, 1995), 54–64.

11. "Candid Conversation with the Evangelist," *Christianity Today*, August 24, 2006. The Billy Graham Crusade film, *His Land*, released in 1970, was publicized by an ad that called the rebirth of Israel "by far the greatest biblical event that has taken place during the twentieth century" (David A. Rausch, *Zionism within Early American Fundamentalism, 1878–1918: A Convergence of Two Traditions* [New York: Edwin Mellen Press, 1979], 336–37).

12. George M. Marsden, *Fundamentalism and American Culture* (Oxford: Oxford University Press, 2006), 249 and 328 n56; See Grant Wacker, *Heaven Below: Early Pentecostals and American Culture* (Cambridge, Mass.: Harvard University Press, 2001).

13. Michael Cromartie in "God's Country? Evangelicals and U.S. Foreign Policy," The Pew Forum on Religion & Public Life, Washington, D.C., September 26, 2006.

14. Todd Hertz, "*The* Evangelical View of Israel?" *Christianity Today,* June 11, 2003. In 2006, almost exactly the same percentage of American Jews (54%) favored establishing a Palestinian state (2006 Annual Survey of American Jewish Opinion, American Jewish Committee [http://www.ajc.org/site/apps/nl/content3.asp?c=ijITI2PHKoG&b=846741&ct=3152877]).

15. Interview with Robert Stearns, May 16, 2005.

16. This "double perspective" characterizes evangelical thought on other topics as well. They see voluntary school prayer, for example, as a matter of First Amendment rights but also as a matter of the primacy of divine over human authority (Simon Coleman, "An Empire on a Hill? The Christian Right and the Right to be Christian in America," *Anthropological Quarterly* 78 [3] Summer 2005, 653–71).

17. Interview with Richard Land, September 27, 2005.

18. Hertz, "*The* Evangelical View of Israel?"; Hertz, "God's Country?" Land believes that it would be lunacy for Israel to go all the way back to its pre-1967 borders, though, since that would leave it indefensible (interview with Richard Land, September 27, 2005).

19. Interview with Susan Michael, January 23, 2006.

20. Tovah Lazaroff, "'Evangelicals the World Over Are Praying Fervently for Israel," *Jerusalem Post,* August 9, 2006. See also Zev Chafets, *A Match Made in Heaven: American Jews, Christian Zionists, and One Man's Exploration of the Weird and Wonderful Judeo-Evangelical Alliance* (New York: HarperCollins, 2007), 204. In March 2008, John McCain reported that John Hagee had assured him that he favored a peace process and was committed to peace between Palestinians and Israelis (Rob Eshman, "20 Questions with John McCain," *Jewish Journal of Greater Los Angeles,* April 4, 2008).

21. Merrill Simon, *Jerry Falwell and the Jews* (Middle Village, New York: Jonathan David, 1984), 63.

22. Chafets, *A Match Made in Heaven,* 67 and 192.

23. Inhofe cited Genesis 13:14–17. "Peace in the Middle East Speech by U.S. Sen. James M. Inhofe R-Okla," Washington, D.C. March 4, 2002 (http://inhofe.senate.gov/public/index. cfm?FuseAction=PressRoom.Speeches&ContentRecord_id=73a47d47-802a-23ad-4d61-336bcd0c370f&Region_id=&Issue_id=&CFID=5872324&CFTOKEN=81269357).

24. Interview with Ted Haggard, June 26, 2006.

25. Interview with Ray Sanders, July 25, 2005.

26. David Parsons, "Swords into Ploughshares: Christian Zionism and the Battle of Armageddon," International Christian Embassy Jerusalem (http://icej.org/data/Images/File/News/ Swords.pdf).

27. Speech by Hedding at the October 2004 Feast of Tabernacles in Jerusalem, in "The Biblical Basis for Christian Zionism" (fp.thebeers.f9.co.uk). Victoria Clark reports that the ICEJ "loudly opposed Prime Minister Sharon's decision to dismantle the Gaza settlements in the summer of 2005." She cites as proof Hedding's online warning that Israel was placing itself in danger, and his call for Israelis to devote a day to "Humility and Repentance" (*Allies for Armageddon: The Rise of Christian Zionism* [New Haven, Conn.: Yale University Press, 2007], 217). Hedding's statement also said, however, that "We will never tell you what to do because we respect your democracy." He exhorted Israelis to turn to God (Malcolm Hedding, "ICEJ Disengagement Statement," July 21, 2005 [http://www.icej.org/article.php?id=2808]).

28. Interview on condition of anonymity, February 8, 2006.

29. "Where Are the Christians?" *Jerusalem Newswire,* August 16, 2005.

30. Interview with Malcolm Hedding, July 20, 2005.

31. Speech by Hedding at the 2004 Feast of Tabernacles in Jerusalem, in "The Biblical Basis for Christian Zionism" (fp.thebeers.f9.co.uk).

32. Malcolm Hedding and Jurgen Buhler, "A Biblical Stand on Zionism—Part 2," *Christian Zionism,* October 1, 2006 (http://www.christian-zionism.org/analysis_articles_body.asp?Title =A+Biblical+Stand+on+Zionism+%2D+Part+2).

33. Interview with Rebecca Brimmer, August 8, 2005.

34. Jack W. Hayford, "A Decisive Dilemma," *Jerusalem Post Christian Edition,* November 2006.

35. John Hagee, "Our Jewish Roots," *JH Magazine,* Summer 2002.

36. Saul Elbein, "Evangelicals Raise $8.5 m. for Jewish State." *Jerusalem Post,* October 17, 2007.

37. David Horowitz, "Most Evangelicals Are Seeing the Error of 'Replacement Theology,'" *Jerusalem Post,* March 20, 2006. CUFI was not the first evangelical pro-Israel lobby intended to be a Christian AIPAC. The Christians' Israel Public Action Campaign (CIPAC), established in the 1980s, enjoyed the support of then-senator Jesse Helms (Jakov Ariel, *Philosemites or Antisemites?: Evangelical Christian Attitudes toward Jews, Judaism, and the State of Israel* [Jerusalem: Hebrew University, Vidal Sassoon International Center for the Study of Antisemitism, Analysis of Current Trends in Antisemitism, 20, 2002]), 24. Its current president is Richard A. Hellman.

38. Not all religious leaders in San Antonio admire Hagee. Rabbi Barry Block, senior rabbi at Temple Beth-El in that city, warns that Jews are tarnished by association with CUFI. He notes that no Jew can hear Hagee's sermons series "Allah and America" and support him, and observes that to the Christian colleagues with whom he works most closely, Hagee is a charlatan (Rabbi Barry Block, "When Friends Aren't Really Friends: Be Wary of Evangelical Support for Israel," JTA, July 9, 2006).

39. Jerry Gordon, "What a 'Night to Honor Israel': The CUFI Washington Summit Dinner in DC," *Israpundit,* July 20, 2006; Michelle Vu, "U.S. Christian Leaders Defend Israel, Decry 'Islamic Fascism,'" *Christian Post,* July 20, 2006; Jim VandeHei, "Congress Is Giving Israel Vote of Confidence," *Washington Post,* July 19, 2006; "Commentary and News Briefs," *Agape Press,* July 19, 2006; Andrew Higgins, "Holy War: A Texas Preacher Leads Campaign to Let Israel Fight," *Wall Street Journal,* July 27, 2006; Margot Patterson, "Evangelicals Rally for Israel, Warn of Iran Threat," *National Catholic Reporter,* July 28, 2006; Jake Tapper and Dan Morris, "Save Israel, for Jesus?" ABC News, July 31, 2006 (www.abcnews.go.com/Nightline/print?id=2258864); Max Blumenthal, "Birth Pangs of a New Christian Zionism," *The Nation,* August 8, 2006.

40. A third talking point was in favor of the Iran Libya Sanctions Act, which prohibits American investments in Iran (Richard Allen Greene, "Evangelical Christians Plead for Israel," BBC News, July 19, 2006 [http://newsvote.bbc.co.uk/mpapps/pagetools/print/news.bbc.co.uk/2/hi/americas/5193092.s.]); Unity Coalition for Israel (voices@israelunitycoalition.org), July 19, 2006; Gordon, "What a 'Night to Honor Israel'").

41. Blumenthal, "Birth Pangs of a New Christian Zionism"; VandeHei, "Congress Is Giving Israel Vote of Confidence"; Jonathan Weisman, "Congress Cautioned on Support of Israel," *Washington Post,* July 26, 2006; David D. Kirkpatrick, "For Evangelicals, Supporting Israel Is 'God's Foreign Policy,'" *New York Times,* November 14, 2006.

42. Terence Hunt, "White House Plays Down Mideast Meeting," AP, July 17, 2007.

43. Nathn Guttman, "Pro-Israel Christians Mobilize in D.C.," *The Forward,* July 18, 2007; Ron Kampeas, "Bush seeks Support for Peace Plan," JTA, July 17, 2007; Yitzhak Benhorin and AP, "Christian Zionists: Ahmadinejad Is new Hitler," *Ynet,* July 18, 2007; James D. Besser, "'Not One Inch' Still Alive and Well," *Jewish Week,* July 20, 2007.

44. Hunt, "White House Plays Down Mideast Meeting"; "Sen. McCain Tells Israel Supporters U.S. Withdrawal from Iraq Would Be Disaster," AP, July 17, 2007; "Sen. McCain Addresses National Convention of Christians United for Israel," U.S. Fed News Service, July 17, 2007; "Lieberman Address to Christians United for Israel," July 16, 2007 (http://lieberman.senate.gov/newsroom/release.cfm?id=279110); Sarah Posner, "Theocrats Deny 'End Times' Theology Is Cause of Their Push for War with Iran," *Alternet,* July 23, 2007.

45. Abe Levy, "Hagee, Israel Backers Push a Get-tough Policy," *San Antonio Express-News,* July 22, 2007.

46. Greene, "Evangelical Christians Plead for Israel."

47. Max Blumenthal, "Birth Pangs" and "Israel, the US, and the Christian Right: The Menage a Trois from Hell," *Huffington Post,* August 10, 2006. The articles by Sarah Posner are "Pastor Strangelove," *American Prospect Online,* June 6, 2006; "Holy War," *The American Prospect Online,* July 19, 2006; and "Lobbying for Armageddon," August 3, 2006.

48. Larry Cohler, "Evangelical Split over Israel Batters Bush."

49. James D. Besser, "New Evangelical Group Could Buck Promised West Bank Pull-outs," *Jewish Week,* April 7, 2006; Eric Yoffie, "When We Let John Hagee Speak for Us," *The Forward,* May 18, 2006; Michal Lando, "Reform Leader: 'Christians for Israel' hurt country," *Jerusalem Post,* April 3, 2008.

50. Derek Prince, *Promised Land: God's Word and the Nation of Israel,* (1978; reprint, Charlotte, N.C.: Derek Prince Ministries, 2003), 76; Jim Kuhnhenn, "Televangelist John Hagee Apologizes to Catholics," *Washington Post,* May 14, 2008; Neela Banerjee and Michael Luo, "McCain Cuts Ties to Pastors Whose Talks Drew Fire," *New York Times,* May 23, 2008; Laurie Goodstein, "Spotlight Recasts Church Leaders and Their Support," *New York Times,* May 24, 2008; "Help Us Respond to the Attacks on Pastor Hagee!" CUFI e-mail, May 26, 2008; Robert D. Nova, "McCain's Evangelical Problem," *Washington Post,* June 9, 2008. McCain also repudiated an endorsement by Pastor Rod Parsley after it became known that Parsley had called Islam a false anti-Christ religion that intended to conquer the world. That, of course, is familiar Christian Zionist discourse, as we have seen.

51. Daniel Levy, "Israeli Labor Leader Calls for Severing of Ties with Hagee/CUFI," June 4, 2008 (www.prospectsfor peace.com/2008/06/Israeli_labor_leader_calls_for.html); David Saperstein, "Hagee's Jewish Endorsers," *Washington Post,* May 23, 2008; James D. Besser, "Breaking: Foxman Calls for 'Hold' on Hagee Ties," *Jewish Week,* May 21, 2008; Nathan Guttman, "Hagee's a No-Show at Israel Lobby Meet, But He Has Plenty of Friends There," *The Forward,* June 3, 2008.

52. James D. Besser, "New Evangelical Group Could Buck Promised West Bank Pull-outs," *Jewish Week,* April 7, 2006; Eric Yoffie, "When We Let John Hagee Speak for Us," *The Forward,* May 18, 2006; Besser, "'Not One Inch' Still Alive and Well.'"

53. Horovitz, "Most Evangelicals Are Seeing the Error of 'Replacement Theology.'"

54. Guttman, "Pro-Israel Christians Mobilize in D.C."

55. Lonnie Mings, "Christian Group Warns U.S. against Pressuring Israel," Christian Friends of Israel, *Israel News Digest,* July 31, 2007.

56. David Brog, *Standing with Israel: Why Christians Support the Jewish State* (Lake Mary, Fla.: Frontline, 2006), 179–80, 193; Julia Duin, "Christian Group to Advocate More Support for Israel," *Washington Times,* July 13, 2006.

57. Etgar Lefkovits, "Robertson Warns Bush against Dividing Jerusalem," *Jerusalem Post,* October 5, 2004; Laurie Copans, "Pat Robertson Warns Bush against Dividing Jerusalem," AP, October 5, 2004.

58. Interviews with Richard Land, September 27, 2005, June 6, 2006.

59. John Hagee, *Final Dawn over Jerusalem* (Nashville: Thomas Nelson, 1998), 42, and *Jerusalem Countdown; a Warning to the World* (Lake Mary, Fla.: Frontline, 2006), 25–26. The Temple is not typically considered one of the Seven Wonders of the World. At his 2007 Night to Honor Israel in San Antonio, Hagee warned that giving the Palestinians control of holy sites in Jerusalem "would be the death-knell of Christian tourism in Israel" (Abe Levy, "Hagee Cautions on Mideast talks," *My San Antonio,* October 14, 2007).

60. Hagee, *Final Dawn over Jerusalem,* 119–20.

61. "Evangelist Pat Robertson Leads Pilgrims to Israel," AP, October 4, 2004; Daphna Berman, "If Bush 'Touches' Jerusalem, We'll Form Third Party," *Haaretz,* October 4, 2004; Lefkovits, "Robertson Warns Bush against Dividing Jerusalem."

62. See patrobertson.com, no date (but after December 17, 2003) (www.patrobertson.com/Teaching/TeachingRoadMap.asp).

63. Interview with Mike Pence, September 25, 2006.

64. Interview with Robert Stearns, May 16, 2005.

65. Paul Charles Merkley, *Christian Attitudes towards the State of Israel* (Montreal: McGill-Queen's University Press, 2001), 188–89.

66. Parsons, "Swords into Ploughshares"; Gershom Gorenberg, "Danger: Millennium Ahead," *Jerusalem Report*, February 19, 1998.

67. Parsons, "Swords into Ploughshares."

68. Malcolm Hedding, "Fundamental Mistakes," *Ynet*, December 13, 2006; interview with Hedding, July 20, 2006.

69. Ron Kampeas, "Jews Urged to Embrace Evangelicals," *Jerusalem Post*, February 27, 2007.

70. Interview with Rebecca Brimmer, August 8, 2005.

71. "Hagee, Falwell, Deny Endorsing 'Dual Covenant' Theology," *Jerusalem Post*, March 2, 2006.

72. Horovitz, "Most Evangelicals Are Seeing the Error of 'Replacement Theology.'"

73. Interview with Gary Bauer, October 14, 2005.

74. Gary Bauer, Fifth Annual Israel Solidarity Event, Israeli embassy, Washington, D.C., June 9, 2006.

75. Besser, " 'Not One Inch' Still Alive and Well."

76. Ralph Reed, "Evangelical Christians and Zionism," Talk Today in *USA Today*, May 23, 2002.

77. Jonathan Falwell, "Christians and Muslims in Historic Meeting." At the meeting were Reed, Jonathan Falwell, Benny Hinn, Gordon Robertson of the *700 Club*, Paul Crouch, Jr., of Trinity Broadcasting Network, Richard Cizik, and Vernon Brewer of WorldHelp, among others.

78. Delinda C. Hanley, "The Armageddon Vote in Election 2004," *Washington Report on Middle East Affairs*, 23 (July/August 2004), 87; George Monbiot, "Their Beliefs are Bonkers, but They Are at the Heart of Power," *The Guardian*, April 20, 2004; Stephen Sizer, "The Origins of Christian Zionism," *Cornerstone*, 31 (Winter 2003); Jimmy Carter, *Our Endangered Values: America's Moral Crisis* (New York: Simon and Schuster, 2005) , 114. The title alone of Wagner's *Anxious for Armageddon* captures his endorsement of this charge against dispensationalists.

79. Brog, *Standing with Israel*, 80–87.

80. "The Rebirth of Ralph Reed," *Atlanta Jewish Times*, July 23, 1999; David D. Kirkpatrick, "What Next for Ralph Reed?" *New York Times*, July 21, 2006; Marvin Olasky, "The Ralph Reed Scandal," *World* magazine, February 22, 2006 (http://www.worldmagblog.com/blog/archives/022805.ht,l).

81. Craig Unger, "American 'Rapture,'" *Vanity Fair*, December 2005. The first volume in Tim LaHaye and Jerry B. Jenkins's series, *Left Behind: A Novel of the Earth's Last Days*, appeared in 1995. The sixteenth and final book in the series, *Kingdom Come: The Final Victory*, was published in 2007.

82. George Eliot, "Evangelical Teaching: Dr. Cumming," *Westminster Review* 64 (October 1855), 455, cited by Mark A. Noll, *The Scandal of the Evangelical Mind* (Grand Rapids, Mich.: Eerdmans, 1994), 143. Noll says that the extreme partisanship fostered by Rapture theology is a "wooden interpretation" of 1 Thessalonians 4 that causes damaging intellectual attitudes.

83. Jason Boyett, "Apocalypse Soon," *Salon.com*, August 7, 2006; "The End?," Beliefwatch, *Newsweek*, August 7, 2006.

84. Eric J. Greenberg, "Graham Apology Not Enough," *Jewish Week*, March 1, 2002.

85. Interview with Martin E. Marty, January 11, 2006. Mark Noll agrees. Evangelicals support Israel for many reasons, he notes, including the fact that it is a staunch ally of the United States and an outpost of democracy in an important and difficult part of the world. But the eschatological element is there as well, says Noll, and that complicates the picture ("Understanding American Evangelicals: A Conversation with Mark Noll and Jay Tolson," Ethics and Public Policy Center, Washington, D.C., June 2, 2004.

86. Interview with Marty, January 11, 2006.

87. Ted Haggard, Fifth Annual Israel Solidarity Event, Embassy of Israel, Washington, D.C., June 9, 2006.

88. Tim Stafford, "Good Morning, Evangelicals!" *Christianity Today*, November 4, 2005.

89. Paul Nussbaum, "An Evangelical Voice Strikes Different Notes," *Philadelphia Inquirer*, June 19, 2005.

90. Interview with Ted Haggard, June 26, 2006.

91. Zev Chafets, "I Want Falwell in My Foxhole," *Los Angeles Times*, July 23, 2006.

92. Brian Braiker, "Are These the End Times?" *Newsweek*, MSNBC.com, July 28, 2006.

93. Interview with Ted Haggard, June 26, 2006.

94. Ibid.

95. Chafets, *A Match Made in Heaven*, 210–13.

96. Ori Nir, "Evangelicals Eye Middle Ground on Middle East," *The Forward*, July 1, 2005.

97. The three NAE board members who signed the 2007 letter to Bush were Joel Hunter, David Neff, the editor of *Christianity Today;* and Berten Waggoner. Don Argue, a former NAE president, also signed.

98. E-mail interview with John Green, July 4, 2006.

99. Chafets, *A Match Made in Heaven*, 67.

CHAPTER 9

1. Todd Hertz, "*The* Evangelical View of Israel?" *Christianity Today*, June 11, 2003.

2. Green, "Evangelical Protestants and Jews: A View from the Polls," in *Uneasy Allies?* (Lanham, Md.: Lexington Books, 2007), 35–36.

3. "Religion, Belief, and Policy," Pew Research Center for the People & the Press, Washington, D.C., July 24, 2003, and "Many Americans Uneasy with Mix of Religion and Politics," Pew Research Center for the People and the Press, Washington, D.C., August 24, 2006. A Gallup survey in February 2006 found that 59 percent of Americans sided with Israel and 15 percent with the Palestinians (The Gallup Poll, February 6–9, 2006). Christian weekly worship attenders across denominations also tend to favor Israel over the Palestinians by 52 percent to 8.7 percent, according to Pew survey data (John Green, conference on "Evangelical-Jewish Relations: Politics, Policy, and Theology," Temple University, November 29, 2007).

4. The Pew Center found in 2003 that only 26 percent of Americans who sympathized with Israel did so for religious reasons, as compared with 34 percent because of media coverage and 18 percent because of education (Andrew Kohut and Bruce Stokes, "The Problem of American Exceptionalism," Pew Research Center, Washington, D.C., May 9, 2006).

5. "American Christians and Support for Israel," The Tarrance Group, Alexandria, Virginia, October 9, 2002. A second set of questions found that twice as many evangelicals are motivated by God's promise to bless those who bless the Jews than are driven by anticipation of the end-times. Whether respondents support Israel's policies against terrorism is a different question from the one asked by the Pew survey, and the results may have been affected by the severity of Palestinian attacks on Israel in 2002.

6. Yechiel Eckstein, at "Straight Talk: Evangelicals and the Jews," 92nd Street Y, March 7, 2006.

7. Gallup poll, May 30–June 1, 2003. The Gallup survey found that 19.8 percent said that Israel has personal religious significance for them for reasons other than prophecy of future events there; nearly 47 percent said that Israel is not religiously significant for them.

8. Interview with Frank Newport, January 4, 2006. In his 1993 book, *Redeeming America,* Michael Lienesch offered a similar explanation for the New Christian Right's support of Israel (230).

9. Slightly more than one-third of all American Christians believe that the final events will unfold in this pattern (Pew Research Center for the People & the Press, July 2006 Religion and Public Life Survey, Final Topline, July 6–19, 2006, Q. 80).

10. Interview with Green, December 15, 2005. D. Michael Lindsey, author of *Faith in the Halls of Power*, observes that evangelical support of Israel has more to do with God's preference for Israel and Jews in the Bible than with apocalyptic theology ("The Halls of Power," *Sh'ma.com,* May 2007 [http://www.shma.com/may_07/halls_power.htm]).

11. John Green, e-mail, December 6, 2005. A 2006 Zogby poll found that 16 percent of Americans strongly believed that Israel must keep all of the Promised Land in order to facilitate the Second Coming; another 15 percent believe that somewhat (http://www.cnionline.org/learn/polls/czandlobby/). Green considers those numbers to be suspiciously high (e-mail, November 12, 2007).

12. A 2004 *Newsweek* survey reported that 55 percent of all Americans (not just evangelicals) believed that the faithful will be taken up to heaven in the Rapture (David Gates, "The Pop Prophets," *Newsweek,* May 24, 2004).

13. Denison added that in his previous church in Atlanta, a theologically conservative Baptist church, no one had a rapture doctrine and there never was a dispensationalist pastor (interview with Denison, February 13, 2006).

14. Christian Smith, e-mail, January 5, 2006.

15. Christian Smith, *Christian America? What Evangelicals Really Want* (2000; paperback, Berkeley: University of California Press, 2002), 9.

16. "Omar's" name and other identifying information have been changed.

17. Interviews with Omar, January 27 and February 6, 2006.

18. Eckstein was inspired to ally with conservative Christians by his experience with them during a threatened neo-Nazi march in Skokie, Illinois, in 1977. He founded the Holyland Fellowship of Christians and Jews in 1983, which became the International Fellowship of Christians and Jews in 1991. It is now Israel's second-largest charitable foundation, having raised $48 million from some 400,000 donors in 2005 and $72 million in 2006. Its On Wings of Eagles program is dedicated to facilitating aliyah, chiefly from the former Soviet Union but also from other venues, notably Ethiopia and India. Its Isaiah 58 program directs aid to elderly and poor Jews in the former Soviet Union. Its Guardians of Israel program aids needy Jews in Israel. It's Stand for Israel program, co-chaired by Eckstein and Ralph Reed, educates Christians about Israel and seeks to motivate their support for the Jewish state (Ministry Watch.com [www.ministrywatch.org/mw2.1F_SumRpt.asp?EIN=363256096]; International Fellowship of Christians and Jews 2006 Annual Report (http://www.ifcj.org/site/DocServer/2006-Fellowship-Annual-Report.pdf?docID=2561); interview with Eckstein, April 15, 2005; Zev Chafets, *A Match Made in Heaven: American Jews, Christian Zionists, and One Man's Exploration of the Weird and Wonderful Judeo-Evangelical Alliance* (New York: HarperCollins, 2007), 120; Mike Dorning, "Ad Pitch for Israel Aimed at Christians," *Chicago Tribune,* August 16, 2006).

19. Interview on condition of anonymity, December 29, 2005.

20. See Zev Chafets's "The Rabbi Who Loved Evangelicals (and Vice Versa)," *New York Times Magazine,* July 24, 2005, which was incorporated into Chafets's *A Match made in Heaven,* 117–34. Chafets's account is the best profile of Eckstein. See also Josef Federman, "Rabbis Express Unprecedented Criticism of American Evangelical Support for Israel," AP, in Information Clearing House, May 10, 2004. In 2006 and 2007, the IFCJ funded Israeli Arabs as well, providing assistance for their local councils (Yoav Stern and Yair Sheleg, "Private Charity Pledges Welfare Assistance to Arab Local Councils," *Haaretz,* August 10, 2007). In late 2007, Eckstein pledged $45 million to the Jewish Agency over the next three years and was made a voting member of the Agency's executive board and given a seat on the budget and finance committees. He said that this recognized evangelicals as full partners in the Zionist enterprise. The Anti-Defamation League's Abe Foxman called this arrangement disturbing (Anthony Weiss, "Jewish Agency Gives

Boardroom Clout to Ally of Evangelicals," *The Forward,* December 20, 2007; Joshua Mitnick, "Evangelicals' New Reach in Jewish Agency Criticized," *Jewish Week,* December 26, 2007).

21. "Orthodox Rabbi Meets with Evangelicals in Colorado Springs," AP, January 30, 2006.

22. Catholics and most Lutherans and Episcopalians consider anyone who has been baptized to be Christians, but evangelicals have always had a narrow understanding of the term, says historian of religion Mark Noll. For evangelicals, baptism is merely an initiation. In their view, a Christian is one whose heart is changed through trust in Christ. Noll says that seventy-five years ago, Baptists would question if a Catholic was Christian. Now they would question whether a supporter of abortion rights is (Dan Gilgoff, "What Is a 'Real' Christian?" *USA Today* blog, May 21, 2007 [http://blogs.usatoday.com/oped/2007/05/what_is_a_real_.html]).

23. Rausch, *Communities in Conflict: Evangelicals and Jews* (Philadelphia, Pa.: Trinity Press International, 1991), 66–67 passim. Falwell's wisecrack was reported by Edward E. Plowman, "Is Morality All Right," *Christianity Today,* 1979, cited by Lienesch, 232.

24. Fire is representative of the transforming power of the Holy Spirit, as in Acts 2:3. Blaise Pascal spoke of spiritual rebirth as fire.

25. Hal Lindsey with C.C. Carlson, *The Late Great Planet Earth* (Grand Rapids, Mich.: Zondervan, 1970), 154–57. The Dead Sea has been a major source of minerals for over eighty years but is not the only source of potash. Canada and China also extract it and the Russian federation is becoming a major producer (e-mail, Reuven Merhav, former director-general of the Israeli Foreign Ministry, May 23, 2007).

26. Pat Robertson, *New Millennium* (Dallas, Tex.: Word, 1990), 288.

27. 1 Corinthians 1:22. See also Matthew 12:38, 16:1, Mark 8:11, Luke 11:16, John 2:18.

28. Interview with Susan Michael, January 23, 2006.

29. David Brog, "Jews and Evangelicals Together," nationalreview.com, May 22, 2006, and *Standing with Israel: Why Christians Support the Jewish State,* (Lake Mary, Fla.: Frontline, 2006), 166–67, 170.

30. Robertson later objected that he had not meant that he personally was going to bring about Jesus' return (Cal Thomas and Ed Dobson, *Blinded by Might: Can the Religious Right Save America?* [Grand Rapids, Mich.: Zondervan, 1999], 55).

31. "Proclamation of the Third International Christian Zionist Congress" (http://christian actionforisrael.org/congress.html). Evangelicals, alarmed by Iranian President Ahmadinejad's anti-Israel statements, donated $1.4 million to Eckstein's International Fellowship of Christians and Jews to subsidize the aliyah from Iran. The group offered $5,000 to each Iranian Jew who agreed to go to Israel, then raised the amount to $10,000 when the response was low (Regan E. Doherty, "Christians Bring Iranian Jews to Israel," AP, October 22, 2007.

32. See Derek Prince, *Promised Land: God's Word and the Nation of Israel* (1978; reprint, Charlotte, N.C.: Derek Prince Ministries, 2003), 76.

33. Timothy P. Weber, *On the Road to Armageddon: How Evangelicals Became Israel's Best Friend* (Grand Rapids, Mich.: Baker Academic), 2004, 223–24.

34. Yaakov Ariel, *Philosemites or Antisemites? Evangelical Christian Attitudes toward Jews, Judaism, and the State of Israel* (Jerusalem: Hebrew University, Vidal Sassoon International Center for the Study of Antisemitism, Analysis of Current Trends in Antisemitism, 20 [2002]), 23.

35. John Hagee Ministries Web site, retrieved August 17, 2007 (http://www.jhm.org/exodus2.asp). This site informs potential donors that transportation costs from the former Soviet Union can be as low as $300 per person.

36. This passage from Isaiah was a central part of the message in the IFCJ's first infomercial. Narrated by Pat Boone, it appeared across America in 1993 and 1994, mostly on Christian stations, and raised millions of dollars (Chafets, "The Rabbi Who Loved Evangelicals").

37. Gershom Gorenberg, *End of Days: Fundamentalism and the Struggle for the Temple Mount* (2000; paperback, Oxford: Oxford University Press, 2000), 127; Bill Moyers, "Democracy in the Balance," *Sojourners Magazine,* 33 (August 2004).

38. "Many Americans Uneasy with Mix of Religion and Politics."

39. Interview with Ted Haggard, June 26, 2006.

40. Matthew 24:36–42, Mark 13:32.

41. A Pew poll, from 2003, found that 51 percent of blacks hold this view as well ("Religion, Belief, and Policy").

42. E-mail interview with David Parsons, August 13, 2007.

43. Thomas and Dobson, *Blinded by Might*, 55.

44. Louis Sahagun, "End Is Not Near Enough for Pastors," *Los Angeles Times*, February 8, 2006; "Global Pastors Network Draws 2,000 in Evangelism Focus," Baptist Press, in *Florida Baptist Witness*, February 23, 2006.

45. Lindsey, *The Late Great Planet Earth*, 50–51.

46. See, for example, Gush Emunim rabbi Eleazer Waldman's 1983 statement, "The Redemption is not only the Redemption of Israel, but the Redemption of the Whole World. . . . The blessing will come to all of humanity from the people of Israel living in the whole of its land" (cited in Ian Lustick's *For the Land and the Lord: Jewish Fundamentalism in Israel* [New York: Council on Foreign Relations, 1988]), 82–83). See also Armstrong, *Battle for God*, 286, 348).

47. Lawrence Wright, "Forcing the End," *The New Yorker*, July 20, 1998; Benny Morris, *Righteous Victims: A History of the Zionist-Arab Conflict, 1881–2001* (New York: Vintage Books, 1999), 584–85. Cf. Ehud Sprinzak, *The Ascendance of Israel's Radical Right* (New York: Oxford University Press, 1991), 287.

48. Gershom Gorenberg, "More Faithful Than Ever," *Jerusalem Report*, October 25, 1999; Suzanne Goldenberg, "Israelis Storm Muslim Holy Site," *The Guardian*, July 30, 2001.

49. Gorenberg, *End of Days*, 139, 171.

50. Ariel, *Philosemites or Antisemites?*, 37.

51. Gorenberg, *End of Days*, 171–72.

52. Ibid., 99–100; Michael B. Oren, *Six Days of War: June 1967 and the Making of the Modern Middle East* (New York: Ballantine Books, 2002), 243–46.

53. Gershom Gorenberg, *The Accidental Empire: Israel and the Birth of the Settlements, 1967–1977* (New York: Times Books, 2006).

54. Wright, "Forcing the End."

55. *Mishneh Torah*, Laws Concerning the Moshiach, chapter 11, number 4.

56. Wright, "Forcing the End"; Sprinzak, *The Ascendance of Israel's Radical Right*, 265.

57. The estimate was by Nadav Shragai, reporter for Haaretz and author of *The Temple Mount Conflict* (cited by Wright, "Forcing the End."

58. Lustick, *For the Land and the Lord*, 69–71. Gorenberg adds that one of the chief actors in the plot, Menachem Livni, became ill. By 1982, Israel had in any case completed its withdrawal from the Sinai, which the Gush terrorists had hoped to prevent (Gorenberg, *End of Days*, 134–35). Ariel notes that premillennial Christians in America were accused of sponsoring the Lifta Gang, another group that planned to bomb the mosques on the Temple Mount (*Philosemites or Antisemites?*, 38).

59. Wright, "Forcing the End"; Gorenberg, *End of Days*, 7–29.

60. Weber, *On the Road to Armageddon*, 262.

61. Wright, "Forcing the End." Don Stewart and Chuck Missler affirm that the Third Temple has been predicted and will be built, but they urge evangelicals to take no part in planning or funding such an effort. "This is not our cause," they say. The New Testament predicts that the Temple will be built in unbelief, say Stewart and Missler, and Christians who participated in constructing it would be tainted by that. The Temple has in any case been superseded by Jesus (Matthew 12:6), they note (*The Coming Temple: Center Stage for the Final Countdown* [Orange, Calif.: Dart Press, 1991], 189–90). Missler, the former chairman of Western Digital Corporation, does regard it as legitimate to discover the original site of the Temple, though. In 1983, he and Pastor Chuck Smith donated up to $100,000 to fund

an X-ray exploration of the Temple Mount by physicist Lambert Dolphin (Gorenberg, *End of Days*, 124–25).

62. Ibid.

63. Baxter's Web site claims that *Endtime* is the most widely read prophecy magazine in the world, with an active readership of over 110,000 (http://www.endtime.com/aboutus.asp).

64. The televangelist Perry Stone, a premillennial dispensationalist, anticipates the building of the Third Temple but does not believe a red heifer is necessary. Rather, in another illustration of the individuality and variety of evangelical belief, Stone reads the sacrifice of the heifer as the perfect foreshadowing of the Crucifixion. Since this has been fulfilled, he says, a red heifer's ashes are no longer needed (Perry Stone Ministries, Manna-Fest, 383).

65. Ariel, *Philosemites or Antisemites?*, 39.

66. Gorenberg, *End of Days*, 15.

67. Jeffrey Goldberg, "Israel's Y2K Problem," *New York Times Magazine*, October 3, 1999. Don Stewart and Chuck Missler, despite their fascination with locating the site of the Temple, agree that destroying the Muslim buildings on the Temple Mount would invite the destruction of Israel. They consider it unthinkable that any Israeli government would permit any such attack on the shrines (*The Coming Temple*, 172).

68. Zechariah 2:8.

69. Brog, "Jews and Evangelicals Together."

70. Interview with John C. Green, November 30, 2005; Meachem, "The Prodigal Returns," *Newsweek*, November 20, 2006; Bush, *A Charge to Keep: My Journey to the White House* (1999; paperback, New York: Perennial, 1999), 138.

71. Interviews with Richard Land, September 27 and 28, 2005.

72. C. S. Lewis, *Mere Christianity* (1943; reprint, Nashville, Tenn.: Touchstone, 1980), 6.

73. D. Michael Lindsay, *Faith in the Halls of Power: How Evangelicals Joined the American Elite* (Oxford: Oxford University Press, 2007), 25–26.

74. Jacob Weisberg, *The Bush Tragedy* (New York: Random House, 2008), 87.

75. Interview with Ted Haggard, June 26, 2006. David Aikman cites a White House observer who believes that Bush is the first mere Christian to serve as president (*A Man of Faith: The Spiritual Journey of George W. Bush* [Nashville, Tenn.: W Publishing, 2004], 198).

76. "The Jesus Factor." Interview Doug Wead. *Frontline*, PBS, November 18, 2003.

77. Interview with David Frum, September 30, 2005.

78. Guy Lawson, "George W.'s Personal Jesus," *GQ*, September 2003; Ron Hutcheson, "Bush's Attachment to Israel Started with Trip to Holy Land," *McClatchy Newspapers*, August 3, 2006.

79. Deanne Stillman, "Onward, Christian Soldiers," *The Nation*, June 3, 2002.

80. Edward Said, "Europe versus America," *Al-Ahram*, November 14–20, 2002.

81. See Chapter 8 above.

82. Robert Dreyfuss, "Reverend Doomsday," *Rolling Stone*, January 28, 2004.

83. Esther Kaplan, *With God on Their Side: How Christian Fundamentalists Trampled Science, Policy, and Democracy in George W. Bush's White House* (New York: New Press, 2004), 30. Paul S. Boyer points out that prophecy believers saw some Bush policies as being in perfect harmony with God's plan: hostility to multinational cooperation and agreements, acquiescence on the Israeli-Palestinian conflict, the growth of Israeli settlements in the occupied territories, and the focus on Iraq. Boyer notes that it was Saddam who launched a grandiose plan in the 1970s to rebuild Babylon. That, said author Charles Dyer, signaled the approaching end of time and offered proof of the infallibility of biblical prophecy (in Paul S. Boyer, "When U.S. Foreign Policy Meets Biblical Prophecy," *AlterNet*, July 21, 2005).

84. Interviews, August 17, 2005, and February 8, 2006, quoted on condition of anonymity. One Christian who did protest the disengagement from Gaza was Pastor Jim Vineyard, an Oklahoma City preacher who declared that Bush doesn't understand Scripture. To prove his

point, Vineyard cited Genesis 16.11–12, in which God says that Ishmael, the putative ancestor of the Arabs, "shall be a wild ass of a man, his hand against every man and every man's hand against him." The implication was that Arabs are too uncivilized to deserve the land. Rabbi Eric Yoffie, president of the Union for Reform Judaism, spoke for many Jews when he called such statements utterly unacceptable (James D. Besser, "Jewish Right Confronts Post-Gaza Era," *Jewish Week,* August 19, 2005).

85. "Robertson Predicts 'Mass Killing'; Hal Lindsey, "Desperate Search for 'Peace-loving' Palestinians."

86. Unger, "American 'Rapture.'"

87. Carter, *Our Endangered Values,* 113–15; Jennifer Siegel, "Carter Discusses New Book on Israel and the Middle East," *The Forward,* November 16, 2006.

88. Karen Armstrong, "Bush's Fondness for Fundamentalism Is Courting Disaster at Home and Abroad," *The Guardian,* July 31, 2006.

89. Michael Gerson, "Seeds of Anti-Semitism," *Washington Post,* September 21, 2007.

90. Lindsay, *Faith in the Halls of Power,* 51–52.

91. Interview with Don Poage, January 18, 2006.

92. Interview with Mark Leaverton, January 23, 2006.

93. Aikman, *A Man of Faith: The Spiritual Journey of George W. Bush* (Nashville, Tenn.: W Publishing, 2004), 126.

94. Interview with Richard Land, September 27, 2005. Stephen Mansfield reaches the same conclusion (*The Faith of George W. Bush* [New York: Jeremy P. Tarcher/Penguin, 2003], 160–61).

95. "President Bush addresses members of the Knesset," May 15, 2008 (http://www.whitehouse.gov/news/releases/2008/05/print/20080515-1.html).

96. The White House transcript of Bush's speech suggests that he either didn't know about Phillips's assertion or had never heard before about the application of biblical prophecy to the current events. The CNN transcript punctuates the sentence to denote the opposite: "First, I've heard of that, by the way" ("President Discusses War on Terror and Operation Iraqi Freedom, Renaissance Cleveland Hotel, Cleveland, Ohio," White House transcript, March 20, 2006 [(http://www.whitehouse.gov/news/releases/2006/03/20060320–7.html#]; Sidney Blumenthal, "Apocalyptic President," *Guardian,* March 23, 2006).

97. *Lou Dobbs Tonight,* CNN.com, March 20, 2006. According to John Green, white evangelical Christians make up a smaller percentage of Bush voters than Phillips said: 41 percent of all Republican identifiers in 2004 (e-mail interview, May 6, 2006). It is uncertain how many of them believe in the Antichrist.

98. Interview with Faith, December 2005.

99. Max Blumenthal, "Born-agains for Sharon," Salon.com, October 30, 2004. Eckstein would not divulge who went with him on that occasion, except to say that Gary Bauer was not invited. This may be the same meeting to which Faith referred.

100. Geraldine Hawkins, "Pat Robertson Speaks on Israel to Appreciative Audience at Framingham Temple," MassNews.com, April 16, 2003 (http://www.massnews.com/2003_Editions/10_October/4_April/041603_robertson_speaks_on_israel.shtml).

101. Press Briefing by Tony Snow, July 27, 2006 (www.whitehouse.gov/news/releases/2006/07/20060727–8.html). "Never have we had a war that is so specifically following the pattern of the scripture" said LaHaye of the Middle East conflict that was then under way (Brian Braiker, "Are These the End Times?" *Newsweek,* MSNBC.com, July 28, 2006).

CHAPTER 10

1. Interview with Thomas Pickering, January 17, 2006.

2. Ron Hutcheson, "Bush's Attachment to Israel Started with Trip to the Holy Land," *McClatchy Newspapers,* August 3, 2006.

3. Michael Lindsey argues that mass telephone campaigns and similar political pressure tactics are characteristic of "populist" evangelicalism and are an important aspect of the activism of an older generation. More sophisticated "cosmopolitan" evangelicals, by contrast, seek to influence the culture in the long term (*Faith in the Halls of Power: How Evangelicals Joined the American Elite* [Oxford and New York: Oxford University Press, 2007]; "Evangelicals in the Public Square," Pew Forum on Religion and Public Life, October 11, 2007).

4. Interview with Chas. W. Freeman, December 12, 2005.

5. David Frum, *The Right Man: An Inside Account of the Bush White House* (New York: Random House, 2003), 254–55.

6. Bob Woodward, *State of Denial: Bush at War, Part III* (New York: Simon and Schuster, 2006), 75–76.

7. James Bennett, "Far-Right Leader Is Slain in Israel; A Blow to Peace," *New York Times,* October 18, 2001.

8. Uri Dan, "Israel Warns: 'Do Not Appease the Arabs at Our Expense,'" *New York Post,* October 5, 2001; Alan Sipress and Lee Hockstader, "Sharon Speech Riles U.S.," *Washington Post,* October 6, 2001; Lee Hockstader, "Sharon Apologetic over Row with U.S.," *Washington Post,* October 7, 2001.

9. Ze'evi's call for transfer legitimized the position of Meir Kahane, whose Kach party campaigned for the expulsion of Arabs from Israel and the occupied territories.

10. "MP's Anti-Arab Slur Sparks Furor in Knesset," Reuters, October 25, 1989.

11. "About 100 Arabs Wounded in Occupied Territory Violence," UPI, November 4, 1990.

12. "The Extreme Right Quits the Government," *Mideast Mirror,* October 15, 2001; Greg Myre, "Israel's Tourism Minister Killed by Palestinians," AP, October 17, 2001; Laurie Copans, "Israel's Tourism Minister Killed in Shooting Clamed by Palestinian Militants," AP, October 17, 2001; Jack Katzenell, "Slain Cabinet Minister Was One of the Most Controversial Figures in Israeli Politics," AP, October 17, 2001; Jacques Pinto, "Zeevi Assassination Dents Shin Beth's Reputation Anew," *Agence France Presse,* October 17, 2001; "PFLP Claims Revenge Killing of Israeli Minister," *Agence France Presse,* October 17, 2001; Montasser Abdallah, "Palestinians at Lebanese Refugee Camps Celebrate Zeevi," *Agence France Presse,* October 17, 2001; "Israel Reaps What It Sows: Hamas," *Agence France Presse,* October 17, 2001; Martin Sieff, "Ugly Man, but Major Stature," UPI, October 18, 2001; "Rehavam Zeevi," *The Times,* October 18, 2001; Ian Fisher, "Uncompromising as Enemy, often Agreeable as Friend," *New York Times,* October 18, 2001; Suzanne Goldenberg, "Profile: Far-right Leader Who Fell Victim to His Own Ideas," *The Guardian,* October 18, 2001; Jonathan Rosenblum, "Rehavam Zeevi Was the Last of a Generation," *Jerusalem Post,* October 26, 2001; "Rehavam Ze'evi: A Controversial Figure," CNN, April 28, 2002 (http://archives.cnn.com/2001/WORLD/meast/10/17/israel.zeevi.profile/index.html?related); Yitzhak Laor, "Loving the Land—but Without Arabs," *Haaretz,* March 16, 2005; "PA Arrests PFLP Spokesman," UPI, October 17, 2001; Bronwen Maddox, "Conflicts that Could Widen the War," *The Times,* October 18, 2001; James Bennett, "Israeli's Slaying Ignites Clashes and New Fears," *New York Times,* October 19, 2001.

13. See http://www.davidhocking.org.

14. Jack Katzenell, "Israel's Tourism Minister Shot and Wounded," AP, October 17, 2001; Tovah Lazaroff, "U.S. Preacher Recalls Ze'evi's Murder," *Jerusalem Post,* October 8, 2002.

15. 5W Public Relations Web site (http://www.5wpr.com/clients.cfm). Torossian no longer represents the Christian Coalition, though he says that he still provides consultation ("The Bad Boy of Buzz and His PR Problem," *Business Week,* November 12, 2007).

16. Interview with Ronn Torossian, January 17, 2005.

17. "Israel Wooing Christian Visitors," AP, June 17, 2003.

18. Haaretz Service, "Tourism Minister: If They Lose War, Arabs Will Be Expelled," *Haaretz,* December 18, 2001; Matthew Gutman, "Hillary's Visit Is 'Transfer' Pol's Latest Coup," *The Forward,* March 1, 2002; Benny Elon, "Principle Positions: Solve the Palestinian Refugee Problem," JPost.com, June 25, 2007; "We Must Combine Activism with Faith," *Jerusalem Post Christian Edition,* July 2007.

19. Clare Tristram, "Benny Elon's Long, Strange Trip," Salon.com, May 14, 2004.

20. Howard Fineman and Tamara Lipper, "A Very Mixed Marriage," *Newsweek,* June 2, 2003.

21. Pat Robertson: "'Road Map' Is Beginning of End for Israel," May 29, 2003 (http://www.cbn.com/CBNNews/News/030529e.aspx).

22. Binyamin Elon, "The Right Road to Peace," *Front Page,* June 9, 2003; Yaakov Katz, "Elon Urges Christians to Convert Muslims," *Jerusalem Post,* February 9, 2004. In 2004 Elon published "God's Covenant with Israel," a brochure that spelled out the biblical justification for Israel to hold onto its "heartland" and reiterated the "Elon Peace Plan." The text was clearly written for an evangelical audience. Elon presented it at the National Religious Broadcasters convention in Anaheim, California, in 2005.

23. Anthony Stroe, "Interview with Israeli MK Benny Elon," August 17, 2005 (www.globalpolitical.com/articles.asp?ID=1098&print=true); "Egypt, Israel Sign Gaza Border Deal," *ISN Security Watch,* September 2, 2005 (http://www.dawn.com.pk/2005/09/02/top10.htm).

24. Nathan Guttman, "Getting Tight with the Bible Belt," *Haaretz,* February 15, 2005.

25. Victoria Clark says that a Christian Zionist delegation confronted Tim Goeglien, Bush's liaison with evangelicals, in the White House in July 2001. The "posse of Israel's defenders" reportedly threatened to engineer an evangelical revolt against Bush unless he supported Sharon's actions in the territories 100 percent (*Allies for Armageddon: The Rise of Christian Zionism* [New Haven, Conn.: Yale University Press, 2007], 217). Clark's source is an article published on a conspiracy-oriented Larouche Web site. If the White House confrontation did happen as reported, the Bush administration was hardly 100 percent supportive of Sharon that summer and fall, as Clark correctly notes. Nor was there an evangelical revolt against him.

26. James Bennett, "Israeli's Slaying Ignites Clashes and New Fears," *New York Times,* October 19, 2001; Steven Mufson, "U.S. Calls for Israeli Withdrawal," *Washington Post,* October 23, 2001; Steve Huntley, "Israel Doves on Brink of Extinction," *Chicago Sun-Times,* October 23, 2001; Aluf Benn, "Sharon's Fatal Trip," *The Guardian,* October 25, 2001; Daniel Williams, "Israel Says Troops Will Leave if Palestinians Meet Demands," *Washington Post,* October 26, 2001; Uzi Mahnaimi, "Israel Calls Halt to Troop Pull-out," *Sunday Times,* October 28, 2001; Larry Derfner, "A Fearsome Reply to an Assassin," *U.S. News & World Report,* November 5, 2001.

27. Joel Brinkley, "Bomb Kills at Least 19 in Israel as Arabs Meet over Peace Plan," *New York Times,* March 27, 2002; Dan Ephron, "Passover Bomber Kills at least 19 Israelis," *Washington Times,* March 28, 2002; "After Blast, Israel Weighs Its Options," *Washington Post,* March 28, 2002; Lee Hockstader, "Blast Devastates Passover Feast at Israeli Hotel," *Washington Post,* March 29, 2002; Uri Dan, "Inside the Passover Massacre" *New York Post,* March 29, 2002; "Passover Suicide Bombing at Park Hotel in Netanya" (www.mfa.gov.il/MFA/MFAArchive/2000_2009/2002/3/Passover%20suicide%20bo).

28. Todd S. Purdum with David E. Sanger, "Bush Is Said to Expect Israel to Pull Out 'without Delay,'" *New York Times,* April 5, 2002; Andrew Miga, "Bush: 'Enough Is Enough,'" *Boston Herald,* April 5, 2002; David E. Sanger, "As Fighting Rages, Bush Demands Israeli Withdrawal," *New York Times,* April 6, 2002; Serge Schmemann, "Drive Seen Continuing Till Powell Visit," *New York Times,* April 6, 2002; Serge Schmemann, "Fighting Is Fierce," *New York Times,* April 7, 2002; Michele Chabin, "Taking the Pulse on Israel's Military Incursion into Palestinian Areas: Israeli Public Opinion," Jewish Agency for Israel, April 14, 2002 (www.jafi.org.il/education.hasbara/headlines/nb2.html,); Ewen MacAskill, "Israel Promises to Quit Towns by Sunday,"

The Guardian, April 19, 2002; "U.N. Envoy Says Israel 'Lost All Moral Ground' after Jenin," AP, April 19, 2002; James Bennett, "Israel Pulls Back in Two Cities, Saying Offensive Is Over," *New York Times*, April 21, 2002; James Bennett and David Rohde, "In Rubble of a Refugee Camp, Bitter Lessons for 2 Enemies," *New York Times*, April 21, 2002.

29. Serge Schmemann, "Dancing at Arm's Length," *New York Times*, April 8, 2002; David E. Sanger, "An Unhappy Quarterback: Balky Players Are Defying the Bush Game Plan," *New York Times*, April 7, 2002.

30. Frum, *The Right Man*, 260. By 2006, 72 percent of Republicans said that they sympathized more with Israel, as did 47 percent of Democrats and 49 percent of Independents. Seventeen percent of Republicans, 32 percent of Democrats, and 34 percent of independents sympathized more with the Palestinians (Frank Newport and Joseph Carroll, "Republicans and Religious Americans Most Sympathetic to Israel," Gallup News Service, March 27, 2006).

31. Fifty percent said that the Israeli military actions were mostly justified and 66 percent thought that the Palestinian actions were mostly unjustified (Gallup poll, April 5–7, 2002 (http://brain.gallup.com/search/results.aspx?SearchTypeAll=israel&SearchConType=1).

32. Ronald Brownstein, "Drop Peace Effort, Right Urges Bush," *Los Angeles Times*, April 3, 2002.

33. "Let Bush Be Bush," *Wall Street Journal*, April 17, 2002. Charles Schumer, a liberal Democratic senator from New York, said this U.S. approach was muddled, confused, and inconsistent ("Schumer Criticizes Bush on Mideast," *New York Times*, April 10, 2002).

34. Ronald Brownstein, "The Middle East: Hawks Dominate Debate on U.S. Policy in Region," *Los Angeles Times*, April 18, 2002.

35. Carolyn Skorneck, "DeLay: U.S. Must Support Israel, Which Is under Threat that Endangers Civilized World," AP, April 3, 2002; Tom Hamburger and Jim VandeHei, "Chosen People: How Israel Became a Favorite Cause of Christian Right," *Wall Street Journal*, May 23, 2002; Ken Silverstein and Michael Scherer, "Born-again Zionists," *Mother Jones*, 27: September/October 2002, 56–62; "DeLay Rallies Support on Hill," *New York Sun*, May 3, 2002; Michael Duffy and Romesh Ratnesar, "Trapped by His Own Instincts," *Time*, May 6, 2002; Toby Harnden, "Israel Wins Support on Christian Right," *Daily Telegraph*, May 8, 2002.

36. Rod Dreher, "Evangelicals and Jews Together," National Review Online, April 5, 2002.

37. Ilan Chaim, "US Christians Start Massive Prayer Campaign for Israel," *Jerusalem Post*, April 12, 2002.

38. Howard Fineman, and Tamara Lipper. "A Very Mixed Marriage." *Newsweek*, June 2, 2003.

39. The medievalist in me compels me to point out that this dynamic does not appear in *Everyman*, but personifications of temptation and redemption do influence Everyman-like figures in other morality plays.

40. Jerry Falwell, "America's 'Dangerous' Message to Israel," *WorldNetDaily*, April 13, 2002.

41. Duffy and Ratnesar, "Trapped by His Own Instincts"; interview with Gary Bauer, October 14, 2005.

42. Benjamin Netanyahu, "Address to the U.S. Senate," April 10, 2002 (http://www.amer icanrhetoric.com/speeches/netanyahu4–10–02.htm); Ron Dermer, "Israel Could Just Say No," *Jerusalem Post*, June 5, 2003.

43. Marshall Wittmann, formerly a lobbyist with the Christian Coalition, for example, was one of those who made a claim of frequent contact between Christian Zionists and the administration (Silverstein and Scherer, "Born-again Zionists"). See also Duffy and Ratnesar, "Trapped by His Own Instincts," and Fineman and Lipper, "A Very Mixed Marriage."

44. Teresa Watanabe, "Christians Split over Conflict in the Mideast," *Los Angeles Times*, May 5, 2002. This striking motto, which has been voiced by several evangelical leaders, appears

to be an adaptation of the title of a 1987 article by Rabbi Joshua O. Haberman: "The Bible Belt Is America's Safety Belt: Why the Holocaust Couldn't Happen Here," *Policy Review*, 47 (1987) 40–44).

45. Duffy and Ratnesar, "Trapped by His Own Instincts"; "Evangelical Christians and Zionism: Ralph Reed," an interview with Reed in *USA Today*, May 23, 2002; Elisabeth Bumiller, "Seeking to Stem Growing Political Fury, Bush Sends Conservative to Pro-Israel Rally," *New York Times*, April 15, 2002.

46. Yigal Schleifer, "Newfound Friends," *Jerusalem Report*, July 1, 2002.

47. Duffy and Ratnesar, "Trapped by His Own Instincts."

48. Falwell, "America's 'Dangerous' Message to Israel."

49. Janine Zacharia, "Washington Whispers," *Jerusalem Post*, April 19, 2002.

50. References to speeches at the rally are from the National Christian Leadership Conference for Israel Web site (www.nclc.or/washrally.htm). Formerly known as Christians Concerned for Israel, the NCLCI broadened from being a dispensationalist organization to including pro-Israel Catholics and mainline Protestants. Timothy P. Weber says that it organized the 2002 Washington rally (*On the Road to Armageddon: How Evangelicals Became Israel's Best Friend* [Grand Rapids, Mich.: Baker Academic, 2004], 222). The event was sponsored by the Conference of Presidents of Major Jewish Organizations and the United Jewish Communities.

51. Interview with Paul Wolfowitz in James Mann, *Rise of the Vulcans: The History of Bush's War Cabinet* (New York: Penguin, 2004), 325,

52. Ibid; Johann Hari, "In Enemy Territory? An Interview with Christopher Hitchens," September 23, 2004 (http://www.johannhari.com/archive/article.php?id=450).

53. Bumiller, "Seeking to Stem Growing Political Fury, Bush Sends Conservative to Pro-Israel Rally."

54. Yigal Schleifer, "Newfound Friends."

55. Interview with Gary Bauer, October 14, 2005.

56. Duffy and Ratnesar, "Trapped by His Own Instincts."

57. Herb Keinon, "U.S. Christian Leader Bauer: Israel a Priority for Evangelicals," *Jerusalem Post*, July 2, 2002; interview with Gary Bauer, October 14, 2005. Victoria Clark says that Bush abandoned his demand that Sharon withdraw his tanks because Falwell had bombarded the White House with 100,000 e-mails (*Allies for Armageddon*, 217).

58. Todd S. Purdum, "Because It's Necessary," *New York Times*, April 11, 2002.

59. David E. Sanger, "A Late Entry Quickly Hits Mideast Wall," *New York Times*, April 12, 2002; Patrick E. Tyler, "A Rising Toll for Bush: No Peace, More Blame," *New York Times*, April 17, 2002.

60. Peter Slevin and Mike Allen, "Bush: Sharon a 'Man of Peace,'" *Washington Post*, April 19, 2002; Israel 'Responded' to Call for Pullout," *Washington Post*, April 19, 2002. In late April, the Palestinian Authority said that a "military field court" had convicted four of Ze'evi's killers. Israel dismissed the trial, which was hastily conducted by security guards with no training in law. In 2006, when international monitors left the prison in Jericho where the man who shot Ze'evi had been held, Israel took him into custody. In 2007, he was sentenced to two life terms plus 100 years (Serge Schmemann, "Arafat Court Said to Convict 4 Israel Seeks," *New York Times*, April 26, 2002; Colin Nickerson and Globe staff, "Palestinians Convict 4 in Israeli Death; Secret Proceeding Dismissed as Sham," *Boston Globe*, April 26, 2002; Ofra Edelman, "Ze'evi Killer Jailed for Two Life Terms Plus 100 years," *Haaretz*, December 3, 2007).

61. Robin Wright, "Arab Leaders Lean on Bush to Bring about a Withdrawal," *Los Angeles Times*, April 19, 2002; David E. Sanger, "President Praises Effort by Powell in the Middle East," *New York Times*, April 18, 2002.

62. Frum, *The Right Man*, 281.

63. Sanger, "President Praises Effort by Powell in The Middle East"; Thomas M. De-Frank, "Time to Quit, Israel Told Bush Ultimatum after Troops Return to West Bank Town," *New York Daily News*, April 27, 2002; Alan Sipress, "Policy Divide Thwarts Powell in Mideast Effort," *Washington Post*, April 26, 2002; Duffy and Ratnesar, "Trapped by His Own Instincts."

64. Glenn Kessler and Michael Abramowitz, "Eyes Will Be on Bush at Talks on Mideast," *Washington Post*, November 24, 2007.

65. Duffy and Ratnesar, "Trapped by His Own Instincts."

66. It is unclear whether Caldwell was suggesting that Bush shared this belief with Falwell, Robertson, Ralph Reed, the LaHayes, et al. (Deborah Caldwell, "The Rapture Factor: Why Conservative Christians' Love of Israel Is Intertwined with the Battle of Armageddon," *Beliefnet*, May 30, 2002).

67. Fineman and Lipper, "A Very Mixed Marriage"; "Zion's Christian Soldiers," *60 Minutes*, October 6, 2002 (http://www.cbsnews.com/stories/2002/10/03/60minutes/main524268.shtml); Brog, *Standing with Israel*, 145.

68. Interview with Gary Bauer, October 14, 2005.

69. Patrick E. Tyler, "Saudi to Warn Bush of Rupture over Israel Policy," *New York Times*, April 24, 2002; "Today's Meeting between President George Bush and Saudi Crown Prince Abdullah," *All Things Considered*, NPR, April 24, 2002.

70. Ron Suskind, *The One Percent Doctrine: Deep Inside America's Pursuit of Its Enemies Since 9/11* (New York: Simon and Schuster, 2006), 110–11.

71. DeFrank, "Time to Quit"; Andrew Metz, "Arafat Deal Struck," *Newsday*, April 29, 2002; James Bennett, "Israel Lifts Siege as Arafat Yields Six Wanted Men," *New York Times*, May 2, 2002.

72. Alan Sipress, "Attack Highlights U.S. Effort's Vulnerabilities," *Washington Post*, May 8, 2002.

73. Avram Goldstein, "Christian Coalition Rallies for Israel in Comeback Bid," *Washington Post*, October 12, 2002.

74. Ronn Torossian, "The Christian Coalition and the Jewish Community," *Gamla*, October 20, 2002 (www.gamla.org.il/english/article/2002/oct/t1.htm).

75. Interview with Torossian, January 17, 2005.

76. That may have been borne out a year later when Gary Bauer organized a second e-mail blitz. In June 2003, a White House spokesman said that the president was deeply troubled by Israel's attempt to assassinate Hamas leader and co-founder Abdel Aziz Rantisi. Bush, who had launched his peace plan at Aqaba less than a week earlier, was said to be disturbed by the loss of innocent life and the danger that the attack would derail the peace process. Bauer said that he and other evangelical leaders took this up with the president and urged others to write to the White House. "I got thousands of emails the next day that were copies of emails sent to the president," said Bauer. Within twenty-four hours, he noted, the president changed his position, emphasizing Israel's right to defend itself. Then, in April 2004, when Israel did kill Rantisi, the White House was supportive. Bush's posture in 2004 may well have reflected the circumstances at the time: Sharon had informed him one week earlier at the White House of his plan to disengage from Gaza, and the Israelis wanted to inflict punishment on Hamas so the Islamist group would be less likely to claim the withdrawal as a victory. In addition, it was a presidential election year. John Kerry, the Democratic frontrunner, was even more publicly sympathetic to the Israeli action than Bush was (Jane Lampman, "Mixing Prophecy and Politics," *Christian Science Monitor*, July 7, 2004; Laura King and Fayed abu Shammalah, "Israel Kills New Leader of Hamas," *Los Angeles Times*, April 18, 2004; Glen Johnson, "Kerry Attacks and Defends," *Boston Globe*, April 19, 2004).

CHAPTER 11

1. "Evangelical Christians and Zionism: Ralph Reed," *USA Today*, May 23, 2002.

2. "Evangelical Reflections on the U.S. Role in the World," Carnegie Council on Ethics and International Affairs, New York, September 15, 2005. Cizik declined numerous requests to comment on this.

3. Interview with Richard Land, September 27, 2005.

4. David Kuo, *Tempting Faith: An Inside Story of Political Seduction* (New York: Free Press, 2006), 229–30. D. Michael Lindsey says that based on his interviews and observations in the Bush White House, he thinks that such name-calling did happen, though not to the extent that Kuo indicates (*Faith in the Halls of Power: How Evangelicals Joined the American Elite* (New York: Oxford University Press, 2007), 262 n33). But John DiIulio, the first head of Bush's faith-based initiative office, made statements in 2002 that were entirely consistent with Kuo's assertion four years later that Bush administration officials courted but merely tolerated the Christian right. DiIulio had conflicts with evangelicals when he served at the White House. Rove asked him to bury the hatchet with them and DiIulio replied, "I'm not taking any shit off Jerry Falwell. The souls of my dead Italian grandparents are crying out to me, 'That guy's not on the side of the angels.'" Rove's response and DiIulio's subsequent answer confirm Kuo's point: "Look," said Rove, "those guys don't really matter to this president." "Sure, Karl," DiIulio answered, "they don't matter, but they're in here all the time" (Ron Suskind, "Why Are These Men Laughing?" *Esquire*, January 1, 2003). In the face of criticism, DiIulio subsequently made the oblique statement that one unspecified conversation with Rove in the *Esquire* article "did not occur as such" (Scott Lindlaw, "Politics Rules the White House, Former Aide Says," AP, December 2, 2002).

5. Interview with David Frum, September 30, 2005.

6. Bob Woodward, *State of Denial: Bush at War, Part III* (New York: Simon and Schuster, 2006), 4, 6–16.

7. Interview with Frum, September 30, 2005.

8. "Secretary Condoleezza Rice, Remarks at the 88th Annual American Legion Convention," August 29, 2006 (www.state.gov/secretary/rm/2006/71636.htm).

9. Interview with Frum, September 30, 2005.

10. Ron Suskind, *The One Percent Doctrine: Deep Inside America's Pursuit of Its Enemies since 9/11* (New York: Simon and Schuster, 2006), 104–5, 233; Lewis H. Lapham, "The Case for Impeachment," *Harper's* Magazine, February 27, 2006.

11. Sheryl Gay Stolberg, "Bush's Embrace of Israel Shows Gap with Father," *New York Times*, August 2, 2006.

12. E-mail interview with Frum, August 2, 2006.

13. Speech by Condoleezza Rice, "Secretary Rice Speaks at Saban Forum Dinner," US Fed News Service, November 4, 2007.

14. Elisabeth Bumiller, "Bush's Book Club Picks a New Favorite," *New York Times*, January 31, 2005.

15. Efraim Halevy, *Man in the Shadows: Inside the Middle East Crisis with a Man Who Led the Mossad* (New York: St. Martin's, 2006), 206–14.

16. Nahum Barnea, "A New Member in Likud," *Yediot Aharonot*, June 25, 2002.

17. Efraim Halevy, *Man in the Shadows: Inside the Middle East Crisis with a Man Who Led the Mossad* (New York: St. Martin's, 2006), 234–35.

18. Glenn Kessler and Michael Abramowitz, "Eyes Will Be on Bush at Talks on Mideast," *Washington Post*, November 24, 2007.

19. Elisabeth Bumiller, "Behind Rice's Shift on Leading Mideast Peace Efforts," *New York Times*, November 26, 2007.

20. Howard Fineman and Tamara Lipper, "A Very Mixed Marriage," *Newsweek*, June 2, 2003.

21. Ariel Sharon, with David Chanoff, *Warrior: An Autobiography of Ariel Sharon* (New York: Simon and Schuster, 1989), 356; speech by Bush at American Israel Public Affairs Committee Conference, May 22, 2000 (http://www.jewishvirtuallibrary.org/jsource/US-Israel/Bush.html).

22. David Aikman, *A Man of Faith: The Spiritual Journey of George W. Bush* (Nashville, Tenn.: W Publishing, 2004), 122–24.

23. "Secretary Rice Speaks at Saban Forum Dinner."

24. Dennis Ross, *The Missing Peace: The Inside Story of the Fight for Middle East Peace* (2004; paperback, New York: Farrar, Straus and Giroux, 2005), 785; David Frum, *The Right Man: An Inside Account of the Bush White House* (New York: Random House, 2003), 256.

25. Daniel Dombey, "Scowcroft Lambasts Bush's Unilateralism," *Financial Times,* October 14, 2004.

26. Interview with Chas. W. Freeman, December 12, 2005.

27. Interview with Lawrence Wilkerson, December 2, 2005.

28. Aluf Benn, "The Silent Partner," *Haaretz,* December 30, 2006.

29. Nahum Barnea, "Painful Awareness Drives Sharon Move," *Ynet,* January 17, 2005; interview with Pickering, January 17, 2006; interview with Malcolm Hoenlein, February 27, 2006.

30. Ron Hutcheson, "Bush's Attachment to Israel Started with Trip to the Holy Land," *McClatchy Newspapers,* August 3, 2006; "Barbara Walters Interviews President and Mrs. Bush, December 6th, 2001," Wisconsin Republican Party (http://wisgop.org/site/Viewer.aspx?iid=31 89&mname=Article&rpid=1183).

31. Bill Clinton, *My Life* (New York: Knopf, 2004), 938.

32. Ross, *The Missing Peace,* 784, 786.

33. Interview with Frum, September 30, 2005.

34. Interview with Hoenlein, February 27, 2007.

35. "U.S. cautious on Middle East Peace Hopes after Pullout," *Haaretz,* August 14, 2005; Ori Nor, "U.S. To Broker Formula on Hamas Role in Palestinian Elections," *The Forward,* September 20, 2005.

36. Interview with Chas. W. Freeman, December 12, 2005.

37. In January 2004, Bush told a group of American conservative thinkers that removing Saddam would decrease the exportation of terror from Iraq, lending a stability to Israel that would make it easier to achieve peace with the Palestinians (Robert Draper, *Dead Certain: The Presidency of George W. Bush* [New York: Free Press, 2007], 189).

38. James Mann, *Rise of the Vulcans: The History of Bush's War Cabinet* (New York: Penguin, 2004), 322–23.

39. Interview with Frum, September 30, 2005.

40. Interview with Pickering, January 17, 2006.

41. Interview with Freeman, December 12, 2005.

42. J. J. Goldberg, *Jewish Power: Inside the American Jewish Establishment* (Reading, Mass.: Addison-Wesley, 1996), xxi, 276–77.

43. Thomas B. Edsall, "Post-9/11 Drive by Republicans to Attract Jewish Voters Stalls," *Washington Post,* March 6, 2006. Jewish donations, reported by the nonpartisan Center for Responsive Politics, were on track to be the highest percentage given to Republicans since the Center began to track such giving in 1990 (Jim VandeHei, "Congress Is Giving Israel Vote of Confidence," *Washington Post,* July 19, 2006; e-mail correspondence with VandeHei, July 28, 2006).

44. James Kitfield, "The Ties that Bind, and Constrain," *National Journal,* April 20, 2002; Council on Foreign Relations Meeting Subject: Peace versus Democracy in Palestine, with Former U.S. President Jimmy Carter, Federal News Service, March 2, 2006. Carter extended his criticism of Israel and its American supporters in *Palestine: Peace Not Apartheid* (New York: Simon and Schuster, 2006).

45. John Mearsheimer and Stephen Walt, "The Israel Lobby," a summary of their findings in *London Review of Books,* March 23, 2006. In 2007, Mearsheimer and Walt published a book-length version of this argument: *The Israel Lobby and U.S. Foreign Policy* (New York: Farrar, Straus and Giroux, 2007).

46. Michael B. Oren, "Tinfoil Hats in Harvard Yard," *The New Republic* Online, March 31, 2006.

47. Benny Morris, "And Now for Some Facts," *The New Republic,* April 28, 2006.

48. Alan Finder, "Essay Stirs Debate about Influence of a Jewish Lobby," *New York Times,* April 12, 2006.

49. Martin Peretz, "Surveying the Israel Lobby," *The New Republic,* March 30, 2006.

50. Alan Dershowitz, "Debunking the Newest—and Oldest—Jewish Conspiracy: A Reply to the Mearsheimer-Walt 'Working Paper,'" paper, Harvard Law School, April 2006.

51. David Gergen, "An Unfair Attack," *U.S. News & World Report,* April 3, 2005.

52. Frum, e-mail interview, March 17, 2006.

53. David Remnick, "The Lobby," *New Yorker,* September 3, 2007.

54. George P. Shultz, "The 'Israel Lobby' Myth," *U.S. News and World Report,* September 9, 2007.

55. Michael Gerson, "Seeds of Anti-Semitism," *Washington Post,* September 21, 2007.

56. Joseph Massad, "Blaming the Lobby," *Al-Ahram Weekly,* March 23–29, 2006.

57. Goldberg, *Jewish Power,* xvii–xxvi.

58. Akiva Eldar, "America's Man in the Middle East," *Haaretz,* December 16, 2005.

59. "Hamas Says New Government Won't Recognize Israel," Bridges for Peace, *Israel Current News Update and Prayer Focus,* November 17, 2006.

60. Stan Goodenough, "Bush: Israel's Survival Depends on Two-state Solution," *Jerusalem Newswire,* October 31, 2006.

61. Gary Bauer, "President Pushes Palestinian State," *American Values,* July 17, 2007, and "The Annapolis Decision," *American Values,* November 26, 2007.

62. Parsons refuted some Christians' claims that this was dispensationalism's "false peace" of the Antichrist. That would occur only after the Temple is rebuilt, he said (David Parsons, "More Birth Pangs Ahead," *Jerusalem Post Christian Edition,* November 2007).

63. "Olmert Says [He] Believes in Diplomatic Initiatives," Bridges for Peace, *Israel Current News Update and Prayer Focus,* August 17, 2007.

64. "Urgent Action Alert," *Today's News Summaries,* Unity Coalition for Israel, November 14, 2007.

65. Joseph Farah, "Annapolis Insanity," *World Net Daily,* November 13, 2007, reprinted by the Unity Coalition for Israel (http://www.israelunitycoalition.org/news/article.php?id=2040).

66. Edgar Lefkovits, "Evangelicals Blast Any J'lem Division," *Jerusalem Post,* November 28, 2007.

67. Carolyn Jacobson, "The Spirit of Antichrist," Christian Friends of Israel, *Watchmen's Prayer Letter,* November 26, 2007.

68. Gary Bauer, CUFI's David Brog, the Southern Baptist Convention's Barrett Duke joined with Orthodox Jewish leaders in the meeting (Hana Levi Julian, "Olmert to World Jewry: Israel Makes Sole Decision on Jerusalem," *Arutz Sheva,* November 28, 2007.

69. Khaled Abu Toameh, "Fatah's Collapse in Gaza Rocks Its W. Bank Status," *Jerusalem Post,* June 15, 2007.

70. Fouad Ajami, "Brothers to the Bitter End," *New York Times,* June 19, 2007.

71. "Israeli Intelligence: Abbas Is Too Weak," *Jerusalem Post,* November 8, 2007.

72. Barak Ravid, "Olmert Seeks Agreement with PA on Core Issues during Bush Administration," *Haaretz,* November 2, 2007; Steven Erlanger, "U.S. Pushes for Turnout at Middle East Conference," *New York Times,* November 19, 2007.

73. Kessler and Abramowitz, "Eyes Will Be on Bush at Talks on Mideast"; Steven Lee Myers, "Seeking a Mideast Path, Bush Offers a Nudge," *New York Times,* November 26, 2007.

74. "Letter from President Bush to Prime Minister Sharon," April 14, 2004 (http://www.whitehouse.gov/news/releases/2004/04/20040414–3.html).

75. "President Bush Discusses the Middle East," July 16, 2007 (http://www.whitehouse.gov/news/releases/2007/07/20070716–7.html).

76. Hilary Leila Krieger, "Bush: US to Be 'Actively Engaged,' " *Jerusalem Post,* November 28, 2007.

77. "Poll Shows Peace Pessimism," AP, December 25, 2007. The poll was conducted by Hebrew University's Truman Center and the Palestinian Center for Policy and Survey Research.

78. Yossi Verter, "Poll: Most Israeli Public Believes Annapolis Summit Was a Failure," *Haaretz,* November 29, 2007; Roee Mandel, "Israeli Arabs: Abbas Lacks Mandate to Make Concessions," *Ynet,* November 28, 2007; Ephraim Yaar and Tamar Hermann, "Just Another Forgotten Peace Summit," *Haaretz,* December 11, 2007.

79. "Secretary Rice Speaks at Saban Forum Dinner." In this speech, Rice referred five times to "violent extremism" and once to "unbridled extremism" as the danger. She pointedly did not speak of "Islamic" extremism.

80. Aluf Benn, David Landau, Barak Ravid, Shmuel Rosner , "Olmert: Two-state Solution, or Israel Is Finished," *Haaretz,* November 29, 2007. The Unity Coalition for Israel called on its readers to endorse a declaration that Olmert's statement was outrageous ("Urgent Action Alert: Many in U.S. Oppose Israeli Surrender," UCI, Today's News Summaries, December 5, 2007).

81. David Neff, "Evangelical Leaders Reiterate Call for Two-State Solution for Israel and Palestine," *Christianity Today,* November 29, 2007. The signatories included several who had signed letters to Bush in 2002 and July 2007 urging him to pursue an even-handed policy in the conflict and a two-state solution: Gary Burge, Tony Campolo, Joel Hunter, Richard Mouw, David Neff, Ron Sider, and Don Wagner; Jim Wallis joined them this time.

82. Ron Sider on *Bill Moyers' Journal*, PBS, November 30, 2007; "Secretary Rice Speaks at Saban Forum Dinner."

83. "Annapolis: Having Tea with the Mad Hatter," Olive Trees Ministry, November 29, 2007.

84. Mike Evans, "BETRAYED: The Conspiracy to Divide Jerusalem," Jerusalem Prayer Team, November 29, 2007. A former PLO official, Muhammad Daoud Oddeh, said that Abbas was involved in the Black September organization that perpetrated the massacre of Israeli athletes at the 1972 Munich Olympics (Michael Young, "Did Mahmoud Abbas Finance the 1972 Munich Olympic Takeover?" *Slate,* July 24 2003).

85. Mike Evans, "Bush Announces PLO State in '08," e-mail from Jerusalem Prayer Team, January 29, 2008; Jerusalem Prayer Team Action Alert, January 30, 2008.

86. "Day after Annapolis: PA Television Palestinian Authority TV Show 'Palestine' Map Erasing Israel" and "Power Struggle Shakes PA," Bridges for Peace, *Israel Current News Update and Prayer Focus,* November 30, 2007.

87. Hal Lindsey, "Shades of Munich at Annapolis," The Hal Lindsey Report, late November 2007 (http://hallindsey.org/index.php?option=com_content&task=view&id=220&Itemid=28).

Selected Bibliography

Unless noted otherwise, all biblical citations are from *The Oxford Annotated Bible, with the Apocrypha* (Revised Standard Version). Herbert G. May and Bruce M. Metzger, eds. New York: Oxford University Press, 1965.

Abelove, Henry. *The Evangelist of Desire: John Wesley and the Methodists.* Stanford: Stanford University Press, 1990.

Abrams, Elliott. *Faith or Fear: How Jews Can Survive in a Christian America.* New York: Free Press, 1997.

Aikman, David. *A Man of Faith: The Spiritual Journey of George W. Bush.* Nashville: W Publishing, 2004.

"American Attitudes Hold Steady in Face of Foreign Crises," Pew Research Center for the People and the Press, Washington, D.C., August 17, 2006.

"American Christians and Support for Israel," The Tarrance Group, Alexandria, Virginia, October 9, 2002.

"American Piety in the 21st Century." Baylor Institute for Studies of Religion, Waco, Texas, September 2006.

"The American Religious Landscape and Politics, 2004." Pew Forum on Religion & Public Life, Washington, D.C.

Ariel, Yaakov. *On Behalf of Israel: American Fundamentalist Attitudes toward Jews, Judaism, and Zionism, 1865–1945.* Brooklyn: Carlson, 1991.

———. *Evangelizing the Chosen People: Missions to the Jews in America, 1880 to 2000.* Chapel Hill: University of North Carolina Press, 2000.

———. *Philosemites or Antisemites? Evangelical Christian Attitudes toward Jews, Judaism, and the State of Israel.* Jerusalem: Hebrew University, Vidal Sassoon International Center for the Study of Antisemitism, Analysis of Current Trends in Antisemitism, 20 (2002).

———. "An Unexpected Alliance: Christian Zionism and Its Historical Significance," *Modern Judaism,* 26.1 (2006), 74–100.

Armstrong, Karen. *The Battle for God.* New York: Ballantine Books, 2000.

———. *Islam: A Short History.* New York: Modern Library Chronicles, 2000.

————. "Bush's Fondness for Fundamentalism Is Courting Disaster at Home and Abroad." *The Guardian,* July 31, 2006.

Ateek, Naim Stifan. *Justice and Only Justice: A Palestinian Theology of Liberation.* Maryknoll, N.Y.: Orbis Books, 1989.

Ateek, Naim Stifan, Cedar Duaybis, and Maurine Tobin, eds. *Challenging Christian Zionism: Theology, Politics and the Israel-Palestine Conflict.* London: Melisende, 2005.

Aumann, Moshe. *Conflict & Connection: The Jewish-Christian-Israel Triangle.* Jerusalem: Gefen, 2003.

Baker, Joel. "Christian Zionism." In Matt Johnson and Nicola Goodenough, eds., *Christians and Israel: Essays on Biblical Zionism and on Islamic Fundamentalism.* Jerusalem: International Christian Embassy, 1996.

Balmer, Randall. *Mine Eyes Have Seen the Glory: A Journey into the Evangelical Subculture in America.* New York: Oxford University Press, 1989.

————. *Thy Kingdom Come: How the Religious Right Distorts the Faith and Threatens America.* New York: Basic Books, 2006.

Bebbington, David W. *Evangelicalism in Modern Britain: A History from the 1730's to the 1980's.* London: Unwin Hyman, 1989.

————. "Not So Exceptional after All." *Christianity Today,* May/June 2007.

"Benedict XVI Viewed Favorably but Faulted on Religious Outreach." Pew Research Center for the People and the Press, Washington, D.C., September 25, 2007.

Birnbaum, Jeffrey H., and Laurence I. Barrett. "The Gospel according to Ralph." *Time,* May 15, 1995.

Blackstone, William E. (W.E.B.). *Jesus Is Coming.* London: Fleming H. Revell, 1878.

Bloesch, Donald G. *Essentials of Evangelical Theology.* San Francisco: Harper and Row, 1978.

Blumenthal, Max. "Born-agains for Sharon." Salon.com, October 30, 2004.

————. "Birth Pangs of a New Christian Zionism." *The Nation,* August 8, 2006.

————. "Israel, the US, and the Christian Right: The Ménage à Trois from Hell." *Huffington Post,* August 10, 2006.

Boyer, Paul S. *When Time Shall Be No More: Prophecy Belief in Modern American Culture.* Cambridge, Mass.: Belknap Press of Harvard University Press, 1992.

————. "When U.S. Foreign Policy Meets Biblical Prophecy." *AlterNet,* July 21, 2005.

Brimmer, Rebecca, Ray Sanders, and Malcolm Hedding. "The Jerusalem Declaration of Christian Zionism." Reprinted in *The Jerusalem Connection,* December 2007.

Brog, David. *Standing with Israel: Why Christians Support the Jewish State.* Lake Mary, Fla: Frontline, 2006.

————. "Jews and Evangelicals Together." National Review Online, May 22, 2006.

Brueggemann, Walter. *The Land.* Philadelphia: Fortress Press, 1977.

Bush, George W. *A Charge to Keep: My Journey to the White House.* 1999; paperback, New York: Perennial, 1999.

Caldwell, Deborah. "The Rapture Factor: Why Conservative Christians' Love of Israel Is Intertwined with the Battle of Armageddon." *Beliefnet,* May 30, 2002.

————. "How Islam-Bashing Got Cool." *Beliefnet,* August 8, 2002.

Caner, Ergun Mehmet, and Emir Fethi Caner. *Unveiling Islam.* Grand Rapids, Mich.: Kregel, 2002.

Carter, Jimmy. *Our Endangered Values: America's Moral Crisis.* New York: Simon and Schuster, 2005.

————. *Palestine: Peace Not Apartheid.* New York: Simon and Schuster, 2006.

Casanova, José. *Public Religions in the Modern World.* Chicago: University of Chicago Press, 1994.

Chafets, Zev. "The Rabbi Who Loved Evangelicals (and Vice Versa)." *New York Times Magazine,* July 24, 2005.

————. *A Match Made in Heaven: American Jews, Christian Zionists, and One Man's Exploration of the Weird and Wonderful Judeo-Evangelical Alliance.* New York: HarperCollins, 2007.

Cimino, Richard. "New Boundaries—Evangelicals and Islam after 9/11" (www.religionnews.com/press02/PR121405.html).

Clark, Victoria. *Allies for Armageddon: The Rise of Christian Zionism.* New Haven: Yale University Press, 2007.

Clinton, Bill. *My Life.* New York: Knopf, 2004.

Cohler-Esses, Larry. "Evangelical Split over Israel Batters Bush." *Jewish Week,* August 3, 2007.

Dershowitz, Alan. "Debunking the Newest—and Oldest—Jewish Conspiracy: A Reply to the Mearsheimer-Walt 'Working Paper.'" Cambridge, Mass.: Harvard Law School, April 2006.

Didion, Joan. "Mr. Bush & the Divine." *The New York Review of Books,* November 6, 2003.

Draper, Robert. *Dead Certain: The Presidency of George W. Bush.* New York: Free Press, 2007.

Dreyfuss, Robert. "Reverend Doomsday." *Rolling Stone,* January 28, 2004.

Duffy, Michael, and Romesh Ratnesar. "Trapped by His Own Instincts." *Time,* May 6, 2002.

Durham, Martin. "Evangelical Protestantism and Foreign Policy in the United States after September 11." *Patterns of Prejudice,* 38 (2004), 145–58.

Eidsmore, John. *God and Caesar: Biblical Faith and Political Action.* Westchester, Ill.: Crossway Books, 1984.

Elon, Amos. *Herzl.* New York: Holt, Rinehart and Winston, 1975.

Esposito, John L. *Unholy War: Terror in the Name of Islam.* Oxford: Oxford University Press, 2002.

"Evangelical Reflections on the U.S. Role in the World." Carnegie Council on Ethics and International Affairs, New York, September 15, 2005.

"Evangelicalism, Islam, and Humanitarian Aid: A Conversation with Lamin Sanneh." Ethics and Public Policy Center, Washington, D.C., December 15, 2003.

"Evangelicals and Israel: A Conversation with Gerald R. McDermott." Ethics and Public Policy Center, Washington, D.C., November 20, 2003.

"Evangelicals and the Public Square." Pew Forum on Religion and Public Life, Washington, D.C., October 11, 2007.

"Evangelical Views of Islam." EPPC-*Beliefnet*, April 7, 2003.

Evans, Mike, and Jerome R. Corsi. *Showdown with Nuclear Iran: Radical Islam's Messianic Mission to Destroy Israel and Cripple the United States.* Nashville: Thomas Nelson, 2006.

Falk, Gerhard. *The Restoration of Israel: Christian Zionism in Religion, Literature, and Politics.* New York: Peter Lang, 2006.

Falwell, Jerry. *Listen, America!* Toronto: Bantam Books, 1980.

————. "The Twenty-First Century and the End of the World." *Fundamentalist Journal,* May 1988.

————. "America's 'Dangerous' Message to Israel." *WorldNetDaily,* April 13, 2002.

————. "Bible History, Prophecy and 'World War III.'" *Falwell Confidential,* July 21, 2006.

Finch, Henry. *The World's Great Restauration, or Calling of the Jews and with them of all Nations and Kingdoms of the Earth to the Faith of Christ.* London: William Gouge: 1621; reprinted, Early English Books Online. Ann Arbor: University of Michigan, 1999.

Fineman, Howard. "Religion: Apocalyptic Politics." *Newsweek,* May 24, 2004.

Fineman, Howard, and Tamara Lipper. "A Very Mixed Marriage." *Newsweek,* June 2, 2003.

Finto, Don. *Your People Shall Be My People: How Israel, the Jews, and the Christian Church Will Come Together in the Last Days.* 1973; reprint, Ventura, Calif.: Regal Books, 2001.

"Five Years after 9/11: The Clash of Civilizations Revisited." The Pew Forum on Religion & Public Life," Washington, D.C., August 18, 2006.

Foxman, Abe. *Never Again? The Threat of the New Anti-Semitism.* New York: HarperCollins, 2003.

Frum, David. *The Right Man: An Inside Account of the Bush White House.* New York: Random House, 2003.

Gerson, Michael. "Seeds of Anti-Semitism." *Washington Post,* September 21, 2007.

Gibbs, Nancy, and Michael Duffy. "Leveling the Praying Field." *Time,* July 12, 2007.

Gilgoff, Dan. *The Jesus Machine: How James Dobson, Focus on the Family, and Evangelical America Are Winning the Culture War.* New York: St. Martin's Press, 2007.

———. "What Is a 'Real' Christian?" *USA Today* blog, May 21, 2007 (http://blogs.usatoday. com/oped/2007/05/what_is_a_real_.html).

"God's Country? Evangelicals and U.S. Foreign Policy." The Pew Forum on Religion & Public Life, Washington, D.C., September 26, 2006.

Goldberg, Jeffrey. "Israel's Y2K Problem." *New York Times Magazine,* October 3, 1999.

Goldberg, J. J. *Jewish Power: Inside the American Jewish Establishment.* Reading, Mass.: Addison-Wesley, 1996.

Goldberg, Michelle. *Kingdom Coming: The Rise of Christian Nationalism.* New York: W. W. Norton, 2006.

Gorenberg, Gershom. "Danger: Millennium Ahead." *Jerusalem Report,* February 19, 1998.

———. "More Faithful Than Ever." *Jerusalem Report,* October 25, 1999.

———. *The End of Days: Fundamentalism and the Struggle for the Temple Mount.* 2000; paperback, Oxford: Oxford University Press, 2000.

———. "Unorthodox Alliance." *Washington Post,* October 11, 2002.

———. *The Accidental Empire: Israel and the Birth of the Settlements, 1967–1977.* New York: Times Books, 2006.

Graham, Billy. "Billy Graham on Key '73." *Christianity Today,* March 16, 1973.

Graham, Franklin, with Bruce Nygren. *The Name.* Nashville: Nelson Books, 2002.

"The Great Divide: How Westerners and Muslims View Each Other." The Pew Global Attitudes Project, Washington, D.C., June 22, 2006.

Green, John C. "Evangelical Protestants and Jews: A View from the Polls." In *Uneasy Allies?* Lanham, Md.: Lexington Books, 2007, 19–38.

Gregerman, Adam. "Old Wine in New Bottles: Liberation Theology and the Israeli-Palestinian Conflict." *Journal of Ecumenical Studies,* 41 (Summer/Fall 2004), 313–40.

Grossman, Lawrence. "The Organized Jewish Community and Evangelical America: A Brief History." In *Uneasy Allies?,* 49–72.

Haberman, Joshua O. "The Bible Belt Is America's Safety Belt: Why the Holocaust Couldn't Happen Here." *Policy Review,* 47 (1987), 40–44.

Hagee, John. *Beginning of the End: The Assassination of Yitzhak Rabin and the Coming Antichrist.* Nashville: Thomas Nelson, 1996.

———. *Day of Deception.* Nashville: Thomas Nelson, 1997.

———. *Final Dawn over Jerusalem.* Nashville: Thomas Nelson, 1998.

———. "Our Jewish Roots." *JH Magazine,* Summer 2002.

———. *Jerusalem Countdown; a Warning to the World.* Lake Mary, Fla.: Frontline, 2006.

———. *In Defense of Israel.* Lake Mary, Fla.: Strang, 2007.

———. AIPAC Policy Conference, March 11, 2007 (http://www.aipac.org/about_AIPAC/ Learn_About_AIPAC/2841_2859.asp).

Haggard, Ted. *Primary Purpose: Making It Hard for People to Go to Hell from Your City.* Lake Mary, Fla.: Charisma House, 1995.

Halevy, Efraim. *Man in the Shadows: Inside the Middle East Crisis with a Man Who Led the Mossad.* New York: St. Martin's, 2006.

Halsell, Grace. *Prophecy and Politics: Militant Evangelists on the Road to Nuclear War.* 1986; reprint, Bullsbrook, Western Australia: Veritas Publishing, 1987.

Hedding, Malcolm. Speech at the October 2004 Feast of Tabernacles in Jerusalem. In "The Biblical Basis for Christian Zionism" (fp.thebeers.f9.co.uk).

———. "ICEJ Disengagement Statement." July 21, 2005 (http://www.icej.org/article.php? id=2808).

———. "The Saga of the Vulture." *Jerusalem Post Christian Edition,* May 2006.

———. "Fundamental Mistakes." *Ynet,* December 13, 2006.

———. "The Root of Anti-Semitism." *Jerusalem Post Christian Edition,* May 2007.

Hedding, Malcolm, and Jurgen Buhler. "A Biblical Stand on Zionism—Part 2." Christian Zionism. October 1, 2006 (http://www.christian-zionism.org/analysis_articles_body.asp? Title=A+Biblical+Stand+on+Zionism+%2D+Part+2).

Henry, Carl F. H. *The Uneasy Conscience of Modern Fundamentalism.* Grand Rapids. Mich.: Eerdmans, 1947.

Hertz, Todd. "The Evangelical View of Israel?" *Christianity Today,* June 11, 2003.

Hodgson, Marshall. *The Venture of Islam.* Chicago: University of Chicago Press, 1974.

Hoffman, Martin L. *Empathy and Moral Development: Implications for Caring and Justice.* Cambridge: Cambridge University Press, 2000.

Horowitz, Craig. "Israel's Christian Soldiers." newyorkmetro.com, September 29, 2003.

Huntington, Samuel P. *The Clash of Civilizations and the Remaking of World Order.* New York: Simon and Schuster, 1996.

"In Pursuit of Values Voters." Event Transcript, Pew Research Center for the People and the Press, Washington, D.C., October 11, 2006.

"In Search of the Spiritual." *Newsweek,* September 5, 2005.

"The Iran Phenomenon in the Middle East—An Israeli Perspective." Saban Center; reprinted in *Jewish Council for Public Affairs Briefing,* November 1, 2006 (http://www.brookings.edu/ events/2006/1019iran.aspx).

"Islam and the West: A Conversation with Bernard Lewis." Pew Forum on Religion & Public Life, April 27, 2006.

"The Jerusalem Declaration on Christian Zionism," August 29, 2006 (http://www.hcef.org/ index.cfm/mod/news/id/16/subMod/NewsView/NewsID/1595.cfm).

"The Jerusalem Sabeel Document: Principle for a Just Peace in Palestine-Israel" (www.fosna. org/index.php?display=jerusalemsabeel).

"The Jesus Factor." Interview Doug Wead. *Frontline,* November 18, 2003 (http://www.pbs.org/ wgbh/pages/frontline/shows/jesus/interviews/wead.html).

———. Interview Richard Cizik. *Frontline,* November 12, 2003 (http://www.pbs.org/ wgbh/pages/frontline/shows/jesus/interviews/cizik.html).

———. Interview Richard Land, *Frontline,* November 18, 2003 (http://www.pbs.org/ wgbh/pages/frontline/shows/jesus/interviews/land.html).

Johnson, Matt, and Nicola Goodenough, eds. *Christians and Israel: Essays on Biblical Zionism and on Islamic Fundamentalism.* Jerusalem: International Christian Embassy, 1996.

Kaplan, Esther. *With God on Their Side: How Christian Fundamentalists Trampled Science, Policy, and Democracy in George W. Bush's White House.* New York: New Press, 2004.

Kean, Thomas H., and Lee H. Hamilton with Benjamin Rhodes. *Without Precedent: The Inside Story of the 9/11 Commission.* New York: Knopf, 2006.

Keeter, Scott. "Evangelicals and the GOP: An Update." Pew Research Center for the People and the Press, Washington, D.C., October 18, 2006.

Kelsay, John. *Arguing the Just War in Islam.* Cambridge, Mass.: Harvard University Press, 2007.

Kjaer-Hansen, Kai, and Bodil F. Skjott. "Facts and Myths about the Messianic Congregations in Israel, 1998–1999." *Mishkan,* Caspari Center for Biblical and Jewish Studies, Jerusalem, 1999.

Koenig, William. *Eye to Eye: Facing the Consequences of Dividing Israel.* Alexandria, Va.: About Him Publishing, 2004.

Kohut, Andrew, and Bruce Stokes. "The Problem of American Exceptionalism." Pew Research Center for the People and the Press, Washington, D.C., May 9, 2006.

Korn, Eugene. "The Man of Faith and Religious Dialogue: Revisiting 'Confrontation.'" *Modern Judaism,* 25 (2005), 290–315.

Kuo, David. *Tempting Faith: An Inside Story of Political Seduction.* New York: Free Press, 2006.

Kuttab, Jonathan. "The Challenge of Christian Zionism." *Cornerstone,* 32 (Spring 2004).

LaHaye, Tim. *The Coming Peace in the Middle East.* Grand Rapids, Mich.: Zondervan, 1984.

LaHaye, Tim, and Jerry B. Jenkins. *Left Behind: A Novel of the Earth's Last Days.* Carol Stream, Ill.: Tyndale House, 1995.

———. *Kingdom Come: The Final Victory.* Carol Stream, Ill.: Tyndale House, 2007.

Guy Lawson, "George W.'s Personal Jesus" *GQ,* September 2003.

Leppakari, Maria. "The End Is a Beginning: Contemporary Apocalyptic Representations of Jerusalem." Abo, Finland: Abo Akademi University Press, 2002.

"Letter from President Bush to Prime Minister Sharon." April 14, 2004 (http://www.whitehouse. gov/news/releases/2004/04/20040414-3.html).

"Letter to President Bush." July 23, 2002 (http://campus.northpark.edu/centers/middle/midest. letter_to_bush.htm).

"Letter to President Bush from Evangelical Leaders." *New York Times,* July 29, 2007.

Lewis, Bernard. *Islam and the West.* New York: Oxford University Press, 1993.

———. "Allah Will Know His Own." *Wall Street Journal* (Europe), August 8, 2006.

Lewis, C. S. *Mere Christianity.* 1943; reprint, Nashville: Touchstone, 1980.

"Lieberman Address to Christians United for Israel." July 16, 2007 (http://lieberman.senate. gov/newsroom/release.cfm?id=279110).

Lienesch, Michael. *Redeeming America.* Chapel Hill: University of North Carolina Press, 1993.

Lindsay, D. Michael. "Is the National Prayer Breakfast Surrounded by a 'Christian Mafia'? Religious Publicity and Secrecy within the Corridor of Power." *Journal of the American Academy of Religion,* 74.2 (June 2006), 390–419.

———. *Faith in the Halls of Power: How Evangelicals Joined the American Elite.* Oxford: Oxford University Press, 2007.

———. "The Halls of Power," *Sh'ma.com,* May 2007 (http://www.shma.com/may_07/halls_ power.htm).

Lindsey, Hal. *The Everlasting Hatred: The Roots of Jihad.* Murrieta, Calif.: Oracle, 2002.

Lindsey, Hal, with C. C. Carlson. *The Late Great Planet Earth.* Grand Rapids, Mich.: Zondervan, 1970.

Lustick, Ian. *For the Land and the Lord: Jewish Fundamentalism in Israel.* New York: Council on Foreign Relations, 1988.

Malachy, Yona. *American Fundamentalism and Israel: The Relation of Fundamentalist Churches to Zionism and the State of Israel.* Jerusalem: Graph Press, Institute of Contemporary Jewry, Hebrew University, 1977.

Mann, James. *Rise of the Vulcans: The History of Bush's War Cabinet.* New York: Penguin, 2004.

Mansfield, Stephen. *The Faith of George W. Bush.* New York: Jeremy P. Tarcher/Penguin, 2003.

"Many Americans Uneasy with Mix of Religion and Politics." Pew Research Center for the People and the Press, Washington, D.C., August 24, 2006.

Marsden, George M. *Understanding Fundamentalism and Evangelicalism.* Grand Rapids, Mich.: W.B. Eerdmans, 1991.

———. *Fundamentalism and American Culture.* Oxford: Oxford University Press, 2006.

Marty, Martin E. "What Is Fundamentalism? Theological Perspectives." In Hans Kung and Jurgen Moltmann, eds. *Fundamentalism as an Ecumenical Challenge,* Concilium 1992/93. London: SCM Press, 1992, 3–13.

———. *When Faiths Collide.* Malden, Mass.: Blackwell, 2005.

Meacham, Jon. "Pilgrim's Progress." *Newsweek,* August 14, 2006.

———. "The Prodigal Returns," *Newsweek,* November 20, 2006.

Mead, Walter Russell. "God's Country?" *Foreign Affairs,* September/October 2006.

Mearsheimer, John, and Stephen Walt. "The Israel Lobby" *London Review of Books,* March 23, 2006.

———. *The Israel Lobby and U.S. Foreign Policy.* New York: Farrar, Straus and Giroux, 2007.

Merkley, Paul Charles. *The Politics of Christian Zionism, 1891–1948.* London: Frank Cass, 1998.

———. *Christian Attitudes towards the State of Israel.* Montreal: McGill-Queen's University Press, 2001.

Metlitzki, Dorothee. *The Matter of Araby in Medieval England.* New Haven: Yale University Press, 1977.

Miller, Donald E. *Reinventing American Protestantism: Christianity in the New Millennium.* Berkeley: University of California Press, 1997.

Missler, Chuck, and Don Stewart. *The Coming Temple: Center Stage for the Final Countdown.* Orange, Calif.: Dart Press, 1991.

Mittleman, Alan, Byron Johnson, and Nancy Isserman, eds. *Uneasy Allies? Evangelical and Jewish Relations.* Lanham, Md.: Lexington Books, 2007.

Morris, Benny. *Righteous Victims: A History of the Zionist-Arab Conflict, 1881–2001.* New York: Vintage Books, 1999.

———. "And Now for Some Facts." *The New Republic,* April 28, 2006.

———. "Hamas: Alms and Arms." *The New Republic,* July 11, 2006.

"Most Evangelical Leaders Favor 'Evangelizing Muslims Abroad.'" Ethics and Public Policy Center press release, Washington, D.C., April 7, 2003.

Mouly, Ruth W. *The Religious Right and Israel: The Politics of Armageddon.* Chicago: Political Research Associates, 1985.

Mouw, Richard. "The Chosen People Puzzle." *Christianity Today,* March 5, 2001.

———. "How to Bless Israel." *Beliefnet,* May 31, 2002.

Moyers, Bill. "Democracy in the Balance." *Sojourners Magazine,* volume 33, August 2004.

"Muslim Americans: Middle Class and Mostly Mainstream." Pew Research Center for the People and the Press, Washington, D.C., May 22, 2007.

"Muslim Public Opinion on US Policy, Attacks on Civilians and al Qaeda." World Public Opinion.org, University of Maryland, April 24, 2007 (http://www.worldpublicopinion.org/pipa/pdf/apr07/START_Apr07_rpt.pdf).

Nafisi, Azar. "America's Best Weapon Is the Iranian People." *The New Republic,* April 23, 2007.

Nasr, Vali. *The Shia Revival: How Conflicts within Islam Will Shape the Future.* New York: W.W. Norton, 2006.

———. "After Lebanon, There's Iran." *Christian Science Monitor,* August 9, 2006.

———. "The New Hegemon." *The New Republic Online,* December 12, 2006.

Neff, David. "From an Evangelical Perch." *Sh'ma.* May 2007.

———. "Evangelical Leaders Reiterate Call for Two-State Solution for Israel and Palestine." *Christianity Today,* November 29, 2007.

Noll, Mark A. *The Scandal of the Evangelical Mind.* Grand Rapids, Mich.: Eerdmans, 1994.

———. *The Rise of Evangelicalism: The Age of Edwards, Whitefield and the Wesleys.* Downers Grove, Ill.: InterVarsity Press, 2003.

Nussbaum, Paul. "An Evangelical Voice Strikes Different Notes." *Philadelphia Inquirer,* June 19, 2005.

———. "The Surprising Spectrum of Evangelicals." *Philadelphia Inquirer,* June 19, 2006.

Olasky, Marvin. "The Panda in Winter." *World* Magazine, February 18, 2006.

O'Leary, Stephen D. *Arguing the Apocalypse: A Theory of Millennial Rhetoric.* New York: Oxford University Press, 1994.

Oren, Michael B. *Six Days of War: June 1967 and the Making of the Modern Middle East.* New York: Ballantine Books, 2002.

———. "Tinfoil Hats in Harvard Yard." *The New Republic,* March 31, 2006.

———. *Power, Faith, and Fantasy: America in the Middle East, 1776 to the Present.* New York: W. W. Norton, 2007.

Oz, Amos. *How to Cure a Fanatic.* Princeton: Princeton University Press, 2006.

Pagels, Elaine. *The Origin of Satan.* New York: Random House, 1995.

Pape, Robert A. *Dying to Win: The Strategic Logic of Suicide Terrorism.* New York: Random House, 2005.

Park, Miriam Rodlyn. "Watchmen on the Wall: A Practical Guide to Prayer for Jerusalem and Her People." Robert Stearns, gen. ed. (Training manual.).

Parsi, Trita. *Treacherous Alliance: The Secret Dealings of Israel, Iran and the United States.* New Haven: Yale University Press, 2007.

Parsons, David. "Swords into Ploughshares: Christian Zionism and the Battle of Armageddon." International Christian Embassy Jerusalem (http://icej.org/data/Images/File/News/Swords. pdf).

———. "Witness to Prophecy: An Interview with Dr. Jack Hayford." *Jerusalem Post Christian Edition,* October 2006.

———. "Killing Off the Messenger." *Jerusalem Post Christian Edition,* August 2007.

———. "What Better Place than in Israel?" *Jerusalem Post Christian Edition,* September 2007.

———. "Preaching to the President." *Jerusalem Post Christian Edition,* October 2007.

———. "More Birth Pangs Ahead." *Jerusalem Post Christian Edition,* November 2007.

"Peace Index: December 2006." JCPA Middle East Briefing, January 10, 2007.

"Peace versus Democracy in Palestine: A Conversation with Jimmy Carter." Council on Foreign Relations, March 2, 2006.

Perlstein, Rick. "The Jesus Landing Pad." *Village Voice,* May 18, 2004.

Phillips, Kevin. *American Theocracy.* New York: Viking, 2006.

———. "How the GOP Became God's Own Party." *Washington Post,* April 2, 2006.

"Poll: America's Evangelicals More and More Mainstream, But Insecure." Religion and Ethics Newsweekly, PBS, April 16, 2004.

Posner, Sarah. "Pastor Strangelove." *American Prospect Online,* June 6, 2006.

———. "Holy War." *American Prospect Online,* July 19, 2006.

———. "Lobbying for Armageddon." *Alternet,* August 3, 2006.

———. "Theocrats Deny 'End Times' Theology Is Cause of Their Push for War with Iran." *Alternet,* July 23, 2007.

Poupko, Yehiel. "Protestants Talking about Israel." Unpublished paper, May 5, 2005.

Pragai, Michael J. *Faith and Fulfilment: Christians and the Return to the Promised Land.* London: Vallentine Mitchell, 1985.

"President Bush Addresses Members of the Knesset," May 15, 2008 (http://www.whitehouse. gov/news/releases/2008/05/print/20080515-1.html).

Prince, Derek. *Promised Land: God's Word and the Nation of Israel.* 1978; reprint, Charlotte, N.C.: Derek Prince Ministries, 2003.

"Proclamation of the Third International Christian Zionist Congress" (http://christianactionforisrael. org/congress.html).

Rausch, David A. *Zionism within Early American Fundamentalism, 1878–1918: A Convergence of Two Traditions.* New York: Edwin Mellen Press, 1979.

———. *Communities in Conflict: Evangelicals and Jews.* Philadelphia: Trinity Press International, 1991.

"Religion, Belief, and Policy." Pew Research Center for the People and the Press, Washington, D.C., July 24, 2003.

The Religious Right: The Assault on Tolerance and Pluralism in America. New York: Anti-Defamation League, 1994.

"Results of Palestinian Public Opinion Poll No. 30." Al-Najah National University, Center for Opinion Polls and Survey Studies, September 13–15, 2007 (http://imra.org.il/story.php3?id-36073).

Richardson, Joel. *Antichrist: Islam's Awaited Messiah.* Enumclaw, Wash.: Pleasant Word, 2006.

Richardson, Louise. *What Terrorists Want: Understanding the Enemy, Containing the Threat.* New York: Random House, 2006.

Riggans, Walter. *Israel and Zionism.* London: Handsel Press, 1988.

Robertson, Pat. *The New Millennium.* Dallas: Word, 1990.

———. "'Road Map' Is Beginning of End for Israel." CBN, May 29, 2003.

———. "Praying for a 'Decisive' Victory." Pat Robertson.com (http://www.patrobertson.com/PressReleases/JPCE0906.asp).

Rosen, David. "Orthodox Judaism and Jewish-Christian Dialogue" (http://www.bc.edu/research/cjl/meta-elements/texts/center/conferences/soloveitchik/sol_rosen.htm).

Rosenberg, Joel C. *Epicenter: Why the Current Rumblings in the Middle East Will Change Your Future.* Carol Stream, Ill.: Tyndale House, 2006.

Ross, Dennis. *The Missing Peace: The Inside Story of the Fight for Middle East Peace.* 2004; paperback, New York: Farrar, Straus and Giroux, 2005.

———. "The Can't-Win Kids." *The New Republic,* December 11, 2007.

Rossing, Barbara. *The Rapture Exposed Exposed: The Message of Hope in the Book of Revelation.* Boulder, Colo.: Westview Press, 2004.

Ruether, Rosemary Radford. "Christian Zionism and Main Line Western Christian Churches." In Naim Ateek, Cedar Duaybis, and Maurine Tobin, eds. *Challenging Christian Zionism: Theology, Politics and the Israel-Palestine Conflict.* London: Melisende, 2005, 154–62.

———. "Challenging Christian Zionism." *Catholic New Times,* May 9, 2004.

Ruether, Rosemary Radford, and Herman J. Ruether. *The Wrath of Jonah: The Crisis of Religious Nationalism in the Israeli-Palestinian Conflict.* Minneapolis: Fortress Press, 2002.

Ruthven, Malise. *Islam in the World.* London: Penguin, 1994.

———. *Fundamentalism: The Search for Meaning.* Oxford: Oxford University Press, 2004.

Ryrie, Charles Caldwell. *Dispensationalism Today.* Chicago: Moody Press, 1965.

Safa, Reza F. *Inside Islam: Exposing and Reaching the World of Islam.* Lake Mary, Fla.: Charisma House, 1996.

Said, Edward W. *Peace and Its Discontents: Essays on Palestine in the Middle East Peace Process.* New York: Vintage Books, 1996.

———. "Europe versus America." *Al-Ahram,* November 14–20, 2002.

Sandeen, Ernest. *The Roots of Fundamentalism: British and American Millenarianism, 1800–1930.* Chicago: University of Chicago Press, 1970.

Schindler, Colin. "Likud and the Christian Dispensationalists: A Symbiotic Relationship." *Israel Studies,* 5 (2000), 153–82.

Scofield, Cyrus Ignatius. *The Scofield Reference Bible.* 1909; reprinted as *The Scofield Study Bible,* New York: Oxford University Press, 1945.

Segev, Tom. *One Palestine Complete: Jews and Arabs under the British Mandate.* Haim Watzman, trans. New York: Holt, 1999.

Shapiro, Ian. *Containment: Rebuilding a Strategy against Global Terror.* Princeton: Princeton University Press, 2007.

Sharlett, Jeff. "Soldiers of Christ: Inside America's Most Powerful Megachurch with Pastor Ted Haggard," *Harper's,* May 2005.

Sharon, Ariel, with David Chanoff. *Warrior: An Autobiography of Ariel Sharon.* New York: Simon and Schuster, 1989.

Shepherd, Naomi. *Teddy Kollek: Mayor of Jerusalem.* New York: Harper and Row, 1988.

Shoebat, Walid. *Why I Left Jihad: The Root of Terrorism and the Rise of Islam.* Newtown, Penn.: Top Executive Media, 2005.

———. "Why I Left Jihad." *Jerusalem Post Christian Edition,* October 2006.

Sider, Ronald J. *The Scandal of the Evangelical Conscience: Why Are Christians Living Just Like the Rest of the World?* Grand Rapids, Mich.: Baker Books, 2005.

Sikand, Yoginder. "The Faith of George W. Bush; Christian Supremacy, American Imperialism and Global Disaster." *The American Muslim,* May 10, 2006.

———. "Christian Zionism: Terror in Jesus' Name." July 8, 2006 (www.mukto-mona.com/Articles/yogi_s/christian_zionism011205.htm).

Silk, Mark. *Spiritual Politics: Religion and America since WW II.* New York: Simon and Schuster, 1988.

Silverstein, Ken, and Michael Scherer. "Born-again Zionists." *Mother Jones,* 27 (September/October 2002), 56–62.

Simon, Merrill. *Jerry Falwell and the Jews.* Middle Village, N.Y.: Jonathan David, 1984.

Sizer, Stephen. "The Origins of Christian Zionism." *Cornerstone,* 31, Winter 2003.

———. *Christian Zionism: Road-map to Armageddon?* Leicester, England: Inter-Varsity Press, 2004.

Smidt, Corwin E., and James M. Penning, eds., *Sojourners in the Wilderness: The Christian Right in Comparative Perspective.* Lanham: Rowman and Littlefield, 1997.

Smith, Christian. *American Evangelicalism: Embattled and Thriving.* Chicago: University of Chicago Press, 1998.

———. *Christian America? What Evangelicals Really Want.* 2000; paperback, Berkeley: University of California Press, 2002.

Snobelen, S. "'The Mystery of This Restitution of All Things': Isaac Newton on the Return of the Jews." In J. E. Force and R. H. Popkin, eds. *Millenarianism and Messianism in Early Modern European Culture: The Millenarian Turn.* Dordrecht, The Netherlands: Kluwer Academic, 2001, 95–118.

Soloveitchik, J. B. "Confrontation." *Tradition,* 6 (Spring/Summer 1964), 5–28.

Spencer, Robert. *The Politically Incorrect Guide to Islam (and the Crusades).* Washington, D.C.: Regnery Publishing, 2005.

———. "The War Is Over; the Jihad Isn't." *Front Page,* August 18, 2004.

Sprinzak, Ehud. *The Ascendance of Israel's Radical Right.* New York: Oxford University Press, 1991.

Stewart, Don, and Chuck Missler. *The Coming Temple: Center Stage for the Final Countdown.* Orange, Calif.: Dart Press, 1991.

Stillman, Deanne. "Onward, Christian Soldiers." *The Nation,* June 3, 2002.

"Survey: America's Evangelicals." *Religion and Ethics Newsweekly,* April 16, 2004.

Suskind, Ron. "Why Are These Men Laughing?" *Esquire,* January 1, 2003.

———. *The One Percent Doctrine: Deep Inside America's Pursuit of Its Enemies since 9/11.* New York: Simon and Schuster, 2006.

Tamney, Joseph B. *The Resilience of Conservative Religion: The Case of Popular, Conservative, Protestant Congregations.* New York: Cambridge University Press, 2002.

Tanenbaum, Marc H. "No, They Have Forsaken the Faith." *Christianity Today,* April 24, 1981.

Thomas, Cal, and Ed Dobson. *Blinded by Might: Can the Religious Right Save America?* Grand Rapids, Mich.: Zondervan, 1999.

Tolson, Jay. "Aiming for Apocalypse." *U.S. News & World Report,* May 22, 2006.

Tristram, Clare. "Benny Elon's Long, Strange Trip." Salon.com, May 14, 2004.

Tuchman, Barbara W. *Bible and Sword: England and Palestine from the Bronze Age to Balfour.* 1956; reprint, New York: Ballantine Books, 1984.

2006 Annual Survey of American Jewish Opinion, American Jewish Committee (http://www.ajc.org/atf/cf/{42D75369-D582-4380-8395-D25925B85EAF}/2006_FINAL_QUESTIONNAIRE_SURVEY_FULL.PDF).

"2007 Annual Survey of Jewish Opinion." American Jewish Committee (http://www.ajc.org/site/c.ijITI2PHKoG/b.3642857/).

"Understanding American Evangelicals: A Conversation with Mark Noll and Jay Tolson." Ethics and Public Policy Center, Washington, D.C., June 2, 2004.

Unger, Craig. "American 'Rapture.'" *Vanity Fair,* December 2005.

Uslaner, Eric, and Mark Lichbach. "Why the GOP Can't Convert the Jewish Vote." *The Forward,* February 24, 2006.

———. "The Two Front War: Jews, Identity, Liberalism, and Voting" (undated, http://www.bsos.umd.edu/gvpt/uslaner/uslanerlichbachjewishvotingbehavioriii.pdf).

Van Biema, David. "The 25 Most Influential Evangelicals in America." *Time,* February 7, 2005.

van der Hoeven, Jan Willem. *Babylon or Jerusalem?* Shippensburg, Penn.: Destiny Image, 1993.

———. "Allah Is Not God." March 30, 2004 (www.isrealmybeloved.com/history_prophecy/islam_arabs/God_allah.htm).

———. "A Clever People, yet So Self-destructive!" International Christian Zionist Center, January 30, 2007; reprinted in Unity Coalition for Israel, *Today's News Summaries* (http://www.israelunitycoalition.org/news/article.php?id=816).

Van Zile, Dexter. "Sabeel's Teachings of Contempt." *Judeo-Christian Alliance,* June 30, 2005.

Wagner, Clarence H., Jr. "The Error of Replacement Theology." Bridges for Peace, May 9, 2002.

Wagner, Donald. E. *Anxious for Armageddon.* Scottdale, Penn.: Herald Press, 1995.

———. *Dying in the Land of Promise: Palestine and Palestinian Christianity from Pentecost to 2000.* London: Melisende, 2001.

———. "A Christian Zionist Primer (Part II): Defining Christian Zionism." *Cornerstone,* 31 (Winter 2003).

———. "Christians and Zion: British Stirrings." *Information Clearing House,* October 9, 2003.

Wald, Kenneth D., and Lee Sigelman. "Romancing the Jews: The Christian Right in Search of Strange Bedfellows." In Smidt and Penning, eds. *Sojourners in the Wilderness: The Christian Right in Comparative Perspective.* Lanham, Md.: Rowman and Littlefield, 1997.

Wallis, Jim. *God's Politics: Why the Right Gets It Wrong and the Left Doesn't Get It.* San Francisco: Harper San Francisco, 2005.

———. "Pat Robertson: An Embarrassment to the Church." *Sojourners,* August 25, 2005.

Walvoord, John F. *Israel in Prophecy.* Grand Rapids, Mich.: Zondervan, 1962.

———. "The Amazing Rise of Israel." *Moody Monthly* 68 (October 1967).

———. *Armageddon, Oil, and the Middle East: What the Bible Says about the Future of the Middle East and the End of Western Civilization.* Grand Rapids, Mich.: Zondervan, 1974.

Weber, Timothy P. *On the Road to Armageddon: How Evangelicals Became Israel's Best Friend.* Grand Rapids: Baker Academic, 2004.

Weisberg, Jacob. *The Bush Tragedy.* New York: Random House, 2008.

"What It Means to Love Israel." *Christianity Today,* September 5, 2007.

Wiesel, Elie. "The Missionary Menace." In Gary D. Eisenberg, ed. *Smashing the Idols: A Jewish Inquiry into the Cult Phenomenon.* Northvale, N.J.: Jason Aronson, 1988, 161–63.

Wills, Garry. *Under God: Religion and American Politics.* New York: Simon and Schuster, 1990.

Wilson, Dwight. *Armageddon Now! The Premillenarian Response to Russia and Israel since 1917.* 1977 ; reprint, Tyler, Tex.: Institute for Christian Economics, 1991.

Wolfe, Alan. *The Transformation of American Religion: How We Actually Live Our Faith.* New York: Free Press, 2003.

Woodward Bob. *State of Denial: Bush at War, Part III.* New York: Simon and Schuster, 2006.

Wright, Lawrence. "Forcing the End." *New Yorker,* July 20, 1998.

Yoffie, Eric H. "When We Let John Hagee Speak for Us." *The Forward,* May 18, 2006.

———. "Remarks as Prepared for the Islamic Society of North America 44th Annual Convention, Chicago, Illinois, Friday, August 31st, 2007" (http://urj.org/yoffie/isna/index.cfm?&printable=1).

Zertal, Idith, and Akiva Eldar. *Lords of the Land: The War over Israel's Settlements in the Occupied Territories, 1967–2007.* Vivian Eden, trans. New York: Nation Books, 2007.

"Zion's Christian Soldiers." *60 Minutes,* October 6, 2002 (http://www.cbsnews.com/stories/2002/10/03/60minutes/main524268.shtml).

Zoba, Wendy Murray. *The Beliefnet Guide to Evangelical Christianity.* New York: Doubleday, 2005.

INTERVIEWS

Gary Ackerman: March 30, 2006, Queens, N.Y.

Said Arjomand: December 7, 2006, Stony Brook, N.Y.

Gary Bauer: October 14, 2005, Arlington, Va.

Shmuel Ben-Shmuel: August 11, 2005, Washington, D.C.

Ben Bixby: August 31, 2005, Washington, D.C.

Peggy Booker: August 17, 2005, Woodlands, Tex.

Richard Booker: August 17, 2005, Woodlands, Tex.

Rudy Boschwitz: June 15, 2005, Plymouth, Minn.

Rebecca Brimmer, August 8, 2005, Jerusalem, Israel

Matt Brooks: July 8, 2005, Washington, D.C.; August 16, 2005, Washington, D.C.

Herman Cohen: June 14, 2005, Washington, D.C.

Jim Denison: February 13, 2006, Dallas, Tex.

Shari Dollinger: September 28, 2005, Washington, D.C.; December 28, 2005, Atlanta, Ga.

Barrett Duke: September 27, 2005, Washington, D.C.

Yechiel Eckstein: April 15, 2005, Chicago, Ill.

David Elcott: December 29, 2005, Washington, D.C.

John Esposito: May 3, 2007, Washington, D.C.

"Faith": February 8, 2006, New York, N.Y.

Ethan Felson: September 28, 2005, Washington, D.C.; November 17, 2005, New York, N.Y.

Abe Foxman: February 27, 2007, New York, N.Y.

Alan Freeman: October 31, 2007, Jerusalem, Israel

Chas. Freeman: December 12, 2005, Washington, D.C.

David Frum: September 30, 2005, Washington, D.C.

John Green: November 30, 2005, New York, N.Y.; December 15, 2005, Akron, Ohio

Lawrence Grossman: January 17, 2006, New York, N.Y.

Ted Haggard: June 26, 2006, Colorado Springs, Colo.

Malcolm Hedding: July 20, 2005, Jerusalem, Israel; December 17, 2007, Jerusalem, Israel

Richard Hellman: September 28, 2005, Washington, D.C.

Malcolm Hoenlein: January 30, 2006, New York, N.Y.; February 27, 2006, New York, N.Y

Martin Hoffman: November 14, 2006, Stony Brook, N.Y.

Joel James: March 22, 2005, Clarence, N.Y.; September 28, 2005, Washington, D.C.; January 19, 2006, Clarence, N.Y.

David D. Kirkpatrick: December 15, 2005, Washington, D.C.

Bill Koenig: July 25, 2005, Jerusalem, Israel

Richard Land: September 27, 28, 2005, Washington, D.C.; June 6, 2006, Washington, D.C.

Mark Leaverton: January 23, 2006, Austin, Tex.

Esther Levens: August 25, 2005, Shawnee Mission, Kans.; September 28, 2005, Washington, D.C.

JoAnn Magnuson: September 23, 2005, South Burnsville, Minn.; September 28, 2005, Washington, D.C.

George Mamo: October 17, 2005, Chicago, Ill.

Martin E. Marty: January 11, 2006, Riverside, Ill.

Gerald Meister: June 27, 2005, Suffern, N.Y.

Susan Michael: January 23, 2006, Washington, D.C.

Frank Newport: January 4, 2006, Princeton, N.J.

"Omar": January 27, 2006, Queens, N.Y.

Miriam Rodlyn Park: March 23, 2005, Wyckoff, N.J.

Mike Pence: September 25, 2006, Washington, D.C.

Thomas Pickering: January 17, 2006, Alexandria, Va.; September 5, 2006, Alexandria, Va.

Glenn Plummer: September 28, 2005, Washington, D.C.; October 17, 2005, Southfield, Mich.

Don Poage: January 18, 2006, Midland, Tex.

Yehiel Poupko: November 18, 2005 New York, N.Y.

Josh Reinstein: August 3, 2005, Jerusalem, Israel

David Roet: August 3, 2005, Jerusalem, Israel

David Rosen: December 29, 2005, Jerusalem, Israel

James Rudin: December 28, 2005, New York, N.Y.

Karen Sackville: July 28, 2005, New York, N.Y.

Alex Safian: July 8, 2005, Washington, D.C.

Ray Sanders July 25, 2005, Jerusalem, Israel

Michael Schneider: November 11, 2004, New York, N.Y.

Amir Shaviv: November 11, 2004, New York, N.Y.; September 7, 2007, New York, N.Y.

Myrna Shinbaum: February 27, 2007, New York, N.Y.

Robert Stearns: May 16, 2005, Clarence, N.Y.

Bill Sutter: September 28, 2005, Washington, D.C.

Ronn Torossian: January 17, 2005, New York, N.Y.

Elaine Urban: September 27, 2005, Washington, D.C.

Robert Urban: September 27, 2005, Washington, D.C.

Lawrence Wilkerson: December 12, 2005, Washington, D.C.

Eric Yoffie: January 30, 2006, New York, N.Y.

Belaynesh Zevadia: September 19, 2005, Houston, Tex.

E-MAIL INTERVIEWS AND CORRESPONDENCE

Said Arjomand: January 21, 2007

Rudy Boschwitz: June 21, 2006; June 23, 2006

George H.W. Bush: December 29, 2005; May 17, 2007

Alan Cooperman: May 22, 2007

David Frum: March 17, 2006; August 2, 2006; August 30, 2006; September 9, 2007

John Green: March 6, 2006; March 30, 2006; July 4, 2006; June 8, 2007; July 5, 2007; June 2, 2008

Ellen W. Horowitz: August 9, 2007; September 25, 2007

Robert Malley: July 6, 2006

Reuven Merhav: May 23, 2007

David Parsons: August 9, 2007; August 13, 2007

Tom Segev: September 7, 2007

Walid Shoebat: March 24, 2007

Christian Smith: January 5, 2006
Tom W. Smith: January 6, 2006

Interviews were conducted in person, by phone, and through e-mail. Several people spoke and corresponded on condition of anonymity and so are not listed here.